"Many have wondered how Christians who read the same Bible can come to such different conclusions about what it means. Rhyne Putman not only provides a thorough answer to that question; he also helps us live more peaceably and fruitfully amidst our differences. This helpful book will encourage Christians to hold their convictions with greater irenicism, humility, awareness, and wisdom."

Gavin Ortlund, Senior Pastor, First Baptist Church of Ojai; author, *Finding the Right Hills to Die On*

"With keen historical and philosophical insight, Rhyne Putman probes deeply the roots of Protestantism's disputatious and division-making nature. He asks the right questions and addresses the roots of the problems that have prevented even evangelical Christians with a high view of Scripture from uniting in common causes for the sake of the gospel. Without diminishing or downplaying our differences and their consequences, he calls us to once more heed the call of Wesley in his famous 'Catholic Spirit' letter and reach across the theological divides and say 'if your heart is as my heart, give me your hand' in things we can do together for the sake of Christ. Here is a practical study of how to disagree in love, without becoming disagreeable, much less foes. Highly recommended!"

Ben Witherington III, Jean R. Amos Professor of New Testament for Doctrinal Studies, Asbury Theological Seminary

"Rhyne Putman is one of the best Baptist theologians writing today, and he has given us a superb study on two themes central to Scripture: Christian unity and doctrinal diversity. Seldom have these topics been dealt with together in a more coherent way. This is an important book."

Timothy George, Research Professor, Beeson Divinity School, Samford University

"This book by Rhyne Putman is superbly done. I will be quick to commend it to others who want to understand how to navigate Christian differences with conviction and compassion, with both a love for truth and a heart of love. The chapter on Wesley and Whitefield and their complicated relationship alone makes the book worth the price! Buy it and be blessed."

Daniel L. Akin, President, Southeastern Baptist Theological Seminary

D1226131

"*When Doctrine Divides the People of God* is one of the most important books written since the turn of the twenty-first century. Biblically faithful, wise, and humane in his reflections, Putman addresses two of the most important questions of our time: First, how can faithful evangelical Christians come to such drastically different conclusions on matters of doctrine? Second, how should we handle those disagreements? Given that evangelical Christians will likely experience increased attacks from the antagonists of our secular age, we should take Putman's advice to heart, uniting whenever and however we can, to bear witness to the gospel once for all delivered to the saints. Recommended highly and without reservation."

Bruce Riley Ashford, Provost and Professor of Theology and Culture, Southeastern Baptist Theological Seminary; coauthor, *The Gospel of Our King*

"In this fascinating book, Rhyne Putman models not only erudition and breadth of study but also a necessary concern for the union of doctrine and practice. This work needs to be read by evangelicals and nonevangelicals alike. It teaches and models epistemic humility in the face of scriptural authority, thus showing how we can foster both confessional commitment and unity in the gospel across confessional lines."

Matthew Pinson, President and Professor of Theology, Welch College

"If evangelicals share a commitment to the gospel and a high view of Scripture, then why isn't there more agreement on theological matters? This is the thorny question that Rhyne Putman takes on and answers so ably in *When Doctrine Divides the People of God*. I wish I had read this book when I was a seminarian who thought he had all the answers! Like Putman, I long for a deeper sense of catholicity and a greater spirit of cooperation with fellow believers in other traditions. This book will help pastors, theologians, and other leaders work toward a greater embodiment of Jesus's high priestly prayer of John 17 with conviction and civility."

Nathan A. Finn, Provost and Dean of the University Faculty, North Greenville University

When Doctrine Divides
the People of God

When Doctrine Divides the People of God

An Evangelical Approach to Theological Diversity

Rhyne R. Putman

Foreword by David S. Dockery

WHEATON, ILLINOIS

Library of Congress Cataloging-in-Publication Data
Names: Putman, Rhyne R., author.
Title: When doctrine divides the people of God : an evangelical approach to theological diversity / Rhyne R. Putman ; foreword by David S. Dockery.
Description: Wheaton : Crossway, 2020. | Includes bibliographical references and index.
Identifiers: LCCN 2019023079 (print) | LCCN 2019023080 (ebook) | ISBN 9781433567872 (trade paperback) | ISBN 9781433567889 (pdf) | ISBN 9781433567896 (mobi) | ISBN 9781433567902 (epub)
Subjects: LCSH: Bible—Evidences, authority, etc. | Bible—Hermeneutics. | Bible—Criticism, interpretation, etc. | Church controversies. | Interdenominational cooperation.
Classification: LCC BS480 .P88 2020 (print) | LCC BS480 (ebook) | DDC 230/.04624—dc23
LC record available at https://lccn.loc.gov/2019023079
LC ebook record available at https://lccn.loc.gov/2019023080

Crossway is a publishing ministry of Good News Publishers.

VP   30   29   28   27   26   25   24   23   22   21   20
15   14   13   12   11   10   9   8   7   6   5   4   3   2   1

For my parents,
Glen and Diane Putman,
model peacemakers,
children of God (Matt. 5:9)

Contents

Foreword

Jesus prayed for unity for his followers in what many consider the greatest prayer recorded in Holy Scripture. In our Lord's own prayer, which he offered just before he was arrested, we see Jesus Christ pouring out his heart to the Father for his followers on the night before he died for us (John 17). This prayer was not only for the disciples and immediate followers of Christ, but for the church through the ages. Elsewhere, we are reminded that Jesus still prays for his own today from his exalted position at the right hand of God (Rom. 8:34; Heb. 7:25). His prayers for believers today surely reflect the words of John 17, which is a prayer for unity and a prayer for truth, a prayer for a holy uniqueness and a unique holiness for his followers.

In verses 20–26 of John 17, we read that Jesus prayed for his followers to experience a spiritual unity that exemplifies the oneness of the Father and the Son. Yet, far too often the followers of Christ throughout the centuries have been characterized by controversy, infighting, disagreement, and disunity. It is to this tension that Rhyne Putman has applied his insightful theological skills, wrestling with the issues and questions associated with doctrinal divisions among the people of God. In this extraordinarily well-written and well-designed volume, Putman explores not only why we disagree about doctrinal matters but what we should do about these doctrinal disagreements.

If the church believes the Bible and if the words of John 17 are seriously taken to heart, then why do these doctrinal differences seem not only to continue, but to multiply and expand? Putman brilliantly examines perspectives on the nature of Scripture and the hermeneutical questions involved in moving from Bible to theology. This careful treatment is followed by a thoughtful look at the role of reason, tradition, experience, and emotion in the formulation of Christian doctrine. Such a wide-ranging exploration will certainly prove to be helpful to readers.

The second half of the book encourages readers to move beyond explanation, taking steps toward application. Putman engages the thorny issues of when to change one's mind about previously held positions, and when and where to draw the lines regarding these doctrinal matters. The practical outworking of these challenging questions are given careful attention. *When Doctrine Divides the People of God* concludes on a hopeful note as Putman provides guidance on *how* we should disagree, offering a historically informed pathway regarding fellowship, shared service, cooperation, and collaboration.

The Nicene Creed, an important fourth-century confession, describes the church as one, holy, catholic or universal, and apostolic. Living out these creedal convictions and applying Putman's framework are much needed in our day. We should not, however, be naive to the difficulties involved especially when sorting out differences that arise over first-order theological issues, not to mention secondary and tertiary matters, requiring much prayer and wisdom.

Christ's followers are called to exemplify love and truth, oneness and holiness, catholicity and apostolicity. Certainly, we are to promote Christian unity at every opportunity. True believers belong to the same Father and are called to the same service. Believers trust the same Savior and have received the same gift of God's grace, thus sharing a common salvation. Ultimately, true unity must be built on true truth. Any other kind of unity is earthly, worldly, temporal, and thus falls short of the John 17 ideal.

Putman has offered beneficial guidance for his readers, doing so with exemplary exegetical skill, historically informed reasoning, and pastoral sensitivity. Taking seriously the reality of doctrinal differences that have developed over the years, he recognizes that a unity that exists without truth is mushy, misguided, and meaningless. The yearning for unity is real, as heard from those who ask, "Why can't we all just get along?" Putman, however, enables us to see that those who promote a kind of unity not grounded in truth and those who champion truth without a concern for love and unity are hardly consistent with scriptural teaching or the aspirations of the Nicene Creed.

As we reflect on Jesus's prayer in John 17, we see that his desire is not only for spiritual unity but also for sanctified truth (John 17:17). So, as affirmed in the historical creed, the church is not only one and universal, but also holy and apostolic. True holiness is based on truth taught by the apostles and made known to us in Holy Scripture (John 14:6; 16:13; 17:17). Just as it saddens the Father and the Son and harms the witness of the church when we fail to love one another and demonstrate biblical unity, so, likewise, the witness of the church is harmed when we look to the world to be our guide rather than to the truthfulness of God's word and the best of the Christian tradition.

How then do we know when our calling to truth and holiness is a call to be different not only from the world but from other professing believers? Putman provides a wise resource for those struggling with this question. After all, the question is not new. As early as the time of Tertullian (155–220) and the Montanists in the late second century, and especially with the debate surrounding Augustine (354–430) and the Donatists two centuries later, these questions were raised and have continued to be raised through the years. In American Christianity, the Fundamentalist-Modernist controversy in the early twentieth century brought about splits in major denominations, and parallel splits between conservatives and liberals took place in a number of churches in the United States and Canada. Putman's work is designed to strengthen theological convictions, foster Christian unity, and provide guidance for those who tend to divide or separate from others too quickly. Putman knows that such unnecessary fragmentation diminishes opportunities for genuine church reform and renewal.

Christians are thus called to live in tension emphasizing both truth and love, holiness and unity. It seems paramount in our polarized and fragmented world for followers of Christ to not only balance commitments to truth and love, but to pursue genuine Christian unity informed by authentic doctrinal conviction. The apostle Paul exhorts us not to take a wait-and-see attitude, but to be eager to preserve the "unity of the Spirit in the bond of peace" (Eph. 4:3). God's Spirit energizes the church to exemplify unity to an observing world. When believers cultivate and practice the virtues described in Ephesians 4:1–6, they display and preserve the unity of the Spirit. Paul's admonition to unity also includes the basis for this unity.

Paul continues his appeal in verses 4 and 5 of Ephesians 4 by claiming that "one hope," "one faith," and "one baptism" exist because there is "one Lord." The "one hope" of our calling points to the confident expectation of Christ's coming glory. The "one faith" refers to the sum and substance of the church's belief. No long-term Christian unity will be possible unless believers share a common commitment to apostolic doctrine, the "faith that was once for all delivered to the saints" (Jude 3). This "one faith" reflects the common experience of faith in Christ and the same access to him shared by all believers. "One baptism" pictures the outward expression of faith in the "one Lord." The larger context of Ephesians 4 indicates that true Christian unity expresses itself through variety (Eph. 4:7–12), bringing about maturity (vv. 13–16) and purity (vv. 17–32) in the body of Christ.

Rhyne Putman is to be commended for offering this superb and substantive volume, which in many ways provides a thoughtful and engaging blueprint for living out the expectations of scriptural teaching found in John 17 and Ephesians 4, doing so with a thorough exploration of the challenges and issues associated with hermeneutics, reason, epistemology, experience, tradition, bias, boundary-making, all informed by his grasp of the history of Christian doctrine.

Putman's exercise in theological method is ever so much more than ivory tower discussion. Readers will be blessed by this work, enabling them to be the people of God before a watching world. We are reminded afresh that visible unity grounded in theological truth is God's expectation for Christ's followers. Let us pray and work for renewal and unity not only in our theological commitments but in our worship, in our fellowship, in our educational efforts, in our shared service and social engagement, and ultimately in our gospel proclamation. We trust that Putman's work will not only help us take steps toward theological understanding and maturity but will lead us toward renewal to hear afresh and live out the words of Jesus himself: "that they may all be one, just as you, Father, are in me, and I in you, that they also may be in us, so that the world may believe that you have sent me" (John 17:21).

David S. Dockery
Professor of Theology, Theologian-in-Residence,
and Special Consultant to the President,
Southwestern Baptist Theological Seminary

Abbreviations

AT   Descartes, René. *Oeuvres de Descartes*. Vols. 1–12. Rev.
            ed. Edited by Charles Adam and Paul Tannery. Paris: J.
            Vrin/C.N.R.S., 1964–1976.

BECNT   Baker Exegetical Commentary on the New Testament

CP   Peirce, Charles S. *The Collected Papers of Charles Sand-
            ers Peirce*. 8 vols. Edited by Charles Hartshorne and Paul
            Weiss (vols. 1–6) and Arthur W. Burks (vols. 7–8). Cam-
            bridge, MA: Harvard University Press, 1931–1958.

ICC   International Critical Commentary

JETS   *Journal of the Evangelical Theological Society*

JGRChJ   *Journal of Greco-Roman Christianity and Judaism*

LW   Luther, Martin. *Luther's Works*. Edited by Jaroslav
            Pelikan, Helmut T. Lehmann, and Christopher Boyd
            Brown. 75 vols. Philadelphia: Fortress; St. Louis: Con-
            cordia, 1955–.

NIDNTTE   Moisés Silva, ed. *New International Dictionary of New
            Testament Theology and Exegesis*. 2nd ed. 4 vols. Grand
            Rapids, MI: Zondervan, 2014.

NPNF[1]   *Nicene and Post-Nicene Fathers*, Series 1. Edited by Al-
            exander Roberts, James Donaldson, Philip Schaff, and
            Henry Wace. 14 vols. Peabody, MA: Hendrickson, 1994.

NPNF[2]   *Nicene- and Post-Nicene Fathers*, Series 2. Edited by Al-
            exander Roberts, James Donaldson, Philip Schaff, and
            Henry Wace. 14 vols. Peabody, MA: Hendrickson, 1994.

S   Zwingli, Ulrich. *Huldreich Zwingli's Werke*. Edited by
            M. Schuler and J. Schulthess. 7 vols. Zurich, 1828–1842.

TDNT   Friedrich, Gerhard and Gerhard Kittel, eds., *Theological Dictionary of the New Testament* [*Theologisches Wörterbuch zum Neuen Testament*]. Translated by Geoffrey W. Bromiley. Grand Rapids, MI: Eerdmans, 1965–1976.

WA   Luther, Martin. *D. Martin Luthers Werke*. Kritische Gesamtausgabe. 73 vols. Weimar: Hermann Böhlaus Nachfolger, 1883–2009.

WBC   Word Biblical Commentary

Z   Zwingli, Ulrich. *Huldreich Zwinglis sämtliche Werke*. 10 vols. Berlin, Leipzig, Zurich: Heinsius, 1905–1991.

Introduction

When Doctrine Divides
the People of God

"Behold, how good and pleasant it is when brothers dwell in unity!"
Psalm 133:1

"For everything there is a season, and a time for every matter under heaven: . . . a time to embrace, and a time to refrain from embracing."
Ecclesiastes 3:1, 5b

"Protestant Leader Refutes Other 'Protestant' Heretic over His Erroneous Doctrine of the Lord's Supper."

Had there been a thing called the internet five centuries ago when Martin Luther and Ulrich Zwingli had their famous feud over Christian Communion, the blogosphere might have lit up with clickbait headlines like this one. The armchair commentators of social media could have rushed to publish their underdeveloped musings on the whole affair, either by taking sides in the debate or by asserting their moral superiority over the whole debacle. Luther and Zwingli may have taken shots at each other in their respective podcasts, exchanged a series of combative tweets and blog posts, debated in a YouTube simulcast, and then followed the whole thing up with a conciliatory book tour.

But in the actual sixteenth century, less than a decade after the Reformation began, the German and Swiss pastor-theologians engaged each other in a series of tracts and written disputations made publicly available through the new mass media technology of the moveable type printing press.[1] They were eventually called to an intervention by Philip of Hesse—a young German prince convinced that a face-to-face meeting would help resolve their conflict. Though political motives drove his efforts at reconciliation, Philip may very well be considered the first Protestant *ecumenist*. He longed for the sparring Reformers to make nice so that Protestants across Europe could take a stand together against the bullying of the papacy and the Holy Roman Empire. Philip wanted to see a united Protestant movement that could rival Rome in its scope and power.

Team Luther and Team Zwingli met at Marburg Castle in the first three days of October 1529. This meeting of the minds, known by history as the Marburg Colloquy, was a defining moment in the early years of the Reformation, not because it was successful but because it was such a letdown. To Philip's chagrin, no political alliance of German and Swiss Protestants would emerge. But the greater tragedy may be the fracas that kept these giants from personal fellowship and cooperation in a time of ecclesial and social upheaval.[2]

So, what went wrong? Both of these pastors *practiced* the Supper in virtually the same way. Unlike many late medieval Catholics, both believed that the sacrament was for both laypersons and the priestly class. Yet they were poles apart in their understandings of the *meaning*

---

1. Zwingli began the engagement with Luther with his *Amica exegesis, id est exposition eucharistiae negotii ad Martinum Lutherum* (1527; Z 5:562–758). Luther responded with *Daß diese Worte Christi: Das ist mein Leib, noch feststehen wider die Schwarmgeister* (1527; WA 23:64–283; *The Annotated Luther*, vol. 3: *Church and Sacraments*, ed. Paul W. Robinson [Minneapolis: Fortress, 2016], 163–274). Zwingli responded to Luther with *Daß diese Worte: Das ist mein Leib usw. ewiglich den alten Sinn haben werden usw* (1527; S 2.2:16–93; Z 5:805–977). Luther's final written contribution to the debate was his book *Vom Abendmahl Christi, Bekenntnis* (1528; WA 26:241–509). Zwingli and Johannes Oecolampadius countered this tome with *Über D. Martin Luthers Buch, Bekenntnis genannt* (1528; Z 6.2:22–248).

2. The most comprehensive account of the controversy between Luther and Zwingli is in Walther Köhler, *Zwingli und Luther. Ihr Streit über das Abendmahl nach seinen politischen und religiösen Beziehungen*, vol. 1, *Die religiöse und politische Entwicklung bis zum Marburger Religionsgespräch 1529* (Leipzig, 1924); and vol. 2, *Vom Beginn der Marburger Verhandlungen 1529 bis zum Abschluss der Wittenberger Konkordie 1536* (Gütersloh, 1953). The most detailed treatment of the controversy available in English is Hermann Sasse, *This Is My Body: Luther's Contention for the Real Presence in the Sacrament of the Altar* (Philadelphia: Augsburg Fortress, 1959). Whereas Köhler treats Zwingli more favorably, Sasse defends Luther's stance.

of the Supper. Luther rigorously argued that the risen, glorified body of Christ was present "in," "with," and "under" the bread and the wine of Communion.[3] Zwingli, on the other hand, insisted that the bread and the wine are merely symbolic representations of Christ's body and blood. For the Swiss Reformer, the Supper served as an important reminder of Christ's great sacrifice for our sin, but for the German, the Supper was an actual means by which God imparted grace into the lives of those who believe.

The kerfuffle between Luther and Zwingli began with different assumptions and starting points. First, they disagreed about the nature of the sacraments.[4] Second, they clashed over Christology, with each accusing the other of holding a heretical position on the union of Christ's human and divine natures.[5] Third, each took issue with the other's hermeneutics. They debated over what Jesus meant when he took the bread at the Last Supper and said, "This is my body, which is given for you" (Luke 22:19; 1 Cor. 11:24; cf. Matt. 26:26; Mark 14:22). Luther took Jesus's words "This is my body" quite *literally*. Because he believed the human nature of Jesus is present everywhere, he contended Jesus is bodily present in the bread and wine of Communion. Zwingli, who contended Jesus was using figurative language here, thought Luther's interpretation had a whiff of the Roman Catholic doctrine of transubstantiation that both men claimed to reject.[6]

Aside from the colorful rhetorical jabs fired at each other, the colloquy was principally a debate about key biblical texts and the

---

3. This language appears in the seminal Lutheran confessions. See The Augsburg Confession 10.1; The Small Catechism 6.2; The Large Catechism 5.8; The Apology of the Augsburg Confession 10.

4. Luther wanted to reform Catholic sacramentalism, and Zwingli wanted to abandon it. Zwingli believed the sacraments were mere signs of grace, not vessels of it. See Sasse, *This Is My Body*, 164–177; Sasse, "The Lutheran Understanding of the Consecration," in Hermann Sasse, *We Confess*, vol. 2, *The Sacraments*, trans. Norman Nagel (St. Louis: Concordia, 1985), 113–138; W. P. Stephens, *Zwingli: An Introduction to His Thought* (Oxford: Clarendon, 1994), 76–84.

5. On the communication of properties (*communicatio idiomatum*) between Christ's two natures, Luther contended that whatever one says of Christ's divine nature is also applicable to his human nature. Zwingli made a sharper distinction between the properties of the natures. Consequently, Luther accused Zwingli of Nestorianism and Zwingli accused Luther of Eutychianism. See Ryan Tafilowski, "Marburg Colloquy," in *Encyclopedia of Martin Luther and the Reformation*, vol. 2, ed. Mark A. Lamport (Lanham, MD: Rowman & Littlefield, 2017), 500; Z 5:930–932; S 2.2, 71; Sasse, *This Is My Body*, 121–122; Sasse, "The 1,500th Anniversary of Chalcedon," in Hermann Sasse, *We Confess*, vol. 1, *Jesus Christ*, trans. Norman Nagel (St. Louis: Concordia, 1984), 62–65; WA 26:332.

6. Anthony C. Thiselton, *The Hermeneutics of Doctrine* (Grand Rapids, MI: Eerdmans, 2007), 531–534.

interpretive rules for distinguishing between metaphorical and literal descriptions. It was first and foremost a dispute between men who *read the same Bible differently*. They reasoned differently about the texts. They felt differently about their respective theological positions. They interacted differently with the tradition that had gone before them. Even though Luther and Zwingli were both staunch defenders of the clarity of Scripture, they disagreed adamantly about what the biblical text meant on this point.

At the end of the colloquy, the two Reformers and their associates acknowledged their agreement with one another on fourteen out of fifteen tenets of the faith in a document known as the Marburg Articles. It could have been the making of a beautiful friendship, but one article—the final article on the Lord's Supper—drove a permanent wedge between the two groups and even kept Luther from acknowledging Zwingli as his Christian brother at the time. A weeping Zwingli pleaded with Luther for his right hand in fellowship, which the German Reformer denied him. For many contemporary readers, the differences between these positions on the Lord's Supper may seem trivial, but in the minds of these sixteenth-century Reformers, the gospel itself was on the line.[7]

Though historians like to ruminate on what might have happened had the Marburg Colloquy gone another direction, only God knows what the Protestant world would look like if Luther and Zwingli had been able to work through this matter. Protestants, who share a core conviction that every individual should be able to read the Bible for himself or herself, more than likely would have found themselves in another equally divisive conflict a few months later.[8]

Why Can't We All Just Get Along?

Nearly five centuries later, the spirit of dissent that permeated the Marburg Colloquy still haunts Protestantism and evangelicalism. We

---

7. For Luther, "This sacrament is the Gospel" (Sasse, *This Is My Body*, 405; cf. 281). Luther's emphasis on the sacramental nature of the Supper "led Zwingli to contrast two ways of salvation: the one by eating the flesh of Christ and the other by believing in him" (Stephens, *Zwingli*, 100). The former option was, for Zwingli, a return to papist religion that rendered the death of Christ unnecessary (Z 5:576, 659–661, 706–708).

8. Even if Luther and Zwingli had forged the union Philip wanted, these Magisterial Reformers still would have been at odds with the so-called "Radical Reformers" like the Anabaptists.

still quarrel over how best to understand the beginning of the Bible (Genesis 1–3), its ending (Revelation 19–22), and a good deal of what is in between.[9] We fight over which existing structure of church government most closely conforms to the biblical pattern (1 Tim. 3:1–13; Titus 1:5–9). We can be contentious over the proper candidates for baptism. We wag our tongues over speaking in tongues and the so-called miraculous spiritual gifts (Mark 16:17; Acts 2:1–13; 1 Corinthians 12–14; Heb. 2:3–4). We can have heated disagreements about predestination, election, and human freedom (Romans 8–9; Eph. 1:3–14). We have extended discussions about the extent of the atonement (Isa. 53:6; John 3:16; 10:15; Col. 1:20; 1 John 2:2). We even spar over what method of counseling or approach to apologetics is most faithful to Scripture. When we are not arguing about our theological traditions, we are caught up in more academic controversies like the recent scholarly debates over Paul's relationship to Judaism, the extent of God's foreknowledge, or the eternal relations within the Trinity.

Even as society becomes increasingly antagonistic toward traditional Christian beliefs and practices, many followers of Jesus remain gridlocked over the doctrinal matters that separate them. Though we live in what is becoming a post-Christian culture, some segments of the church have never been more theologically engaged—or divided. Never before in the history of the church have our theological disputes been so public, so accessible. The Reformation may have put the Bible in the hands of every individual, but the digital age has given everyone an open platform to discuss doctrine. Through the blessing (or the curse) of social media, everyone who has an opinion has an opportunity to air their viewpoints and project their disagreements to the world. Yet even with all of this ability to communicate, we still gravitate toward echo chambers that protect us from the risks of having open dialogue. We love protecting our tribes, our labels, and the self-assuring safety that comes in numbers. Though we should be modeling civility for our deeply divided political and cultural climate, we who are the people of God have done very little to set ourselves

---

9. Alister McGrath identifies at least nineteen Protestant approaches to Darwin's theory of evolution, all of which claim to be the correct interpretation of Scripture. See McGrath, *Christianity's Dangerous Idea* (New York: HarperOne, 2007), 208–209, 372–386.

apart from the broader culture. Instead of embodying the gospel of grace, we have just been part of the problem.

It comes as no surprise that we are at odds with the unbelieving world—Jesus promised that would happen (Matt. 10:22, 34; John 15:18)—but why do we "devour one another" (Gal. 5:15) with our infighting over doctrine? Jesus told his disciples that they would prove themselves to be his followers by their love for one another (John 13:35). On the night of his betrayal, he asked the Father to give his followers perfect unity—that they would be "one" as the Father and the Son are one—so that "the world may know" he was indeed sent by God (John 17:23). In essence, Jesus wanted his people to reflect the perfect union of the Father and the Son in the immanent Trinity. Given this kind of mandate, why do Christ-followers seem to revel in the "narcissism of minor details"? Should we continue sparring in an increasingly anti-Christian context?

One answer to these questions comes from ecumenists who have dedicated themselves to the visible unity of all Christian traditions as an essential element of Christian witness. Ecumenists get their name from a Greek term meaning "the inhabited world" or "universal" (*oikoumenikos*)—the same term (*oikoumenē*) used to describe the ecumenical councils of the early church. Ecumenists seek to stage a "sneak preview" on earth of the future eschatological reconciliation of all followers of Christ throughout history. In their quest for visible (and sometimes institutional) unity, ecumenists are sometimes accused of making too little of the convictions that set these traditions apart. Though building bridges between various traditions and denominations can bear much fruit, the tendency of some ecumenists to overlook or ignore doctrine is deeply troubling.

Other evangelical scholars have written excellent works on the possibility and parameters of evangelical ecumenism, issues I do not plan to explore here in detail.[10] I am more interested in the theologi-

---

10. See Michael Allen and Scott Swain, *Reformed Catholicity: The Promise of Retrieval for Theology and Biblical Interpretation* (Grand Rapids, MI: Baker, 2015); Christopher W. Morgan, "Toward a Theology of the Unity of the Church," in *Why We Belong: Evangelical Unity and Denominational Diversity*, ed. Anthony L. Chute, Christopher W. Morgan, and Robert A. Peterson (Wheaton, IL: Crossway, 2013), 19–36; Curtis Freeman, *Contesting Catholicity: Theology for Other Baptists* (Waco, TX: Baylor University Press, 2014); Steven R. Harmon, *Toward Baptist Catholicity* (Eugene, OR: Wipf & Stock, 2006); Harmon, *Ecumenism Means You, Too: Ordinary*

cal processes that led to these divergent traditions. However, I wish to preface this book on theological disagreement with a disclaimer about ecumenism. Many within my evangelical tradition cringe at the very mention of the term *ecumenical* because of the bad taste left in their mouth from twentieth-century ecumenical movements.[11] While some evangelicals suggest that we should recover the term *ecumenism* in a way that is consistent with our convictions about the gospel,[12] others maintain it is wiser to refrain from using it altogether because of its association with the ecumenical movements of the past.[13] Others prefer the related term *catholicity*, which doesn't come with all the sociopolitical baggage of *ecumenism*.[14]

I share many of the concerns my evangelical forebears had about ecumenical endeavors of the past. First, several (but not all) of the twentieth-century ecumenical efforts sought a tawdry peace through surrender and compromise. Evangelicals have felt that the social focus of many ecumenists undermined commitment to the gospel and personal evangelism. They were also uncomfortable with the easy peace made with some in these movements who denied essential tenets of the faith.[15] Of the eighteenth-century Latitudinarians, who shared with modern ecumenicists a penchant for theological accommodation, John Wesley wrote, "This unsettledness of thought, this being 'driven to and fro, and tossed about with every wind of doctrine,' is a great curse, not a blessing, an irreconcilable enemy, not

---

Christians and the Quest for Christian Unity (Eugene, OR: Cascade, 2010); Peter J. Leithart, *The End of Protestantism: Pursuing Unity in a Fragmented Church* (Grand Rapids, MI: Brazos, 2016); and Luder G. Whitlock Jr., *Divided We Fall: Overcoming a History of Christian Disunity* (Philipsburg, NJ: P&R, 2017).

11. Kenneth Scott Latourette, "Ecumenical Bearings of the Missionary Movement and the International Missionary Council," in *A History of the Ecumenical Movement, 1517–1948*, 2nd ed., ed. Ruth Rouse and Stephen C. Neil (Philadelphia: Westminster, 1967), 353.

12. Timothy George, for example, contends for an "ecumenism of conviction, not an ecumenism of accommodation." See "Baptists and Ecumenism: An Interview with Timothy George," interview by Everett Berry and Winston Hottman, Center for Baptist Renewal, April 6, 2017, http://www.centerforbaptistrenewal.com/blog/2017/4/6/baptists-and-ecumenism-a-discussion -with-timothy-george.

13. The historical theologian Gregg Allison suggests that evangelicals use the term *gospel connectionalism* instead of *ecumenism* so that evangelicals who pursue unity can (1) avoid the negative connotations of the ecumenical movement and (2) make the gospel the central element of their agreement (Gregg Allison, interview by author, Louisville, KY, September 8, 2016).

14. The term *catholicity* shares a very similar etymology to *ecumenism* (*katholikē* and *oikoumenē* both speak to something universal).

15. This criticism appears in William R. Estep, *Baptists and Christian Unity* (Nashville: Broadman, 1966), 108–123.

a friend, to true catholicism."[16] Unity without truth is no actual unity at all because it is devoid of a common purpose. For this reason, Paul told first-century believers to be "of the same mind" (Phil. 2:2; cf. 1:27) and Peter told persecuted believers to "have unity of mind" (1 Pet. 3:8).

Second, many evangelicals are skeptical of post-Vatican II efforts to forge ecumenical dialogue with Roman Catholics, especially when something as central as the doctrine of justification by faith still divides them. As the controversy surrounding the 1994 statement *Evangelicals and Catholics Together* illustrated, evangelicals do not all agree with one another about how precisely they relate to Roman Catholicism.[17] On the other side of the aisle, Roman Catholics disagree with one another about whether the condemnations of the Protestant doctrine of justification made by the Council of Trent (1545–1563) still apply.[18]

Third, evangelicals rebuff the anti-realism of some ecumenical efforts. One of the most significant (and most controversial) works in contemporary theological method was George Lindbeck's 1984 book, *The Nature of Doctrine*. In it, the Lutheran ecumenist suggested one way of getting around our doctrinal disputes would be recognizing that doctrine is merely a culturally conditioned way of regulating our belief systems. Lindbeck denied that doctrine depicts reality. Instead, it is just a set of rules or grammar that shape the way we believe. By conceiving of doctrine in this way, he hoped to resolve conflicts between Protestants, Catholics, and Orthodox Christians who present contrary doctrinal assertions.[19] However, evangelical theologians reacted strongly, asserting that such an anti-realist way of reading Christian doctrine undermined its ability to speak truthfully about God and his world.[20]

---

16. John Wesley, "The Catholic Spirit," in *The Works of John Wesley*, ed. Thomas Jackson, 14 vols. (London, 1872), 5:502.

17. See "Evangelicals and Catholics Together: The Christian Mission in the Third Millennium," *First Things* (May 1994); Timothy George and Thomas G. Guarino, eds., *Evangelicals and Catholics Together at Twenty: Vital Statements on Contested Topics* (Grand Rapids, MI: Brazos, 2014); R. C. Sproul, *Getting the Gospel Right: The Tie That Binds Evangelicals Together* (Grand Rapids, MI: Baker, 2003).

18. See Karl Lehmann, Michael Root, and William G. Rusch, eds., *Justification by Faith: Do the Sixteenth-Century Condemnations Still Apply?* (London: Bloomsbury, 1997).

19. George A. Lindbeck, *The Nature of Doctrine* (Louisville: Westminster John Knox, 1984).

20. See Kevin J. Vanhoozer, *The Drama of Doctrine* (Louisville: Westminster John Knox, 2006); Alister E. McGrath, *A Passion for Truth: The Intellectual Coherence of Evangelicalism* (Downers Grove, IL: InterVarsity Press, 1996), 119–162.

Fourth, some evangelicals equate ecumenism with normative religious pluralism or compromising interreligious dialogue between Christian and non-Christian religions.[21] The term *ecumenical* typically signifies attempts at visible or organizational unity between self-described Christians, not agreement with other world religions. Though this pluralistic use of *ecumenical* is not the ordinary sense of the word, evangelicals are right to be concerned about any attempt to normalize religious pluralism. The centrality of Christ and exclusivity of the Christian gospel are central tenets of our worldview (John 14:6; Acts 4:12).

Finally, evangelicals in Free Church traditions like mine are particularly wary of any talk of institutional unions because of the often contrary ways Christians think about church government. The Baptists in my faith tradition emphasize the independence of local churches that enables them to make decisions for themselves under the authority of Scripture and the direction of the Holy Spirit without an outside governing body. This vision of church leadership is incompatible with top-down, hierarchical models of church government where local churches take marching orders from a central office.[22]

While I do have reservations about some ecumenical movements in recent history, I want to stress the great need for *catholicity* rooted in the biblical gospel. Catholicity is a celebration of the things that all gospel-loving Christians share in common. All who have been justified by Christ through faith believe the same gospel and belong to the same family. As Paul asserted, "There is one body and one Spirit—just as you were called to the one hope that belongs to your call—one Lord, one faith, one baptism, one God and Father of all, who is over all and through all and in all" (Eph. 4:4–6). We may have our differences, but we must recognize that among followers of Jesus, there is only one body, one hope, and one calling. We share a common charge to go and make disciples of all nations, teaching them to obey all that our Lord commanded (Matt. 28:19–20).

---

21. See John MacArthur and Richard Mayhue, eds., *Biblical Doctrine: A Systematic Summary of Bible Truth* (Wheaton, IL: Crossway, 2017), 688. MacArthur describes ecumenism as a strategy from Satan where "all sincere religions involve valid expressions of worshiping the true God."

22. See Robert G. Torbet, *Ecumenism: The Free Church Dilemma* (Valley Forge, PA: Judson, 1968).

Rivalry, discontent, and disagreement may be part of every natural family, but an adopted family rooted in divine forgiveness should extend that same forgiveness to one another, even if they cannot simply overlook all the things that set them apart. We should make every effort "to maintain the unity of the Spirit in the bond of peace" (Eph. 4:3). We should strive toward "unity of the faith and of the knowledge of the Son of God" (v. 13). Though we recognize this as our ideal, we are on the lookout for "gospels" contrary to the gospel of Christ that cannot provide this true catholic unity (Gal. 1:8).

On occasion, Protestants and evangelicals must engage in *polemic theology*, an expression of Christian doctrine that explains and defends the distinctive beliefs of a particular theological tradition. Polemics serves an important and necessary function in maintaining and replicating belief. It stresses the importance of biblical truth and the need for coherence in a theological system. It eschews accommodation and can increase confidence in one's tradition.

The word *polemic* has its origins in a Greek word meaning "war" or "warlike" (*polemikos*). Sometimes such warring is necessary when opposing doctrines pose a danger to the faith and to the flock that God has entrusted the shepherds to protect (Acts 20:28; Titus 1:10–16). We must guard diligently those doctrines that we believe are *essential* to the Christian faith. But a polemic theology lacking wisdom or love can create more problems than it fixes. In the same way that a war can be justified with a just cause and righteous conduct, polemics can and should be carried out with Christian virtue and kindness. We must be willing to speak truth but always with love and with the building up of the body as our end (Eph. 4:15–16).

Other times, we must practice *irenic theology*. Irenicists, who draw their name from a Greek word meaning "peace" (*eirenikos*), seek peace with fellow believers from other traditions in their theological discourse. In so doing, they embody Jesus's blessing as the sons and daughters of God (Matt. 5:9). An irenic and graceful spirit should characterize our intramural disagreements. But just as polemic theology without love can be an abuse of polemics, irenic theology without a commitment to biblical truth can become imbalanced and distorted. The preacher of Ecclesiastes says that there is "a time for war, and a time for peace"

(Eccles. 3:8b). We might add that there is *a time for polemics* and a *time for irenics*. We can fight false teaching without being contentious, and we can be peacemakers without waving the white flag in the surrender of our biblical convictions. Christian unity is a good, valuable thing to pursue, but not at the expense of essential truth.

Unlike the spirit of theological minimalism that permeates so much of the ecumenical conversation, the discussion of doctrinal disagreement in this book celebrates both *doctrine* and *difference*. Protestants and evangelicals need teaching rooted in God's self-revelation. They need to be able to articulate the theological content of the Bible in a manner that is clear and concise and fitting for their context. They also need to be free to read the Bible for themselves without a church magisterium (or a popular blog) simply telling them what to believe.

As lovers of the truth, we should not reduce our doctrinal disagreements to much ado about nothing. Healthy disagreements are an important part of sanctification and growth in "grace and knowledge of our Lord and Savior Jesus Christ" (2 Pet. 3:18). The doctrinal distinctives of our traditions and denominations are important, giving shape to who we are. To force conformity of thought or the capitulation of beliefs would work against the grain of what it means to be a Protestant. If I may misquote John Henry Newman, to be deep in uniformity of thought is to cease to be Protestant.[23]

The Plan of This Book

This book is a work in *theological method* that explores the nature of doctrinal diversity from a distinctly evangelical point of view. Theological method (sometimes called *theological prolegomena*) is an area of theology that addresses big-picture questions about the nature of doctrine, the sources of theology, and the processes by which we develop doctrine. It is a philosophy of theology. This book is meant to be an interdisciplinary exploration of doctrinal disagreement that borrows from the rich resources of hermeneutics, philosophy,

---

23. See John Henry Newman, *An Essay on the Development of Christian Doctrine* (London, 1893), 8. Accusing Protestants of being detached from history and tradition, the future Roman Catholic cardinal quipped, "To be deep in history is to cease to be a Protestant."

tradition, and other academic disciplines such as psychology and the social sciences.

Here, I will seek to answer two fundamental questions about theological diversity: First, how do Christ-followers with similar convictions about Scripture and the gospel come to such drastically different points of view in matters of faith and practice? Second, what should otherwise like-minded Christians do about the doctrines that divide them? This is not an exhaustive survey of every factor behind our theological diversity—I'm confident there are many important matters I don't address here—but a summary of the major factors I see at work in the divide among evangelical Christians.

The focus here is on theological diversity among Protestant evangelicals who affirm *sola Scriptura*—the Reformation doctrine that Scripture is the supreme source and only normative standard for Christian doctrine. Evangelicals confess Scripture as the only inspired, inerrant, and infallible revelation of God.[24] Roman Catholic and Orthodox Christians give tradition a more prominent place of authority than their Protestant and evangelical counterparts do. For some in these traditions, ecclesial tradition is often placed alongside Scripture as an equal authority.[25] By contrast, *sola Scriptura* Protestants recognize tradition as a valuable resource for Christian theology but understand its authority to be derivative, not primary. In other words, tradition is not an independent, primary authority and is authoritative for the Christian only when it correctly conveys the message of Scripture.

Those in faith traditions that gauge religious beliefs by personal experiences (e.g., some in Pentecostal traditions or some liberal Protestants) are very likely to have differences of opinion because of the uniqueness of personal life experiences, and it should come as no surprise when such competing individual religious authorities yield

---

24. My working definition of *evangelical* leans heavily on the "Bebbington Quadrilateral" found in David W. Bebbington, *Evangelicalism in Modern Britain: A History from the 1730s to the 1980s* (London: Routledge, 1989), 2–3. The four characteristics Bebbington identifies in all evangelicalism are: *conversionism*, the belief that lives can and should be changed through the gospel; *biblicism*, an unwavering commitment to the unique authority of Scripture; *activism*, the missionary and sociopolitical impetus of evangelical ministry; and *crucicentrism*, the emphasis on Jesus Christ's atoning work on the cross.

25. See *Catechism of the Catholic Church*, 2nd ed. (New York: Doubleday, 2012), 31. "Sacred Tradition and sacred Scripture . . . flowing out of the same divine well-spring, come together in some fashion to form one thing and move towards the same goal. . . . Both Scripture and Tradition must be accepted and honored with equal sentiments of devotion and reverence."

diverse results. Some might assert the "Holy Spirit" is leading them to a new belief or practice contrary to Scripture, but the Holy Spirit cannot contradict what he inspired as inerrant truth. One may claim the experience of having been on a tour through heaven or of receiving a personal message from Jesus, but such claims are not provable by Scripture and therefore cannot be binding on all believers. They may be genuinely spiritual experiences without being from the Spirit of God (1 John 4:1–6). Again, *sola Scriptura* Protestants may recognize the value of experience in Christian theology without giving experience primacy in the formation of beliefs. Experience can confirm the truth of Scripture in the life of the believer, but experience does not dictate what Christians should believe about belief and practice.

I also will not address disagreements with other Protestant groups who downplay or outright dismiss the unique authority of Scripture in the formation of Christian doctrine or practice. Dissent with readers of Scripture who endorse its piecemeal application is inevitable for those who unequivocally invoke its authority on disputed matters. Those who deny the full truthfulness of the Bible usually claim conflicting opinions among biblical authors themselves. They will pit Jesus against Paul or Paul against "deutero-Paul" and take sides with one author or another on the issues most important to them. Though important conversations need to be had with those from these liberal and progressive traditions, those discussions are well beyond the scope of my project here.

I am more concerned with this question: how do evangelical Christians who claim the same final authority come to their opposing views, especially when they share common convictions about the sufficiency, clarity, and inerrancy of Scripture? Why do believers who agree that the whole Bible is true still disagree about the truth it teaches? In what way can we say Scripture is "clear" if what it says seems so foggy to us?

The first part of this book is an exploration of the question, "Why are the people of God divided over doctrine?" This section is primarily *descriptive*, meaning I am only describing what happens in theological disagreement, not necessarily what *should* happen. Just like the controversy between Luther and Zwingli, I submit that most doctrinal disputes among Protestants and evangelicals today begin as disagreements over how best to understand the Bible, though other social, psychological, and rational factors are also key in understanding these feuds. I remain convinced that a better awareness of our own interpretive processes and the way we come to our theological beliefs can change the tenor of our debates.

I begin Part One with a description of the *interpretive limitations* of every Bible reader that builds on the insights of contemporary hermeneutical theory (chapter 1). This chapter is an exploration of the *general hermeneutics* of our interpretive differences, i.e., an exploration of how all human interpretation works. In Luther and Zwingli's day, the charge made by their Roman Catholic opponents was that Scripture was in need of a formal interpreter because ordinary people could not be entrusted with the responsibility of discovering its proper meaning. Today, the postmodern temptation is to blame this diversity of opinion on an unstable text without meaning, pronouncing authorial intent irrelevant and locating ultimate authority in the reader or the reading community. The realities of hermeneutical diversity— what Christian Smith has provocatively called "pervasive interpretive pluralism"[26]—pose a real challenge to the evangelical affirmation of the clarity of Scripture. Using the insights of evangelical hermeneutics scholars, I will suggest that traditional Protestant affirmations of the clarity of Scripture and the illuminating activity of the Holy Spirit in biblical interpretation can be maintained even in the face of pervasive hermeneutical diversity.

Chapter 2 is an introductory overview of the specific types of *exegetical difference* between Christians that can contribute to doctrinal disagreement. Whereas the focus of chapter 1 is general hermeneutics, the focus here is *special hermeneutics*, i.e., the specific ways readers approach biblical texts. Here I offer an introductory overview of specific ways in which differences at the level of biblical exegesis and historical interpretation can shape our various theological outcomes, something that gets surprisingly little treatment in many discussions of theological method. Much of what is covered here is material covered

---

26. Christian Smith, *The Bible Made Impossible: Why Biblicism Is Not a Truly Evangelical Reading of Scripture* (Grand Rapids, MI: Brazos, 2012).

in Biblical Hermeneutics 101: textual criticism, the role of semantics, syntax, and literary and historical criticism. I intend to show ways in which each step in the process of biblical interpretation can impact our understanding of biblical doctrines.

The more constructive arguments of the book begin with chapter 3, which addresses the role *reason* plays in our interpretive conflicts. Poor deductive and inductive reasoning may have some explanatory power with regards to our theological differences, but faults of the individual mind cannot account for all the differences. I will contend that abductive reasoning, a type of informal logic that depends on creative thinking, is the primary way we create and choose theological models for interpreting the thematic unity of Scripture. Differences are inevitable given the sizable role human creativity plays in interpreting Scripture and developing doctrine. Some of this discussion is unavoidably technical, but I have tried to address these issues in a way that will benefit nonspecialists who are patient enough to follow the argument through to its conclusion.

The role *human psychology* plays in our interpretive and theological disagreements is the subject of chapter 4. I interact extensively with the work of social psychologist Jonathan Haidt, who argues that people quarrel over ethics, politics, and religion because they begin with fundamentally different intuitions or feelings about morality. I critically employ Haidt's research to talk about the way in which *experience* and *personality* can shape our biblical interpretation and theological construction. I will suggest that emotion and intuition may have a powerful effect on the interpretive choices we make, even if we believe we are being completely rational in our reading of the Bible.

I conclude Part One with a discussion about the ways *bias* and *tradition* have tremendous sticking power in our theological formation and doctrinal disagreements (chapter 5). Tradition is an important formative tool in the life of any Christian, but uncritical engagement with tradition can foster unhelpful biases in theological formation. Using research from cognitive psychology, I address ways in which our reading of the Bible frequently tends to reinforce our previously held theological assumptions rather than producing faithful exegesis.

I conclude the chapter with suggestions drawn from the same research to minimize theological confirmation bias.

The second part of this book is more *prescriptive* than descriptive, and it addresses a more practical question: "What should the people of God do about doctrinal division?" In chapter 6, I engage with philosophers working in the area of "epistemology of disagreement" to help address the question "When should we change our minds about our theological disagreements and when should we agree to disagree?" As I hope to show, the practical advice offered by these philosophers can be useful for our in-house theological debates.

In chapter 7, I ask an ecclesiological question: When should doctrine divide the people of God and when should it unite them? When should we be joined together in cooperative fellowship and when should we go our separate ways? I explore the concept of doctrinal taxonomy, the way in which Christians tend to rank doctrines according to their importance. Here I explore the ecclesiological convictions which draw lines around our tribal fellowships and attempt to define the gospel in its simplest biblical expression. I offer three tests for determining where a particular tenet should fit in a doctrinal taxonomy.

The book concludes with a constructive Christian ethic of doctrinal disagreement informed by Scripture, church history, and pastoral theology. How should we act toward one another while we await the future eschatological event wherein God finally resolves all our differences of opinion? I appeal to the religious conflict and subsequent personal reconciliation of early evangelical leaders George Whitefield and John Wesley as models for a contemporary evangelical praxis for theological disagreement.

I pray this book helps some think more clearly about how we disagree about doctrine and how we respond to our parochial skirmishes. I contend that clarity in this matter requires a better understanding of how we move from the Bible to our theological systems of belief. I am convinced that appropriate respect for differing traditions and beliefs can honor the Lord Jesus and improve our gospel witness to the watching world. More than anything else, I want God's word, not a favorite theological tradition or denominational distinctive, to be the master of our thinking when we talk about doctrine.

PART ONE

WHY WE DISAGREE ABOUT DOCTRINE

1

We Read Imperfectly

General Hermeneutics and
the Clarity of Scripture

Protestants and evangelicals who quarrel over Christian doctrine and practice read the same Bible, the same sixty-six-book canon.[1] We may hail from divergent denominations or traditions, but we claim a common authority. We may have particular ways of doing church but all appeal to the same standard to defend our distinctive practices. We sometimes need to go our separate ways because we can't agree about the implications of the gospel, but all of us want to get the gospel right. We who affirm the Reformation principle of *sola Scriptura* agree, at least in principle, that Scripture is the supreme source and only guiding norm of Christian theology.

As evangelicals, we long to be "biblical" in what we teach and practice. We want our doctrine—our normative expression of Christian truth—to be rooted in the Bible. We all agree Scripture should have the final word in our disputes, but Scripture must be interpreted (Neh. 8:8; Acts 8:30). We want to be obedient to God's voice in the

---

1. Roman Catholics acknowledge seventy-three books (including the Apocrypha). The Greek Orthodox canon contains seventy-nine. The canon of the Orthodox Tewahedo Church in Ethiopia has a whopping eighty-one-book canon! But while these canons contain apocryphal or deuterocanonical books, even these traditions give their additional books a lesser authority in the formation of doctrine.

text and sensitive to the Spirit's leading, but even those shared desires do not guarantee uniformity in our interpretations of Scripture. Something about our reading (or our nature) keeps us from coming into the Bible in the same way, from making the same judgments about the text. Though we eagerly await the future day in which all of our hindrances to knowing God fully are removed, now, in the interim period, we see the written word of God through a glass darkly (1 Cor. 13:12).[2]

Theologians have long recognized the role our interpretive differences play in doctrinal diversity. The fifth-century Gallic theologian Vincent of Lérins said, "All do not accept [Scripture] in one and the same sense. . . . One understands its words in one way, another in another; so that it seems to be capable of as many interpretations as there are interpreters."[3] Interpretive diversity—and the ever-present threat of heresy—led Vincent to believe "the rule for the right understanding of the prophets and apostles should be framed in accordance with the standard of Ecclesiastical and Catholic interpretation."[4] Though Vincent believed Scripture to be a sufficient source of divine revelation in need of no other additional content, he suggested interpreters read the Bible with church tradition so they wouldn't become heretics. Building on this germ of an idea, later medieval theologians insisted the church needed a formal teaching office to decipher the meaning of Scripture and the will of God for the people.[5]

The Reformers gave neither the church nor tradition such primacy in biblical interpretation. They conceded the potential for human error in individual interpreters, but they also realized the magisterium and church councils were also made up of people prone to the same kinds of mistakes.[6] Luther and the other Reformers maintained Scripture is

---

2. See Wayne Grudem, *Systematic Theology* (Grand Rapids, MI: Zondervan, 2000), 1162n7. Paul does not mean that glorified believers will have omniscience or exhaustive knowledge of all things, only that our knowledge will be "without any error or misconceptions."

3. Vincent of Lérins, *Commonitory* 2.5; *NPNF*[2] 11:132.

4. Vincent of Lérins, *Commonitory* 2.5; *NPNF*[2] 11:132.

5. For a history of this development, see Heiko Oberman, *Forerunners of the Reformation: The Shape of Late Medieval Thought*, trans. Paul L. Nyhus (New York: Holt, Rinehart & Winston, 1966).

6. Luther boldly charged the Fathers with the same potential for interpretive error: "Since the Fathers have often erred, as you yourself confess, who will make us certain as to where they have not erred, assuming their own reputation is sufficient and should not be weighed and judged ac-

We Read Imperfectly   39

clear enough for every Christian to interpret it without the need of a divinely instituted teaching office. Scripture has an intellegible meaning communicated by its human and divine authorship. The Reformers presumed that the Holy Spirit involves himself in the interpretation process, helping *illuminate* the meaning of Scripture for its readers.

Yet these affirmations pose an interesting problem: In what sense can we call the Bible clear if its meaning is so disputed? And why do believers reach conflicting conclusions if the same Holy Spirit is at work in each of their lives? This chapter breaks ground on the larger theme of this book: the relationship between our claims about Scripture as the definitive authority for the people of God and the reality of evangelical theological diversity.

In this chapter I lay out basic evangelical presumptions about the nature of biblical interpretation which will shape the discussion in the following chapters. Here I will borrow liberally from the work of more qualified hermeneutics scholars who defend the ability of authors to convey meaning and who acknowledge the fallibility of interpreters striving to make sense of authorial intentions. Theological diversity does not diminish or take away from the doctrines of the clarity of Scripture and the illumination of the Spirit when these claims are properly understood.

The Nature of Interpretation

How do we know what the Bible—or any text, for that matter—really means? Before tackling the big issues like ecclesiology, eschatology, or election, we must explore the more fundamental questions about interpretation. The term *hermeneutics* (from the Gk. *hermēneuō*, meaning "to interpret") has many uses. Most who hear the word associate it with the rules for interpreting biblical genres (what we also call *biblical hermeneutics* or *special hermeneutics*). The term can also refer to a branch of philosophy which examines how human beings make meaning and communicate through texts (*general hermeneutics* or *philosophical hermeneutics*).

---

cording to the divine Scriptures? They have (you say) also interpreted the Scriptures. What if they erred in their interpretation, as well as in their life and writings?" WA 8:484; translation appears in Mark D. Thompson, *A Sure Ground on Which to Stand: The Relation of Authority and Interpretive Method in Luther's Approach to Scripture* (Eugene, OR: Wipf & Stock, 2006), 254–255.

General hermeneutics is a close cousin to other important areas in philosophy: the study of how we know what we know (*epistemology*), the search for what it means to be a human being (*anthropology*), and the field that examines how we use signs in human communication (*semiotics*). Here, I want to leverage the tools of general hermeneutics to defend the clarity of Scripture and a commonsense approach to biblical interpretation. Though some of the hermeneutical philosophers who shape my thinking here do not share my evangelical worldview, many of the assertions they make about texts and readers are consistent with what Scripture says about God's self-communication, about human nature, and about the world God has made.[7]

Theologians sometimes ignore the detours through philosophy so they can jump straight into the fray of exegetical debate, but questions related to general hermeneutics loom large over everything we do in interpreting the Bible and developing doctrine: *What are texts? What is the role of the reader in interpretation? Where does the meaning of a text come from—the author, the reader, or the text itself? What is the right way to read a text? The wrong way?* Answers to these questions usually fall into one of two categories: *author-oriented* or *reader-centered* hermeneutical approaches. Author-oriented approaches to interpretation seek to understand the meaning of a text created by the author. Reader-centered approaches put the onus of creating meaning on the individual reader or reading community. Clarity on these matters is crucial in a postmodern climate where exclusive truth claims are ignored or dismissed, sometimes even among self-described Christians.

Most Christian theologians throughout the history of interpretation have gravitated toward a commonsense hermeneutic that gives the authorship of biblical texts pride of place in interpretation. Before the dawn of modernity, readers usually took for granted the ability of authors to convey meaning through written texts. Even the medieval theologians who affirmed the "fourfold sense of Scripture" (i.e., its literal, typological, moral, and analogical senses) prioritized the "literal sense"

---

7. Truth shared between believers and nonbelievers flows out of common grace. The inclusion of hermeneutical philosophy in a discussion on theological method does not make theology or the interpretation of Scripture subservient to such philosophical discussions. Instead, my aim is to appropriate the tools of "hermeneutical realism" as an ancillary complement to the truth of God's word. See Alister E. McGrath, *A Scientific Theology*, vol. 2, *Reality* (Grand Rapids, MI: Eerdmans, 2002), 200–201.

of the authors in their interpretation of the Bible. As Thomas Aquinas explains, "The literal sense is indeed what the author intends."[8] Hugh of St. Victor encouraged readers of Scripture to give preference to the meaning "which appears certain to have been intended by the author."[9] Medieval interpreters may have believed the Bible can mean more than what its original human authors intended, but certainly not any less.

The Protestant Reformers downplayed the other three senses of interpretation but agreed with medieval theologians that interpreters should seek to understand Scripture's literal sense.[10] The Reformers' approach to biblical texts later came to be known as the *grammatical-historical method*. Contrary to what its name might imply, the grammatical-historical "method" is not so much a step-by-step methodology for biblical interpretation as it is a general orientation toward Scripture. Advocates of the grammatical-historical method see their primary task to be interpreting Scripture in its original linguistic and historical contexts without calling into question its claims. Interpreters in this vein presume the truthfulness of Scripture and receive the claims of biblical authorship in good faith.

In the eighteenth and nineteenth centuries, however, the practice of biblical interpretation began drifting away from the grammatical-historical emphasis on the discovery of authorial intent toward a *historical-critical method*. Modernists asserted that human beings were capable of mastery over their world, which entailed taking the Bible captive as an object of critical study. Instead of taking the intentions of biblical authors at their face value, these modernist interpreters sought to reconstruct the message of the Bible for Enlightenment-era humanity.[11]

The theologians and biblical scholars of modernity did not deny biblical texts the ability to convey authorial meaning, but they did deny these authors any authority over their lives. They rejected the

---

8. Aquinas, *Summa Theologica* 1.1.10; quoted in Thompson, *Sure Ground on Which to Stand*, 41–42.

9. Hugh of St. Victor, *De Scripturis et Scriptoribus Sacris* 6; quoted in Thompson, *Sure Ground on Which to Stand*, 41–42.

10. For a brief overview of this development in Protestant hermeneutics, see Anthony C. Thiselton, *Hermeneutics* (Grand Rapids, MI: Eerdmans, 2009), 124–133.

11. For an excellent critical history of this period in hermeneutics and biblical scholarship, see Stephen Neil and N. T. Wright, *The Interpretation of the New Testament, 1861–1986*, 2nd ed. (Oxford: Oxford University Press, 1988).

supernatural worldview of biblical authors as an artifact from the primitive past—something that needed to be "demythologized" rather than embraced.[12] They presumed they were in a place to understand biblical texts even better than the authors because they were in a better place to judge the authors' historical and cultural biases.[13] Many of these modernist figures embraced *positivism*, the belief in an individual's ability to have indisputable knowledge of the world around them. But they naively (and ironically) believed biblical writers were tainted by subjective, imperfect knowledge from an archaic worldview while maintaining that they themselves were being neutral, objective, and empirical in their own beliefs. Modernists asserted their ability to read Scripture without presuppositions while grumbling about the biased, "dogmatic" interpretations of orthodox Christians.[14]

On the other side of the hermeneutical spectrum lies a group of interpreters who stress subjectivity to the point that they deny the ability to know anything about what a text really means. Traditional notions about authorial intent came under scrutiny in twentieth-century literary criticism, in wave after wave of text-centered and reader-centered literary approaches such as the New Criticism, Deconstruction, Poststructuralism, and radical Reader-Response Criticism. Representatives of these schools believe readers or reading communities, not authors, ultimately determine the meaning of texts. They maintain that the structure of human language and the nature of interpretation prevents us from discovering the meanings of texts as intended by their authors.

Biblical scholars and theologians under the influence of these postmodern theories reject the notion that the Bible has a fixed meaning that its readers can discover.[15] In the words of the postmodern New Testament scholar Dale Martin,

---

12. When I teach about demythologization in twentieth-century New Testament scholarship, I require my students to read Rudolf Bultmann, *Jesus Christ and Mythology* (Upper Saddle River, NJ: Prentice Hall, 1958). This book gives readers a clear introduction to the thought of one of the most influential voices of twentieth-century neo-liberal theology. As with many other liberal writers of his time, Bultmann believes himself to be doing Christianity a favor by providing an apologetic for the faith appealing to the scientific, modern mind.

13. Friedrich Schleiermacher, *Hermeneutics: The Handwritten Manuscripts*, ed. Heinz Kimmerle, trans. James Duke and Jack Forstman (Atlanta: Scholars, 1999), 113.

14. N. T. Wright, *The New Testament and the People of God* (Minneapolis: Fortress, 1992), 32–34. Wright calls this modernist mind-set "naïve realism."

15. Dale B. Martin, *Biblical Truths: The Meaning of Scripture in the Twenty-First Century* (New Haven, CT: Yale University Press, 2017), 96.

Learning to interpret the Bible in seminary is pictured as learning how to open the box, unpack and perhaps discard the rather useless packing materials, and pull the meaning out of the text. . . . The meaning . . . is objectively in there, simply hidden in the container of the text. . . . Texts are not just containers that hold meaning. The meaning of a text is a result of the interpretive process itself, which is not possible apart from the activities of human interpreters. . . . All readings of texts in fact are the making of meaning.[16]

Martin insists we can't get into the minds of authors, nor can we capture their intentions. We come to texts with our own interpretive frameworks and agendas. Interpreters do not "discover" meaning; they *create* it every time they take up a book to read.[17]

By denying an author his or her place of determining the meaning of a text, text-centered and reader-centered hermeneutics undermine the prospect of recovering a "correct" reading of a text. Appeals to the author or the text itself cannot resolve our feuds about the meaning of the text because meaning is not in the text. For radical Reader-Response interpreters, one reading of a text is just as valid as another.[18] This means the Bible offers no "right" answers for our doctrinal disputes. There is no "biblical position" on marriage or human sexuality, or any other subject for that matter.[19] The atheist, the right-wing Catholic, and the left-wing Protestant can all come to the same passage and create drastically different meanings if neither the text nor the author provides a means to adjudicate between the readings.

These postmodern biblical scholars claim our hermeneutical and theological diversity as evidence for their belief that texts have no meaning and no way of communicating authorial purpose. But

---

16. Dale B. Martin, *Pedagogy of the Bible: An Analysis and Proposal* (Louisville: Westminster John Knox, 2008), 30.

17. Dale B. Martin, *Sex and the Single Savior: Gender and Sexuality in Biblical Interpretation* (Louisville: Westminster John Knox, 2006), 4–7.

18. More moderate versions of Reader-Response Theory speak of ways in which authors intentionally invite readers in to actualize potential meanings latent in the texts. For an overview of the differences between radical and moderate forms of Reader-Response Theory, see Anthony C. Thiselton, *Systematic Theology* (Grand Rapids, MI: Eerdmans, 2015), 25; Thiselton, *Hermeneutics*, 29–34, 306–325.

19. For a sampling of these postmodern readings on sexuality in the Bible, see Martin, *Sex and the Single Savior*; Jennifer Knust, *Unprotected Texts: The Bible's Surprising Contradictions about Sex and Desire* (New York: HarperOne, 2011).

interpretive disputes need not lead to the drastic conclusion that texts have no meaning or that authors are incapable of expressing their desires. Far from it. The very fact that we have impassioned debates about the meanings of literary works shows that we intuitively presume them to bear meaning and purpose. We have dissenting opinions because we intuitively believe there is a right way and a wrong way to make sense of what we read.

Evangelicals reject both the modernist claim that we can lord it over the biblical text via the historical-critical method and the postmodernist assertion that biblical texts have no meanings apart from the meanings we give them. As John Webster and others have shown, the evangelical doctrine of Scripture flows out of the doctrine of God.[20] The triune God is a communicative agent who has willed to disclose himself to his creatures through the means of human language to bring about his desired ends.[21] In his sovereign providence, God inspired people with unique personalities in various historical settings to produce a clear message that is wholly his. Our affirmation of biblical authority is not the claim that an autonomous text has authority over our lives but an affirmation of God's authority expressed through human writers. The twin interpretive heresies of modernism and postmodernism which deny the divine authorship of Scripture are ultimately denials of the lordship of Christ.

Our interpretation of Scripture begins with two important hermeneutical assumptions that are true of every form of human communication. The first is *hermeneutical realism*. On this view, all texts have meanings "independent of the process of interpretation" because authors create those meanings.[22] The implication for biblical interpretation is clear: Belief in the inspiration and authority of Scripture would be futile if its divine authorship could not convey meaning through human language. If human language is incapable of communicating the intentions of authors, then God sent the prophets on a fool's errand when he commanded them to write down his word (1 Sam.

---

20. John Webster, *Holy Scripture: A Dogmatic Sketch* (New York: Cambridge University Press, 2003).

21. Kevin J. Vanhoozer, *Remythologizing Theology: Divine Action, Passion, and Authorship* (New York: Cambridge University Press, 2012), 179–294.

22. Kevin J. Vanhoozer, *Is There a Meaning in This Text? The Bible, the Reader, and the Morality of Literary Knowledge* (Grand Rapids, MI: Zondervan, 1998), 48.

10:25; Isa. 30:8; Hag. 1:3). Worse yet, we are powerless to "hear the word of the LORD" (2 Kings 7:1; cf. Isa. 1:10; Jer. 10:1; Hos. 4:1). If authors cannot communicate meaning through texts, then reader or reading community would have the final say on matters of doctrine and practice, not the "men [who] spoke from God as they were carried along by the Holy Spirit" (2 Pet. 1:21).

Second, we must own our *limits and shortcomings* as interpreters of Scripture.[23] The second principle complements the first. As Richard Lints explains, "If truth can be known, then there must be some mechanism to explain why everyone does not agree with that truth."[24] This commonsense approach to interpretation is both an affirmation of *objective meaning* in texts and a recognition that understanding must come through *subjective interpretation*. The objective nature of texts means they can be read either correctly or incorrectly. The subjective nature of interpretation means that comprehension is fallible and open to revision or correction.[25]

"Let the Reader Understand"

Hermeneutical realism is in step with both premodern and modern intellectual traditions, which, despite their considerable differences, share affirmation of a real world outside of the mind of the observer. When applied to written texts and speech, hermeneutical realism entails the belief that authors and speakers are at least capable of communicating their meanings and intended purposes through writing and speech. Texts have meaning independent of their interpreters.

Biblical authors themselves testify to their ability to communicate their purposes through written texts. Commonplace writings and historical documents detailed in the Bible evidenced their belief in the ability of texts to convey the meaning of authors.[26] Elsewhere, God commanded Moses to write down clear words that would become the

---

23. Carl F. H. Henry, *God, Revelation, and Authority*, 6 vols. (Wheaton, IL: Crossway, 1999), 4:316.

24. Richard Lints, *The Fabric of Theology: A Prolegomenon to Evangelical Theology* (Grand Rapids, MI: Eerdmans, 1993), 21.

25. Wright, *New Testament and the People of God*, 32–37; Vanhoozer, *Is There a Meaning in This Text?*, 300–302; 320–323.

26. See 1 Samuel 10:25; 2 Samuel 1:18; 11:14–15; 1 Kings 11:41; 14:19, 29; 16:14, 20; 2 Kings 1:18; 8:23; 1 Chronicles 28:19; 2 Chronicles 2:11; 35:4; Ezra 4:7; Esther 4:8; 8:8, 13; Ezekiel 13:9; Malachi 3:16.

basis of the covenant with Israel (Ex. 34:27). To his original audience in Corinth, Paul writes, "For *we do not write you anything other than what you can read and also understand*. But I hope that you will understand completely" (2 Cor. 1:13 NET; cf. 1 Cor. 4:14). The gospel of John has a clear statement of purpose: "These [things] are written *so that you may believe* that Jesus is the Christ, the Son of God, *and that by believing you may have life* in his name" (John 20:31). Luke unambiguously states his intention to write clear and orderly accounts of the life of Jesus and his earliest followers (Luke 1:1–4; Acts 1:1). Consequently, the postmodern rejection of authorial intention is contrary to the explicit statements of biblical authors.

Premodern and modern thinkers also believed that the world was inherently rational, meaning it was capable of being perceived by the mind. Because hermeneutical realists presume that all written texts are the products of their authors, laden with the intentions of authors to do something with their words, they likewise assert that normally functioning human minds are at least capable of retrieving or reconstructing meaning in a way that is faithful to an author's design for a text. This assertion does not mean that readers climb deep into the psyche of authors or that they necessarily understand their unstated motivations for writing. Rather, it means that interpreters are capable of receiving the communication writers and speakers intend to express.

Using the resources of philosophy and literary criticism, evangelical biblical scholars and theologians have mounted numerous lines of defense against the postmodern critics of hermeneutical realism.[27] Many have built upon the work of American literary critic E. D. Hirsch Jr., whose 1967 publication *Validity in Interpretation* served as an apologetic for the intent of the author and the determinate meaning of texts. There, Hirsch advocated a strict distinction between the *meaning* of a text and its *significance*. For the early Hirsch, the *meaning* of a text was something fixed by the author by his or her particular use of language. *Significance*, by contrast, is the unique way a reader approaches the fixed meaning of a text, how she applies it to her life situation. The

---

27. The most comprehensive defense of hermeneutical realism to date is Vanhoozer's *Is There a Meaning in This Text?*, in which Vanhoozer systematically responds to the reader-centered approaches of New Criticism, Deconstruction, and Reader-Response Theory.

author-intended meaning of a text does not change, but a text can be applied in numerous ways in new contexts.[28]

Though appreciative of Hirsch's work as a whole, Christian hermeneutics scholar Anthony Thiselton calls Hirsch's dichotomy between meaning and significance "grossly over-simple, over-general" and incapable of serving as "a panacea for all hermeneutical headaches."[29] Thiselton understands faithful interpretation of Scripture to be more than the mere rediscovery of a past authorial intent, because the "past" could easily be defined as closed off to the present.[30] Interpreters of the Bible engage with the divine-human authorship of the text and obey it. Though the books of the Bible were written by human authors in historical settings far removed from our own, the divine author of the Bible still speaks directly to us through Scripture. The reader is in a covenantal relationship with the divine author of Scripture, not with an objectified statement about the text's meaning.

To understand the Bible in the way its authorship intends us to, we must seek to *apply* it, not just grasp its cognitive content. Biblical authors commanded this: "Be doers of the word, and not hearers only, deceiving yourselves" (James 1:22; cf. Josh. 1:7–8; 2 Kings 17:37; John 13:17; Rom. 2:13). The reader of the Bible who puts himself under its authority seeks to experience its transforming power. He wants to see the world in the same way the divinely inspired authors of the text see it, not simply recreate its significance for himself in the present.

One helpful amendment to Hirsch's work has been built on the insights of speech-act theory. Developed by philosophers of language, speech-act theory was initially meant to describe the way language works, not to prescribe a model for interpretation, but hermeneutics scholars have called upon its resources to help defend authorial intent. According to speech-act theory, every time a person speaks, writes, or

---

28. E. D. Hirsch Jr., *Validity in Interpretation* (New Haven, CT: Yale University Press, 1967), 8. Hirsch moved away from this clear-cut distinction between *meaning* and *significance* in his later writings, though his modified position still gave authorial intent priority in interpretation. See E. D. Hirsch Jr., "Meaning and Significance Reinterpreted," *Critical Inquiry* 11 (1984): 202–225.

29. Anthony C. Thiselton, "'Behind' and 'in Front of' the Text: Language, Reference, and Indeterminacy," in *After Pentecost: Language and Biblical Interpretation*, ed. Craig Bartholomew, Colin Greene, and Karl Möller (Grand Rapids, MI: Zondervan, 2001), 103. See also Vanhoozer, *Is There a Meaning in This Text?*, 259–265.

30. Thiselton, "'Behind' and 'in Front of' the Text," 332–333.

uses nonverbal communicative signs, he or she intends *to do some-thing with those words or signs.*[31] Every speech-act, whether written or spoken, has at least three components:

- the words said or written (the *locution* or *locutionary act*),
- the intent or purpose of writing (the *illocution* or *illocution-ary act*),
- the intended effect of the words on the hearer or reader (the *perlocution* or *perlocutionary act*).[32]

The sentence you are presently reading is a speech-act intended by this author to illustrate the way speech-acts work. If it succeeds, then the words written on my laptop (the locutionary act) will accomplish my communicative purpose (illocutionary act) and the reader will have a better grasp on the subject (perlocutionary act). Not every speech act is an effort to inform or explain. With words, speakers/authors can also attempt to persuade, question, challenge, taunt, threaten, mis-lead, deceive, insult, promise, bless, or curse.[33] Some speech-acts can even *create new worlds* or *new states of affairs*, such as God speaking creation into being with the phrase "Let there be" (Gen. 1:3, 6, 14), a judge delivering a guilty verdict, or a minister pronouncing a couple "husband and wife."

When the purpose of the writer and the effect on the reader align, what J. L. Austin calls a "happy" speech-act occurs.[34] A happy speech-act does not mean that the reader/hearer always agrees with the author/speaker, but it does mean that the reader/listener has suc-cessfully understood the author's/speaker's intent or purpose. On other occasions, the intended effect and the actual effect did not align, resulting in miscommunication. Even when miscommunica-tion occurs, it does not mean that author/speakers are incapable of communicating their meanings.

---

31. J. L. Austin, *How to Do Things with Words*, 2nd ed. (Cambridge, MA: Harvard University Press, 1962); John Searle, *Speech Acts* (Cambridge: Cambridge University Press, 1969).

32. A fourth component I could list is the *propositional act*, a development made by Searle that de-scribes the extra-linguistic reference of a speech-act. See Searle, *Speech Acts*, 24–25. This element simply means that every speech-act has reference to some state of affairs, real or imaginary. The imperative statement "Sit in the chair" makes sense only if the speaker believes the proposition, "Chairs exist."

33. Anthony C. Thiselton, *New Horizons in Hermeneutics: The Theory and Practice of Trans-forming Biblical Reading* (Grand Rapids, MI: Zondervan, 1992), 299.

34. Austin, *How to Do Things with Words*, 14ff.

Biblical scholars and theologians have made use of speech-act theory to describe the nature of texts, the nature of interpretation, and the theological task in new ways.[35] One of the key figures in this trend, Kevin Vanhoozer, defines a text as a "communicative action fixed by writing."[36] In general hermeneutics, every reader is responsible for working to understand what the author is trying to do with his or her text. In special or biblical hermeneutics, the interpreter is trying to make sense of Scripture's "human-divine communicative actions that do many different things."[37] The Bible presents us with many different genres, and the divine-human authorship of Scripture seeks various responses from its readership, depending on the genre and the text. The reader under biblical authority desires to understand the illocutions (communicative purposes) of Scripture and to act or react in ways consistent with the perlocutionary acts that the authors desire.

Though speech-act theory has its limitations and is not in and of itself a be-all, end-all method of biblical interpretation, it can be a helpful supplement to traditional author-oriented hermeneutics. It does not account for whether authors/speakers are telling the truth, nor does it prescribe a step-by-step method of interpretation. Speech-act theory modestly offers a commonsense description of the way writers use words to convey meaning or produce results. It not only describes the place of the author/speaker but accounts for how misinterpretation can take place.[38] Both are important for the present discussion.

"Lean Not unto Thine Own Understanding"

Though human beings are capable of communication through words and sentences, not every attempt at such communication succeeds. Writers sometimes fail to communicate their intentions. (I have seen

---

35. See Richard S. Briggs, *Words in Action: Speech Act Theory and Biblical Interpretation, Toward a Hermeneutic of Self-Involvement* (Edinburgh: T&T Clark, 2001); Dietmar Neufeld, *Reconceiving Texts as Speech Acts: An Analysis of John* (Leiden: Brill, 1994); Daniel J. Treier, *Virtue and the Voice of God: Toward Theology as Wisdom* (Grand Rapids, MI: Eerdmans, 2006); James Wm. McClendon Jr. and James M. Smith, *Convictions: Defusing Religious Relativism* (Valley Forge, PA: Trinity, 2002), 47–79.

36. Vanhoozer, *Is There a Meaning in This Text?*, 229.

37. Kevin J. Vanhoozer, *First Theology: God, Scripture, and Hermeneutics* (Downers Grove, IL: InterVarsity Press, 2002), 151.

38. Speech-act theory is not without its evangelical critics. See Gregory Alan Thornbury, *Recovering Classical Evangelicalism: Applying the Wisdom and Vision of Carl F. H. Henry* (Wheaton, IL: Crossway, 2013), 112–114. I respond to some of these criticisms in my book, *In Defense of Doctrine: Evangelicalism, Theology, and Scripture* (Minneapolis: Fortress, 2015), 276–279.

my own unintended mistakes in print!) Diplomacy fails because of linguistic and cultural misunderstanding. Lovers can spat when they don't successfully communicate their intentions and feelings. (Sometimes, in a disagreement, I tell my wife that her perlocutionary act isn't matching up with my illocutionary act. That always goes over very well!) Bottom line: both human speakers and human hearers are capable of error and misunderstanding. The purpose of words spoken or written can be lost in the shuffle, because of either the incompetence of the speaker/writer or the misunderstanding of the hearer/reader.

Human interpreters are creatures gifted with rationality, intelligence, creativity, self-awareness, and adaptability, but they also have limitations and impediments to their understandings of written and spoken texts. This is true in every instance of human communication, including our attempts to make sense of Scripture. Though Christians make unique claims about Scripture's full truthfulness and infallibility, this affirmation does not guarantee infallible and inerrant interpretations on our part. We assert the inerrancy of Scripture, but we cannot make the same claims about its readership. Readers are prone to error and are limited in their capacity for understanding.[39]

Our interpretation is fallible for several reasons. *First, human reason is limited.* We are flawed, fragile creatures in the presence of an almighty God who is unfathomable through ordinary means. Scripture talks plainly about the inability of human beings to have complete understanding of the world or of God's works:

> When I applied my heart to know wisdom, and to see the business that is done on earth, how neither day nor night do one's eyes see sleep, then I saw all the work of God, that man cannot find out the work that is done under the sun. However much man may toil in seeking, he will not find it out. Even though a wise man claims to know, he cannot find it out. (Eccles. 8:16–17)

No matter how much we may toil in seeking the knowledge of God in this world, there are things we cannot know or understand (Job 11:7;

---

39. In the words of John Locke, "Though every thing said in the [Old and New Testament] Text be infallibly true, yet the Reader may be, nay cannot chuse but be, very fallible in the understanding of it" (Locke, *An Essay Concerning Human Understanding*, ed. Peter H. Nidditch [New York: Oxford University Press, 1975], 3.10.23 [489–490]).

Isa. 55:8–9; Rom. 11:33–34). Our knowledge of God is already limited to what he reveals, but on top of that, we are capable of altogether misconstruing his revelation!

Hermeneutical philosophers label this creaturely limitation the *finitude* of the interpreter. The interpreter is finite in intellect, limited to his time and place, and did not choose the culture that shaped his thinking.[40] We interpret Scripture with our fallible reasoning processes, and we can misinterpret Scripture even when we have the best of intentions. Some Christian theologians blame these interpretive limitations on the brokenness of the world following the fall of humanity, while others suggest that this interpretive finitude reflects our essential creatureliness. Some theologians submit that God can help us overcome our limitations as interpreters by the work of his Spirit, while others propose that God purposely made us with innate epistemic limitations to remind us of our status as creatures.[41]

The mind is *selective* in its attentions and limited in its *capacity* to retain information.[42] This pervasive inability to recollect details casts a shadow over interpretation. The brain, like a computer with low RAM, also has difficulty *processing too many details at once*, which means we cannot always consider every significant factor in interpretation at the same time. A lack of *topical knowledge* can hinder our ability to reason through the meaning of a biblical text.[43] Some interpreters have more *procedural knowledge* than others.[44] (I know many Hebrew and Greek scholars far more adept than I am at translation and syntax! I also know several analytic theologians whose brains seem to work much, much faster than mine.) Education can help overcome some of these limits of intelligence, but these handicaps still affect our ability to grasp some texts.

Second, we interpret texts with our own ingrained cultural and personal perspectives that color our readings. Every reader must acknowledge his or her own subjectivity, even when trying to make

---

40. See Martin Heidegger, *Being and Time*, trans. John Macquarrie and Edward Robinson (New York: Harper & Row, 1962); Hans-Georg Gadamer, *Truth and Method*, rev. ed., trans. Joel Weinsheimer and Donald G. Marshall (New York: Continuum, 2004).

41. For an evaluation of these competing perspectives, see James K. A. Smith, *The Fall of Interpretation: Philosophical Foundations for a Creational Hermeneutic*, rev. ed. (Grand Rapids, MI: Baker, 2012).

42. See Stephen K. Reed, *Cognition*, 4th ed. (Pacific Grove, CA: Brooks/Cole, 1996), 50–78.

43. Raymond S. Nickerson, *Reflections on Reasoning* (Hillsdale, NJ: Lawrence Erlbaum, 1986), 15.

44. Nickerson, *Reflections on Reasoning*, 16.

sense of biblical or doctrinal statements that are objectively true. We do not read books, watch television, or look at art as blank slates, nor do we come to the biblical text as neutral observers who passively receive what it offers us. Instead, we are active readers who come to texts with our own unique questions, experiences, and presuppositions. Years of enculturation, family background, language training, and personality development coalesce to create our subjective *horizon* or frame of reference.

In its most literal sense, the word *horizon* refers to the line in a field of vision where earth and sky seem to touch. Metaphorically, horizon describes an individual's perception of the world.[45] When someone tells us that we need to "broaden" our horizons, we typically take this to mean that we need to try a new experience, like a new food or a new hobby, or that we need to try looking at things from another point of view. In the same way that a visual horizon is limited by a person's field of vision, her perspective of reality is constrained by her geography, her culture, and her milieu. God makes the sovereign choice of when and where in history and culture his creatures will live and develop intellectually (Acts 17:26). We cannot see future events, and we can only make sense of the past through the point of view of our present horizon.

Our experiences, our families, our education, and our cultures can have a cumulative effect in shaping not only our points of view on particular issues but also our entire worldview. In the same way that the literal horizon can change with the earth's rotation beneath our feet, the passing of time can change our metaphorical horizons. A change in our cultural location can change the vantage point of our beliefs.[46] The evangelical missiologist Lesslie Newbigin recognized the challenges that our cultural limitations impose on our reading of Scripture:

> We read the Bible in our own language and it is full of resonances which arise from past cultural experience. Where do I find the stance from which I can look at myself from the point of view of

---

45. Since the nineteenth century, philosophers have used the metaphor of *horizon* to portray the limitations of our perspectives and the way our perspectives change. According to Gadamer, Friedrich Nietzsche, Wilhelm Dilthey, and Edmund Husserl all use *Horizont* to "characterize the way in which thought is tied to its finite determinacy, and the way one's range of vision is gradually expanded" (Gadamer, *Truth and Method*, 301).

46. Ben F. Meyer, *Reality and Illusion in New Testament Scholarship: A Primer in Critical Realist Hermeneutics* (Collegeville, MN: Liturgical Press, 1994), 50.

the Bible when my reading of the Bible is itself so much shaped by the person that I am, formed by my culture? . . . All our reading of the Bible and all our Christian discipleship are necessarily shaped by the cultures which have formed us.[47]

Though our cultural backgrounds and settings shape who we are as readers, they are not deterministic rulers over our interpretation of the Bible. As we grow in our knowledge, our frame of reference and cultural presuppositions can change as well.[48]

Everyone reads the Bible through a kind of *narrative framework*, or story. Scour through Amazon reviews of any best-selling Christian book on traditional marriage and you will find a litany of complaints for any author who takes seriously Paul's command for wives to submit to their own husbands (Eph. 5:22). These readers find traditional views of sex and marriage oppressive and outmoded ways of thinking. They reject Paul's instruction here, believing it to be "patriarchal," "fundamentalist," or "misogynistic." Believing marriage to be primarily about personal fulfillment, they might also wince at the suggestion that husbands should love their wives self-sacrificially like Jesus loves the church (v. 25). As evangelical Christians, we also recognize that we read the Bible within a narrative framework. But we have consciously chosen the narrative we believe the Bible to be spelling out for us: creation, fall, redemption, and consummation. We take these commands seriously because we buy into the narrative Paul is laying out for us.

The people of God want Scripture, not culture or tradition, to have the final say over the content of doctrine, but the natural limitations posed by our horizons mean that theology is an exercise always shaped by time, place, and culture. Our readings of Scripture are always laden with presuppositions.[49] We never think or write about God in a vacuum or from some remote, detached location. Many of the questions we seek to answer in theology are shaped by our cultural settings.

---

47. Lesslie Newbigin, *The Gospel in a Pluralist Society* (Grand Rapids, MI: Eerdmans, 1989), 196.

48. William W. Klein, Craig L. Blomberg, and Robert L. Hubbard Jr., *Introduction to Biblical Interpretation*, 3rd ed. (Grand Rapids, MI: Zondervan, 2017), 239–241.

49. Evangelicals consciously embrace presuppositions like the authority of Scripture, inerrancy, etc., when reading the Bible. Rather than presupposing the possibility of error, we presume that any tensions or apparent contradictions can be resolved when the text is interpreted properly.

The way in which we proclaim the unchanging gospel message is always contingent on our setting and audience. We have good precedent for this type of contextual presentation. Biblical authors, too, wrote in human languages and from specific cultural settings to address real-world problems. Yes, these authors spoke for God, and yes, the truthfulness of what they wrote extends far beyond their original time, intended audiences, and cultural settings, but they also model for us ways of making God's word speak in fresh and relevant ways to our own ministry contexts.

Third, the historical, cultural, geographical, and linguistic distance between biblical authors and their contemporary readers can make grasping the meaning of biblical texts difficult.[50] Years ago I had a student from Taiwan who told me that he took it upon himself to learn the rules of American football so that he could understand the sermon illustrations at the church he attended during seminary. Not only was this student having to listen to sermons in a second language, but he also had to learn the rules of the sport to decipher the pastor's sermon! (Gridiron football is, after all, an important staple here in the southern United States.) The distance between the Taiwanese seminary student and the pastor from the southern United States was more than geographical; it was cultural. If this interpretive difficulty is true of people who live in the same time and place, it is even more complicated for readers of the Bible who are trying to understand two- and three-millennia-old books!

Interpretation happens where our horizons meet the horizons of the text. Contemporary Westerners do not view the world in the same ways ancient Near Eastern and first-century Christians did. In order to come into the Bible in the right way, we have to understand the ways in which its setting and its cultures are unlike our own.[51] The historical distance between the reader and the Bible means that the interpreter should spend considerable time developing the skills and ascertaining the background knowledge needed to make sense of the text.[52] Biblical

---

50. See Klein, Blomberg, and Hubbard, *Introduction to Biblical Interpretation*, 53–59.

51. For a helpful overview of particular ways in which Western culture distorts biblical interpretation, see E. Randolph Richards and Brandon J. O'Brien, *Misreading Scripture with Western Eyes: Removing Cultural Blinders to Better Understand the Bible* (Downers Grove, IL: InterVarsity Press, 2012).

52. Grant R. Osborne, *The Hermeneutical Spiral: A Comprehensive Introduction to Biblical Interpretation*, rev. ed. (Downers Grove, IL: InterVarsity Press, 2006), 25.

interpreters can always benefit from a better grasp of ancient agrarian cultures, honor and shame dynamics, economies in the biblical world, purity practices, and a host of other issues phone-addicted twenty-first-century Christians normally have difficulty fathoming.[53]

Fourth, we have our own unique preunderstandings of texts that we bring to them. That is to say, we begin with assumptions about a text before we start to read or interpret it. We don't usually start a book or a movie or a biblical passage without some sort of "big-picture" concept of what it is about, even if that preunderstanding is completely incorrect. We have an initial preunderstanding of a text as a whole that we bring to its particular parts. When we interpret the parts, it reshapes the way we understand the whole. This is what is sometimes called the "hermeneutical circle" or "hermeneutical spiral."

Oftentimes postmodern scholars suspect these preunderstandings have a determining influence that keeps us from ever getting at the authorial meaning of a text. As noted above, I do not believe that to be the case. However, we must work to be keenly aware of our assumptions, whether they are shaped by a culture or a theological tradition, and we must be willing and ready to make sense of the text on its own terms. When we read those with whom we disagree, we should practice charitable reading that seeks to understand the author in the fairest light. When we read Scripture, we must be willing to lay aside our presumptions and let the text correct our misunderstandings.

Finally, we can also admit that sin can affect our interpretation of Scripture by distorting its meaning with our selfish desires and prejudices. The Bible repeatedly stresses the negative effects of the fall on human thinking, what theologians call the "noetic effects of sin." Those who live according to their sinful desires have minds set on those desires, and their minds are hostile to God (Rom. 8:5–7). Unbelievers are incapable of "seeing the light of the gospel of the glory of Christ" because the god of this age has blinded their minds (2 Cor. 4:4). As a result of their sin, they regard the word of God a

---

53. For introductory surveys of these topics, see David A. deSilva, *Honor, Patronage, Kinship, and Purity: Unlocking the New Testament Culture* (Downers Grove, IL: InterVarsity Press, 2000); Richard L. Rohrbaugh, ed., *The Social Sciences and New Testament Interpretation* (Peabody, MA: Hendrickson, 1996).

"strange thing" (Hos. 8:11–12). Believers also endure the effects of sin on the mind, and their minds are in need of renewal (Rom. 12:1–2; Eph. 4:20–24). But as Stephen Moroney remarks, the Bible does not explicitly say how human thinking is corrupted by sin and what the renewal of the mind does to alleviate these effects.[54]

The human heart is prone to self-deception (Jer. 17:9; cf. Prov. 14:12; 28:26). Interpreters can likewise be guilty of reading texts in self-serving ways. For this reason, biblical interpreters need to practice something akin to what Paul Ricoeur called a *hermeneutic of suspicion*. By a "hermeneutic of suspicion," I do not mean readers should mistrust Scripture itself or that they should call into question its truthfulness (i.e., the kind of suspicion modeled by Nietzsche).[55] Rather, Bible readers should be aware of the ways in which their own motives and prejudices can keep them from a correct understanding of the Bible. Every follower of Jesus should practice a *hermeneutic of submission* that minimizes the role of self in interpretation and submits to the divine authority behind the text. In this way, we truly practice the authority of Scripture, by prayerfully acknowledging our weakness and asking God to correct our faulty or sinful assumptions about the content of Scripture.

Our doctrinal disputes are indicative of the fact that readers can be wrong about their respective interpretations of the Bible, but followers of Christ are not without hope. Not only do we receive God's grace in interpretation—grace that enables us to know God despite our frailties and weaknesses as interpreters—we also have the promise of a day when we will understand more completely. Paul depicts our present knowledge of God as a pale reflection our future, more complete knowledge of God. One day, instead of looking into the mirror, we shall see God face to face, and our knowledge of God will be without dispute among one another. "Now I know in part; then I shall know fully, even as I have been fully known" (1 Cor. 13:12b).

---

54. Stephen K. Moroney, *The Noetic Effects of Sin: A Historical and Contemporary Exploration of How Sin Affects Our Thinking* (Lanham, MD: Lexington, 2000), 90.

55. Alan Jacobs contrasts this unhealthy hermeneutic of suspicion with healthy discernment in *A Theology of Reading: The Hermeneutic of Love* (Boulder, CO: Westview, 2001), 88–89. Jacobs notes that in a Christian worldview, everyone is a "neighbor" but not every neighbor is a good neighbor, nor should every neighbor be trusted as a friend. Discernment, not a hermeneutic of suspicion, helps us make that distinction.

The Clear Meaning of Scripture and Interpretive Disagreement

The contemporary affirmation of hermeneutical realism is consistent with a doctrine held dearly by Luther, Zwingli, Calvin, and most within the Protestant tradition: the *clarity* (or *perspicuity*) *of Scripture*.[56] The doctrine of the clarity of Scripture is a statement about Scripture's sufficiency as a source of divine truth. It developed as a response to the late medieval Roman Catholic Church's claim that the Bible is in need of authoritative ecclesial interpretation because it is too obscure and too complicated for untrained laypersons to interpret for themselves.[57] To the contrary, Zwingli declares, "God's Word can be understood by a man without any human direction."[58] For Luther, this doctrine was "the very first principle . . . by which everything else has to be proved."[59] But if Scripture is so clear, then why do Christians so often disagree about how best to interpret it?

Somewhat ironically, the doctrine of the clarity of Scripture can be easily misunderstood. An oversimplified version of the doctrine parallels simplistic and unhelpful versions of the doctrines of inspiration. In the same way in which the inspiration of Scripture is not mere dictation, the clarity of Scripture is not a promise of perfect comprehension apart from the hard and fallible work of hermeneutics. Furthermore, anyone who would suggest that all of Scripture is plain to anyone who reads it fails to appreciate the humanity of the Bible or its complexity.[60] Even the classical Protestant formulation plainly states that the Scriptures are "not alike plain in themselves, nor alike clear unto all."[61]

Consider the following definitions of scriptural clarity from contemporary evangelical theologians. For Wayne Grudem, the doctrine

---

56. Luther lays out his doctrine of the clarity or perspicuity of Scripture in his *Bondage of the Will*. Zwingli articulates his doctrine in his 1522 sermon, "On the Clarity and Certainty of the Word of God."

57. For a masterful exposition of the development of this doctrine and a robust contemporary defense of it, see Gregg R. Allison, "The Protestant Doctrine of the Perspicuity of Scripture: A Reformulation on the Basis of Biblical Teaching," PhD diss. (Trinity Evangelical Divinity School, 1995); cf. Allison, *Historical Theology* (Grand Rapids, MI: Zondervan, 2011), 120–141.

58. Ulrich Zwingli, "Of the Clarity and the Certainty of the Word of God," in *Zwingli and Bullinger*, ed. G. W. Bromiley (Philadelphia: Westminster, 1953), 78.

59. Luther, *On the Bondage of the Will* [*De Servo Arbitrio*], in *Luther and Erasmus: Free Will and Salvation*, ed. E. Gordon Rupp and Philip S. Watson (Philadelphia: Westminster, 1969), 159; WA 18:653.

60. Michael Horton, *The Christian Faith: A Systematic Theology for Pilgrims on the Way* (Grand Rapids, MI: Zondervan, 2011), 196–197.

61. The Westminster Confession of Faith 1.7; see Horton, *Christian Faith*, 197.

of the clarity of Scripture means that *"the Bible is written in such a way that its teachings are able to be understood by all who will read it seeking God's help and being willing to follow it."*[62] Gregg Allison defines the clarity of Scripture as "a property of Scripture as a whole and of each portion of Scripture whereby it is comprehensible to all believers who possess the normal acquired ability to understand oral communication and/or written discourse, regardless of their gender, age, education, language, or cultural background." Allison also adds that Scripture's clarity "requires a dependence on the Holy Spirit for Scripture to be grasped and calls for a responsive obedience to what is understood."[63] Mark Thompson summarizes the doctrine in this way: *"The clarity of Scripture is that quality of the biblical text that, as God's communicative act, ensures its meaning is accessible to all who come to it in faith."*[64] What all three of these contemporary definitions have in common are affirmations (1) that clarity is a quality or property of Scripture itself, (2) that believers can ascertain its basic meaning, and (3) that dependence on God is necessary for its understanding and application.

Yet dissenting opinions in theology and biblical interpretation have always posed a challenge to the concept of biblical clarity. In his debate with Luther over free will, Desiderius Erasmus argued that their differences stemmed from God's choice to leave some ideas in Scripture vague:

> There are some things which God has willed that we should contemplate, as we venerate himself, in mystic silence; and moreover, there are many passages in the sacred volumes about which many commentators have made guesses, but no one has finally cleared up their obscurity: as the distinction between the divine persons, the conjunction of the divine and human nature in Christ, the unforgivable sin; yet there are other things which God has willed to be most plainly evident, and such are the precepts for the good life. . . . These truths must be learned by all, but the rest are more properly committed to God, and it is

---

62. Grudem, *Systematic Theology*, 108, italics original.
63. Allison, "Protestant Doctrine of the Perspicuity of Scripture," 516.
64. Mark D. Thompson, *A Clear and Present Word: The Clarity of Scripture* (Downers Grove, IL: InterVarsity Press, 2006), 169–170, italics original.

more religious to worship them, being unknown, than to discuss them, being insoluble.[65]

Disputed theological issues such as the doctrine of the Trinity, the unity of Christ's natures in one person, the unpardonable sin, and free will are, according to Erasmus, unsettled because Scripture is less than clear on these matters.[66] Rather than highlighting defects in human understanding, Erasmus minimized God's role as a communicative agent.

Luther does not contest Erasmus's claim that much about God remains a mystery to his creatures, but he wholeheartedly rejects Erasmus's claim that Scripture is obscure by divine design. The main subject matter of Scripture is so clear and so accessible that any interpreter who brings due diligence to the duty of interpreting the text can make sense of its meaning. Luther labels this quality of the text the *external clarity of Scripture*. Doctrines like those mentioned by Erasmus have mysterious qualities, yes, but Scripture is not obscure in what it "simply confesses" about them. True, Scripture leaves some mystery to the inner workings of the Godhead. However, the divinely inspired authors do lay out a clear means by which interpreters can affirm the tenets that there is one God and that God is three persons.[67]

Luther's observation here parallels a distinction long held by philosophers and theologians between the *apprehension* and *comprehension* of a subject matter. To *apprehend*, which literally means, "to lay hold upon" or "seize," is the simple recognition of a mental object as truthful or factual. *Apprehension* is the most basic level of understanding. To *comprehend*, by contrast, is to "take it all in," to have exhaustive knowledge or understanding of an object.[68] Luther's distinction between the belief of what Scripture confesses about God

---

65. Desiderius Erasmus, *On the Freedom of the Will* [*De Libero Arbitrio*], in *Luther and Erasmus: Free Will and Salvation*, ed. E. Gordon Rupp and Philip S. Watson (Philadelphia: Westminster, 1969), 39–40.

66. Thiselton, *New Horizons in Hermeneutics*, 181.

67. Luther, *On the Bondage of the Will*, 112; WA 18:551–787.

68. See Richard Chenevix Trench, *On the Study of Words* (New York, 1856), 185. As Trench (1807–1886) distinguishes these categories, "We 'apprehend' many truths which we do not 'comprehend.' The great mysteries of our faith, the doctrine, for instance, of the Holy Trinity—we lay hold upon it (*ad prehendo*), we hang upon it, our souls live by it; but we do not take it all in, we do not 'comprehend' it; for it is a necessary attribute of God that He is incomprehensible; if He were not so He would not be God, or the being that comprehended him would be God also. But it also belongs to the idea of God that He may be 'apprehended,' though not 'comprehended' by His reasonable creatures; He has made them to know Him, though not to know Him all, to 'apprehend' though not to 'comprehend' Him."

and a full understanding of it reflects Augustine's important maxim about theological knowledge: "We are speaking of God; what marvel, if thou do not comprehend? For if thou comprehend, He is not God. Be there a pious confession of ignorance, rather than a rash profession of knowledge. To reach to God in any measure by the mind, is a great blessedness; but to comprehend Him, is altogether impossible."[69] We may be able to apprehend divine truth, but we cannot comprehend God. God cannot be mastered by our finite minds.

Another objection to Scripture's clarity comes from the number of difficult texts in the Bible and the recognition of the need for interpretation in the Bible (Acts 8:30–31; cf. Isa. 53:7–8). How do we harmonize biblical clarity with Peter's observation that the letters of Paul contain "some things in them that are hard to understand" (2 Pet. 3:16)? Luther grants that there are difficult passages in Scripture but maintains that they are difficult to understand because of our own frailties and limitations as interpreters, not because God has in any way failed to communicate clearly.[70] As Allison makes note, the clarity of Scripture does not mean that "all of Scripture and each part of Scripture is easily understandable, only that it is intelligible." Certain portions of Scripture that pose interpretive difficulties to readers are "'hard to understand,' not impossible."[71]

Biblical authors do not explicitly teach a doctrine of the clarity of Scripture, but it is an implication of what they say about inspiration: "All Scripture is breathed out by God and profitable for teaching, for reproof, for correction, and for training in righteousness, that the man of God may be complete, equipped for every good work" (2 Tim. 3:16–17). The Scriptures provide everything needed "to make you wise for salvation through faith in Christ Jesus" (2 Tim. 3:15). The divine inspiration of Scripture ensures its profitableness and sufficiency for doctrine, correction, and obedience. Since "God is not a God of confusion but of peace" (1 Cor. 14:33), his written revelation—intended to equip us for every good work—was inspired with the purpose of expressing everything we need to know in order to be obedient followers of Jesus.[72]

---

69. Augustine, *Sermons* 67.5 [117.3.5]; NPNF[1] 6:459.
70. Luther, *On the Bondage of the Will*, 110; WA 18:606.
71. Allison, "Protestant Doctrine of the Perspicuity of Scripture," 519.
72. Thompson, *Sure Ground on Which to Stand*, 274.

The general clarity of the subject matter of Scripture does not guarantee a perfect, automatic understanding of every difficulty in the biblical text. Vanhoozer observes that "Scripture's clarity does not mean that reading works *ex opere operato* ['from the work worked'], as if simply pronouncing the words magically yields understanding."[73] Kevin DeYoung states, "The doctrine of the clarity of Scripture is not a wild assertion that the meaning of every verse in the Bible will be patently obvious to everyone."[74] Mark Thompson adds, "God does not ensure that understanding is uniformly automatic or intuitive, nor has any serious affirmation of Scripture's clarity ever denied the continuing reality of difficulty at points."[75]

Every dedicated and hardworking teacher has had that student who does not pay attention in class, read his assigned books, or do his homework. The teacher cannot be blamed for that student's failure or incompetence. In the same way, our refusal or inability to listen to God does not reflect back on his ability to speak clearly to us. Biblical interpretation may be hard, messy work, and some of us struggle with it more than others, but that does not entail that God has not spoken in such a way that he can be understood by those who are willing to listen carefully.

The Illumination of the Spirit and Human Fallibility

So, how does the recognition of human fallibility square with Jesus's promises that the Holy Spirit whom he sent will "teach . . . all things" (John 14:26) and "guide . . . into all the truth" (John 16:13)? Theologians sometimes call this work of the Spirit *illumination*, the activity of the Spirit by which "believers are aided in their understanding of particular passages of Scripture."[76] Though Jesus does not speak directly about the illumination of Scripture by the Holy Spirit, the notion of scriptural illumination seems to be a proper inference from the biblical claims that Scripture preserves God's teaching (2 Tim. 3:16–17) and that the Spirit helps us understand divine truth (1 Cor. 2:10; cf. Prov. 2:3–6).

---

73. Kevin J. Vanhoozer, *Biblical Authority after Babel: Retrieving the Solas in the Spirit of Mere Protestant Christianity* (Grand Rapids, MI: Brazos, 2016), 113.
74. Kevin DeYoung, *Taking God at His Word* (Wheaton, IL: Crossway, 2014), 59.
75. Thompson, *Clear and Present Word*, 167.
76. Henry, *God, Revelation, and Authority*, 6:266.

For Luther, the affirmation of the Spirit's illumination goes hand in hand with Scripture's clarity: "For the Spirit is required for the understanding of Scripture, both as a whole and in any part of it." The Spirit's work provides for Luther what he dubs the *internal clarity* of Scripture.[77] Were it not for the external clarity of Scripture, Luther argued, there would be a need for the church to tell untrained Christians what the Bible says and what they should believe. Without the internal clarity of Scripture brought about by the work of the Spirit, men could not understand what the Bible says about their own spiritual conditions.[78]

According to Calvin, the Spirit's primary role in illumination is the confirmation of the word of God in the heart of the believer. In other words, the Spirit testifies to the truthfulness of Scripture and the interpreter's need for that truth.[79] This definition is consistent with Paul's description of divine wisdom, which contrasts the mind of the natural person who "does not accept the things of the Spirit of God" with the "spiritual person" who possesses "the mind of Christ" and the ability to discern the things of God (1 Cor. 2:14–16). The illumination of the Holy Spirit is what separates the reading of the uneducated believer who is convinced of her sin and her need for Jesus from the reading of the skeptical scholar who understands the language, composition, and historical background of the text but does not see how the text or its message fits into his own life.

Some evangelical interpreters have suggested that the illuminating work of the Spirit eliminates subjectivity and supernaturally corrects misunderstandings about the text.[80] However, as Thiselton observes, "The Holy Spirit may be said to work *through* human understanding, and not usually, if ever, through processes which bypass the considerations discussed under the heading of hermeneutics."[81] Illumination is not normally an automatic impartation of knowledge (though it is certainly within God's power to produce such knowledge). Rightly

---

77. Luther, *On the Bondage of the Will*, 112; WA 18:609.
78. Thompson, *Clear and Present Word*, 228–235.
79. John Calvin, *Institutes of the Christian Religion*, 1.9.3.
80. Robert L. Thomas, *Evangelical Hermeneutics: The New Versus the Old* (Grand Rapids, MI: Kregel, 2002), 52–53.
81. Anthony C. Thiselton, *The Two Horizons: New Testament Hermeneutics and Philosophical Description with Special Reference to Heidegger, Bultmann, Gadamer, and Wittgenstein* (Carlisle, UK: Paternoster, 1980), 92.

handling the word of truth is hard work which requires diligence and endurance (2 Tim. 2:15).

Moreover, illumination does not guarantee uniformity of belief, nor does it mean that interpreters are beyond critique or revision. Grant Osborne observes how doctrinal and interpretive dissent makes this reality apparent: "By the very fact that scholars differ so greatly when interpreting the same passage, we know that God does not miraculously reveal the meaning of passages whenever they are read."[82] The desire for an interpreter to experience the illumination of the Spirit does not mean that the interpreter's work is beyond criticism, as Carl Trueman warns: "Too much emphasis on illumination as providing the content of Christian belief can render biblical interpretation an essentially gnostic activity, which places the views of those who have been 'illuminated' beyond the criticism of those who have not."[83]

The Spirit does a work in the life of the believer that enables him to receive God's message with gladness (1 Cor. 2:12–13; cf. Eph. 3:16–19), but this work does not necessarily ensure a perfect understanding of every Scripture in much the same way that the Spirit's ongoing work of sanctification does not result in instantaneous perfection in the life of the Christian. We grow in gradual holiness and in ever-deepening understanding of God's word. In *The City of God*, Augustine details four basic states human beings experience in relationship to sin and salvation, all of which have potential application to our hermeneutical shortcomings:

1. Before the fall, innocent human beings had the ability to sin or not to sin (*posse peccare, posse non peccare*).
2. After the fall and before redemption, man had the ability to sin and was unable not to sin (*non posse non peccare*).
3. After receiving the new birth but before glorification, humans were able to sin or not to sin (*posse non peccare*).
4. After glorification, the redeemed man is finally unable to sin (*non posse peccare*).[84]

---

82. Osborne, *Hermeneutical Spiral*, 24.

83. Carl R. Trueman, "Illumination," in *Dictionary for Theological Interpretation of the Bible*, ed. Kevin J. Vanhoozer, Craig G. Bartholomew, Daniel J. Treier, and N. T. Wright (Grand Rapids, MI: Baker, 2005), 318.

84. Augustine, *City of God* 22.30; NPNF[1] 2:510.

In comparing the various ways humans experience "free will," Augustine implicitly compares the activity of the Spirit in regeneration/sanctification and in glorification. The believer before glorification has a God-given ability to act in obedience but is also capable of sin as someone who still wrestles with his depravity. The Spirit completes his work in glorification, in which a person always freely choses obedience.

It is possible to posit a similar picture of human thinking and interpretation before and after the fall that takes into account creation, grace, redemption, and eschatology. Like any work of God, there is an already/not yet tension between the present age and the age to come (Luke 17:20–21; 20:34–36).[85] The Spirit's illumination in the present age makes it possible for believers to receive the word of God as a word of truth, but this supernatural work does not ensure perfect comprehension or absorption of that word:

1. Before the fall, finite human beings had *the ability to understand and obey God's commands* or *understand and disobey God's commands* (Gen. 2:15–17; 3:1–7).[86]
2. After the fall and before the illuminating work of the Holy Spirit, the natural person was *incapable of understanding the things of God* (Job 17:4; Ps. 14:2; Isa. 6:9; Mic. 4:12; Eph. 4:18; 1 Tim. 6:4; Jude 10).
3. After the illuminating work of the Spirit but before glorification, the interpreter is able either to *grasp the meaning of revelation in Scripture* or to *misinterpret the meaning of revelation in Scripture* (Joel 2:28; Matt. 15:16; 16:11; Mark 9:32; Luke 24:25; John 20:9; 2 Cor. 1:14; 10:11; Gal. 1:4; Eph. 5:17; 2 Pet. 3:16; 1 John 5:20). The interpreter's knowledge is in an eschatological tension, *already* in possession of an imperfect knowledge of God in Christ but *not yet* having the fuller knowledge of God promised in 1 Corinthians 13:12.
4. The glorified saint, who will be able to know fully as he is fully known, is finally *unable to misinterpret God's revelation* (1 Cor. 13:12; 2 Cor. 4:18; Rev. 22:4).

---

85. See George Eldon Ladd, *The Gospel of the Kingdom: Scriptural Studies in the Kingdom of God* (Grand Rapids, MI: Eerdmans, 1959), 24–51.

86. I do not mean to suggest Adam and Eve had a comprehensive understanding of the consequences of their actions—they did not yet know good or evil—but they clearly apprehended God's primary speech act ("You shall not eat"; Gen. 3:3). God's command was intelligible to them, but they chose to believe the serpent before God.

Even with the illuminating activity of the Spirit and a clearly revealed word, biblical interpreters are imperfect readers prone to error and disagreement, and they will remain so until God completes the good work he began in them on the day of Jesus Christ (Phil. 1:6).

The consummation of the kingdom of God in the eschaton will bring a more complete understanding of God to believers and unbelievers alike (Zech. 12:10; 2 Cor. 4:3–4; Phil. 2:9–10). This final removal of hindrances to knowledge will not likely give us godlike omniscience, but we will be free from sinful distortions and creaturely imperfections.[87] In the interim, we can pray for Spirit-led understanding which reflects our future, fuller knowledge in the same way that we pray for the Kingdom to come in the present age as we await its future consummation (Matt. 6:10; Luke 11:10).[88]

Conclusion

In contrast to postmodern thinkers who cast doubt on the ability of authors to communicate meaning, hermeneutical realists affirm that such communication is possible. On the other hand, naive interpreters who dogmatically confuse their understanding of the biblical texts with the texts themselves will often have difficulty coming to terms with those who challenge their opinions. Interpretive diversity abounds because human beings are frail creatures beset by natural limitations and impediments, as well as those imperfections caused by the brokenness of the present age.

True recognition of the authority of Scripture requires *openness* to ways in which it may challenge one's worldview and preconceived notions.[89] Openness to Scripture means readers must put their own interpretive interests and theological agendas under the microscope. Interpretation can be hard work, because of our limitations as readers and the distance between our present world and the world of the Bible. The challenges of interpretation do not prevent the Presbyterian teenager, the Methodist soccer mom, or the uneducated Baptist layman from ascertaining the larger narrative of Scripture summed up

---

87. For thoughtful speculation about the possibilities of learning in heaven, see Randy Alcorn, *Heaven* (Carol Stream, IL: Tyndale, 2004), 317–327.

88. Thiselton, *Systematic Theology*, 5–6.

89. Wright, *New Testament and the People of God*, 97.

in the good news of Jesus. The Spirit often provides these interpreters with a fuller understanding of Scripture than even the most erudite of professional theologians and biblical scholars, those who may be able to grapple with the historical complexities of the Bible but fail to see how its message applies to their own lives. Notwithstanding these challenges, the Bible is clear enough to bring any individual who reads it with an openness to the activity of the Spirit into an understanding sufficient unto obedience and service to God.

2

We Read Differently

The Contribution of Exegesis and Hermeneutics to Theological Diversity

Though there are exceptions in areas such as philosophical theology or natural theology, most doctrinal controversies among evangelicals begin as disagreements over how best to understand the message of the Bible, either in its explicit message or in its implications for a theological system.[1] The evangelical heirs of the Reformation universally choose Scripture—not experience, philosophy, culture, or church teaching—as the starting point and final word of theological construction. Even though other elements such as reason, tradition, experience, history, and science have important roles to play in theological method, the biblical text is the primary arena for those who claim it as the supreme source and only guiding norm of their faith and practice.[2]

---

1. Liberal Protestants who minimize the significance of Scripture in theology have an entirely different set of reasons for their disagreements. As Gary Dorrien describes liberal Protestant theology, "The essential idea of liberal theology is that all claims to truth, in theology as in other disciplines, must be made on the basis of reason and experience, not by appeal to external authority. Christian scripture may be recognized as spiritually authoritative within Christian experience, but its word does not settle or establish truth claims about matters of fact" (Dorrien, *The Making of American Liberal Theology: Idealism, Realism, and Modernity, 1900–1950* [Louisville: Westminster John Knox, 2003], 1).

2. Evangelical philosophers of religion and philosophical theologians tackle numerous metaphysical and epistemological issues not directly addressed by biblical authors (e.g., relations within the Godhead, divine impassibility, the nature of freedom, etc.), but these scholars seek to put their

Consequently, conflicting explanations of biblical texts take center stage in our theological disagreements.

Not all readers of the Bible approach interpretation in the same way or with the same seriousness. In practice, many interpreters use Scripture to prove a preconceived theological system or to reinforce a particular social agenda, slapping a Bible verse on a pet idea to give it some weight or authority. This uncritical use of biblical texts to reinforce one's preconceived beliefs is sometimes called *eisegesis*, which means to read something *into* (from the Greek preposition *eis*) the text that isn't there.

Both novice readers and seasoned scholars of the Bible can fall into this trap. For many readers, eisegesis is an unconscious act stemming from biblical illiteracy. Some are accidental eisegetes, unaware of their own interpretive shortcomings. For others, it is a deliberate strategy arising from a postmodern "reader-centered" approach to the text that makes the reader or reading community, not the author, the final arbiter of the text's meaning.

Eisegetes see what they want to see on the page. They avow that whatever a text means, it cannot mean something that is inconsistent with their presupposed theological or ethical system: Throughout history, interpreters have used the Bible both to justify slavery and to abolish it, to advance racist causes and promote racial equality, to endorse feminism and denounce it, and to defend modern economic theories of every stripe. While the human authors of Scripture do take definitive positions on some of these matters, finite and fallen interpreters have a penchant for abusing texts that do not coincide with their worldviews.

Other readers approach the Bible *mystically*, equating the meaning of the text with an emotional feeling or impression that the text elicits in them. The key question for mystical readers is not "What does it mean in its original context?" but "How does it make me feel?" While it is imperative for readers to make a connection between what a biblical text meant then and what its significance is for them now, mystical readers frequently skip the hard work of trying to understand meaning in proper context and go straight to matters of personal application. Many books in the "Christian" self-help section of local bookstores

---

discussions under the authority of Scripture. See Thomas H. McCall, *An Invitation to Analytic Christian Theology* (Downers Grove, IL: InterVarsity Press, 2015).

exemplify this trait. Instead of taking the voices and concerns of biblical authors seriously, eisegetes treat the Bible like a crystal ball that directly addresses every mundane personal crisis they face.

Neither eisegesis nor mystical interpretation gives adequate attention to the authorial intentions, literary genres, and historical contexts of Scripture. By ignoring the contexts of biblical authors, these approaches effectively make the reader or reading community the authority over the text. The "meanings" of texts become subject to the preferences and whims of their readership.[3] As hermeneutical realists who contend that authors can communicate their intended meanings through texts, evangelicals reject any approach to the Bible that would make readers the authorities over its meaning.

In contrast to these deficient ways of reading the Bible, interpreters in the tradition of the Reformation contend that the central task of biblical interpretation is to draw out the original meaning of the biblical texts without imposing a sense alien to its original authorship. This approach, historically known as the *grammatical-historical* method, is a conscious effort to make sense of the biblical words (*grammatical*) in their ancient setting (*historical*). The grammatical-historical meaning of Scripture has also been called its *literal sense* (*sensus literalis*).

The literal sense of the text does not mean one should interpret everything literally—some passages are meant to be read metaphorically—but that its readers seek to understand the "sense" of the written "letter" (i.e., its authorial intention). Grammatical-historical interpretation is a human process subject to human error and misjudgment, but it is also the best way to approach the Bible. It involves paying close attention to the genres, figures of speech, and historical setting of biblical books in order to grasp the intentions of biblical authorship.

Differences in the way we understand the grammar and context of biblical passages is inevitable given our creaturely limitations of imperfect memory, faulty reasoning, and limited know-how. We could devote several lifetimes to covering all the interpretive debates related to the Bible, but my goal in this chapter is much more modest. Here, I want only to give readers a taste of some of the types of interpretive

---

3. Ralph P. Martin, "Approaches to New Testament Exegesis," in *New Testament Interpretation: Essays on Principles and Methods*, ed. I. Howard Marshall (Exeter, UK: Paternoster, 1977), 220–223.

differences that shape our doctrinal diversity. This chapter is meant to be a basic overview of the practice of biblical hermeneutics for students and nonspecialists. I will introduce practices like textual criticism, semantic studies, syntax analysis, and various forms of literary and historical criticism with the hope of demonstrating ways in which these practices impact theological formation.

Exegetical Differences

The first broad type of interpretive diversity we will explore is the category of *exegetical differences*. *Exegesis*, from an ancient Greek term meaning "interpretation," "exposition," or "explanation,"[4] describes the actual process of interpreting and explaining a particular text. Exegesis here accounts for the minutia of interpretation related to texts, vocabulary, syntax, etc. In some instances, exegetical disagreements lead to drastically divergent theological conclusions. On other occasions, even those who affirm similar doctrinal positions may differ over the meanings and nuances of particular texts.

Biblical exegesis in the grammatical-historical method involves several steps or stages, some of which can be very complicated and all of which create the potential for interpretive diversity. The possibility of interpretive controversy escalates with each successive step in the exegetical process. Exegetical differences discussed here are differences related to textual criticism, word studies, and grammar or syntax.

We Read Different Textual Variants

Sometimes the differences in interpretation are related to *variants of the same biblical passage*. The use of multiple *translations* among lay readers reading the Bible in their native language can affect their respective interpretations of the Bible. Translations are, after all, interpretations of biblical texts. But the differences in modern translations occasionally depend on the choices of translation committees between various *critical texts* of the Bible—the scholarly compilations of the ancient manuscripts. Even professional biblical scholars and theologians working in the original Greek, Hebrew, or Aramaic may clash over which manuscript or manuscript tradition provides the best reading of a particular biblical passage.

---

4. *A Patristic Greek Lexicon* (Oxford: Clarendon, 1961), s.v. ἐξήγησις.

The task of *textual criticism*, a preliminary step in exegesis, helps scholars and theologians identify the best reading(s) of ancient biblical texts. The original handwritten versions of biblical texts—what scholars call the autographs—were lost to history. The surviving manuscripts are replete with scribal errors, corrections, and occasionally, additions—called *glosses*. Textual critics weigh the differences between manuscripts and try to approximate which variant reading of the passage in question is more likely to reflect the earliest attainable wording of the text.

The manuscript tradition of the New Testament contains roughly 400,000 variants, most of which are related to copying issues like spelling differences, differences in word order, or copying errors. The ancient transmission of texts was an imperfect, fluid process dependent almost entirely upon the competency of the scribe or scribes who copied the texts by hand.[5] Even skeptical New Testament scholar Bart Ehrman acknowledges that "the vast majority [of differences between the manuscripts] are purely 'accidental,' readily explained as resulting from scribal ineptitude, carelessness, or fatigue."[6] For the most part, the variants in the New Testament manuscript tradition are of little or no theological significance. Still, a small percentage of variants in the manuscripts do change the meaning of certain texts to some degree.

The most notable textual variants appear in the "Received Text" (*Textus Receptus*) or "Majority Text" tradition on which the King James Version is based but do not appear in the earliest known manuscripts.[7] Some of these debated Majority Text passages include the longer ending of Mark (16:9–20) and the story of the woman caught in adultery (John 7:53–8:11), but perhaps the most theologically germane

---

5. For an overview of these types of errors, see Bruce M. Metzger and Bart D. Ehrman, *The Text of the New Testament: Its Transmission, Corruption, and Restoration*, 4th ed. (New York: Oxford University Press, 2005), 250–271.

6. Bart D. Ehrman, *The Orthodox Corruption of Scripture: The Effect of Early Christological Controversies on the Text of the New Testament* (New York: Oxford University Press, 1993), 27.

7. The majority of biblical scholars consider these variants spurious, despite their prominence in older translations. There are exceptions to this scholarly consensus, as KJV-only advocates contend that the later textual tradition on which the KJV was based better preserves the original writing. For more on this debate, see D. A. Carson, *The King James Debate: A Plea for Realism* (Grand Rapids, MI: Baker, 1979); James R. White, *The King James Only Controversy: Can You Trust Modern Translations?* 2nd ed. (Grand Rapids, MI: Bethany, 2009); Theodore Letis, ed., *Majority Text: Essays and Reviews in the Continuing Debate* (Grand Rapids, MI: Institute for Biblical Textual Studies, 1987); Harry A. Sturtz, *The Byzantine Text-Type and New Testament Textual Criticism* (Nashville: Thomas Nelson, 1984).

variant from the Majority Text tradition is the so-called *Comma Johanneum* in 1 John 5:7. The text reads, "For there are three that bear witness in heaven: the Father, the Word, and the Holy Spirit; and these three are one" (NKJV). The statement is consistent with Trinitarian doctrine but is likely a later scribal gloss on 1 John 5:8. Though the gloss does appear in later versions of the Latin Vulgate, it does not appear in any Greek manuscripts before the fourteenth century. The original context does not seem to speak about the Trinity but about the baptism, death, and resurrection of Jesus.[8] However, the absence of this line from the early manuscripts does not detract from Trinitarian doctrine in the Bible because of the prevalence of its principal ideas elsewhere in the canon.

New Testament textual critics concede that other variants can have some impact on the interpretation of texts related to minor doctrines. "If major teachings of the New Testament are not impacted by viable variants, what about *minor* doctrines? By minor doctrines we mean some non-central belief or practice. Yes, some of those seem to be affected. But these are quite rare."[9] Disputed variants among textual critics that may contribute to differences in interpretation may include things like the number of the beast in Revelation 13:18, which, according to the earliest known manuscript of the passage, is 616 instead of 666. But as Daniel Wallace points out, one would be hard pressed to find a major confession or creed in the church that draws the line of fellowship over the mark of the beast being 666.[10]

In the interpretation of texts like these, biblical scholars make judgment calls about which manuscripts provide the best reading. The choices they make can change the outcome of interpretation, which in turn can result in minor doctrinal dissent. William Klein, Craig Blomberg, and Robert Hubbard add a much-needed warning for theologians: "Perhaps the most important hermeneutical principle to learn from textual criticism is that one must not derive theological and ethi-

---

8. Philip Wesley Comfort, *A Commentary on the Manuscripts and Text of the New Testament* (Grand Rapids, MI: Kregel, 2015), 397.

9. J. Ed Komoszewski, M. James Sawyer, and Daniel B. Wallace, *Reinventing Jesus: How Contemporary Skeptics Miss the Real Jesus and Mislead Popular Culture* (Grand Rapids, MI: Kregel, 2006), 114.

10. This textual witness is in the Codex Ephraimi Rescriptus, P115. See Daniel B. Wallace, "Opening Remarks," in *The Reliability of the New Testament: Bart D. Ehrman and Daniel B. Wallace in Dialogue*, ed. Robert B. Stewart (Minneapolis: Fortress, 2011), 40–41.

cal principles solely from passages that are textually uncertain."[11] For this reason, among many others, I choose to refrain from the textually dubious practices of snake handling and poison drinking (see Mark 16:18; MT, KJV). I advise other interpreters to follow suit!

We Read Biblical Words Differently

Another source of interpretive discrepancy comes from *semantics*, i.e., the search for the lexical meanings of words used in biblical texts. We dispute the meaning of words used by authors who share our language, but these differences are exacerbated when talking about ancient texts written in long-dormant languages that have not been spoken in many years. Even Modern Hebrew and Modern Greek are distinct tongues from Biblical Hebrew and Koine Greek.

Word Study Fallacies and Their Impact on Doctrine

The fallacious handling of word studies can lead to exegetical discrepancies. Teachers and preachers with only a superficial knowledge of the original biblical languages are prone to these types of mistakes. Take the suggestion that, because the English word *dynamite* comes from the Greek word for power (*dynamis*), God's saving power (Rom. 1:16, *dynamis*) is somehow explosive like dynamite.[12] But even trained biblical scholars and theologians can make etymological mistakes. One such common error is what D. A. Carson calls the "root fallacy," which presumes that its composite parts can determine the meaning of a word.[13]

Some scholars have suggested that the word Paul uses for "servant" in 1 Corinthians 4:1 (*hypēretas*) comes from two Greek words meaning "under" (*hypo*) and "to row" (*ēressō*) and that the word describes a slave who rows the oars at the very bottom of a ship. The takeaway, these biblical scholars suggest, is that Paul is painting for us a picture of the lowliest of servants. The problem, however, is that *hypēretas* is used nowhere in antiquity to describe the "under-rower"

11. William W. Klein, Craig L. Blomberg, Robert L. Hubbard Jr., *Introduction to Biblical Interpretation*, 3rd ed. (Grand Rapids, MI: Zondervan, 2017), 190.

12. D. A. Carson, *Exegetical Fallacies*, 2nd ed. (Grand Rapids, MI: Baker, 1996), 33–34; cf. Moisés Silva, *Biblical Words and Their Meaning: An Introduction to Biblical Semantics*, rev. ed. (Grand Rapids, MI: Zondervan, 1994), 44–45.

13. Carson, *Exegetical Fallacies*, 28–29.

of a ship or trireme (i.e., a slave-powered ship like the ones seen in *Ben-Hur*).[14] In the same way that the meaning of *butterfly* is not a fly made of butter and a *strawberry* is not a berry made from straw, the meaning of biblical words cannot be determined solely by their constituent parts.[15]

In earlier generations of biblical scholarship, theological debates often centered on the etymology of ancient words. The so-called Biblical Theology Movement of the mid-twentieth century spent considerable time tracing the treatment of words throughout history, believing such endeavors to be vital for comprehending the theology of biblical writers.[16] Scholars would ask questions like "Does the Hebrew word *'ôlām* (frequently translated as 'everlasting') describe eternity as being in time or outside of time?"[17] "Do New Testament writers use forms of the Greek word *proginōskō* (typically translated 'foreknow') to describe God's simple foreknowledge of future events or the divine foreordination of future events?"[18] While these are interesting questions, simple appeals to biblical Hebrew and Greek lexicons have rarely resolved these debates, since the lexicons offer interpretations of words that are themselves open to dispute.

Just because a word is used in one way in one context, that does not ensure that the word means the same thing in another context. Interpreters should be wary of a semantic fallacy James Barr calls "illegitimate totality transfer,"[19] or what N. Clayton Croy dubs "*the dump-truck fallacy.*" With this fallacy, interpreters take all the known meanings of a given word throughout history and "dump" them in

---

14. J. P. Louw, *Semantics of New Testament Greek* (Atlanta: Scholars, 1982), 26; Carson, *Exegetical Fallacies*, 29.

15. Louw, *Semantics of New Testament Greek*, 27.

16. The most famous example of this obsession with word studies in the Biblical Theology Movement is the *Theological Dictionary of the New Testament* [*Theologisches Wörterbuch zum Neuen Testament*] (originally published in Stuttgart, 1933–1976; see listing for English translation under Kittel in the Bibliography).

17. See Genesis 3:22; 6:3; 17:19; 21:33; Exodus 15:18; Leviticus 24:8; Deuteronomy 5:29; 33:27; Joshua 24:2; Psalm 90:2; 145:13. The debate over biblical words for time in Oscar Cullmann, *Christ and Time: The Primitive Christian Conception of Time and History*, trans. Floyd V. Filson (London: SCM, 1951); and John Marsh, *The Fullness of Time* (London: Nisbet, 1952) led James Barr to his paradigm-shifting critique of the Biblical Theology Movement's use of word studies in *Biblical Words for Time* (London: SCM, 1962). See also Anthony C. Thiselton, *The Hermeneutics of Doctrine* (Grand Rapids, MI: Eerdmans, 2007), 574–581.

18. See Acts 26:5; Rom. 8:29; 11:2; 1 Pet. 1:20; 2 Pet. 3:17. See also Rudolf Bultmann, "προγινώσκω," in *TDNT* 1:715–716; *NIDNTTE* 4:138–139.

19. James Barr, *The Semantics of Biblical Language* (Oxford: Oxford University Press, 1961), 218.

their totality into that word's single usage in a particular passage. As Croy notes, authors rarely have this sort of usage in mind.[20]

If I say to my wife, "Dinner was terrific tonight," I mean that I enjoyed my meal, whether she cooked it or we ate out. However, etymologists could point out that the word *terrific* is a seventeenth-century derivation of the Latin words *terrificus* and *terrere*, which mean "to cause fear" or "to be filled with fear." Someone illegitimately transferring the totality of etymological meaning may suggest to my wife that I enjoyed the food so much that it filled me with fear. Context and good sense should prevent readers from jumping to such conclusions, but this sort of fallacy sometimes rears its ugly head in commentaries, sermons, and so-called "amplified" translations of the Bible.

While scholars today have some appreciation for lexical analysis, they also understand that the sentence, not the individual word, is the most basic unit of meaning.[21] As Daniel Wallace notes, "*Words* in isolation mean next to nothing—simply because they are capable of so many meanings. Given no context, it would be impossible to define, for example, 'bank,' or 'fine,' or 'trust.' . . . Without a context, we are at a loss to decide."[22] An essential step for the biblical interpreter is making sense of a word in a given context, when and where a particular speaker uses the word.

An example from English illustrates this need for context. As George Caird observes, an American speaker and a British speaker may not mean the same thing when saying, "I'm mad about my flat." An American more than likely will use the words "mad" and "flat" to describe his frustration with a deflated tire. A Brit, on the other hand, can use the same words to describe his enthusiasm for his apartment.[23] In this sentence, both the context of the sentence and the context of the speaker are essential for discerning how the words are used.

---

20. N. Clayton Croy, *Prima Scriptura: An Introduction to New Testament Interpretation* (Grand Rapids, MI: Baker, 2011), 67–68, italics original.

21. Anthony C. Thiselton, "Semantics and New Testament Interpretation," in *New Testament Interpretation: Essays on Principles and Methods*, 76.

22. Daniel B. Wallace, *Greek Grammar beyond the Basics: An Exegetical Syntax of the New Testament* (Grand Rapids, MI: Zondervan, 1996), 7–8.

23. George B. Caird, *The Language and Imagery of the Bible* (Philadelphia: Westminster, 1980), 50; cf. N. T. Wright, *The Resurrection of the Son of God* (Minneapolis: Fortress, 2003), 9.

The good news for interpreters is that writers cannot use words arbitrarily *and* successfully convey their intended meaning, so they typically wield words within the conventions of a language used by a society or culture. Word studies focused on the particular time period of the author (*synchronic* word studies) can give us a clue as to what a biblical author means by a precise use of a word, but this process is fallible and open to revision. As H. S. Baldwin explained, "Understanding the meaning of a word in a specific context is a trial-and-error process" that involves testing our knowledge of a word's general use against the context of a passage.[24] Tentative, imperfect lexical methods can yield diverse interpretations of key passages, which in turn can add to doctrinal diversity.

The Challenge of Hapax Legomena

Perhaps the most debated terms are the words (not including proper nouns or names) that appear only once in the whole of biblical literature (i.e., what biblical scholars call *hapax legomena*). These words can pose great difficulty to interpreters, and numerous criteria have been used by specialists to decode them.[25] The Hebrew Bible contains roughly fifteen hundred of these unique words, though the number is much smaller if one counts only words with unique roots.[26] The New Testament contains around two thousand words appearing only once.[27] Even so, its vocabulary presents fewer challenges to interpreters because of (1) the abundance of non-biblical Greek literature containing these words and (2) the ease with which unique words can be explained as cognates within the language.[28]

On occasion, theological debates rest on these one-of-a-kind words. Take the discussion over the meaning of the Greek verb *authentein* in 1 Timothy 2:12 (frequently translated as "assume authority," "have

---

24. Henry Scott Baldwin, "An Important Word: Αὐθεντέω in 1 Timothy 2:12," in *Women in the Church: An Analysis and Application of 1 Timothy 2:9–15*, 2nd ed., ed. Andreas J. Köstenberger and Thomas R. Schreiner (Grand Rapids, MI: Baker, 2005), 44.

25. See Frederick E. Greenspahn, *Hapax Legomena in Biblical Hebrew: A Study of the Phenomenon and Its Treatment since Antiquity with Special Reference to Verbal Forms*, SBL Dissertation Series 74 (Chico, CA: Scholars, 1984).

26. I. M. Casanowicz, "Hapax Legomena—Biblical Data," in *The Jewish Encyclopedia*, 12 vols. (New York, 1906), 6:226–228; cf. Greenspahn, *Hapax Legomena in Biblical Hebrew*, 33.

27. For a comprehensive list, see Warren C. Trenchard, *Complete Vocabulary Guide to the Greek New Testament*, rev. ed. (Grand Rapids, MI: Zondervan, 1998), 198–236.

28. Silva, *Biblical Words and Their Meaning*, 42.

authority," and "exercise authority"), which has considerable ramifications in the intramural Christian debate over the role of women in
ministry. Broadly speaking, evangelicals take two sides in this debate.
The *complementarian* regards men and women as equals in the eyes of
God but created to complement each other with different roles in the
life of the family and the church. The *egalitarian* denies any gender-
specific roles given to men and women, who are equals in Christ.[29] The
traditional, complementarian interpretation of the verb *authentein* in
1 Timothy 2:12 prohibits women from having positions of pastoral
authority over men in churches, but some egalitarian scholars have
offered alternative explanations.

Catherine C. Kroeger initially argued that *authentein* was a
verb meaning "to thrust oneself" on a man in an erotic manner
or "engage in fertility practices," meaning Paul's prohibition was
not against women in authority but against licentiousness in the
church.[30] She later contended that the verb means to "proclaim
herself as author" or "originator," believing that Paul is primarily
addressing women who deny the created order described in the Genesis account.[31] Other alternatives to the traditional interpretation of
authentein are more modest, such as the suggestion that the verb
refers only to women who "dominate" or "domineer."[32] According
to those who interpret the verb in this manner, Paul issued the prohibition in a situation in which "women were acting in a way that
threatened the men."[33]

Complementarian scholars who affirm the traditional reading of
authentein have produced several strong defenses of their position in

29. For a survey of egalitarian arguments, see Ronald W. Pierce and Rebecca Merrill Groothuis,
eds., *Discovering Biblical Equality: Complementarity without Hierarchy* (Downers Grove, IL:
InterVarsity Press, 2005). For the complementarian view, see John Piper and Wayne Grudem, eds.,
Recovering Biblical Manhood and Womanhood (Wheaton, IL: Crossway, 1991).

30. Catherine Clark Kroeger, "Ancient Heresies and a Strange Greek Verb," *Reformed Journal*
29 (1979): 12–15.

31. Richard Clark Kroeger and Catherine Clark Kroeger, *I Suffer Not a Woman: Rethinking
1 Timothy 2:11–15 in Light of Ancient Evidence* (Grand Rapids, MI: Baker, 1992), 103.

32. Carroll D. Osborn, "ΑΥΘΕΝΤΈΩ (1 Timothy 2:12)," *Restoration Quarterly* 25 (1982):
1–12. See also Armin J. Panning, "AUTHENTEIN—A Word Study," *Wisconsin Lutheran Quarterly* (1981): 185–191; Cynthia Long Westfall, "The Meaning of αὐθεντέω in 1 Timothy 2.12,"
JGRChJ 10 (2014): 138–173; I. Howard Marshall and Philip H. Towner, *A Critical and Exegetical Commentary on the Pastoral Epistles*, ICC (Edinburgh: T&T Clark, 1999), 456–459; Ben
Witherington III, *Women in the Earliest Churches* (Cambridge: Cambridge University Press,
1988), 121.

33. Marshall and Towner, *Pastoral Epistles*, 459.

response to these recent proposals.[34] But a more robust case for traditional complementarianism must be made with reference to the whole witness of Scripture and not word studies alone. The theologian must account for all of the gender-related instructions in the Epistles as well as the biblical theology of creation and humanity taught throughout the Scriptures. Though word studies can be a key part of the debate, they are by themselves incapable of yielding definitive results.

We Interpret Biblical Grammar Differently

Interpretive conflict also stems from distinct ways of approaching biblical grammar and syntax. The study of Hebrew and Greek grammars is complex, and exegesis at the level of syntax is prone to multitudes of interpretive complications and mistakes. A language like Biblical Hebrew presents certain interpretive difficulties because, unlike New Testament Greek, there are relatively few examples of the language outside of the biblical text. New Testament Greek, on the other hand, carries with it certain ambiguities and challenges because it is a less formal version of the language than its classical counterparts. Many of the syntactical rules of the classical Greek texts do not apply to the Koine Greek ("common Greek"), the Greek dialect of the New Testament.

Sparring grammarians rarely settle theological debates. Nevertheless, these debates can be used either in support of or in opposition to a theological position. The following examples of disputes over grammar, both from the Pauline letters, can have far-reaching theological repercussions.

Faith in Christ or Christ's Faith?

One of the more theologically significant debates over grammar in recent decades has been the brouhaha over how to translate and

---

34. For a sample of these word studies drawn along traditional lines, see Baldwin, "Important Word," 39–51; Denny Burk, "New and Old Departures in the Translation of Αὐθεντεῖν in 1 Timothy 2:12," in *Women in the Church*, 3rd ed., ed. Andreas J. Köstenberger and Thomas R. Schreiner (Wheaton, IL: Crossway, 2016), 279–296; G. W. Knight III, "AY-ΘΕΝΤ'ΕΩ in Reference to Women in 1 Timothy 2.12," *New Testament Studies* 30 (1984): 143–157; William D. Mounce, *Pastoral Epistles*, WBC 46 (Nashville: Thomas Nelson, 2000), 126–130; Al Wolters, "A Semantic Study of Αὐθέντης and Its Derivatives," *JGRChJ* 1 (2000): 145–175; Wolters, "The Meaning of Αὐθεντέω," in Köstenberger and Schreiner, *Women in the Church*, 3rd ed., 65–115.

understand the Pauline formula *pistis Christou* (Rom. 3:22, 26; Gal. 2:16; Phil. 3:9; cf. Eph. 3:12), which typically has been translated either as "faith in Christ" or "faithfulness of Christ."[35] Both translations hang on a particular understanding of the syntax of the phrase, and both have consequences for Paul's wider theological program.

Greek is an inflected language, meaning that the spelling of words, not word order, is the primary way a reader understands its function in a sentence. A reader usually can determine what function a Greek noun plays in a sentence by its case ending. *Pistis*, translated as "faith" or "faithfulness," is a verb-like noun because of its relationship to the verb *pisteuō*, which means "to believe," "to trust," or "to have faith." Grammarians are in agreement that the case ending of the noun *Christou* (from *Christos*) in *pistis Christou* is genitive, meaning the noun describes or qualifies the noun next to it, which in this case is the verb-like noun *pistis*. However, New Testament scholars take issue over what type of genitive *Christou* is.

Following Luther, the traditional reading of the genitive here is an objective genitive, meaning *Christou* here essentially functions as a direct object of the verb-like noun. According to this interpretation, Christ is the object of the believing. This reading, typically translated as "faith in Christ," stresses *human belief or trust in Christ*. For this reason, it has been labeled by some as the "anthropological" reading of the phrase.

Interpreters who affirm this position believe Paul's primary focus to be on the faith in Christ needed to attain a right standing with God (justification). The "so-what" of these passages becomes an emphasis on our need to respond to the gospel in faith. Mark Reasoner points out that "our stance on the meaning of *pistis Christou* can affect how we draw the circle around those we call saved. Proponents of the objective genitive tend to understand faith in Christ as a requirement for salvation that logically precludes those who do not have such faith from salvation."[36]

---

35. See Michael F. Bird and Preston M. Sprinkle, eds., *The Faith of Jesus Christ: Exegetical, Biblical, and Theological Studies* (Grand Rapids, MI: Baker, 2010).

36. Mark Reasoner, *Romans in Full Circle: A History of Interpretation* (Louisville: Westminster John Knox, 2005), 40.

Other interpreters understand *Christou* here to be a subjective genitive, which would mean that Christ is essentially the subject of the verb-like noun. One possible reading is that Paul speaks of the "faith of Christ."[37] Some have suggested that if Christ is the subject, the verb-like noun *pistis* is not "faith" or "belief," but "faithfulness." If one interprets *pistis Christou* with Christ as the subject of the verb-like noun, then the phrase stresses *Christ's faith* or *Christ's faithfulness*, not the faith of believers in Christ. Because of its emphasis on Christ's character, this reading has been branded the "Christological" reading.

Those who embrace this Christological reading believe Paul to be more focused on telling a theological *story* about Jesus's role in our justification than on giving instruction on how to be justified.[38] Again, according to Reasoner, this affects the very way Christians understand and present the gospel message: "Proponents of the subjective genitive, who hold that Christ's faith is what saves, will not call for a distinct, conversion-constituting act of placing one's faith in Jesus. They will rather call people to join the church that lives out in a concentric pattern the faith that Jesus displayed."[39] Reasoner also adds that this interpretation of *pistis Christou* changes one's reading of Paul's theology, making justification part of the bigger theme of participation in Christ.[40]

Both anthropological and Christological interpretations appear to be valid, at least in the sense that both are grammatical possibilities. However, strong arguments for and against both translations have been made by scholars of every theological stripe.[41] Though grammar plays a key role in the debate over the interpretation of the Pauline phrase *pistis Christou*, larger questions about the wider context of Scripture, hermeneutics, and theology are probably more significant

---

37. Markus Barth, "The Faith of the Messiah," *Heythrop Journal* 10 (1969): 363–370; Richard B. Hays, *The Faith of Jesus Christ: An Investigation of the Narrative Substructure of Galatians 3:1–4:11* (Chico, CA: Scholars, 1983). For an exploration of the implications of this interpretation for systematic theology and Christology, see Gerald O'Collins and Daniel Kendall, "The Faith of Jesus," *Theological Studies* 53 (1992): 403–423.

38. See Richard B. Hays, "ΠΙΣΤΙΣ and Pauline Christology: What Is At Stake?" in *Pauline Theology*, vol. 4, ed. E. Elizabeth Johnson and David M. Hay (Atlanta: Scholars, 1997), 35–60.

39. Reasoner, *Romans in Full Circle*, 39–40.

40. Reasoner, *Romans in Full Circle*, 40.

41. For a summary of these arguments, see Matthew C. Easter, "The *Pistis Christou* Debate: Main Arguments and Responses in Summary," *Currents in Biblical Research* 9, no. 1 (2010): 34–42.

contributors to the debate. The particular meaning of Paul's phrase may be debated, but it is clear from other passages in the New Testament that Jesus is often the object of faith or belief (John 3:16; Acts 16:31; 1 John 5:13).

Did Jesus Descend Into Hell? The Debate over Ephesians 4:9

There is a syntactical controversy surrounding one passage frequently associated with the doctrine of Jesus's descent into hell. Since at least the second century, Christian theologians have asserted that Jesus went to preach to the world of the dead (Hades) in the time between his death on the cross and his resurrection on the third day.[42] The Apostles' Creed, at least in its later recensions, explicitly states that Jesus "descended into hell" (descendit ad infernos).[43] Since the Reformation, Protestants and evangelicals have been divided over the precise meaning of the phrase and the biblical texts commonly associated with this doctrine (Acts 2:27; Rom. 10:6–7; Eph. 4:8–9; 1 Pet. 3:18–20; 4:6).[44]

This debate is more complicated than disparity over the grammar of any single passage, but the question about how best to translate Ephesians 4:9 has contributed to the controversy. One common translation goes like this: "But what does 'he ascended' mean except that he also descended to the lower parts of the earth?" (CSB). This verse and its immediate context continue to mystify interpreters, but three basic explanations have been offered. First, some commentators suggest that Paul is speaking here about Jesus's descent into the world of the dead.[45] Second, some argue that Paul is describing Jesus's descent to

---

42. See Polycarp, Letter to the Philippians 1; Irenaeus, Against All Heresies 4.27.2; 5.31.1; 5.33.1; Tertullian, On the Soul 55.

43. For an examination of the evolution of the Apostles' Creed on this subject, see Wayne Grudem, "He Did Not Descend into Hell: A Plea for Following Scripture instead of the Apostles' Creed," JETS 34, no. 1 (1991): 103–113.

44. See Matthew Emerson, He Descended to the Dead: An Evangelical Approach to Holy Saturday (Downers Grove, IL: InterVarsity Press, 2019).

45. H. M. F. Büchsel, "κάτω," TDNT 3:641–642; James D. G. Dunn, Christology in the Making: A New Testament Inquiry into the Origins of the Doctrine of the Incarnation, 2nd ed. (Grand Rapids, MI: Eerdmans, 1996), 186–187; Frank Thielman, Ephesians, BECNT (Grand Rapids, MI: Baker, 2010), 271–272; Timothy G. Gombis, The Drama of Ephesians: Participating in the Triumph of God (Downers Grove, IL: InterVarsity Press, 2010), 140. For ancient commentators, the almost universal consensus was that Jesus descended into the world of the dead. See Irenaeus, Epideixis 83; Tertullian, Against Praxeas 30. See also Ronald E. Heine, The Commentaries of Origen and Jerome on St. Paul's Epistle to the Ephesians (New York: Oxford University Press, 2002), 173–174.

earth in the incarnation event.[46] Third, a minority of scholars contend the passage means that Jesus has "descended" to us in the gift-giving activity of the Holy Spirit.[47]

In Ephesians 4:8–10, Paul provides a Christ-centered commentary on Psalm 68:18. However, the precise function of this quotation from the psalter in verse 8 and its subsequent explanation in Paul's larger argument about church unity here is unknown. Some suggest that this may just be a digression that honors Christ but has no direct connection to the broader context of unity in his body. Another explanation (the idea that Jesus descended through the Holy Spirit) directly ties the descent to the dispersion of spiritual gifts in verses 11–13.[48]

The grammar of the genitive phrase "of the earth" (*tēs gēs*) in verse 9 adds to the difficulty of interpretation. Remember that the genitive is a noun that has a relationship to another noun, which is, in this case, the substantive phrase "the lower parts" (*ta katōtera merē*). For exegetes, the question is about what type of genitive Paul is using here. Interpreters have offered five basic choices. First, *tēs gēs* is translated as a partitive genitive, meaning the preceding noun is part of the larger whole described here (i.e., "the lower parts of the earth").[49] Second, the interpretive option of *tēs gēs* as a genitive of simple apposition makes "the earth" an explanation of the same referent, "the lower parts" ("the lower parts, namely, the earth").[50] Third, if *tēs gēs* is an attributive genitive, then it works like an adjective that describes the head noun "the lower parts" ("the lower, earthly parts").[51] The fourth option is that of the attributed genitive, which makes the head noun "lower parts" function like an adjective that describes the genitive "the earth" ("lowly earth").[52] Finally,

---

46. F. F. Bruce, *The Epistles to the Colossians, to Philemon, and to the Ephesians* (Grand Rapids, MI: Eerdmans, 1984), 343–344; Ernest Best, *A Critical and Exegetical Commentary on Ephesians* (Edinburgh: T&T Clark, 1998), 383–386.

47. George B. Caird, "The Descent of Christ in Ephesians 4, 7–11," in *Studia Evangelica*, ed. F. L. Cross, 7 vols. (Berlin: Akademie, 1964), 2:535–545; Andrew T. Lincoln, *Ephesians*, WBC 42 (Nashville: Thomas Nelson, 1990), 246–248; W. Hall Harris III, "The Ascent and Descent of Christ in Ephesians 4:9–10," *Bibliotheca Sacra* 151 (1994): 198–214.

48. Lincoln, *Ephesians*, 244.

49. See 4:9 in the KJV, NASB, CSB, and ASV.

50. See 4:9 in the NET, ESV.

51. See 4:9 in the NIV.

52. See 4:9 in the NLT.

there is the option of *tēs gēs* as a comparative genitive ("the parts lower than the earth").[53]

The dissimilarities between these translations are noteworthy.[54] If one interprets *tēs gēs* as a partitive genitive meaning "the lower parts of the earth" or a comparative genitive meaning "the parts lower than the earth," then the likeliest interpretation is that Paul is speaking of Jesus's descent into the world of the dead. Both syntactical options would fit well with an ancient cosmogony that understood Hades to be below the earth.[55] On the other hand, if one interprets the same phrase as a genitive of simple apposition ("the lower parts, namely, the earth") or as an attributed genitive ("the lowly earth"), then Paul is likely speaking of the *incarnation event*, when Jesus came down out of heaven to the earth. Those who advocate that Jesus descended through the Spirit take the same approach to the grammar. Consequently, the syntax can mount evidence either in favor of or against the patristic doctrine of Jesus's descent into Hades. Once more, the grammar plays a sizeable role in this debate, but it is not in and of itself conclusive.

Hermeneutical Differences

Having addressed a few ways in which the exegetical minutia can foster interpretive and theological diversity, I will now turn to larger and more important interpretive matters. Despite the gravity of exegesis for theological diversity, differences in interpretation of biblical texts cannot fall squarely on the shoulders of exegetical methods. The second, weightier category of interpretive difference comes from our *varying hermeneutical approaches* to biblical texts.

Hermeneutics (here in the sense of *special hermeneutics*) describes the specific ways readers approach the particular genres, literary devices, and thematic unity of the Bible. Whereas exegetical differences are differences in the way readers practice the methods of interpretation in individual biblical texts, hermeneutical differences are "big-picture"

---

53. Nigel Turner, *Syntax*, vol. 3 of *A Grammar of New Testament Greek*, 3rd ed., ed. James Hope Moulton (Edinburgh: T&T Clark, 2000), 215–216.
54. See Wallace, *Greek Grammar beyond the Basics*, 99–100.
55. B. F. Westcott, *Epistle to the Ephesians* (Grand Rapids, MI: Eerdmans, 1952), 61; Clinton E. Arnold, *Ephesians*, Exegetical Commentary on the New Testament (Grand Rapids, MI: Zondervan, 2010), 254.

differences about the methods of interpretation themselves. If exegesis is a focus on the tree bark and the trees, hermeneutics attempts to provide a view of the whole forest. It is here where our disagreements become much more substantial. The hermeneutical differences we will consider are differences in literary and historical context, competing understandings of biblical genre, and ways in which newer methods like rhetorical criticism can affect our theological reading of biblical texts.

Broadly speaking, we read for context in two ways: (1) *historical context* and (2) *literary context*. When we ask questions about historical context, we are asking about things like authorship, date, intended audience, and purpose.[56] Looking into the historical background of a biblical passage is like going "behind the scenes" in the making of a movie, trying to understand who the filmmakers are, what they were trying to do, and how they went about making the film. Literary context, by contrast, is trying to make sense of the story itself, how one scene fits into the larger whole of the story or series of stories. In biblical interpretation, literary context is about capturing the flow of thought in a particular passage, what its words mean, and how the passage relates to other parts of the whole context.[57] Conflicting explanations of historical and literary contexts can play crucial roles in our theological debates.

We Read Historical Contexts Differently

Apart from rediscovery or reconstruction of the original historical context, interpreters run a high risk of reading their own cultures, ideologies, and social setting back into the world of the Bible. They can quickly turn the sprawling vistas of ancient texts into bathroom-mirror selfies; that is, these readings speak more about the interpreter than the world of the texts. For this reason, Randolph Tate surmises that "the most effective safeguard against a wholesale imposition of the interpreter's world upon the world of the text is the diligent study of the world that produced the text."[58] Attempts at reconstructing

---

56. Grant R. Osborne, *The Hermeneutical Spiral: A Comprehensive Introduction to Biblical Interpretation*, rev. ed. (Downers Grove, IL: InterVarsity Press, 2006), 37–38.

57. Klein, Blomberg, and Hubbard, *Introduction to Biblical Interpretation*, 295.

58. W. Randolph Tate, *Biblical Interpretation: An Integrated Approach* (Peabody, MA: Hendrickson, 1991), 27.

the historical context of the Bible can be challenging, given the vast distance in time and culture between biblical authors and us.

Without borrowing the assumptions of the historical-critical worldview, the tools of historical criticism may be helpful supplemental tools for grammatical-historical exegesis.[59]

- *Source criticism* and *form criticism* can help us determine the authorship and the dating of biblical books. Whereas source criticism assesses the use of written sources in the final forms of biblical books, form criticism focuses on the oral traditions contained in biblical texts. Evangelicals tend to reject speculative versions of these methods that give greater weight to a hypothetical earlier recension of the text than to its final canonical form.
- *Redaction criticism,* a tool initially created to compare the Synoptic Gospels, seeks to understand the theological themes unique to the arrangement or composition of a book.[60] What distinct theological emphasis does Matthew's Gospel have, for example, and how is it different from Luke, Mark, or John?
- *Social-scientific criticism* can help shed light on social conventions and dynamics in the biblical world.[61]
- *Rhetorical criticism* provides a means for assessing the type of argument and persuasion used in a biblical passage, which in turn can help the reader determine the overall purpose of the book or passage.[62]

While each of these methods can be valuable to biblical scholarship and Christian theology, any approach to the Bible that stops at historical description falls short of the intended purposes of its authorship.

---

59. Others disagree strongly on this point. See Gordon J. Spykman, *Reformational Theology: A New Paradigm for Doing Dogmatics* (Grand Rapids, MI: Eerdmans, 1992), 119–120.

60. Gail Paterson Corrington, "Redaction Criticism," in *To Each Its Own Meaning: An Introduction to Biblical Criticisms and Their Application*, ed. Steven L. McKenzie and Stephen R. Haynes (Louisville: Westminster John Knox, 1993), 87–99. For an evangelical application and critique of redaction criticism, see Craig L. Blomberg, *Interpreting the Parables*, 2nd ed. (Downers Grove, IL: InterVarsity Press, 2012), 119–150.

61. See David A. deSilva, *Honor, Patronage, Kinship, and Purity: Unlocking New Testament Culture* (Downers Grove, IL: InterVarsity Press, 2000); Richard L. Rohrbaugh, ed., *The Social Sciences and New Testament Interpretation* (Grand Rapids, MI: Baker, 2003).

62. See George A. Kennedy, *New Testament Interpretation through Rhetorical Criticism* (Chapel Hill: University of North Carolina Press, 1984); Ben Witherington III, *New Testament Rhetoric: An Introductory Guide to the Art of Persuasion in and of the New Testament* (Eugene, OR: Wipf & Stock, 2009).

Scripture was never meant to be treated like an object in a museum, like a strange artifact of a distant culture in the past. It was and presently is "living and active" and able to discern "the thoughts and intentions of the heart" (Heb. 4:12).

Perspectives on Paul—Old and New

The controversy surrounding the so-called "New Perspective on Paul" provides ample evidence of the way in which scholarly reconstructions of historical context can play a considerable role in theological diversity.[63] For nearly four decades, New Testament scholars have engaged in lively controversy about the essence of Second Temple Judaism and the relationship of Paul to this religion. Since Luther, the prevailing opinion of biblical scholarship was that the Judaism Paul reproached was a rigid, legalistic religion that imposed a heavy burden on its adherents by demanding a works-based righteousness. Consequently, Paul was believed to offer an antithesis to this works-based religion with the free gospel of grace. The apostle answered this legalism with the conviction that we cannot save ourselves and we must rely wholly on the grace of God given to us through our faith in Christ. This trust in the righteousness of Christ, not our own righteous works, is the basis of God declaring us right before him.

But in the late twentieth century, New Testament scholars started calling into question this picture of Paul's theology as interpreted by Luther and his successors. Not only did they have concerns about its potentially anti-Semitic roots, but they also raised questions about whether this is the best historical description of first-century Judaism. It is argued that Luther's reading of Paul's opponents in Romans and Galatians was greatly colored by his criticism of late medieval Roman Catholicism. Following their analysis of Jewish writings from the Second Temple period—many of which were completely inaccessible to Luther—these scholars suggest that the picture of first-century Judaism as a works-based religion is an unhelpful caricature. Based

---

63. For readers wanting a concise overview of the complex exegetical and hermeneutical issues related to the New Perspective, I heartily recommend Kent L. Yinger, *The New Perspective: An Introduction* (Eugene, OR: Wipf & Stock, 2011). Though Yinger is admittedly predisposed toward the New Perspective, I have found no clearer introduction to the main issues of the debate.

on his reading of these texts, E. P. Sanders argued that Jews affirmed *covenantal nomism* (from the Greek *nomos*, meaning "law").[64] According to Sanders, Second Temple Jews did not obey the Torah to make themselves acceptable to God but because they wanted to be faithful to the covenant.[65]

Though many contemporary scholars almost take for granted covenantal nomism as a foundational premise for understanding first-century Judaism, the jury is still out for others. Its critics claim that the literature of Second Temple Judaism paints a far more complex picture than Sanders has advocated.[66] The recent work of John M. G. Barclay on the overlooked concept of "grace" or the "gift" (*charis*) in Judaism and in Paul has important implications for both Old and New Perspectives on Paul. Barclay agrees with Sanders that Judaism may have been a grace religion but observes that not everyone in the ancient world defined "grace" in the same manner. For Barclay, Paul's revolutionary notion of unmerited grace in the Christ-event was in stark contrast with the view of grace held by his Galatian opponents.[67]

Many questions about Paul's historical context remain unsettled in the guild of New Testament scholarship, and these questions have significant implications not only for the interpretation of key texts but for the construction of doctrines based on these texts.

We Read Literary Contexts Differently

The search for literary context is the decisive step in seeing how a particular passage fits the broader context around it. What is the immediate context of the passage, its context in the book, its place in the collection of writings by a particular author, its role in the Old or New Testament, and its relationship to the canon as a whole?[68] Readers are encouraged to read not only the particular passage in question but the entire book around it. They should move from superficial readings of the book to more detailed readings that pick

---

64. E. P. Sanders, *Paul and Palestinian Judaism* (Minneapolis: Fortress, 1977), 75, 422; cf. Sanders, *Judaism: Practice and Belief, 63 BCE–66 CE* (Minneapolis: Fortress, 2016), 430–456.
65. Sanders, *Paul and Palestinian Judaism*, 420.
66. See D. A. Carson, Peter T. O'Brien, and Mark A. Seifrid, eds., *Justification and Variegated Nomism*, 2 vols. (Tübingen: Mohr Siebeck, 2001, 2004).
67. See John M. G. Barclay, *Paul and the Gift* (Grand Rapids, MI: Eerdmans, 2015).
68. Osborne, *Hermeneutical Spiral*, 39; Klein, Blomberg, and Hubbard, *Introduction to Biblical Interpretation*, 301.

up recurring themes and ways in which passages and ideas relate to one another.[69]

For instance, readers trying to make sense of Paul's doctrine of election in Romans 9:6–29 need to understand its literary context in the larger section (chs. 9–11 and chs. 1–11), its place in the whole book of Romans, and its place in Paul's entire corpus. They also need to be familiar with the numerous quotations from Genesis, Exodus, Isaiah, and Hosea and their respective contexts if they want to grasp Paul's argument. Differing explanations of any of these elements of literary context can yield contrary theological conclusions. If a reader posits that the relevant Old Testament texts speak about God's choosing of a corporate group (Israel) to a life of mission rather than the election of individuals unto salvation, then the reader may intuit the same type of corporate election of the church in Paul's argument in Romans 9.[70] A reader who understands Paul to be speaking about God's sovereign predestination of individuals unto eternal salvation may find the same pattern in Old Testament descriptions of the election of Israel.[71]

We Read Literary Genres Differently

Reading literary context also involves attention to the *literary genre* of a particular text. As Tate puts it, "Hermeneutics must concern itself not only with the content [of a biblical passage], but also with the form of the text."[72] In addition to grasping the genres of books, readers must strive to understand the literary features of smaller units or subgenres within larger works, such as parables within the Gospels.[73] Readers also wrestle with questions about how particular books fit into the canon of Scripture. Should we read the Song of Solomon merely as a Hebrew celebration of human sexuality, or does it also have a place in the canon as a description of God's love for Israel and

---

69. Osborne, *Hermeneutical Spiral*, 40–45.

70. See William W. Klein, *The New Chosen People: A Corporate View of Election*, rev. ed. (Eugene, OR: Wipf & Stock, 2015), 3–19, 131–194; Chad Thornhill, *The Chosen People: Election, Paul, and Second Temple Judaism* (Downers Grove, IL: InterVarsity Press, 2015), 229–253.

71. Calvin himself acknowledged that the nation of Israel had a "general election" from God—a special kind of providential privilege given to a particular people—but he maintained that "actual election" in the Old Testament describes the predestination of individual Israelites unto salvation and the reprobation of others to destruction. See John Calvin, *Institutes of the Christian Religion*, 3.21.5–87.

72. Tate, *Biblical Interpretation*, 64.

73. Osborne, *Hermeneutical Spiral*, 181–183.

Christ's love for the church? Evangelical opinion is not uniform on this matter.[74]

Comprehending a genre means knowing the rules or conventions associated with it, or in terms of speech-act theory, understanding the illocutions of a genre. The rules for reading New Testament Epistles are not identical to those for reading Old Testament Law; the parables of Jesus serve different purposes than historical narratives; and so on and so forth. Genre is an important contributor to the *overall purpose or design* of a whole written work. A functional grasp of a text's genre is vital for grasping the authorial design of a book or a segment within a book.[75] Interpretation with an awareness of the different literary conventions of different genres helps the reader understand the "relationship between what is said (content) and how it is said (genre, form)."[76] One major hermeneutical contributor to doctrinal disagreement stems from the numerous approaches taken to biblical genres.

Biblical scholars and theologians have conflicting opinions about the theological functions of genres such as psalms, prophetic literature, and the parables. How are we to understand the theology of the psalter? Does it convey a direct revelation of God or does it simply describe the way human beings relate to God?[77] How do we understand the differences in prophetic oracles concerning Nineveh in Jonah (3:1–10) and Nahum (2:1–12)? Did God change his mind concerning his course of action? Is it ever appropriate to draw eschatological concepts from parables, such as the parable of the rich man and Lazarus (Luke 16:19–31)? These remain debated hermeneutical issues about genres and subgenres that affect theological conclusions.

Perhaps no New Testament genre invites more hermeneutical hullabaloo than its apocalypse, the book of Revelation. The

---

74. Tremper Longman III, "Song of Songs," in *Dictionary for Theological Interpretation of the Bible*, ed. Kevin J. Vanhoozer, Craig G. Bartholomew, Daniel J. Treier, and N. T. Wright (Grand Rapids, MI: Baker, 2005), 758–761; Kevin J. Vanhoozer, "Ascending the Mountain, Singing the Rock: Biblical Interpretation Earthed, Typed, and Transfigured," *Modern Theology* 28, no. 4 (2012): 784–785, 797–798.

75. Kevin J. Vanhoozer, *Is There a Meaning in This Text? The Bible, the Reader, and the Morality of Literary Knowledge* (Grand Rapids, MI: Zondervan, 1998), 340–342.

76. Tate, *Biblical Interpretation*, 64.

77. Eugene H. Merrill, *Everlasting Dominion: A Theology of the Old Testament* (Nashville: B&H Academic, 2006), 570. This question is crucial for understanding imprecatory psalms (e.g., Psalms 5; 58; 79; 137).

interpretation of Revelation is multifaceted because of its relationship to a genre called *apocalyptic writings*, a group of Jewish writings primarily composed between the Old and New Testament books, and because of its *prophetic* character. The book also has the features of New Testament *epistles* written to the churches, particularly in its first three chapters.

The way a reader conceptualizes the genre of Revelation colors everything about her reading of the book. With broad strokes, exegetes must answer whether the book describes events completed in the past (the *preterist* viewpoint), events happening throughout the history of the church (*historicist*), symbolic events that depict timeless truths (*idealist*), future events not yet fulfilled (*futurist*), or some combination thereof.[78] The way a reader chooses to answer these questions will form the outcome of her interpretation of the whole.

For many interpreters, Revelation 20:1–10 serves as a kind of theological center or anchor for the book. How readers choose to understand the "thousand years" (*chilia etē*), or the millennium described by John, can affect their total understanding of the book. This choice relates to another hermeneutical question: how best to understand the figures of speech in the book. Dispensationalists interpret the phrase "thousand years," as well as much of the imagery elsewhere in the book, as a literal one-thousand-year period in the future following a seven-year period of great tribulation derived from Daniel 9:25–27 (cf. Dan. 12:11–12; Rev. 11:2–3; 13:5). Other interpreters understand the thousand years as a figurative image, even if there are some variations between preterist, historicist (e.g., amillennial), and futurist (e.g., historic premillennial) readings.

We Read Literary Devices Differently

Interpreters also tussle over how to understand the various *literary devices* of biblical literature. The central exegetical debate at the Marburg Colloquy over the Lord's Supper was over the literary device used by Jesus when he described the Supper as "my body" (Matt. 26:26; Mark 14:22; Luke 22:19; cf. 1 Cor. 11:24). Luther and his compatri-

---

78. For a summary of these approaches, see C. Marvin Pate, ed., *Four Views on the Book of Revelation* (Grand Rapids, MI: Zondervan, 1998), 9–34.

ots took Jesus's words "This is my body" quite *literally*. The bread is *literally Jesus's body*. Luther believed the meaning of "this is my body" to be so plain that the burden of proof rested solely on those who rejected a literal interpretation. By contrast, Zwingli argued that Jesus's description of the bread as his "body" was figurative or *metaphorical* in the same way he described himself as the "true vine" (John 15:1) or the same way Paul called Christ the "rock" (1 Cor. 10:4; cf. Ex. 17:6; Num. 20:11).[79] These biblical metaphors and symbols are not mere poetic expressions of literal truth; they are literary devices capable of producing new insights in the minds of the reader that plain description could not convey.[80]

No evangelical interpreter of Scripture would deny the existence of hell, but evangelicals do have in-house debates about what the biblical imagery of hell really means. Are the descriptions of the "hell of fire" (Matt. 5:22; 18:9) and the "lake of fire" (Rev. 20:10, 14–15) meant to be taken literally, or are they the best metaphors human language can give us of the horrors of God's judgment? The traditional view (my own view) states that hell is conscious, eternal torment. Other views, such as annihilationism and Christian universalism, offer alternative explanations for this biblical imagery. If the apocalyptic imagery of eternal torture (Rev. 14:9–11) is literal, then one must explain how exactly God can "destroy both soul and body in hell" (Matt. 10:28). All sides have their own interpretive difficulties rooted in the variety of literary devices used to describe God's judgment.[81]

Various approaches to the *rhetoric of the Bible* can also yield a multitude of interpretations of key texts. One example of rhetorical controversy is the dispute over how to understand Paul's use of "I" (*egō*) in the argument of Romans 7:14–25. When Paul says, "I do not understand what I am doing, because I do not practice what I want to do, but I do what I hate" (Rom. 7:15 CSB), is he speaking autobiographically about his past or present experience, or is he

---

79. Hermann Sasse, *This Is My Body: Luther's Contention for the Real Presence in the Sacrament of the Altar* (Philadelphia: Augsburg Fortress, 1959), 232.

80. Anthony C. Thiselton, *Hermeneutics* (Grand Rapids, MI: Eerdmans, 2009), 235–236.

81. For a summary of these positions and the exegetical debates, see William Crockett, ed., *Four Views on Hell* (Grand Rapids, MI: Zondervan, 1996); Preston Sprinkle, ed., *Four Views on Hell*, 2nd ed. (Grand Rapids, MI: Zondervan, 2016). Both editions of this collection provide different and valuable contributions to the debate.

using some other ancient rhetorical convention to make a particular point?[82] Exegetes have offered several explanations for Paul's use of *egō* in this text.[83] Practical and theological outcomes follow whatever choices readers make about Paul's use of "I" here, particularly how one understands the Christian experience with sin.

Taking a relatively straightforward reading of the grammar of the text, the later Augustine and his theological successors contend that Paul is speaking autobiographically about his enduring struggle with sin as a Christian.[84] Augustine's experience with personal sin undoubtedly colors his reading. Following Augustine, Luther concludes that the believer is simultaneously a saint and a sinner (*simul iustus et peccator*), someone who is both justified by faith in Christ but still haunted by sinful desire.[85] For Calvin, Paul's "I" provides a picture of the Christian who is torn between flesh and spirit.[86] If Paul is speaking about his ongoing battle with sin, then even the mature follower of Christ might expect the same sort of experience. After all, besides Jesus himself, who was more spiritually mature than the apostle Paul? If Paul struggled like this, then we can expect the same inevitable tension in our own lives.[87]

Other interpreters have been hesitant to paint Paul in this way. Many of the alternative explanations of "I" in Romans 7:14–25 include Paul using a rhetorical technique called *impersonation (prosopopoeia)*. Impersonation is a rhetorical device wherein the speaker dramatically embodies another persona. Sometimes the only indication of impersonation was in the audience's oral hearing as the

---

82. See Terry L. Wilder, ed., *Perspectives on Our Struggle with Sin: Three Views of Romans 7* (Nashville: B&H Academic, 2011); Ben Witherington III, *The Problem with Evangelical Theology: Testing the Exegetical Foundations of Calvinism, Dispensationalism, Wesleyanism, and Pentecostalism*, rev. ed. (Waco, TX: Baylor University Press, 2016), 19–34.

83. Witherington identifies at least eight ways interpreters read Paul's rhetorical "I" (*egō*) in this passage. See Ben Witherington III and Darlene Hyatt, *Paul's Letter to the Romans: A Socio-Rhetorical Commentary* (Grand Rapids, MI: Eerdmans, 2004), 187–188.

84. Augustine, *Retractions* 1.23.1; 2.1.1; *Against Two Letters of Pelagius* 1.10–11.

85. See WA 56:339–349; LW 25:327–338. The phrase *simul iustus et peccator* (translated "at the same time both a sinner and a righteous man") appears in WA 56:272; LW 25:260.

86. John Calvin, *Commentaries on the Epistle of Paul the Apostle to the Romans*, trans. and ed. John Owen (Grand Rapids, MI: Baker, 2009), 261–265.

87. For more recent exegetical defenses of this position, see Charles E. B. Cranfield, *The Epistle to the Romans*, vol. 1, ICC (Edinburgh: T&T Clark, 1975), 344–347; Thomas R. Schreiner, *Romans*, BECNT (Grand Rapids, MI: Baker, 1998), 379–384; 390–392; Grant R. Osborne, "The Flesh without the Spirit: Romans 7 and Christian Experience," in Wilder, *Perspectives on Our Struggle with Sin*, 7–48.

speaker would change his voice or tone, something obviously missing from the written text alone.[88] If Paul is using this device with *egō* in Romans 7, then he is not being autobiographical but rather embodying another character or group of characters. As "I," Paul does not speak about himself but rather puts himself in the place of another (e.g., unregenerate humanity, Israel, or Adam) to make a persuasive theological case[89]

Strong arguments can be made for and against the traditional Augustinian reading of Romans 7:14–25. The choice to take the Pauline *egō* as a rhetorical device of impersonation can affect the theological choice between Luther's belief that even mature, justified believers continue to struggle with sin and Wesley's belief that Spirit-led believers are capable of holy living apart from deliberate and voluntary acts of sin.[90]

Conclusion

The takeaway from this interpretive menagerie is that the various uses of exegetical and hermeneutical tools can impact the readings of texts key to a theological dispute. Every step in the exegetical process presents possibilities for theological disagreement. However, the exegesis of individual texts is rarely the sole deciding factor in theological debates. The larger and more substantive questions about biblical doctrine are more hermeneutical in nature: questions about historical context, literary context, genre, and how biblical texts from across the canon relate to one another.

This small sampling has also shown that interpreters often tend to favor interpretations of biblical texts favorable to their theological systems or traditions. Even with the best of intentions to be faithful to the pertinent texts, readers often have other interpretive interests at work. Other factors, such as their reasoning processes, their emotions, and their traditional biases can shape their exegetical

---

88. Witherington, *New Testament Rhetoric*, 132–133.

89. The revival of the interpretation of Paul as impersonator is largely credited to the work of Werner Georg Kümmel in his *Römer 7 und Das Bild des Menschen im Neuen Testament* (Munich: C. Kaiser, 1974). See also Karl Hermann Schelkle, *Paulus, Lehrer der Väter: die alkirchliche Auslegung von Römer 1–11* (Düsseldorf: Patmos-Verlag, 1959), 242–248; Witherington, *New Testament Rhetoric*, 133; Witherington, *Problem with Evangelical Theology*, 20–33.

90. For an overview of Wesley's view, see Thomas C. Oden, *John Wesley's Teachings*, vol. 2, *Christ and Salvation* (Grand Rapids, MI: Zondervan, 2012), 267–279.

and hermeneutical work. Exposure to these factors may not completely abate them, but it may minimize their detrimental effects on interpretation and theological construction. I will now turn to these matters, beginning with the way in which our reasoning processes open us up to interpretive diversity.

3

We Reason Differently

The Role of Guesswork in Interpretation

Long before the days of binge watching police procedurals like *CSI* and *NCIS* on Netflix, Arthur Conan Doyle riveted his readers with Sherlock Holmes stories. Doyle crafted a fleshed-out character with a penchant for solving crimes by observing small details and making wild conjectures. No matter how absurd Holmes's hunches initially seemed, Doyle connected the logical dots for the readers in such an effortless way that we were left, like Dr. Watson, wondering how we could have missed the obvious plot twist before us.

In Holmes stories, the great detective often described his method of observation and drawing conclusions as a simple "process of deduction," but his method does not resemble what logicians call "deduction" or "deductive logic."[1] In the real world, deductive reasoning is a branch of logic dedicated to assessing the validity of arguments. When one presents a *valid* deductive argument, the premises of the argument necessarily lead to its conclusion. When someone makes a valid deductive argument with all true premises, they make a *sound* argument with a conclusion that is necessarily true.[2] This is not generally the type of

---

1. See Umberto Eco and Thomas A. Sebeok, eds., *The Sign of Three: Dupin, Holmes, Peirce* (Bloomington: Indiana University Press, 1983); Louis J. Pojman, *Philosophy: The Quest for Truth*, 4th ed. (Belmont, CA: Wadsworth, 1999), 28–30.
2. C. Stephen Layman, *The Power of Logic*, 3rd ed. (New York: McGraw-Hill, 2003), 3.

reasoning Sherlock Holmes used. An event from the short story "A Scandal in Bohemia" illustrates this difference.

The story begins with Watson's account of his reunion with Holmes some months after the events of *A Study in Scarlet*, Holmes and Watson's first case together. On the way home from visiting a patient, Watson decides to drop in on Holmes at his Baker Street flat. The newlywed doctor has not seen his detective friend in some time and has since returned to civil medical practice. Though Watson does not mention this detail to Holmes in his greeting, the detective infers this fact merely from his physical appearance:

> "Wedlock suits you," he remarked. "I think, Watson, that you have put on seven and a half pounds since I saw you."
>
> "Seven," I answered.
>
> "Indeed, I should have thought a little more. Just a trifle more, I fancy, Watson. And in practice again, I observe. You did not tell me that you intended to go into harness."[3]
>
> "Then how do you know?"
>
> "I see it, I deduce it. How do I know that you have been getting yourself very wet lately, and that you have a most clumsy and careless servant girl?"
>
> "My dear Holmes," said I, "this is too much. You would certainly have been burned had you lived a few centuries ago. It is true that I had a country walk on Thursday and came home in a dreadful mess; but as I have changed my clothes, I can't imagine how you deduce it. As to Mary Jane, she is incorrigible, and my wife has given her notice; but there again I fail to see how you work it out."
>
> He chuckled to himself and rubbed his long nervous hands together.
>
> "It is simplicity itself," said he, "my eyes tell me that on the inside of your left shoe, just where the firelight strikes it, the leather is scored by six almost parallel cuts. Obviously they have been caused by someone who has very carelessly scraped round the edges of the sole in order to remove crusted mud from it.

---

3. "Go into harness" is a variation of the idiom "get back in the harness," which means to return to a vocation after an extended time away.

Hence, you see, my double deduction that you had been out in vile weather, and that you had a particularly malignant boot-slicking specimen of the London slavey. As to your practice, if a gentleman walks into my rooms, smelling of iodoform, with a black mark of nitrate of silver upon his right forefinger, and a bulge on the side of his top hat to show where he has secreted his stethoscope, I must be dull indeed if I do not pronounce him to be an active member of the medical profession."

I could not help laughing at the ease with which he explained his process of deduction. "When I hear you give your reasons," I remarked, "the thing always appears to me so ridiculously simple that I could easily do it myself, though at each successive instance of your reasoning I am baffled, until you explain your process. And yet, I believe that my eyes are as good as yours."[4]

After observing Watson's weight, his shoe, his odor, his finger, and his hat, Holmes concludes his doctor friend has gained seven pounds, has returned to his practice, and now employs a bungling housekeeper. The astonished Watson confirms each of Holmes's hunches, exclaiming that Holmes's power of "deduction" almost resembles sorcery.

The logic used here is not what philosophers typically call deduction. Holmes does not present a valid argument because his reasoning by no means guarantees a necessary conclusion. But Holmes, like real-world detectives and forensic scientists, makes creative guesses he believes best explain the clues before him. In the world created by Doyle to display Holmes's genius, the somewhat random conjectures made by the sleuth are spot-on, affirmed by Watson. Yet in the real world, where omniscient narrators do not voice every detail, the guesswork of crime fighting is more complex, more tentative. Though the guesses made by Holmes in the story were the best explanations for Watson's appearance, no rational method he used to make those inferences could guarantee their accuracy.

A real-world investigator could have looked at Watson's weight, his shoe, his odor, his finger, and his hat, and arrived at an altogether different set of conclusions. He might have guessed that Watson got

4. Arthur Conan Doyle, "A Scandal in Bohemia," in *The Adventures of Sherlock Holmes* (London, 1901), 3–4.

his shoes muddy running errands for his wife and scraped them when he attempted to get the mud off his own shoes. Maybe he would think Watson smelled like antiseptic because he used it on his own cuts. Inferences to the best explanation like these are an important part of reasoning, but they are imperfect and can vary from person to person.

The rational process of moving from biblical exegesis to systematic theology is a lot like the guesswork of real detectives. The biblical text presents itself to us like a crime scene, frozen in time. The textual evidence largely remains pristine and untouched. The canon draws lines around the scene like yellow barricade tape, protecting and isolating the most important evidence. The miscellaneous items spread across the room appear to be interconnected, but the investigator (i.e., the theologian) must figure out how the seemingly random items relate to one another and in what order. He must work through the scene delicately, aware that mishandling the evidence could ruin the case or result in false charges.

Sometimes biblical doctrine presents itself like an open-and-shut case, when direct statements from Scripture explain the circumstances like a confession letter left on the scene. Other times, theologians find "smoking guns" that may quickly explain the meaning of a passage or the theological framework of the author. In other moments, the theologian must "think outside of the box" if he is going to understand the scene of the text. He must put himself in the shoes of the inspired writer and reconstruct his argument. From there he can recreate a picture of how the seemingly unrelated books and genres of the Bible relate together in the divine economy of revelation.

We seek out the best explanation for the theological data of Scripture because we presume the text has a meaning capable of being grasped.[5] We try to understand the connections between the books and motifs of Scripture because we affirm its divine inspiration and full truthfulness. But systematic theology, like forensics, is a kind of science that does not guarantee certain, foolproof results. Some take the fallibility of the interpreter as an excuse to be lazy with the biblical text or to refrain from making any commitments to the precepts in it.

---

5. The attempt to offer a "best explanation" presumes a real world that can be known. See Alister McGrath, *The Science of God* (Grand Rapids, MI: Eerdmans, 2004), 131.

However, courts offer no such retreat when weighing criminal cases. Investigation is necessary for justice to be executed.

Some readers may feel uneasy hearing theology described in such tentative terms. "How can we be certain we are coming to the right conclusions?" Disagreement over doctrine gives us pause about having certainty on every biblical theme or teaching. The good news is that *certainty* is not necessary to have general *confidence* in our ability to reason through the Bible. The ground for prosecution in a real-world courtroom is not certainty but rather proof beyond a reasonable doubt. Proof beyond a reasonable doubt entails only *an explanation of the facts so compelling that no other theory seems to satisfy the data.* Just as new evidence or a new conjecture can cast doubt on previous investigations and cause prosecutors to reopen a case or name a new suspect, new evidence and new ways of looking at things can change prior understandings of biblical texts.

As evangelicals, we believe the Bible to be without fault or error, but we have no such opinion of human biblical interpreters and theologians, who are prone to mistakes in judgment. The fallibility of the interpreter is, as we have seen, one of the most significant factors in the diversity of biblical interpretations. But one important factor behind theological diversity may not lie within ourselves at all—our experience, our intelligence, our faithfulness, etc.—but rather in the nature of theological investigation itself. We reason about theology differently. Our reasoning processes, no matter how astute they may be, can sometimes bring us to different perspectives because of the role conjectures play in interpretation. Biblical interpreters and theologians, like detectives and scientists, use their reasoning faculties to make inferences to the explanation that they feel best addresses the data before them.

Reason is a gift from God that can help us make sense of the natural world, make moral decisions, and interpret Scripture (Prov. 1:2–9; Isa. 1:18; Acts 17:17; James 3:17). Carl F. H. Henry described human reason as *"a divinely fashioned instrument for recognizing truth."*[6] Over and against forms of rationalist theology devoid of revelatory

---

6. Carl F. H. Henry, *God, Revelation, and Authority,* 6 vols. (Wheaton, IL: Crossway, 1999), 1:225, italics original.

content, Henry insisted reason is *"not a creative source of truth."*[7] Revelation has primacy over our creative faculties, but we need reason to understand revelation. Without reason, we could not make sense of individual biblical texts—their use of language, their historical settings, their arguments, etc. Apart from reason, a theologian could not make inferences about how the whole of biblical revelation fits together systematically. While reason is tremendously important for what theologians do, there is no uniformity in its exercise. Because theologians reason in different ways, different doctrinal conclusions are inevitable.

In this chapter I will explore the forms of reasoning used in biblical studies and theology, focusing on the role hypothesis-making plays in theological method. I argue here that much of biblical interpretation and theological construction is more like investigative guesswork than mathematics or repeatable, empirical experiments. Philosophers generally call this kind of creative conjecture-making *abduction* or "abductive reasoning." The move from Bible to theology is both an art and a science. The interpreter and theologian work with the data of divine revelation at their disposal. They do not always have the luxury of certainty in disputed interpretive or theological matters, but reasonable confidence in a compelling interpretation of the text is achievable. But if the creative process of abductive reasoning is the primary way we come to our conclusions in biblical interpretation and in systematic theology, then interpretive and theological differences are inevitable.

Reasoning Backwards to a Hypothesis

Throughout the history of Western thought, logicians, philosophers, and theologians universally have recognized two modes of reasoning: *deductive* reasoning and *inductive* reasoning. While both deduction and induction have their proper place in investigation, neither form of reasoning describes the creative process needed to formulate theories. As I shall argue, *abductive* reasoning or *abduction* more accurately describes the normal rational process in moving from the Bible to doctrine than does deductive or inductive reasoning.

---

7. Henry, *God, Revelation, and Authority*, 1:225, italics original.

Abductive reasoning is the primary way that investigators work through a crime scene, scientists think about the world, and doctors make preliminary diagnoses. It is "reasoning backwards" because it moves from an effect to a cause, and it is an imperfect science that can yield many different conclusions. Because abductive reasoning can yield such tentative hypotheses, there needs to be a back-and-forth dialogue between conjecture-making and testing those conjectures. This is how Dr. Gregory House—Sherlock Holmes's twenty-first-century medical doppelgänger—solved his most bizarre cases at the Princeton–Plainsboro Teaching Hospital: by beginning with a creative conjecture, then testing it, rethinking it, and working until he found a suitable diagnosis and cure.[8]

Philosophers have reached no consensus on how precisely abduction works, though it appears to play a crucial role in everyday reasoning. Even though people have always reasoned abductively, the formal study of this type of reasoning has a relatively short history when compared with its more widely recognized counterparts of deduction and induction. Most associate its development with the writings of the nineteenth-century American philosopher Charles Sanders Peirce, who coined the term *abduction*.[9] The work of Peirce (pronounced "purse") has gained renewed interest in the last few decades, sparking new discussions in a wide array of philosophical subdisciplines.

So, how exactly does abduction relate to the traditional logical categories of deductive and inductive reasoning? Some logicians place abduction, sometimes called "inference to the best explanation,"[10] under the category of induction, as merely another type of induction.[11]

---

8. Jerold J. Abrams, "The Logic of Guesswork in Sherlock Holmes and *House*," in *House and Philosophy: Everybody Lies* (Hoboken, NJ: John Wiley & Sons, 2009), 60–61.

9. In discussing Peirce, I will refer to *The Collected Papers of Charles Sanders Peirce*, 8 vols., ed. Charles Hartshorne and Paul Weiss (vols. 1–6) and Arthur W. Burks (vols. 7–8) (Cambridge, MA: Harvard University Press, 1931–1958), abbreviated as "CP." Throughout his corpus, Peirce also uses the terms *hypothesis*, *retroduction*, *presumption*, and *originary argument* to describe the same general logical process as abduction. For purposes of clarity, I have chosen to amalgamate the terms by simply using *abduction*.

10. The phrase "inference to the best explanation" comes from the influential article by Gilbert H. Harman (b. 1938). See Harman, "Inference to the Best Explanation," *Philosophical Review* 74 (1965): 88–95; Harman, "Enumerative Induction as Inference to the Best Explanation," *Journal of Philosophy* 64 (1967): 529–533. As Alister McGrath remarks, the name "inference *to* the best explanation" is "somewhat misleading" because "one can infer *that* A is the best explanation, but not *infer* to A as the best explanation" (McGrath, *Science of God*, 131).

11. Peter Lipton labels this kind of inference a type of induction. See Lipton, *Inference to the Best Explanation*, 2nd ed. (New York: Routledge, 2004), 4–20.

Nevertheless, Peirce has shown that abduction is a distinct form of reasoning that has characteristics of both deduction and induction. Unlike deductive logic, abductive reasoning entails guesswork and hunches, not certain conclusions. Unlike induction, it cannot even demonstrate the likelihood of a truth claim. In fact, Peirce has described abduction as "nothing more than guessing."[12]

Deduction, a branch of logic dedicated to assessing the *validity* of arguments, can *prove* a hypothesis. Induction, a type of reasoning that estimates the *probability* of arguments, can *test* a hypothesis. According to Peirce, abduction is the only process of reasoning by which we *form a new hypothesis*: "Abduction is the process of forming an explanatory hypothesis. It is the only logical operation which introduces any new idea; for induction does nothing but determine a value, and deduction merely evolves the necessary consequences of a pure hypothesis."[13] Abduction "furnishes the reasoner with a problematic theory which induction verifies."[14]

Peirce suggests that every argument, whether deductive, inductive, or abductive, has three parts: the *rule* (the major premise), the *case* (the minor premise), and the *result* (the conclusion). The way these parts relate to one another determines what type of reasoning is being used.[15] In *deductive* arguments, we always infer a *result* from a *rule* and a *case*. The one making the argument always assumes the *rule*, deploys a *case* or particular instance of a *rule*, and draws a necessary conclusion or inference from the *rule* and the *case*. Peirce tells his readers to think about walking into a room where someone is holding up a bag of beans in one hand and a closed fistful of beans in the other hand. The man then gives us a *rule* that describes the bag of beans, and he describes the *case* of the beans in his other hand:

> *Rule.*—All the beans in this bag are white.
> *Case.*—The beans in the closed fist are from this bag.
> ∴ *Result.*—The beans in the closed fist are white.

---

12. Peirce, CP 7:219.
13. Peirce, CP 5:171.
14. Peirce, CP 2:776.
15. C. S. Peirce, "Deduction, Induction, Hypothesis," in *Popular Science Monthly* 13 (1878): 472.

From the *rule* and the *case*, we can infer a *result*: the beans in the closed fist are white. Deductive arguments work backward to *prove* the *result* implied in the *rule* and the *case*. Peirce calls the inferences of deductive arguments *explicative* because they make explicit what is implicit in the *rule* and the *case*.[16]

Unlike deductive arguments, *inductive* arguments do not "prove" claims but demonstrate their probability. In a deductive argument, we make explicit what is implicit in the rule and the case, but in an inductive argument, our conclusion contains information not found in the premises of the argument. The same elements (*case*, *result*, and *rule*) are present in an inductive argument but in a different order, and the different order produces a different type of inference. Unlike the deductive syllogism that begins by assuming a *rule* about the bag—that all the beans in the bag are white—we start here with only a *case* and a *result*:

> *Case.*—These beans are from this bag.
> *Result.*—These beans are white.
> ∴ *Rule.*—All the beans from this bag are white.

The man in the room tells us that the beans in his hand are from the bag, and when he opens his hand, we see that all the beans are white. From this particular *case*—that we have been told the beans are from the bag—and this *result*—these beans are all white—we infer that the beans in the bag are also all white. Then, we begin to test our inductive inference. With each successive extraction of a bean from the bag, we find that all the beans are in fact white (the *result*). This form of reasoning does not guarantee a necessarily true conclusion in the way a valid deductive argument would—a stray black bean could have slipped into the mix—but the inductive inference of this *rule* becomes more and more probable with every successive white bean removed from the bag.[17] As Peirce observes, induction only tests theories; it

---

16. Peirce, "Deduction, Induction, Hypothesis," 470–471.

17. Umberto Eco adds, "As we know, all it takes is one trial in which one of the beans drawn from the sack is black, and my entire inductive effort vanishes into thin air. This is why epistemologists are so suspicious with regard to Induction.

"Actually, since we don't know how many trials are necessary before an Induction can be considered a good one, we really don't know what a valid Induction is." See Umberto Eco, *The Limits of Interpretation* (Bloomington: Indiana University Press, 1990), 157.

cannot prove them: "Induction consists in starting from a theory, deducing from it predictions of phenomena, and observing those phenomena in order to see *how nearly* they agree with the theory."[18]

Abduction occurs when we infer a *case* from a *rule* and a *result*. Abduction accounts for how scientists leap from experience to hypothesis, or in the event of theology, how biblical interpreters jump from the text to theories about its theological content.[19] Peirce returns to the white beans analogy to demonstrate the type of guesswork and mystery that goes into abductive reasoning: "Suppose I enter a room and there find a number of bags, containing different kinds of beans. On the table there is a handful of white beans; and, after some searching, I find one of the bags contains white beans only. I at once infer as a probability, or as a fair guess, that this handful was taken out of that bag. This sort of inference is called *making an hypothesis*."[20] We were not witnesses to this handful of white beans being placed on the table—and it is at least possible that they came from another source other than this bag of white beans—but we use abduction to make the reasonable guess that the white beans on the table did in fact come from the bag. Like Sherlock Holmes, we observe the evidence and form a hypothesis. This type of inference is abduction:

> *Rule.*—All the beans from this bag are white.
> *Result.*— These beans on the table are all white.
> ∴ *Case.*—These beans are from this bag.[21]

Abduction, like induction, makes inferences based on observation. Unlike induction, however, abduction works with a less complete set of data. It offers an explanation of the data—in this case, the beans that are white *possibly* come from the bag of all white beans—but it cannot prove that explanation or even show its probability. In contrast to strong inductive arguments, abductive arguments are weak arguments.[22] The abducted hypothesis leaves even less room for certainty

---

18. Peirce, CP 5:171, italics original.
19. Peirce, CP 2:755.
20. Peirce, "Deduction, Induction, Hypothesis," 471–472.
21. Peirce, "Deduction, Induction, Hypothesis," 472.
22. Abductive arguments like this one commit the formal logical fallacy of *affirming the consequent*, and as a result, the concluding case is just one of many possible inferences—not a necessary conclusion.

than inductive inferences. Induction strives to show us what is prob-able, but abduction can only show us what is possible. All three types of reason, Peirce observes, are indispensable steps of the same reasoning process. "Deduction proves that something *must* be; Induction shows that something *actually* is operative; Abduction merely suggests that something *may* be."[23]

Peirce, who himself wrote extensively in the philosophy of religion, was quite skeptical of systematic theology as an academic or scientific enterprise, largely because of the closed-mindedness he perceived in a discipline he believed was being used to prove established dogmas.[24] In defiance of Peirce's objections, however, it seems that a Christian theology committed to the text as the primary datum before traditions or creeds—a truly Protestant or evangelical theological method—closely resembles the abductive science he wished to see in theology.

The theological task is more like abductive reasoning—like guess-work—than deductive or inductive logic. The abstraction of theological content from the historically contingent writings and placement of such content in systems necessarily requires creative arrangement. Theology also involves reasoning backwards from Scripture and going back and forth between biblical texts and our conjectures about what they mean.[25]

How Theological Abduction Works

We often come to some biblical texts like a detective to a crime scene. We were not eyewitnesses, but we are trying to evaluate the evidence and make well-educated guesses as to the events and significance of the texts. We are attempting to reconstruct the theological framework of biblical authors so that it may have authority over our own beliefs about God, the gospel, and our world. We do not do this only by de-duction, which proves an established premise, or by induction, which shows the probability of an established premise. We have hunches. We make educated guesses. We are like the television detective Adrian

---

23. Peirce, CP 5:171.
24. Douglas Anderson, "Peirce's Common Sense Marriage of Religion and Science," in *The Cambridge Companion to Peirce*, ed. Cheryl Misak (Cambridge: Cambridge University Press, 2004), 181–185.
25. David K. Clark, *To Know and Love God: Method for Theology* (Wheaton, IL: Crossway, 2003), 48–52.

Monk, who begins an investigation with a simple abduction: "I don't know how he did it. But *he* did it." We make guesses about what we think a biblical passage or doctrine means and reason toward or away from such explanations. We make these types of inference whenever we are trying to make sense of the syntax of a passage at the exegetical level or of the literary context at the hermeneutical level.

We also make inferences to the best explanation in trying to ascertain the worldview and theological beliefs of biblical authors. We are trying to make sense of the "horizon" of the text from within our own "horizons." The theological concepts of Scripture rarely appear in syllogistic forms.[26] They are part of a worldview or symbolic universe expressed through storytelling and situation-specific ethical discourse.[27] Even Paul, known for the didactic elements of his letters, nowhere offers his readers a systematic explanation of his core beliefs. (Much to the chagrin of systematic theologians, God did not opt to inspire a systematic theology textbook!) Rather than giving us a comprehensive exploration of his thought world, Paul writes *occasional theology*—ad hoc expressions of his theological beliefs directed toward particular situations and crises in the churches to which he ministers. The same could be said of all other biblical writers in the Old and New Testaments.

The occasional nature of Paul's theology by no means indicates any inconsistency in his expressed beliefs. As J. Christiaan Beker observes, readers of Paul's letters encounter two poles: *contingency*, a particular expression of Paul's worldview relative to the needs of a given faith community; and *coherence*, the systematic framework from which Paul addresses these needs.[28] Simply put, Paul thought coherently about the gospel, but the specific occasions addressed in his letters raised unique responses and applications.

Because Paul writes occasional theology, he does not give us every detail of his theological system. For example, Paul does not *explicitly define* the governmental structure of the church, nor does he detail how church

---

26. There are exceptions to this rule. For example, 1 Corinthians 15 contains a series of syllogisms about the resurrection, indicated by Paul's "if . . . then" formula (vv. 13, 14, 15, 16, 17, 19, 44).

27. Ben Witherington III, *The Problem with Evangelical Theology: Testing the Exegetical Foundations of Calvinism, Dispensationalism, Wesleyanism, and Pentecostalism*, rev. ed. (Waco, TX: Baylor University Press, 2016), 244–246.

28. See J. Christiaan Beker, *Paul the Apostle: The Triumph of God in Life and Thought* (Philadelphia: Fortress, 1980), 11ff.

business meetings should be run. Instead, he simply describes the qualifications of those who hold established offices (1 Tim. 3:1–13; Titus 1:5–9). Paul does not *explain* what he means by the gift of tongues; he only addresses abuses of the gift in worship (1 Cor. 14:1–20). As interpreters, we must make hypotheses about what Paul believed about these issues from the extant evidence. I compare this logical exercise to putting a puzzle together without having the picture on the top of the box. This process can be arduous work, especially when we try to reconstruct the opinion of a biblical writer on a topic infrequently addressed in his corpus.

At this point it is worth mentioning that abductive reasoning might give us a helpful way to think about the differences between *biblical theology* and *systematic theology*. Biblical theology may be defined many different ways, and sometimes it seems as if there as many definitions of biblical theology as there are biblical theologians.[29] What is common to most types of biblical theology, however, is the way biblical scholars attempt to reconstruct the historical beliefs of individual authors in their unique historical situations. This is an abductive process like the one described above with the process of making sense of Paul's coherent thought world.

By contrast, the systematic theologian works to understand what the "whole Bible" says to any contemporary topic.[30] Like biblical theologians, systematic theologians must make abductive hypotheses about what individual writers believed in their original historical context, but they must also make hypotheses about how these individual beliefs and doctrines fit together across the canon of Scripture. They must also make creative conjectures about how the worldviews of biblical authors would respond to the theological questions raised today. No two systematic theologies are exactly alike because systematic theology, unlike biblical theology, consciously speaks to the *present context*, which is always changing. Systematic theologians arrange doctrines differently based on their view of what doctrine comprises the "central motif" of Scripture (e.g., God's sovereignty, God's love, etc.).[31]

---

29. For a helpful summary of some major positions in biblical theology, see Edward W. Klink III and Darian R. Lockett, *Understanding Biblical Theology: A Comparison of Theory and Practice* (Grand Rapids, MI: Zondervan, 2012).

30. Wayne Grudem, *Systematic Theology* (Grand Rapids, MI: Zondervan, 2000), 21.

31. Millard J. Erickson, *Christian Theology*, 3rd ed. (Grand Rapids, MI: Baker, 2013), 63–64; cf. Stanley J. Grenz and Roger E. Olson, *Who Needs Theology? An Invitation to the Study of God* (Downers Grove, IL: InterVarsity Press, 1996), 115–117.

Though all theologians use abductive reasoning, not all abductions or inferences to the best explanation are of the same type. The Italian novelist and semiotician Umberto Eco further developed Peirce's theory of abduction with a taxonomy that identifies four types of abduction: (1) *overcoded*, (2) *undercoded*, (3) *creative*, and (4) *meta-abduction*.[32] These types of abduction make up a spectrum of varying degrees of critical engagement and original thought. Some of these guesses happen automatically, while others take serious reflection and creativity.[33] Each type of abduction plays a role in the process of theological construction. Sometimes in theology we state the obvious, while other times we choose between a set of interpretive opinions. Occasionally, theologians need to offer original solutions to theological problems.

When We State the Obvious

The first category, *overcoded* abduction, occurs intuitively with little or no conscious reflection on the guesswork. When we make overcoded abductions, we are stating the obvious. We arrive at overcoded abductions almost instinctively because of "codes" or "rules" we presume in the reasoning process.[34] Overcoded abductions based on presumed, universally recognized rules help us identify facts in the data.[35] When a friend walks in the door with wet hair and drenched clothing, we can easily infer she had physical contact with liquid somewhere. We make the inference based on a rule we all presume, namely contact with liquid makes dry things wet. Using this presumed rule, we can make an argument like this:

> *Rule (major premise)*.—Physical contact with liquid makes something wet.
> *Result (conclusion)*.—Her hair and clothes are wet.
> ∴ *Case (minor premise)*.—Her hair and clothes had physical contact with liquid.

---

32. Umberto Eco, "Horns, Hooves, Insteps: Some Hypotheses on Three Types of Abduction," in Eco and Thomas A. Sebeok, *Sign of Three*, 206–220. Eco's taxonomy of four is a further development of one put forward by Massimo A. Bonfantini and Giampaolo Proni, "To Guess or Not to Guess?," in *Sign of Three*, 119–134.

33. Bonfantini and Proni, "To Guess or Not to Guess?," 133.

34. Eco describes the intuitive quality of overcoded abductions as "quasi-automatic" and insists they are not automatic in the sense that the one reasoning/interpreting still has to make some decision about the way the rule relates to the case. See Umberto Eco, *Semiotics and the Philosophy of Language* (Bloomington: Indiana University Press, 1984), 41.

35. Eco, "Horns, Hooves, Insteps," 212.

The rule here is so ubiquitous that one can make the inference in an "automatic or semi-automatic way."[36] Overcoded abductions do not always produce certain conclusions but one may reasonably hold these hypotheses with high confidence because of the universal acceptance of the codes presumed.

Overcoded abductions in Christian theology are usually those interpretive "hunches" that are almost universally recognized as the plain meaning of Scripture. Overcoded abductions in biblical interpretation also offer the most confident readings. We may disagree about when Jesus received the final transformation of his resurrection body—immediately upon his resurrection or at his ascension—but no one who takes the text at face value denies that the crucified Christ was raised to new life. Virtually no honest biblical scholar disagrees that the writers of the New Testament believed Jesus died for sins and was raised from the dead on the third day. Whether a person chooses to believe that for himself is a different matter entirely, but it is easy to surmise what biblical authors thought about the topic.

When We Choose between Prominent Interpretive Options

The second kind of abduction, *undercoded* abduction, is what happens when someone must choose a rule from a group of probable solutions.[37] As Eco explains, "Since the rule is selected as the more plausible among many, but it is not certain whether it is the 'correct' one or not, the explanation is only *entertained*, waiting for further tests."[38] This type of abduction is "coded" in the sense that it appeals to an already established code or *rule* in making an inference to the best explanation, but unlike overcoded abduction, it is a *debated* rule rather than a *universally recognized* rule. Rather than creating a new hypothesis, undercoded abduction entertains a previously established rule that possibly addresses the problem or data.[39] Almost all of the examples of exegetical and hermeneutical debates explored in the previous chapter fit this bill. Readers who choose between one of the existing interpretive options in those debates make undercoded abductions.

---

36. Bonfantini and Proni, "To Guess or Not to Guess?," 134.
37. Eco, *Semiotics and the Philosophy of Language*, 42.
38. Eco, "Horns, Hooves, Insteps," 206, italics original.
39. Eco, "Horns, Hooves, Insteps," 206.

We also use undercoded abduction any time we choose from a group of established theological models to explain a disputed biblical passage. Grant Osborne defines a *theological model* as "a heuristic device that is used to organize and structure related ideas."[40] They are "in essence blue prints of a community's beliefs as well as representations of biblical truths" that "have a creedal function and thereby shape as well as describe the belief system."[41] Anytime a theologian chooses one established model or theory to explain a biblical concept or passage (e.g., penal substitutionary atonement, the nature of the gift of tongues, young-earth creation, etc.), he is making an undercoded abduction.

A reader may encounter several conventional models for explaining debated biblical texts such as 1 Corinthians 14:1–40, Hebrews 6:1–8, or Revelation 20:1–10. The theological debate over spiritual gifts in 1 Corinthians 14 overlaps with a question about historical context: What model of interpretation best explains what Paul means by "tongues" (*glossa*) in this passage? Interpreters have ways of understanding the warning passages in Hebrews 6 that confirm or deny the possibility of actual apostasy. Readers of Revelation divide themselves into tribes over the theological model they embrace for reading Revelation 20, an issue related to the literary context of the whole book.[42] After reading established opinions, the reader will make an inference as to which established interpretation offers the best explanation of these passages. This inference will not provide the same level of confidence that an overcoded abduction can afford, but it can provide a coherent way of thinking about a biblical text.

Consider the debates over the doctrines of election and predestination. We read the same texts and choose a theological model for how best to understand those texts. We then put that model or rule to the test. So, if one assumes a rule that "'Election' means God's free,

---

40. Grant R. Osborne, *The Hermeneutical Spiral: A Comprehensive Introduction to Biblical Interpretation*, rev. ed. (Downers Grove, IL: InterVarsity Press, 2006), 391.

41. Osborne, *Hermeneutical Spiral*, 392.

42. Books that outline multiple interpretive positions for these passages are available. See Herbert W. Bateman IV, ed., *Four Views on the Warning Passages in Hebrews* (Grand Rapids, MI: Kregel, 2007); Robert G. Clouse, ed., *The Meaning of the Millennium: Four Views* (Downers Grove, IL: InterVarsity Press, 1977); Darrell L. Bock, ed., *Three Views on the Millennium and Beyond* (Grand Rapids, MI: Zondervan, 1999).

unconditional choice of certain individuals unto salvation" (i.e., unconditional election), the exegesis of Romans 9:1–33 will look much different than for someone who assumes the rule "'Election' is God's choice to elect a covenant community on the condition of faith in Christ" (i.e., conditional election).

> *Rule (major premise).*—Election means God's free, unconditional choice of certain individuals unto salvation.
> *Result (conclusion).*—Paul describes election in Romans 9:1–33.
> ∴ *Case (minor premise).*—Paul describes God's free, unconditional choice of certain individuals unto salvation in Romans 9:1–33.

Both individual and corporate models of election are attempts to make sense of the whole of Paul's theology, and both are inferences made upon observing the text. The text does not *explicitly* rule out either position, making them both *possible* (but not necessarily equiprobable) rules for making sense of the text. The undercoded abduction selected by the interpreter is mostly dependent on how he understands the historical and literary context of the passage.

When We Develop New Solutions

The third type of abduction categorized by Eco, *creative abduction*, occurs when someone offers a new, innovative explanation to explain the data or the problem. Instead of making the choice between what is in Door #1 or Door #2 (what we do in undercoded abduction), an investigator cuts a new door in the wall and offers a creative solution to the problem. Rather than appealing to a previously established theological model, as one does in overcoded and undercoded forms of abduction, the investigator invents a solution *de novo* that she believes best explains the data or problem. This type seems to be the kind of abduction Peirce has in mind when he writes, "No new truth can come from induction and deduction. . . . It can only come from abduction; and abduction is . . . nothing but guessing."[43]

Eco cites Copernicus's heliocentric thesis as a creative abduction that challenged the geocentric cosmology of Ptolemy:

---

43. Peirce, CP 7:219.

Rule (*major premise*).— Planetary objects in our solar system that re-
volve around the sun experience conditions of daylight and night.

Result (*conclusion*).—The earth, rotating daily on its axis, experiences conditions of daylight and night.

∴ *Case* (*minor premise*).— The earth, with the rest of the planetary
objects in our solar system, revolves around the sun.

Copernicus did not select this rule from the available body of human
knowledge at the time but had to invent it. From this rule, he created
a new hypothesis or *case*—that our experiences of daylight and night
come from the earth rotating around its axis as it makes its solar
revolutions, not from the sun moving around the earth as the geocentric system would have us believe. One key criterion for assessing
a creative abduction is its "elegance."[44] Eco associates this type of
abduction with the creative hypotheses that lead to what philosopher
of science Thomas Kuhn calls "paradigm shifts" in a given field of
inquiry.[45]

When someone invents a new explanation for the passage not listed
among traditional interpretations, this invention is a creative abduction. (Note, creative abduction in biblical interpretation is not the
same as inventing revelatory content; it is a new approach to making
revelatory content intelligible.) Interpreters occasionally use creative
abduction to explain biblical texts because none of the available interpretive options seems to provide the best explanation. Because these
creative abductions are untested and unproven, they are tentative and
open to revision or critical reconstruction.

The current debate over the doctrine of justification highlights the
use of creative abduction in biblical theology. Interpreters following
Luther typically understand the Pauline phrase *dikaiosynē theou* ("the
righteousness of God") to refer to the "righteousness of Christ" imputed to us by our faith in his active and passive obedience. In other
words, the righteousness of God refers to Jesus's obedience to the Mo-
saic Law (active obedience) and his obedience unto death on the cross
(passive obedience). We are justified—declared right by God—when we

---

44. Eco, "Horns, Hooves, Insteps," 216.
45. Eco, "Horns, Hooves, Insteps," 207; see also Thomas S. Kuhn, *The Structure of Scientific Revolutions* (Chicago: University of Chicago Press, 1962).

place our faith in Christ, and the merits of his active and passive obedience are imputed or transferred to us. We are declared right because the riches of Christ's obedience are now in our name. Though it now properly fits in the category of undercoded abduction, this traditional Reformed position of the imputation of Christ's righteousness was once a creative abduction because it did not conform to the established interpretation of *dikaiosynē theou* of late medieval Catholicism.

N. T. Wright's rendition of *dikaiosynē theou* as God's "faithfulness to the covenant" is a creative abduction because it does not appeal to any previously held scholarly understanding of the phrase.[46] His position belongs to a "New Perspective" on Paul because it rejects traditional theological models.[47] His creative abduction works like this:

> *Rule (major premise).—* *Dikaiosynē* ("righteousness") harkens back to the covenant made with Abraham (Gen. 15:6), where Abraham's faith was seen as "faithfulness to the covenant."
>
> *Result (conclusion).*—Paul's doctrine of justification in the book of Romans is built around the theme of *dikaiosynē* that grows out of the Old Testament.
>
> ∴ *Case (minor premise).—* Paul's doctrine of justification in the book of Romans builds on a notion of God's righteousness related to covenant faithfulness.

This creative abduction is a rejection of the traditional Reformed conception of *dikaiosynē theou* as the righteous acts of Christ imputed to believers.[48] Instead of choosing from a list of previously established models for reading these texts, Wright has created a new model entirely, but one he believes best describes the thought-world of Paul and other biblical writers.

We Make Guesses to Test Our Guesses

Finally, Eco recognizes a type of abduction he calls *meta-abduction*. Meta-abduction is the process by which we evaluate and test our

---

46. N. T. Wright, *Paul and the Faithfulness of God* (Minneapolis: Fortress, 2013), part 3, 841.

47. Wright rejects monolithic descriptions of the "New Perspective on Paul" because his position, while bearing important similarities to the positions of E. P. Sanders and James D. G. Dunn, has different emphases. Wright's own perspective has developed in different trajectories over time. See his *Pauline Perspectives: Essays on Paul, 1978–2013* (Minneapolis: Fortress, 2013).

48. Wright, *Pauline Perspectives*, 69–71.

hypotheses. As Peirce observes, abductive inferences do "not afford security. The hypothesis must be tested."[49] In meta-abduction, we assess whether the possible worlds and solutions proffered in our creative abductions match real-world experience. We rarely need meta-abduction for our obvious guesses (overcoded abductions) because they borrow from conventional knowledge and experience, but we must always assess our interpretive choices and our creative, out-of-the-box solutions.

As Eco observes, meta-abduction is much easier in detective fiction than in real-world theory making. The world on the page built by Arthur Conan Doyle exists to demonstrate Holmes's genius, and Watson serves the role of verifying Holmes's hypotheses.[50] The process of meta-abduction—the abduction by which we evaluate our creative abductions—is much easier in a small world of few details, few possibilities, and most importantly, omniscient narration. Scientific theorization and real-life detective work offer no such certain confirmation, and their respective theories always remain tentative to some degree.[51] As Peirce himself acknowledges, "Our knowledge is never absolute but always swims, as it were, in a continuum of uncertainty and of undeterminacy [sic]."[52]

Louis Pojman offers four helpful criteria for assessing our hypotheses. Each is applicable to our interpretive and theological explanations:

(1) *Predictability*—Does the abduction in question help explain future events?[53] While this particular test is crucial for scientific theories, it is of lesser use in our attempt to infer the meaning of historical texts.[54]

(2) *Coherence*—Is the abduction internally coherent—i.e., not self-defeating or contradictory—and does it cohere "with ev-

---

49. Peirce, CP 6:470.
50. Eco, "Horns, Hooves, Insteps," 218–219.
51. Eco, "Horns, Hooves, Insteps," 220.
52. Peirce, CP 1:171.
53. Pojman, *Philosophy*, 30.
54. In the place of this criterion of predictability, one might appeal to something like Ernst Troeltsch's (1865–1923) *principle of analogy*—the historiographical principle that in order to assess the events of the past, they must be analogous to the present. See Ernst Troeltsch, "Über historische und dogmatische Method in der Theologie," in *Gesammelte Schriften*, vol. 2 (Tübingen: J. C. B. Mohr, 1913), 729–753. Because the principle of analogy is contingent upon repeatable events, Troeltsch recognizes its limited usefulness in assessing the unique, miraculous events of the Gospels. Wolfhart Pannenberg (1928–2014) offers important criticisms of Troeltsch's method

erything else we hold true in the field"?[55] As we have seen, we do this almost instinctively in overcoded abduction, but this requires careful inquiry and reflection when assessing creative abductions. Theologians who apply this principle will call into question creative abductions they believe to be inconsistent with the whole of Christian truth elsewhere.

(3) *Simplicity*—Is the abduction simpler than other hypotheses? Does it require more or less ad hoc explanations than other theories? This criterion is essentially the application of Ockham's razor in the analyses of undercoded and creative abductions.

(4) *Fruitfulness*—Does the abduction lead to further insights and explanations? In other words, does this abduction also aid in explaining related problems?

In addition to Pojman's four criteria, Robert B. Stewart adds (5) *comprehensiveness* and (6) *consistency*. With the criterion of comprehensiveness, we ask whether the abduction accounts for all of the available data. The criterion of consistency, or credibility, asks whether the abduction has the "ring of authenticity."[56]

Theologians use meta-abduction to assess our undercoded and creative abductive inferences from Scripture. The criteria of meta-abduction are helpful for evaluating every theological position based on Scripture. Is a new or previously established explanation of a biblical text internally *coherent*? Does it cohere with other true statements about the text? Is it *simpler* than other expositions, requiring fewer ad hoc solutions? Is this inference *fruitful* in that it helps address other problems related to the text, or does it create more problems? Does this abduction *comprehensively account for all the available data*? Is it a *credible* theory?

Established theological claims, such as the claim that Jesus is divine, may be inferred through an undercoded abduction of the Gospels. That is, we choose from a group of previously established explanations that

---

in "Redemptive Event and History," in *Basic Questions in Theology*, vol. 1, trans. G. H. Kelm (Philadelphia: Fortress, 1970), 40–50.

55. Pojman, *Philosophy*, 30.

56. Pojman, *Philosophy*, 30; Robert B. Stewart, "The Case of the Unexpected Sermon: Discovering the Value (and Dangers) of Abductive Preaching," *Preaching: The Professional Journal for Preachers* 19, no. 1 (July–August 2003): 17.

help us make sense of what New Testament writers say about Jesus. But Kevin Vanhoozer suggests that something like meta-abduction provides a way of assessing this traditional belief: "We infer, for example, that Matthew is claiming that Jesus is the Messiah promised in the Old Testament, not by citing one verse, but rather by applying the same criteria that science uses to appraise theories—correspondence, comprehensiveness, coherence, and compellingness—to the whole of the Gospel."[57] This, in large part, is the work of "historical Jesus" research—at least as evangelicals do it. New Testament scholars, philosophers, and theologians use the criteria of meta-abduction to test the claims surrounding Jesus's identity.

The same sort of meta-abduction is useful for testing new theories or creative abductions in hermeneutics and theology as well. When assessing a new approach such as Wright's attempt to explain the "righteousness of God" in Pauline theology, we might ask questions about (1) its fruitfulness as a theory (i.e., does it explain other aspects of Pauline thought?), (2) its coherence (i.e., does it cohere with other known elements of Pauline thought?), (3) its simplicity as a theory, or (4) its credibility (i.e., would a first-century Jew have thought in these terms?). If the hypothesis formed in meta-abduction does not satisfy these interpretive criteria, it is time for the reader to go back to the text, make observations, and attempt to either employ an undercoded solution (such as Luther's interpretation of *dikaiosynē theou*) or engage in creative conjecture-making once more.

Concluding Reflections

I conclude this chapter by summarizing ways in which reason—in its deductive, inductive, and abductive forms—contributes to theological diversity. *First, differences in Christian doctrine are occasionally products of fallacious deductive reasoning.* Even if deductive reasoning has not been the focus of this chapter, I am aware that some theological mistakes come from formally invalid deductions (e.g., logical errors). D. A. Carson has provided a helpful summary of some of these types of logical fallacies in biblical interpretation, including, but not limited

---

57. Kevin J. Vanhoozer, *Is There a Meaning in This Text? The Bible, the Reader, and the Morality of Literary Knowledge* (Grand Rapids, MI: Zondervan, 1998), 334.

to, false disjunctions, invalid syllogisms, and non sequitur reasoning. Carson also provides numerous examples of these logical mistakes found in the writings of contemporary Protestant and evangelical theologians.[58]

Second, our differences in abductive reasoning better explain our theological differences than our differences in inductive reasoning. I recognize that this statement is somewhat dependent on a particular conception of "inference to the best explanation" that makes a clear distinction between inductive logic and abductive reasoning. Some philosophers tend to categorize "inference to the best explanation" as a type of inductive reasoning.[59] However, Peirce's threefold distinction is, in my opinion, clearer and better defined.

Third, doctrinal disagreement is often related to the creative nature of our reasoning processes. As psychologist Raymond Nickerson explains,

> The role of inventiveness or creativity in reasoning is far more important than generally acknowledged. Often we think of reasoning as a process of working with information that is given. That may mean evaluating the logical validity of an argument, explicating information that is given only implicitly, piecing together isolated bits of information so as to clarify the justification of an inference, and so on. . . . In contrast, the reasoning demanded of us by the problems of everyday life often requires that much of the information used in the reasoning process come from our own heads. Moreover, for many of the problems we deal with every day, there is no single correct solution, or if there is, there is no sure way to tell whether or not we have found it.
>
> Much of reasoning involves debating with ourselves.[60]

We use creative reasoning like this in formulating the hypotheses of science and theology. The diversity of human creativity unavoidably yields differing results.[61]

---

58. D. A. Carson, *Exegetical Fallacies*, 2nd ed. (Grand Rapids, MI: Baker, 1996), 87–123.

59. See Lipton, *Inference to the Best Explanation.*

60. Raymond S. Nickerson, *Reflections on Reasoning* (Hillsdale, NJ: Lawrence Erlbaum Associates, 1986), 7–8.

61. Nickerson, *Reflections on Reasoning*, 9–10.

This creativity drives the way in which different systematic theologies select, arrange, and prioritize their doctrinal categories. But this creative reasoning is also essential in the selection of what texts and what motifs become central for the interpreter of the Bible. There is no explicit passage in Scripture that says the "covenant" is the central motif of the Bible, or that the "love of God" is the center. These are creative interpretive judgments made by abductive reasoning. Because of their dependence on the creativity of the thinker or theologian, they are fallible judgments, tentative and open to revision.

Fourth, doctrinal disagreement is often over issues that remain provisional because of the limitations on our reasoning and interpretive processes. Readers of the Bible work within a "hermeneutical circle" or "hermeneutical spiral." This means that they move from an initial, more tentative preunderstanding of what a text means to a better understanding through the hard work of exegesis. Our understandings of biblical texts sometimes change over time, not because the authorial meaning changes but because our faculties of reason are limited and prone to error and revision.[62] This initial preunderstanding can be an abductive inference about what we think the text will mean. Abductive reasoning does not give us certain conclusions but a number of possible explanations that merit further consideration. Not all abductions come with the same degree of confidence. When we make overcoded abductions that state the obvious, we can be more confident in our reasoning. Undercoded abductions made when we select one of a number of available options are more tentative. Creative abductions, which are newer and still untested theories, have the most uncertainty attached to them.

Fifth, creative abductions are occasionally necessary for the attempt to better understand Scripture, but theologians should move here with caution. With good reason, Thomas Oden swore to promote "nothing new" in theology when he moved out of twentieth-century

---

62. Anthony C. Thiselton, *Hermeneutics* (Grand Rapids, MI: Eerdmans, 2009), 13. In the last century, hermeneutics scholars have added a variety of metaphors to describe this interpretive process: the "fusion of horizons" (Gadamer), the "hermeneutics of suspicion" (Ricoeur), and the "hermeneutical spiral" (Osborne). See Hans-Georg Gadamer, *Truth and Method*, 2nd rev. ed., trans. Joel Weinsheimer and Donald G. Marshall (New York/London: Continuum, 2004), 268–382; Paul Ricoeur, *Freud and Philosophy: An Essay on Interpretation*, trans. Denis Savage (New Haven, CT: Yale University Press, 1970), 32–36; Osborne, *Hermeneutical Spiral*.

neo-liberal theology into evangelicalism.[63] Neophilia, which values novelty for the sake of novelty, should be rejected at all costs. However, there is a time for creative answers to old problems when the old answers no longer seem to be the most fitting ones. For evangelical Christians, this means returning to the primary source, to the fountain (*ad fontem*) of Christian theology: Scripture itself. The Reformers, discontent with many of the interpretive options presented to them by the theologians of their tradition, presented new (and improved) interpretations of key biblical texts.

Sixth, creative abduction can also be a valuable tool for contemporizing the biblical message. While I am not suggesting transforming the message of the Bible—an approach celebrated in liberal theology—I am suggesting that twenty-first-century readers, operating in different horizons than ancient writers, have questions unique to their time and place in history. Today's Christians must ask questions that probably would have been unimaginable to first-century followers of Jesus. What is a biblically faithful way of tackling hot-button issues not explicitly addressed in Scripture, such as climate change, gun control, immigration, socialism, stem-cell research, and transgenderism? Taking biblical authority seriously means asking questions about how the divinely inspired authors of Scripture would respond to the ethical dilemmas of our day. We must *translate the message of the Bible* in such a way that it addresses these types of concerns. We may never have the same horizon as biblical writers, but we must let them inform how we see our own. This task requires some imagination and yields somewhat tentative results.

Finally, all forms of reasoning have their limitations in Christian theology. Though deductive and creative forms of reasoning are crucial parts of interpretation and theological construction, they are of limited appeal in the broader context in which Christian theologians now minister. As Ben Witherington advises, "In a postmodern and mostly biblically illiterate situation, the power of one's rhetoric counts far more than the power of one's logic. Persuasion is far more

---

63. For more on Oden's "nothing new" conversion, see his memoir, *Change of Heart: A Personal and Theological Memoir* (Downers Grove, IL: InterVarsity Press, 2014).

likely to happen by means of powerful and evocative images than by syllogisms."[64] Feeling and intuition are major driving factors in our cultural disagreements, and the same goes for our theological disputes. That's why we must now explore the *emotional* dimensions of Christian theological formation and disagreement.

---

64. Witherington, *Problem with Evangelical Theology*, 244.

4

We Feel Differently

The Role of Emotions in Theological Diversity

Theology can be a messy affair. Parochial feuds over doctrine can split denominations or even incite violence. Debates over the identity of Jesus in the fourth century sometimes broke out in fistfights. The Catholic Inquisitors put tens of thousands to death for teaching things they believed to be heretical. Millions died in wars stemming from the Protestant Reformation in Europe. Even academicians revered for their thoughtfulness can display intense emotion in their published disagreements.[1] In the twenty-first century, social media and theological blogging has exposed to the world new levels of cruelty and vile speech among professing Christians.

Rarely are our intramural debates over doctrine disinterested intellectual exercises. We often feel frustrated when our dialogue partners cannot see in Scripture what appears to be so clear to us. We deal with disappointment when those who share our beliefs come to reject them. We can bottle up anxiety when our own theological beliefs start to shift. While our disagreements can be the subject of cordial and

---

1. Karl Barth titled his retort to Emil Brunner's natural theology *Nein!* (*No!*) and its opening chapter "An Angry Introduction." See Emil Brunner and Karl Barth, *Natural Theology: Comprising 'Nature and Grace' by Professor Dr. Emil Brunner and the reply 'No!' by Dr. Karl Barth*, trans. Peter Fraenkel (Eugene, OR: Wipf & Stock, 2002), 70–73.

mutually edifying discussions among members of Christ's body, they can also resemble the schoolyard squabbles of petty children exchanging insults and empty threats. Fearmongers promote an unhealthy suspicion of anyone who doesn't conform to their narrowly defined set of beliefs. Those enslaved by a spirit of timidity may have strong feelings of shame when speaking truth into controversial situations (2 Tim. 1:7–8).

Doctrinal disagreements are heated for the same sorts of reasons devoted parents have difficulty being impartial in matters that concern their own children. We cherish our beliefs, especially our most deeply held beliefs. We will work hard to protect and sustain them and even fight to the bitter end when we feel compelled to defend them. We do not approach truth or falsehood dispassionately. Like our Creator, we are wired to delight in truth (Ps. 51:6). But mistruths can cause us sorrow, grief, or anger (Prov. 12:22; Hos. 4:2).

Christian theologians have long recognized the role *experience* plays in our theological formation, but seldom mentioned in our hermeneutical and theological discussions is the crucial role *emotions* and *intuitions* play in the formation of Christian doctrine.[2] Otherwise-agreeable Christians who share similar convictions and hermeneutical methods can come to divergent conclusions because of *nonrational*, emotional factors that shape their thinking. These nonrational factors can have as much influence on theology as exegesis or well-reasoned arguments, sometimes even more so. At times we are more unwittingly swayed by our emotional responses to theological statements than we are by conscious, rational arguments.

The distinction here between *nonrational* and *irrational* is important. To say one is being *irrational* means that one is thinking in ways contrary to reason or elementary laws of logic. Blatant logical contradictions, like saying "up is down" or "2+2=5," are irrational. The term *nonrational*, on the other hand, simply describes factors in human decision making that are not part of the formal reasoning pro-

---

2. Experience is a secondary authority in Christian theology that can be used to confirm or reject doctrinal positions, such as the claim that believers never experience suffering. See Anthony N. S. Lane, "*Sola Scriptura?* Making Sense of a Post-Reformation Slogan," in *A Pathway into the Holy Scripture*, ed. Philip E. Satterthwaite and David F. Wright (Grand Rapids, MI: Eerdmans, 1994), 306–310, 321.

cess. When people make irrational arguments and irrational decisions, they leave themselves open to formal criticism and correction, but no one can reasonably fault a person for *nonrational* issues like matters of taste or preference. I'm not being irrational when I say I prefer Tex-Mex to sushi just because I did not reason my way to my specific (and I think vastly superior) culinary tastes. Though I would never want to reduce something as important as Christian doctrine to a mere matter of taste—we are, after all, striving to make sense of God's revealed *truth*—I do believe nonrational factors such as intuition, personal preference, and some need for social conformity can play a significant role in shaping our framework of interpreting Scripture.

As evangelicals who affirm *sola Scriptura*, we do not consciously look to experience or feelings as the basis for our approach to doctrine, but we are still emotional creatures. Because we have hearts, souls, and minds (Luke 10:27), our emotions and intuitions can play a considerable role in the way we read Scripture and the creeds and confessions we choose to affirm. Emotions also color the way we treat our distinctive theological positions and those positions that contradict them. The present chapter is a descriptive exploration of this theme, bringing contemporary research in social psychology and neuroscience into dialogue with biblical hermeneutics to address the larger issue of doctrinal disagreement.

My primary dialogue partner in this chapter is social psychologist Jonathan Haidt, whose 2012 best-seller *The Righteous Mind: Why Good People Are Divided by Politics and Religion* is a popular-level introduction to the field of moral psychology with a particularly ambitious objective: explaining some of the key differences in the ways liberals and conservatives think about morality, politics, and religion. The result is an eminently readable marriage of empirical research and philosophical discourse.[3] Rather than *prescribing* a moral system, Haidt simply *describes* the intricate biological, psychological, and sociological factors at work in the formation of moral systems.[4] In his approach, which he labels the "social intuitionist" model, he offers

---

3. Jonathan Haidt, *The Righteous Mind: Why Good People Are Divided by Politics and Religion* (New York: Vintage, 2012).
4. Jonathan Haidt, "Morality," *Perspectives on Psychological Science* 3 (2008): 70.

explanatory principles behind moral judgments.[5] Haidt suggests that emotional, nonrational factors play a larger role in the formation of our moral beliefs than we commonly acknowledge. Where Haidt primarily applies these principles to differences of political opinion in the United States, I suggest that they may have application in understanding the nonrational factors at play in doctrinal disagreement between otherwise like-minded Christians.

Haidt and I are worlds apart in our respective worldviews. He is to my far left politically and a committed atheist whose naturalistic beliefs shape his views about human morality. Unlike Haidt, I do not believe neo-Darwinian evolutionary theory can adequately explain human consciousness and rationality (though I am aware of some theologians who feel otherwise).[6] While I don't agree with the sum of Haidt's project—a naturalistic explanation of human morality—I can appreciate his observation of the parts. He makes claims and presents data about the roles emotion and intuition play in belief formation which are compatible with a thoroughly Christian view of human beings as complex spiritual beings made in the image of God.

I intend most of this chapter, like Haidt's discussion of moral disagreements, to be a *description* of ways in which nonrational factors such as emotions *might* shape our doctrinal disagreements. I am not prescribing a theological method where feelings take center stage. I am only attempting to describe what can and often does happen with some of our religious intuitions. However, I conclude the chapter with some *normative* suggestions drawn from Scripture and the Christian tradition about how to wrangle our passions in interpretation and doctrinal disagreement.

One important disclaimer: because I am not a trained psychologist, this chapter is more about theological conjecture–making informed by psychology than it is a scientific, empirical study making proven claims. I have not tested my claims with sample groups and demographics. I leave that sort of labor to much more capable hands. My

---

5. Jonathan Haidt, "The Emotional Dog and Its Rational Tail: A Social Intuitionist Approach to Moral Judgment," *Psychological Review* 108 (2001): 814–834.

6. See J. Wentzel Van Huyssteen, *The Shaping of Rationality: Toward Interdisciplinarity in Theology and Science* (Grand Rapids, MI: Eerdmans, 1999); Philip Clayton, *Explanation from Physics to Theology: An Essay in Rationality and Religion* (New Haven, CT: Yale University Press, 1989).

only hope here is to give some consideration to ways in which nonrational factors shape our theological contests.

Brains, Minds, and Emotions

How we understand the role of emotions in intellectual disagreements over subjects like morality, politics, or religion is in large part dependent on our most fundamental beliefs about human nature, our *philosophical anthropology* (or *theological anthropology*). Do human beings have immaterial souls or minds, and if they do, how do these immaterial minds relate to their material brains? How do emotions and impulses relate to reason? Philosophers, scientists, and theologians proffer a continuum of answers to these questions related to the mind-body problem.

A significant portion of the Western philosophical tradition going back to Plato has primarily understood the human person as a rational being. In other words, we are essentially immaterial "souls" or "minds"—these words are frequently interchangeable—who occupy and direct the physical characteristics of the body, including the brain. On this view, human passions and habits ideally should take their marching orders from the more capable, sovereign sphere of immaterial reason. Emotions and tastes are merely peripheral features associated with our embodiment, and they must be tamed and subjugated by the mind.[7]

Plato understood that the relationship between our reason and emotions is complex. He knew that we battle "inconsistent desires."[8] He believed the soul has three parts: a logical or rational part with which human beings reason and learn; a "spirited" (*thymoeides*) part with which they experience emotions like anger; and an "appetitive" (*epithymetikon*) part that can make people hungry, sexually aroused, or compulsive shoppers.[9] In one analogy, Plato compared the three-part soul to a charioteer driving a chariot pulled by two winged horses—one white and noble, the other dark and ignoble.[10]

---

7. Plato, *Timaeus* 69d–e.
8. David Armstrong, *The Mind-Body Problem: An Opinionated Introduction* (Boulder, CO: Westview, 1999), 23.
9. Plato, *Republic* 439d, 580d.
10. Plato, *Phaedrus* 246a–257b.

The white, noble horse represents the best qualities of the spirited part of the soul—love, beauty, righteous anger—while the other, darker horse represents the appetitive lust for pleasure, food, or sex.[11] The charioteer represents reason or intellect, which, in the case of mortal human beings, has the "painfully difficult business" of trying to drive these horses that are desiring to move in opposite directions.[12] Though he acknowledges the weakness of human reason, Plato suggests that reason, with the right training, can attain mastery over both emotions and appetites on the path to enlightenment.[13] Only the small portion of people who have attained this mastery over emotions and appetites are the fit to rule in Plato's idealized notion of the Republic.[14]

This view of reason as the preeminent characteristic of the human being gained new traction in the seventeenth century under René Descartes, the father of modern philosophy. He suggests that reason "alone makes us men and distinguishes us from animals."[15] Out of his apprehension and uncertainty about his knowledge, Descartes sought to create a method of reasoning that would establish a foundation for all knowledge that was "indubitable" or beyond doubt.[16] One day while sitting alone in a stove-heated room, he reached a crucial moment in the development of his method. He decided to cast a skeptical eye on everything he had ever learned, his senses, and his intuitions. Descartes wanted to begin his quest for knowledge with certain, indubitable truths. Here, he landed on his famous *cogito* ("I think therefore I am") and found it "so firm and so certain" that he could "accept it without scruple."[17] Because Descartes was *reasoning*, he could surmise one fact he believed was beyond doubt: that his mind existed, that the human being is principally a "thinking thing."[18]

For Descartes, like Plato before him, the immaterial mind is the rightful master of the body and brain. But as contemporary philosophers of mind observe, Descartes's radical form of dualism makes the

---

11. Plato, *Phaedrus* 253rd–254b.
12. Plato, *Phaedrus* 246b.
13. Plato, *Phaedrus* 254e.
14. Plato, *Republic* 442a–b.
15. René Descartes, AT 6:2. All quotations of Descartes come from *Discourse on Method and Meditations on First Philosophy*, trans. Donald A. Cress (Indianapolis: Hackett, 1980).
16. Descartes, AT 6:31–32.
17. Descartes, AT 6:32.
18. Descartes, AT 7:8.

notion of mind-body interaction difficult because "minds are unextended, nonmaterial substances and bodies are extended, material substances."[19] In other words, bodies are corporeal entities that extend through physical space, and minds are noncorporeal entities that take up no space. Consequently, the body (or the brain contained therein) plays no necessary or vital role in the formation of beliefs held by the immaterial mind. The immaterial mind controls the body and the brain, not the reverse. Gilbert Ryle famously called this kind of radical separation so lauded by Plato and Descartes "the dogma of the Ghost in the Machine."[20]

On the opposite side of the continuum, some maintain humans are merely material beings whose emotions, moralities, and religious beliefs are by-products of physiological processes at work in the brain. According to *reductive physicalists*, human beings are merely animals with high-functioning brains that enable them to have complex thoughts and the illusion of consciousness. Emotions are simply by-products of physical activity in the body. Many who are enamored with contemporary evolutionary neuroscience take this position, asserting the primacy of the material brain in moral decision making and belief formation.

In its reductive forms, a physicalist view of human nature reduces human belief formation to a sum of material causes. Neuroscientist and leading atheistic spokesperson Sam Harris makes this point emphatically clear: "Your brain is making choices on the basis of preferences and beliefs that have been hammered into it for a lifetime—by your genes, your physical development since the moment you were conceived, and the interactions you have had with other people, events, and ideas."[21] The reductive physicalist contends that the physical brain—not an autonomous, immaterial mind—ultimately determines belief. Consequently, free will and personal identity are sheer illusions caused by these physical operations.[22]

---

19. John Heil, *Philosophy of Mind*, 2nd ed. (New York: Routledge, 2004), 27.

20. Gilbert Ryle, *The Concept of Mind* (Chicago: University of Chicago Press, 1949), 15–16.

21. Sam Harris, *Free Will* (New York: Free Press, 2012), 41.

22. Harris, following Hume, holds what philosophers of mind dub a *nonrealist* view of the will. As Thomas Dixon describes Hume's understanding of the will, it is "just one 'impression'—in other words, a feeling—amongst others, including love, hate, and the other passions; a passive impression received ultimately from the action of external objects and/or the body" (Dixon, *From*

Between these two extremes is a variety of biblically and theologically informed positions on the nature of humanity. Each of these
positions describes human beings as complex unities whose bodies are
more than fleshly marionettes directed by the immaterial mind and
whose immaterial minds are more than smoke and mirrors put on by
the material brain.[23] According to Joel Green and Stuart Palmer, these
positions fall into two broad categories: *holistic dualists* and *nonreductive monists*. Green and Palmer use the term *holistic dualism* to
classify positions that, like their Platonic and Cartesian cousins, see
human beings as unities of body and soul, but unlike their Platonic
and Cartesian counterparts, emphasize a positive, symbiotic relationship between body and soul.[24] On this view, the immaterial mind and
material brain are "highly interactive" and interdependent upon each
other.[25] Conversely, nonreductive Christian monists reject the notion
of a "soul" or a "mind" that is distinct from the essence of the body.
They argue for a psychosomatic unity of the human constitution,
meaning that a human being is incapable of being separated into parts
like body and soul.

Some evangelical theologians have observed that the holistic dualism position is necessary for the eschatological concept of the *intermediate state*—the idea that believers continue to have a conscious
existence with the Lord after physical death but prior to the future and
final resurrection of their bodies (Luke 23:43; 2 Cor. 5:8). If the body
cannot be separated from the mind or the soul, it is argued, then we
cannot consciously be with the Lord before a resurrection event. The
monist must advocate for either *soul sleep*—the idea that we are "unconscious" until the future resurrection—or some kind of *immediate
resurrection upon death*.[26] Monists have responded that a notion of

---

Passions to Emotions: The Creation of a Secular Psychological Category [New York: Cambridge
University Press, 2003], 107).

23. Anthony C. Thiselton, *The Hermeneutics of Doctrine* (Grand Rapids, MI: Eerdmans,
2007), 181–182.

24. For an articulation of four views in these two broad categories, see Joel B. Green and
Stuart L. Palmer, eds., *In Search of the Soul: Four Views of the Mind-Body Problem* (Downers
Grove, IL: InterVarsity Press, 2005).

25. J. P. Moreland, "Restoring the Substance to the Soul of Psychology," *Journal of Psychology
and Theology* 26 (1998): 35.

26. For an extended argument along these lines, see John W. Cooper, *Body, Soul, and Life
Everlasting: Biblical Anthropology and the Monism-Dualism Debate* (Grand Rapids, MI: Eerdmans, 1998).

the intermediate state creates similar problems for the holistic dualist who believes in the interaction of the brain and the mind.[27] Monists also suggest their view of the human constitution better coheres with contemporary developments in the science of the brain.[28]

Nowhere does the Bible give a systematic description of the constitution of human nature. Although biblical authors use a wide array of language to describe humanity—vocabulary translated as "heart," "soul," "body," and "mind"[29]—their usage of these terms is relatively imprecise and does not likely correlate with ancient philosophical uses of the same terms.[30] As a result of this interpretive uncertainty, theologians attempt to make biblical cases in support of both holistic dualist and monist positions. Some of these issues will remain a mystery until we "know fully . . . as [we] have been fully known" (1 Cor. 13:12). What is clear, however, is that Scripture paints human beings made in God's image as complex, embodied individuals who think, feel sensations, experience emotions, and make choices. Neither of the oversimplified explanations offered by radical dualism or reductionistic physicalism can account for the complex relationship between brain and mind, emotions and reason, and spirit and body.

Even with this interdependent relationship between rational thought and emotion, Christian theologians frequently neglect the significant role emotions play in belief formation. As Christian psychologist Keith Edwards elaborates,

> Emotions are one of the most misunderstood and underestimated
> brain functions. . . . We need a better understanding of emotions

---

27. See Kevin Corcoran, "The Constitution View of Persons," in *In Search of the Soul: Four Views of the Mind-Body Problem*, 161–165.

28. See Nancey Murphy, *Bodies and Souls, or Spirited Bodies?* (Cambridge: Cambridge University Press, 2006).

29. Key terms in the Hebrew Bible include *nepeš* ("breath," "soul," "life"), *rûach* ("wind," "spirit"), *bāśār* ("flesh"), *lev* ("heart"), *kelāyôt* ("kidneys"), and *mēʿîm* ("bowels"). New Testament terms include *psychē* ("soul," "life"), *pneuma* ("spirit," "wind," "breath"), *sarx* ("flesh"), *sōma* ("body"), *kardia* ("heart"), *splagchna* ("bowels"), *nephros* ("kidneys"), *nous* ("mind"), *dianoia* ("mind"), and *noēma* ("mind," "thought"). For a systematic exploration of biblical usages of these terms, see James Leo Garrett, *Systematic Theology*, vol. 1, 3rd ed. (North Richland Hills, TX: BIBAL, 2007), 498–507.

30. As James Barr (1924–2006) has shown, attempts to formulate comprehensive doctrines of humanity solely based on how a word has been used across time (a diachronic analysis) is rife with problems. See Barr, *The Semantics of Biblical Language* (New York: Oxford University Press, 1961), 34–39.

and their function if we are going to have an adequate model of human nature. Emotions are concrete experiences with specific informational content. To feel something means to know something. Emotions, feelings, or "vibes" are identified with the tacit or intuitive level of knowing. Emotions are the "royal road" to understanding a person's deeper, core beliefs which may not be consciously recognized.[31]

Edwards states that our minds work toward forming beliefs in two ways. Our left hemisphere provides us with language, conscious conceptual thought, and the ability to reason through issues. The other part our brain consists of a preconscious emotional system that helps us act and react from intuition and memory. The former part of our mind gives verbal expression, while the latter gives emotional expression. Edwards asserts that Christians must make compelling rational cases for the faith but likewise must be equipped to address emotional beliefs that develop through preconscious, nonrational factors.[32]

So, how does theological anthropology relate to doctrinal disagreement? If we believe we are merely rational beings directed by our mind or soul's capacity to reason, as in Platonic or Cartesian dualism, then we will see all disagreement simply as the rational failure by one or more of the parties involved. Then again, if human thoughts are merely the products of material and social causation, as argued by reductionists, we might conceive of our disagreements as brain processes beyond our control.[33] But if we arrive at one of the mediating Christian positions described above, albeit in a more dualistic or monistic framework, we can suggest that both reason *and* emotion contribute to theological conflict. The idiosyncrasies of the brain may contribute to spats about religious belief. The following principles suggested by Haidt may inform us about the role emotional, nonrational factors play in doctrinal diversity.

---

31. Keith J. Edwards, "The Nature of Human Mental Life," in *Christian Perspectives on Being Human: A Multidisciplinary Approach to Integration*, ed. J. P. Moreland and David M. Ciocchi (Grand Rapids, MI: Baker, 1993), 184–185.

32. Edwards, "Nature of Human Mental Life," 196–197.

33. Richard Dawkins calls the ideas about which we disagree "cultural replicators" or "memes." See Dawkins, *The Selfish Gene* (New York: Oxford University Press, 1976), 192; cf. Daniel C. Dennett, *Breaking the Spell: Religion as a Natural Phenomenon* (New York: Viking, 2006), 78–79.

Going with Our Guts

The first principle of Haidt's moral psychology is *"intuitions come first, strategic reasoning second."* In making this claim, Haidt is challenging the traditional belief that persons come to their moral judgments chiefly through conscious reasoning and reflection.[34] "Rather than following the ancient Greeks in worshipping reason," insists Haidt, "we should instead look for the roots of human intelligence, rationality, and virtue in what the mind does best: perception, intuition, and other mental operations that are quick, effortless, and generally quite accurate."[35]

Instead of developing our morality through rational reflection on what is good, Haidt contends that we begin our moral development with instinctive, nonrational intuitions that we only subsequently use moral reasoning to support. Haidt stresses that these intuitions—simple flashes of judgment—are a type of cognition, but not a type of reasoning. Intuition and reasoning make up the two cognitive processes by which we come to moral decisions.[36] *Before we think about what is right and wrong, we have a gut feeling about it.* Our reasoning is often subservient to our intuitions and emotions. Even the way we reason our way to the best possible explanations is often shaped by our feelings.

Whereas Plato compared the soul to the charioteer of reason trying to steer the two wayward horses of emotion and appetite, Haidt compares the mind to an elephant and its rider: The rider represents conscious moral reasoning, while the elephant represents the larger part of the mind consisting of *automatic processes* such as emotion and intuition. It is the elephant and not the rider that determines the direction in which they move.[37] Plato would never suggest that the charioteer exists to serve the horses, but Haidt contends that the rider exists to serve the elephant.

The automatic processes of the elephant in moral reasoning are manifold. As primarily affective entities, human brains continually evaluate the world around them through intuitions. The intuitions are

---

34. Haidt, *Righteous Mind*, xiv, italics original.
35. Haidt, "Emotional Dog and Its Rational Tail," 822. Haidt affirms David Hume's (1711–1776) assumption that "reason is . . . the slave of the passions." See David Hume, *A Treatise on Human Nature*, 2 vols. (London: Longmans, Green, 1874), 2:195.
36. Haidt, "Emotional Dog and Its Rational Tail," 815.
37. Haidt, *Righteous Mind*, 53–54; cf. Haidt, *The Happiness Hypothesis: Finding Modern Truth in Ancient Wisdom* (New York: Basic, 2006), 16–17.

like hunches, positive or negative emotional reactions to situations or ideas.[38] Our bodies play a major role in these automatic processes as feelings of disgust or arousal can shape our moral decision making.[39] The rider on top of the elephant represents the *controlled process of language-based reasoning* that responds to these flashing intuitions. While this process of conscious reasoning has certain advantages that automatic processes such as intuition and emotion do not have— such as being able to reflect on the future and alternative scenarios— conscious reasoning always plays a subordinate role to them.[40]

According to Haidt, conscious moral reasoning is primarily a post hoc process of justifying what one already intuitively believes—what gut feeling tells us. More often than not, reason (at least in moral and religious reasoning) functions "more like a lawyer defending a client than a judge or scientist seeking truth."[41] It almost goes without saying that this sort of rational self-justification can be detrimental to the pursuit of truth. It is an intellectual vice that runs contrary to intellectual honesty. Haidt observes that persons instinctively follow their gut feelings in matters of morality, even when they are not able to justify why.

Haidt likens the mind to an intuitive political machine. In moral decision making, the automatic processes of the unconscious mind operate like a political pollster always examining what others think or feel about their candidate.[42] Conscious moral reasoning, on the other hand, is akin to a White House press secretary whose primary job is to convince members of the press that whatever the president said or did is correct—no matter how contradictory or erroneous it may appear to everyone else in the room. Rationality, like an internal press secretary, strives to convince others and ourselves that what our automatic processes like intuition and emotion tell us about right and wrong is correct.[43] We see this sort of behavior played out frequently when individuals will rationalize or justify the behavior or ideas of their favorite

---

38. Haidt, *Righteous Mind*, 65; cf. Hume, *Treatise on Human Nature*, 2:1. Hume calls automatic processes like intuitions "impressions" and conscious products of reason "ideas."
39. Haidt, *Righteous Mind*, 70–71; Haidt, "Emotional Dog and Its Rational Tail," 825.
40. Haidt, *Righteous Mind*, 54, 59.
41. Haidt, "Emotional Dog and Its Rational Tail," 820.
42. Haidt, *Righteous Mind*, 89–91.
43. Haidt, *Righteous Mind*, 91–92.

political figures or candidates, even when said candidates contradict their own explicit and implicit beliefs about policy and morality.

Experimental psychologists can corroborate the claim that automatic processes play a big role in our moral decision making. Haidt highlights one test widely used by psychologists called the Implicit Association Test (IAT) to exhibit ways in which moral judgments are intuitional. The test measures unconscious or implicit attitudes by measuring automatic responses to pictorial or symbolic representations of particular concepts ("happiness," "race," etc.) paired with descriptors such as "good" or "bad."[44] As one version of the IAT focused on race relations proved, the test can expose a crucial gap in one's expressed, explicit beliefs (e.g., "I do not show preference to persons of my own race") and unconscious attitudes (e.g., a preference to favor persons of the same race).[45] Another version of the IAT used to measure implicit attitudes of politically loaded words such as *Bush*, *Clinton*, *Obama*, *Trump*, *flag*, *taxes*, *welfare*, and *pro-life* illustrates the intuitive nature of partisan political beliefs. For some chunks of the population, the term *pro-life* automatically signaled something very positive; for others, it had a very negative connotation.[46]

Though to my knowledge no such test yet exists, I suspect that word groupings associated with debated theological terms and concepts within evangelical theology might draw the same kinds of automatic responses. An IAT about theological issues may show that doctrinal beliefs relate to automatic responses and intuitions. The term *fundamentalism* might provoke negative emotions for the theological left or for those evangelicals who seek to distance themselves from that term. For others, the same term may be something that evokes a strong sense of moral uprightness and fidelity to the Bible. Some might

---

44. Anthony G. Greenwald, Debbie E. McGhee, and Jordan L. K. Schwartz, "Measuring Individual Differences in Implicit Cognition: The Implicit Association Test," *Journal of Personality and Social Psychology* 74 (1998): 1464–1480. The test is available to take online at http://www.projectimplicit.com.

45. Mahzarin R. Banaji and Anthony G. Greenwald, *Blind Spot: Hidden Biases of Good People* (New York: Delacorte, 2013), 41–46.

46. Haidt, *Righteous Mind*, 68; cf. James P. Morris, Nancy K. Squires, Charles S. Taber, and Milton Lodge, "Activation of Political Attitudes: A Psychophysiological Examination of the Hot Cognition Hypothesis," *Political Psychology* 24, no. 4 (2003): 727–745. Notably, the IAT is not universally accepted by social psychologists as an accurate tool of describing unconscious attitudes. See Jesse Singal, "Psychology's Favorite Tool for Measuring Racism Isn't Up to the Job," *New York Magazine*, January 2017, https://www.thecut.com/2017/01/psychologys-racism-measuring-tool-isnt-up-to-the-job.html.

find the term pejorative while others find it is a badge of honor. Other debated terms within evangelical theology such as *Arminianism, Calvinism, Dispensationalism, postmillennialism, complementarianism, egalitarianism, theistic evolution,* and *young-earth creationism* might elicit similar automatic emotional responses. Many of the issues that we make litmus tests for orthodoxy—or at least for biblically faithful Christianity—are issues about which we have strong intuitive feelings.

Some of the controversy surrounding the resurgence of Calvinistic soteriology among millennial evangelicals may provide evidence for the claim that intuition precedes reason in the formation of theological beliefs. Those who embrace a Reformed or Calvinistic soteriology contend that God has all-determining influence over the minutia of everyday life, including the faith of the elect and the unbelief of the reprobate. The Calvinistic or Reformed camp seems most concerned to defend God's unrivaled sovereignty, believing that unrestrained human freedom somehow diminishes God's glory and power in the world. My Reformed students sometimes make emotional objections to their non-Calvinistic counterparts like this: "Those who reject the doctrines of grace [i.e., Calvinistic soteriological distinctives] are so man-centered in their thinking! They exalt themselves over God, making him hang on their every word!"

Conversely, those in the non-Reformed crowd who shudder at the thought of a God who purposes, without fail, to save some and damn others feel compelled to defend the universal love of God. From passages like 1 Timothy 2:4, they are convinced that God sincerely wants to save every single person from his or her sin and would do nothing to violate that individual's freedom to believe or disbelieve the gospel message. Each of these positions features emotional, admittedly non-rational objections to rival points of view. Both sides will try to make reasonable, persuasive cases for their respective positions, but they seem to *feel* deeply about the beliefs they aim to justify with rational support.

As Collin Hansen noticed in his acclaimed 2006 *Christianity Today* article, "Young, Restless, Reformed," the resurgence of Calvinistic soteriology among millennials did not begin with compelling rational or exegetical arguments, but with the ways in which leaders like pastor-theologian John Piper appealed to their emotions with "unrelenting intensity, demanding discipline, and singular passion—for the glory of God."[47] In his interview with Hansen, Piper himself acknowledged the primacy of emotions in making an appeal for Calvinistic doctrines: "They're not going to embrace your theology unless it makes their hearts sing."[48] The nonrational can have a powerful, persuasive effect, even in theological decision making. Piper's observation goes hand-in-hand with Haidt's notion that "if you want to change someone's mind about a moral or political issue, *talk to the elephant first.*"[49]

Those in the Calvinistic tradition are not the only ones who acknowledge the role nonrational factors such as emotion play in their doctrinal formation. As Roger Olson, a prominent Arminian theologian, somewhat reluctantly admits, his intuition about Reformed doctrines shapes his opinions about them:

> One day, at the end of a class session on Calvinism's doctrine of God's sovereignty, a student asked me a question that I had put off considering. He asked, "*If* it was revealed to you in a way you couldn't question or deny that the true God *actually is* as Calvinism says and *rules* as Calvinism affirms, would you still worship him?" I knew the only possible answer without a moment's thought, even though I knew it would shock many people. I said no, that I would not because I could not. Such a God would be a moral monster. Of course, I realize Calvinists do not *think* their view of God's sovereignty makes him a moral monster, but I can only conclude they have not thought it through to its logical conclusion or even taken sufficiently seriously the things they say about God and evil and innocent suffering in the world.[50]

When posed with the question of great theological and existential significance, Olson claims he "knew the only possible answer *without a moment's thought.*"[51] Like a flashing intuition, Olson reacted with

---

47. Collin Hansen, "Young, Restless, Reformed," *Christianity Today* (September 2006): 32. Hansen explored this issue in further detail in his monograph, *Young, Restless, Reformed: A Journalist's Journey with the New Calvinists* (Wheaton, IL: Crossway, 2008).

48. Hansen, "Young, Restless, Reformed," 35.

49. Haidt, *Righteous Mind*, 59.

50. Roger E. Olson, *Against Calvinism* (Grand Rapids, MI: Zondervan, 2011), 85, italics original.

51. Olson, *Against Calvinism*, 85, italics mine.

a gut feeling from which he proceeded to give reasons for why he felt so strongly about the matter. Olson unequivocally stated that, were it revealed to him that the true God is, in fact, the way Calvinists describe him, he could not willingly surrender himself in worship to this God because such a God is, in Olson's words, "a moral monster." Whereas Hansen describes individuals attracted to Calvinism because of an emotion like "passion" or "intensity," Olson feels sheer disgust for it. Whether doctrines "make . . . hearts sing" or turn our stomachs, they elicit emotional responses that can foster conscious agreement or disagreement.

We Have Different Tastes

The seminary where I teach has a wide array of students. While most if not all of the students with whom I regularly interact are confessing evangelicals who subscribe to the same core nexus of beliefs, they exhibit a wide range of theological and ministerial interests—an observation no doubt congruent with Paul's claim that "the body is one and has many members" (1 Cor. 12:12). Some focus on hands-on ministry projects like evangelism, counseling, or social work, while others gravitate toward preaching, teaching, and researching.

Even among the more cognitively oriented, classical discipline–focused students, the disparity of research interests is great. Some of the biblical studies students revel in the minutia of textual criticism or source criticism, while others appreciate the broader scope of subdisciplines like ancient Near Eastern history or biblical theology. In the small group of theology majors I supervise, I find diverse interests, with some students focusing on historical theology while others gravitate toward systematic or philosophical theology. Now and then, I have to intervene in somewhat esoteric disputes between my philosophical theology students who argue rather heatedly about which philosophical tradition—the rigorously precise analytic tradition or the more existentially oriented continental tradition—best serves the theological enterprise. Subject and procedural interests, even in closely related fields, are largely matters of taste or preference.

Educational psychologists have long observed the way learners gravitate toward one learning style or another, either *cognitive, af-*

fective, or *psychomotor* (practical).[52] The differences in taste between learning styles may explain some differences among theological preferences. We have long recognized that differences in taste are major factors in the choices of churches people attend, especially when worship styles are part of their consideration. The more practically inclined may gravitate toward a church that majors on personal evangelism or community service. The more cognitively inclined may seek out a doctrinally focused church. The emotionally inclined may look for a church that makes them feel like they have had an emotional high point in their week. The aesthetically focused are normally entranced by more liturgical worship styles.

Perhaps our diverse theological conclusions relate to taste or preference in a similar fashion. While we who are evangelicals would like to think we are drawing conclusions solely based on reflection on a particular text or group of texts, a nonrational factor like taste or preference may have a tremendous impact on our exegesis and doctrinal formulation. While theologians and biblical scholars rarely if ever treat this nonrational factor in their methodological discussions, moral philosophers and psychologists have long suggested that preferences shape our beliefs about morality and religion more than pure rational reflection alone.

Haidt, Hume, and Moral Taste Receptors

The philosopher David Hume argued that our moral beliefs begin not with reason but with something akin to "tastes," sentiments that are preferential to some and objectionable to others.[53] Haidt contends that the anthropological evidence of conflicting moral belief systems from across different cultures provides support for Hume's claim that moral beliefs are subjective to individual and cultural tastes.[54] Those who

---

52. For a Christian examination of Benjamin Bloom's taxonomy of learners, see William R. Yount, *Created to Learn: A Christian Teacher's Introduction to Educational Psychology* (Nashville: B&H Academic, 1996), 140–152.

53. In the first edition of the *Enquiry Concerning Human Understanding* (1748), Hume describes morality as "entirely relative to the Sentiment or mental taste of each particular being" (quoted in Haidt, *Righteous Mind*, 135).

54. Haidt, *Righteous Mind*, 119, 127, cf. 116–117. In his descriptive moral pluralism, Richard A. Shweder (b. 1945) identifies three competing moral matrices. First, he identifies an ethic of *autonomy* primarily rooted in individual rights. Second, he identifies an ethic of *community* based on the idea that human beings serve a purpose in the larger community around them. Finally, Shweder finds in cultures an ethic he labels an ethic of *divinity* rooted in the belief that persons

live in Western, highly educated, democratic cultures tend to prioritize personal autonomy and liberty in their assessment of what is right and wrong, while those living within Eastern cultures tend to eschew individualism because of the high value they place on relationships to family and community.[55]

While Haidt considers virtues to be social constructs rooted in one's cultural-historical context, he postulates innate moral "taste receptors" universal to every culture.[56] Every culture may have its own unique moral beliefs, but people from every culture share the same basic capacities for morality: *care, fairness, loyalty, authority, sanctity,* and *liberty*.[57] Haidt illustrates this moral taste analogy with the way in which human cultures across the world produce sweet beverages distinct to their region even though human beings have only one type of sweetness receptor.[58] In the same way that some people have more of a sweet tooth than others, or a greater appreciation for sour tastes, some people are wired with stronger fairness receptors or authority receptors. Moral beliefs develop in a culture when a moral receptor such as *care* is triggered by an issue in the cultural situation.

Though evangelicals will be skeptical of the neo-Darwinist assumptions behind Haidt's description of these moral receptors, the notion of universal moral receptors goes hand in hand with C. S. Lewis's description of the "law of human nature."[59] Men and women have strong moral proclivities endued to them by their Creator, even though they have a wide array of culturally influenced moral codes. As Lewis explained, "Men have differed as regards what people you ought to be unselfish to—whether it was only your own family, or your fellow countrymen, or every one. But they have always agreed that you ought not to put yourself first. Selfishness has never been admired. Men have differed as to whether you should have one wife or four. But they have

are made by God, who has certain requirements or expectations of their behavior. See Richard A. Shweder, "In Defense of Moral Realism: Reply to Gabennesch," *Child Development* 61 (1990): 2060–2067; Richard A. Shweder, Nancy C. Much, Monamohan Mahapatra, and Lawrence Park, "The 'Big Three' of Morality (Autonomy, Community, and Divinity), and the 'Big Three' Explanations of Suffering," in *Morality and Health*, ed. Allan M. Brandt and Paul Rozin (New York: Routledge, 1997), 119–172.

55. Haidt, *Righteous Mind*, 112–113.
56. Haidt, *Righteous Mind*, 142–143.
57. Haidt, *Righteous Mind*, 146, 150–179, 197–205.
58. Haidt, *Righteous Mind*, 145.
59. C. S. Lewis, *Mere Christianity* (New York: HarperOne, 2001), 3–8.

always agreed that you must not simply have any woman you liked."[60] If human beings have a moral compass, it is not the product of chance and time but the design of a God who has written the law on their hearts (Rom. 2:13–16).

Moral receptors play a crucial role in Haidt's differentiation of the competing moral matrices of political conservatives and liberals. While conservatives and liberals share the same innate receptors, they differ on what current triggers evoke their socially constructed virtues. Haidt identifies the *sanctity* receptor that evolved to avoid contamination as essential to Christian objections to sexual immorality, but the same innate receptor, though evoked by very different triggers, drives concerns about environmental pollution on the left.[61] The same fairness receptor that drives the political left to fight for social equality drives those on the right to fight for rewards proportionate to what a person contributes to society (contra socialism).[62] Those on the right find those on the left to be immoral, and vice versa, because of seemingly incommensurable moral taste buds. Haidt alleges political conservatives have an evolutionary advantage because they tend to trigger moral receptors such as loyalty and authority often ignored by the political left.[63]

In a 2009 study, Haidt and his team compiled a long list of words related to each moral receptor and ran a program called LIWC (Linguistic Inquiry and Word Count) and compared the word lists with dozens of sermons from theologically conservative and theologically liberal churches. They used sermon manuscripts and transcripts from Unitarian Universalist churches to represent the liberal group and sermons from Southern Baptist churches to represent the conservative churches.[64] As Haidt and his team expected, the study showed that theologically liberal churches emphasized the care and fairness receptors more than did their conservative counterparts and theologically conservative churches put greater stress on loyalty, authority, and sanctity receptors.[65] This latter

---

60. Lewis, *Mere Christianity*, 6.

61. Haidt, *Righteous Mind*, 175–176.

62. Haidt, *Righteous Mind*, 160–161.

63. Haidt, *Righteous Mind*, 211–214.

64. Jesse Graham, Jonathan Haidt, and Brian A. Nosek, "Liberals and Conservatives Rely on Different Sets of Moral Foundations," *Journal of Personality and Social Psychology* 96 (2009): 1030–1040.

65. Haidt, *Righteous Mind*, 188; cf. Graham, Haidt, and Nosek, "Liberals and Conservatives Rely on Different Sets of Moral Foundations," 1039.

observation comes as no surprise given the evangelical inclination to cite biblical authority—not experience—as the principal guide in debates over sexual ethics or abortion.

Something akin to Haidt's moral receptor paradigm may also shed light on some intramural theological debates. Some find themselves attracted to "social justice" issues (out of a strong *care* receptor?) while others abhor them (perhaps because of a strong *fairness* receptor). It is at least conceivable that something like a strong *liberty* receptor triggers a negative response in the Arminian theologian when he hears the doctrine of unconditional election or that a strong *authority* receptor pushes the Calvinist to embrace it. Something akin to the *fairness* receptor may influence one's decision to take up an egalitarian position in the gender debate, while a *sanctity* receptor may shape a complementarian position. These are only hypothetical suggestions, but we have all seen Christians with strong senses of right and wrong react in various ways to an array of ethical and theological dilemmas.

The Source of Theological Tastes

How might precritical theological tastes akin to these moral receptors develop? In previous generations, psychologists under the influence of Freud's theories related religious belief formation to formative identity crises in early life. In his seminal work, *Young Man Luther*, developmental psychologist Erik Erikson used Martin Luther as a test case for applying Freudian psychoanalysis to significant figures in history. Erikson suggested that Luther's doctrines of both sin and faith were related to the tumultuous relationship he had with his father, Hans Luther.[66] Theologians, church historians, and psychoanalysts have leveled heavy criticisms at Erikson's representation of Luther, citing historical inaccuracies, theological superficiality, and frustrations with the method of psychoanalyzing a long-dead person unavailable for an interview.[67] Still, the science behind our beliefs (and our reactions to the beliefs of others) remains a mystery.

---

66. Erik H. Erikson, *Young Man Luther: A Study in Psychoanalysis and History* (New York: Norton, 1958).

67. See Roger A. Johnson, ed. *Psychohistory and Religion: The Case of Young Man Luther* (Philadelphia: Fortress, 1977).

Another possible explanation may be in the distinction psychiatrist Ana-Maria Rizzuto makes between *God concepts* and *God-images*. According to Rizzuto, God concepts are the products of careful critical analysis in theology and philosophy of religion. God concepts are essentially doctrines explicitly taught by a church or religious organization. God-images, conversely, are precognitive psychological impressions of what one imagines God to be like that take their shape from parental influence and self-image.[68]

Some studies have shown a correlation between personality traits and God images,[69] possibly meaning that personality traits can play a role in theological perspectives. A positive mental representation of a parent can lead to a positive image of God, and a negative image of parents can lead to a negative God-image. Some studies even show that negative parent images associated with negative God-images later can lead to atheistic God concepts.[70] But these parent images are not sole determinants of God-images, since the parent images "can be reversed, or substituted for, or subjected to any of a whole host of defense mechanisms on the way to becoming a God image."[71] Most important for the present discussion, Rizzuto insists that these emotional, preconscious God-images are a necessary precursor to emotional acceptance of these conscious God concepts.[72] In other words, these intuitive, emotional impressions of God can precede conscious and critical theological concepts of God.

Contrary to Rizzuto, and perhaps by extension Haidt, intuitive theological tastes or God-images are not sole determinants of theological concepts. In a recent study by Amy Morgan that began as an assessment of how negative childhood experiences might shape the

---

68. Ana-Maria Rizzuto, *The Birth of the Living God: A Psychoanalytic Study* (Chicago: University of Chicago Press, 1979), 48–51.

69. See Hanneke Schaap-Jonker, Elisabeth Eurelings-Bontekoe, Piet J. Verhagen, and Hetty Zock, "Image of God and Personality Pathology: An Exploratory Study among Psychiatric Patients," *Mental Health, Religion, and Culture* 5 (2002): 55–71; Linda M. Abdelsayed, Joy M. Bustrum, Theresa Clement Tisdale, Kevin S. Reimer, and Claire Allan Camp, "The Impact of Personality on God Image, Religious Coping, and Religious Motivation among Coptic Orthodox Priests," *Mental Health, Religion, and Culture* 16 (2013): 155–172.

70. See Paul C. Vitz, *Faith of the Fatherless: The Psychology of Atheism*, 2nd ed. (San Francisco: Ignatius, 2013).

71. Richard T. Lawrence, "Measuring the Image of God: The God Image Inventory and the God Image Scales," *Journal of Psychology and Theology* 25, no. 2 (1997): 215.

72. Rizzuto, *Birth of the Living God*, 48.

God-images of evangelical Christians, the data showed that among evangelicals, *Christian teaching* was ultimately a stronger influence on a person's personal feelings of God's presence, acceptance, and challenge *than life experience*.[73] This is good news for Christian disciple makers! We may have intuitions and inclinations that form our initial beliefs or preunderstandings of Scripture, but they can be retrained or corrected. Worldviews are not immutable. If they were, the gospel message would never bear real fruit among those who were not born into homes predisposed to a Christian worldview.

The belief that some choose to feel differently about God by following instruction about God seems to indicate that emotions are not simply passive physiological reactions to internal bodily forces or external social forces. In the Christian tradition, Augustine, Thomas Aquinas, Jonathan Edwards, and others have distinguished between *passions*, those involuntary and passive bodily reactions to outside forces, and *affections*, active and voluntary feelings that follow reason and the will. Passions were treated with disdain because of their assault on reason and because of their association with sin. Affections, by contrast, are God-honoring feelings that flow out of reason and choice. Only in modernism was the distinction between passion and affection amalgamated in the singular concept of *emotions*.[74] Christians must refuse slavery to our passions (Rom. 6:12; 7:5; Eph. 2:3) and grow in our affections toward God and one another (Phil. 1:8; 1 Thess. 2:8; 2 Pet. 1:7).

To return to Haidt's metaphor of tastes, it may very well be the case that we have certain emotional reactions that drive our reactions to different theological positions. But these reactions are not *causes* of belief; they are *motives* of belief trained by our minds and our wills. These moral and theological tastes are fed by choices of the mind and can be starved in the same manner. For this reason, the apostle Paul encouraged conscious dwelling or reflection on "excellent and praiseworthy" things (see Phil. 4:8). Such thoughts free the believer from anxiety (v. 6) and fill him with peace and guard his heart and mind (v. 7).

---

73. See Amy C. Morgan, "The Impact of Adverse Childhood Experiences on God Images" (PhD diss., New Orleans Baptist Theological Seminary, 2017), 89.

74. Kevin J. Vanhoozer, *Remythologizing Theology: Divine Action, Passion, and Authorship* (New York: Cambridge University Press, 2012), 400–404.

Tribes, Groupthink, and Solidarity

Biblical scholars and theologians have long recognized that time, place, and tradition can have distorting (or enhancing) effects on an individual's reading of the Bible. Often the sorts of interpretive distortions associated with traditions are products of irrational thinking, such as special pleading, question-begging, and genetic fallacies.[75] All these are *irrational* ways tradition can distort interpretation, but some interpretive distortions caused by tradition may be the result of automatic, *nonrational* processes.

Haidt's principle that "morality binds and blinds" may shed some light on the nonrational factors at work in this hermeneutical concept. Haidt suggests that we live in "hives," and our moral systems and sense of moral reasoning take their shape from this group or hive interaction. As Haidt explains, human beings are *"groupish"* and hardwired in the brain in such a way that they are attracted to being part of a team, a political group, or a religion.[76] In sum, this principle means that once people make an intuitive decision about right and wrong—something based largely on their moral taste receptors—they attach themselves to a group of like-minded individuals. They attach themselves to a tribe, a group, or a hive. They buy into a "shared moral narrative" which makes it difficult for them to see or perceive alternative moral explanations.[77]

A pro-choice feminist may get a sense of belonging in a tribe of fellow "patriarchy-smashers," and with it a strong sense of the moral uprightness of her cause. With her group identity, she finds a common enemy in those who disagree with her beliefs. She finds the "anti-choice" (or alternatively, the "pro-life") position a repulsive invention of white men trying to control her body. She cannot grasp the "anti-science," "anti-women" anti-abortion position. This binding and blinding happens in part because she has a particular moral taste that shapes her outlook on the matter (such as "fairness" to women),

---

75. *Special pleading* occurs in biblical interpretation when one applies certain criteria to another interpreter but inexplicably does not make the same application to her own interpretation. Interpreters *beg the question* when they assert the meaning of a text rather than give sufficient reasons for considering that meaning. Theologians commit the *genetic fallacy* when they dismiss an idea out of hand simply because of negative associations with the person or school of thought from whom it came.

76. Haidt, *Righteous Mind*, 221.

77. Haidt, *Righteous Mind*, xxiii.

but also because she receives emotional satisfaction from being part of a movement or cause larger than herself. (The latter is also true for her pro-life counterpart.) Tribe membership is both cathartic and empowering.

Group association might have psychological benefits, but it can be detrimental to the pursuit of truth. As Haidt remarks, "We can believe almost anything that supports our team."[78] The Yale research psychologist Irving Janis made a similar observation in his detailed study of a phenomenon he dubbed "groupthink."[79] Janis developed this idea in his study of the decision making bodies involved in some of the major political and military fiascoes of the twentieth century, but groupthink could also explain why European nations turned a blind eye to the genocide of the Holocaust or why hundreds would drink poisoned Kool-Aid in Jonestown.[80]

According to Janis, groupthinkers rationalize poor decisions and discount information contrary to their key beliefs. They are firmly convinced in the morality of their corporate cause, even if there are people from other groups who call their activity evil. They stereotype their opponents as evil or stupid. (Think of the Facebook memes produced by both sides of any major political debate.) Groupthinkers enforce loyalty by putting pressure on any member who would doubt their beliefs, and consequently, members of the group censor themselves from expressing doubts or counterarguments. Janis also observed the emergence of "mindguards" who protect the group from contrary beliefs or information that might affect their decision making.[81] Because we receive emotional and psychological benefits from a group dynamic, we sometimes prefer an echo chamber to critical thinking.

We encounter this sort of "groupish" rationalization and self-censorship almost every day in social media, where persons on both the

---

78. Haidt, *Righteous Mind*, 100.

79. See Irving L. Janis, *Victims of Groupthink: A Psychological Study of Foreign Policy Decisions and Fiascoes* (New York: Houghton Mifflin, 1972); Janis, *Groupthink: Psychological Studies of Policy Decisions and Fiascoes*, 2nd ed. (New York: Houghton Mifflin, 1982).

80. Ramon Aldag and Sally Riggs Fuller question many of Janis's assumptions and contend that group-based problem solving has greater value than he recognizes. See Aldag and Fuller, "Beyond Fiasco: A Reappraisal of Groupthink Phenomenon and a New Model of Group Decision Processes," *Psychological Bulletin* 113, no. 3 (1993): 533–352.

81. Irving L. Janis and Leon Mann, *Decision Making: A Psychological Analysis of Conflict, Choice, and Commitment* (New York: Free Press, 1977), 130–131.

left and right sides of the political spectrum will post articles that make their favorite candidates look good and demonize their opponents. Social media users are quick to re-post or "re-tweet" these articles, frequently before they have read them closely or given adequate attention to verifying their contents. Sometimes we want to convince others of our points of view, but other times we just seek praise from people who share our beliefs. Unfortunately, groupthink can have the same sort of distorting effect in theology. As evangelical Protestants committed above all to the supreme authority of Scripture, we recognize the possibility that tradition—however helpful it may be in shaping us as believers—is not beyond revision or correction. I will explore this theme further in the next chapter.

Emotional Creatures under Biblical Authority

This chapter has explored, but not exhausted, possible nonrational or psychological factors at work in the disagreement between otherwise like-minded Christian believers. Because human beings are complex creatures with reason, will, and emotion, no reductionistic scheme that pigeonholes us as purely intuitive or purely rational beings can explain why we reason or why we dissent the way we do. Insights from neuroscience and social psychology, such as Haidt's social intuitionist model of moral psychology, may aid in explaining the nonrational dimension of beliefs and disagreement. Nevertheless, Haidt's model, built on neo-Darwinian and naturalistic assumptions, invites some critical assessment informed by Scripture and Christian tradition.

First, God created human beings with reason indivisible from emotion. While Plato understands emotions as a necessary evil tied to human embodiment, and Descartes understands them as something to be doubted and tamed, Scripture presents reason and emotion as inseparably linked gifts from God. The Hebrew term *lev* (most frequently translated "heart") is a "comprehensive term for the personality as a whole, its inner life, its character."[82] The Greek term for the heart used in both the Septuagint and the New Testament, *kardia*,

---

82. Walter Eichrodt, *Theology of the Old Testament*, vol. 2, trans. J. A. Baker (Louisville: Westminster, 1967), 143.

speaks to the inseparable yet distinguishable relationship of reason, emotion, and volition. The term describes the "inner life, the center of the personality, and the place in which God reveals himself to human beings."[83] Biblical authors use these terms to describe the way people reason (Judg. 5:15; Ps. 74:8; Prov. 2:2, 10; Luke 5:22), feel gladness and joy (Judg. 16:25; Ruth 3:7; Est. 5:9; Pss. 16:9; 19:8; Prov. 15:13), feel distress (Pss. 22:14; 55:4; Nah. 2:10), desire (Pss. 10:3; 37:4), worship (Pss. 28:7; 33:1), trust (Prov. 3:5; 31:11), hate (1 Chron. 15:29), do good (Ps. 32:11), and do evil (Pss. 36:1; 140:2; Zeph. 1:12; Zech. 8:10; Rom. 2:25). It is with the heart that people chose to obey or disobey the Lord (Mal. 2:2; Rom. 10:10). The Bible does not compartmentalize emotion and reason in its treatment of human decision making and behavior.

Christian tradition likewise affirms the complex relationship between reason and emotion. The rejection of human beings as purely rational beings in Haidt's social intuitionism closely parallels a stream of Christian theological anthropology going back to Augustine that envisions human beings as "fundamentally oriented and identified by love."[84] According to James K. A. Smith, Augustine views human beings as "fundamentally noncognitive, affective creatures"[85] who "make their way through the world by feeling [their] way around it."[86] Haidt and Augustine both agree that we *feel* around our world before we reason about it.[87]

Second, emotion plays a vital role in Christian experience. Emotion can reinforce the reasonable truths of Scripture and theology by making them personal. As John Wesley describes his own conversion experience, "I felt my heart strangely warmed. I felt I did trust in Christ, Christ alone for salvation. And an assurance was given me, that he had taken away *my* sins, even mine, and saved me from the law of sin and death."[88] With the God-given gifts of

---

83. Καρδία, in *NIDNTTE* 2:625.

84. James K. A. Smith, *Desiring the Kingdom: Worship, Worldview, and Cultural Formation*, Cultural Liturgies, vol. 1 (Grand Rapids, MI: Baker, 2009), 46.

85. Smith, *Desiring the Kingdom*, 53.

86. Smith, *Desiring the Kingdom*, 47.

87. Smith, *Desiring the Kingdom*, 47–52; Haidt, *Righteous Mind*, 48–52

88. *The Journal of John Wesley*, May 24, 1738; quoted in Thomas C. Oden, *John Wesley's Teachings*, vol. 1, *God and Providence* (Grand Rapids, MI: Zondervan, 2012), 112.

emotion and experience, we can move from orthodoxy (right thinking about God) to doxology (the praise of God). These emotions
are what theologians consider *affections* trained by reason, not
passions of the flesh.

Third, emotions alone are incapable of producing genuine faith.
Wesley writes extensively about a type of irrational enthusiasm that
prioritizes excessive emotional experience over the reasonable interpretation of Scripture. This enthusiastic impulse eschews reason in
favor of heightened emotions and religious experience. Wesley insists
that this is "some falsely imagined influence or inspiration of God
. . . from imputing something to God which ought not to be imputed
to him, or expecting something from God which ought not to be expected from him."[89] In other words, emotional experiences alone are
an insufficient foundation for Christian living. While emotions can
confirm scriptural truth, they are no replacement for it.

*Fourth, Scripture teaches that sin can distort our emotions and
intuitions, and as a result, our beliefs.* Intuitions normally precede
conscious reasoning, and they can be helpful guides. Because we live
in a world broken by sin and wrestle with a flesh opposed to the things
of God, we should be wary of always following our passions. "There
is a way that seems right" to naturally selfish human beings but "its
end is the way to death" (Prov. 14:12). People devise evil and violence
in their hearts and minds contrary to God's design and purpose (Ps.
140:2). Sin darkens the mind with its noetic effects and can create
distorting biases against biblical truth.

The human heart (i.e., the complex relationship between reason,
will, and emotion) can deceive because of its inclination toward wick-
edness (Jer. 17:9; Obad. 3). Sin has noetic effects on the reasoning
faculty of human beings. Self-rationalization of sinful behavior is
an ever-present temptation (1 John 1:10). Calvin says that sin has
corrupted emotions, and this corruption of the emotions extends to
reason: "For not only did a lower appetite seduce [Adam], but un-
speakable impiety occupied the very citadel of his mind, and pride
penetrated the depths of his heart. Thus it is pointless and foolish to

---

89. John Wesley, "The Nature of Enthusiasm," quoted in Oden, *John Wesley's Teachings,*
vol. 1, 117.

restrict the corruption that arises thence only to what are called impulses of the senses."[90] The real danger of a theological system rooted
only in one's personal feelings is that it becomes a shortcut to recreat-
ing gods in our own image. Though we recognize the impact of emotions on our beliefs on an unconscious level—we *describe* it as being
the case—we do not *prescribe* theology driven solely by one's feelings.

*Fifth, we should be wary of irrational emotional responses in the
heat of debate.* Because we are creatures affected by sin, we can be victims of our own unrestrained passions, especially amid conflict. Out
of insecurity, pride, or fear we can overreact to those who challenge
or criticize our points of view. We become irrational when we choose
to attack the person rather than the idea. Irrationality also leads us to
hasty decision making, and as we shall see, patience is an intellectual
virtue much needed in theological disagreements. With disagreements,
there is a time to respond, and there is also a time to back up and let
things breathe.

*Sixth, psychological and emotional factors can influence—but do
not determine—our rational beliefs.* Though I suspect intuitions and
emotions are at work in our belief formation and doctrinal development, I want to reject a kind of doxastic determinism that says our
automatic intuitions *determine* all of our beliefs and reasoning. Such a
notion is incompatible with traditional Christian beliefs about human
freedom and volition. Intuitions have a strong influence on our reasoning processes but not an inescapable influence. The frustration
experienced by some when they discover a conflict between their unconscious attitudes and explicitly held values illustrates that people are
at least capable of *desiring* to overcome these intuitions.[91]

*Seventh, other nonrational, precritical tastes or preferences can
color interpretation.* For example, *neophilia*, a psychological preference for the new or the novel, can shape the outcome of interpretation.
Biblical studies students in search of thesis or dissertation topics feel
the pressure to discover "new perspectives" on ancient texts, as do
established scholars seeking tenure or publication. Theological *obscu-
rantism*, by contrast, is a preference for tradition that is suspicious of

---

90. John Calvin, *Institutes of the Christian Religion*, 2.1.9.
91. Banaji and Greenwald, *Blind Spot*, 41–47, cf. 53–70.

any or all newfound explanations of biblical texts.[92] Sociologists also observe how some religious ideas gain traction simply because they *deviate* from commonly held beliefs, interests, and lifestyles, particularly those commonly held beliefs which seem to present ongoing problems in a cultural context.[93]

Eighth, the mere recognition of a plurality of moral and interpretive intuitions does not entail normative hermeneutical relativism—the idea that all interpretations are equally valid or sound. Anthropological evidence of contradictory moral systems leads Haidt to affirm a kind of *descriptive moral pluralism*. He is careful to point out that he does not affirm a normative moral relativism—the idea that "all moral visions are equally good"—but his descriptive moral pluralism does point out ways in which various cultures seem to have moral matrices that cannot be compared because of their radically diverse starting points. The atheism presumed in Haidt's program prevents him from acknowledging an objective moral law writ large in the created order, but the Christian worldview says otherwise. The fact that men do what is right in their own eyes (Judg. 17:6; 21:25) does not mean they have no King.

Diverse interpretations of Scripture similarly indicate a *descriptive hermeneutical pluralism*—a mere observation of multiple ways people have interpreted biblical texts—but the inevitability of conflicting interpretations does not entail that all interpretations are true or equally valid approaches to biblical texts or that biblical authors wrote without any discernible meaning or purpose. Divinely inspired biblical writers write with intentions that interpreters should seek to make sense of and respond to appropriately. But, as Kevin Vanhoozer has contended, hermeneutical pluralism can be beneficial to the body of Christ when it increases the probability of understanding texts correctly.[94]

---

92. M. James Sawyer, *The Survivor's Guide to Theology: Investigation of the Critical Issues, Survey of Key Traditions, Biography of Major Theologians, Glossary of Terms* (Grand Rapids, MI: Zondervan, 2006), 190–192.

93. New Testament scholars have applied deviance theory to the formation of early Christianity. See John M. G. Barclay, "Deviance and Apostasy: Some Applications of Deviance Theory to First-Century Judaism and Christianity," in *Modelling Early Christianity: Social-Scientific Studies of the New Testament in Its Context*, ed. Philip F. Esler (New York: Routledge, 1995), 114–127; Ekkehard W. Stegemann and Wolfgang Stegemann, *The Jesus Movement: A Social History of the First Century* (Minneapolis: Fortress, 1999), 151–157.

94. See Kevin J. Vanhoozer, *The Drama of Doctrine* (Louisville: Westminster/John Knox, 2005), 274–275; Vanhoozer, *Is There a Meaning in This Text?* (Grand Rapids, MI: Zondervan, 1998), 419–420.

Finally, the Christian believer must ultimately submit his or her emotions to the authority of Scripture and the lordship of Christ. Were someone to put me on truth serum, I would have to admit that some traditional Christian doctrines, such as the doctrine of everlasting punishment or the exclusivity of the Christian gospel, make me *feel* uneasy.[95] This comes as no surprise, given what the Bible says about my depravity and my need for the gospel. Regardless of how I feel about these matters, at the end of the day I want to submit myself to God's authority expressed through the biblical text.

If I have an intuition about a biblical passage that leads me to a particular doctrinal belief, I still must place that intuition under Christ's lordship and biblical authority. My trust is in the person and work of Christ, not in my ability to fully comprehend the person and work of Christ. I must practice epistemic humility and emotional maturity. If my intuition is wrong, I want the Holy Spirit to make that apparent to me, or at least prevent me from sinfully applying my incorrect interpretation. My goal in reading the text should never be to find a reading I'm comfortable with emotionally. My goal is not to be "conformed to this world" or even my present state of mind, but to experience transformation through the renewal of my mind in order that I may "discern what is the will of God, what is good and acceptable and perfect" (Rom. 12:2).

---

95. Several key texts are used in support of a doctrine of eternal punishment: Isaiah 66:22–24; Daniel 12:2; Matthew 18:8; 2 Thessalonians 5:9; Jude 13; Revelation 14:9–11; 20:10.

5

We Have Different Biases

Tradition, Belief, and Confirmation Bias

Differences in the way individuals feel, reason, and read Scripture are major contributing factors to our doctrinal diversity, but it would be misleading to suggest that the theological enterprise is merely an exchange of our personal interpretations of the Bible. Theology is, after all, a *communal activity* rooted in local churches, denominations, and the broader faith "believed everywhere, always, by all."[1] This passing on of the Christian message from one person or group of persons to another is what the New Testament calls *tradition (paradosis)*.

We cannot escape tradition. Unless we have a Damascus Road–like experience, our first encounter with the good news of Jesus usually comes through someone else: a pastor, an evangelist, a teacher, a family member, a friend, or a coworker.[2] Whatever the setting, whatever the context, someone *explained* the gospel to us (e.g., Col. 1:6–7). Without these disciple makers, we might be like the Ethiopian eunuch, struggling to make sense of how the puzzle pieces of biblical narrative, epistle, poetry, prophecy, and law fit together. But we have

---

1. Vincent of Lérins, *The Commonitory* 2.6; NPNF[2] 11:132.
2. Even though Saul of Tarsus had a direct encounter with Jesus (Acts 9:1–11) and "received [the gospel] through a revelation of Jesus Christ" and no human teaching (Gal. 1:12), he acknowledged the role tradition had in shaping his former life in Judaism (Gal. 1:13–14; cf. Acts 22:3) and the message he "delivered" to the churches (1 Cor. 15:3).

been blessed with those like Philip who came alongside us, helping us see the grand narrative of redemption sown from Genesis to Revelation (see Acts 8:26–40).

Though the term *tradition* occasionally connotes something negative in Scripture (Matt. 15:2–3, 6; Mark 7:9; Col. 2:8), it can also positively describe the transmission of Christian revelation and its interpretation (1 Cor. 11:2; 2 Thess. 2:15; 3:6). Paul himself insisted that the gospel he "handed over" (*paradidōmi*) was the same apostolic tradition he "received" (*parelabon*; 1 Cor. 15:3ff.).[3] In the broader historical sense of the word, tradition is the total depository of Christian knowledge, belief, and custom throughout time and space, including the Bible itself. In a more narrow theological sense, tradition refers to the ever-expanding collection of Christian teaching based on the Bible.[4]

Early Christian creeds were explanations of Scripture that developed mostly in response to the heresies faced by the church. They provided "guardrails" by which Christians read the Bible. Later confessions like the Augsburg Confession, the Westminster Confession, the Second London Baptist Confession, and the United Methodist Confession of Faith arose out of the need for particular Christian groups to give verbal expression to their unique theological identities. Contemporary confessions like the Baptist Faith and Message 2000 give theological parameters for denominational affiliation and organization. Some confessions, like the Westminster Confession, make very specific statements about what their tradition teaches (in this case, Reformed theology). The Westminster divines took a very clear stance on debated theological matters such as divine simplicity.[5] Other confessions, such as the Baptist Faith and Message, are much broader and can describe a number of different soteriological perspectives within the broader Baptist family.

In its ongoing development, the Christian tradition has flourished at times and floundered at others. It continues to grow with new theological treatises, sermons, and even the occasional combative blog post. Along the way, some theologians have made explicit the beliefs

---

3. This term is also related to the Hebrew *leqach*, which literally means "something received" but is often translated "teaching" or "doctrine" (e.g., Deut. 32:2; Job 11:4; Prov. 4:2; Isa. 29:24).
4. See Michael F. Bird, *What Christians Ought to Believe: An Introduction to Christian Doctrine through the Apostle's Creed* (Grand Rapids, MI: Zondervan, 2016), 29–42.
5. The Westminster Confession of Faith 2.1.

implicit in Scripture. At other times, believers have needed to formulate new answers—new applications of biblical teaching—to the
particular doctrinal, social, and ethical challenges unique to their day.[6]

Many theologians in Roman Catholic and Eastern Orthodox traditions venerate church teaching to the level of being co-authoritative with
Scripture, insisting that Scripture is in need of the Church as its interpreter. For many within these traditions, this authoritative church teaching also includes apostolic folklore, Christian pseudepigrapha, ecclesial
histories, hagiographies, and "revelations" of new details and facts not
disclosed in the books of the Old and New Testaments.[7] Protestants and
evangelicals have shown great appreciation for forms of tradition that
explain the teaching of Scripture but great resistance to forms of tradition like these that would add to its substantial meaning. Though they
have argued for the clarity of Scripture, they have recognized the value
of tradition as an aid to interpretation. As Wesley explains,

> The Scriptures are a complete rule of faith and practice; and they
> are clear in all necessary points. And yet their clearness does not
> prove that they need not be explained; nor their completeness, that
> they need not be enforced. . . . Esteeming the writings of the first
> three centuries, not equally with, but next to, the Scriptures, never
> carried any man yet into dangerous errors, nor probably ever will.[8]

As valuable as the tradition can be in helping readers find their footing
in Scripture, it does not have the same final authority as the Bible itself.
Creeds, confessions, councils, and various theological works written
throughout history are open to revision and criticism because of the
interpretive fallibility of their authors.

Whereas theologians in some traditions err in over-venerating tradition, some theologians in other camps fail to see its importance or
impact on their own projects. Enlightenment theologians elevated
reason and experience over the external authorities of Scripture and

---

6. See Rhyne R. Putman, *In Defense of Doctrine: Evangelicalism, Theology, and Scripture* (Minneapolis: Fortress, 2015).

7. Heiko Oberman calls this type of tradition "Tradition II." See his *Forerunners of the Ref-ormation: The Shape of Late Medieval Thought* (New York: Holt, Rinehart, & Winston, 1966), 54–56, 58–60, 72–73.

8. John Wesley, "Letter to the Rev. Dr. Conyers Middleton (January 4, 1749)," quoted in Thomas C. Oden, *John Wesley's Teachings*, vol. 1, *God and Providence* (Grand Rapids, MI: Zondervan, 2012), 86.

tradition. They envisioned theology as an autonomous exercise best performed by individual thinkers freed to think without the constraints of other opinions. However, this total rejection of tradition, what philosopher Hans-Georg Gadamer called "prejudice against prejudice itself," is self-defeating and internally incoherent.[9] Reason, experience, and language are shaped by the individual's time and place in history and her most fundamental assumptions about reality. Our inevitable place in tradition means that there is no neutral starting point for doing theology.

The ability to understand the authorial intention of Scripture can be distorted by our tradition as well. In the words of the late hermeneutics scholar Grant Osborne, "We rarely read the Bible to discover truth; more often, we wish to harmonize it with our belief system and see its meaning in light of our preconceived theological system."[10] Or, more lyrically put, "Wonderful things in the Bible I see, most of them put there by you and me."[11] Interpreters can and frequently do read their Bibles with the intention of proving the teaching of their theological tradition true rather than giving an honest assessment of the text's meaning and purpose. While interpreters do not read texts without presuppositions, they should strive to be aware of them.

Have you ever gone to a biblical text *hoping to find support* for a theological position to which you already subscribed? I know I have. Before I darkened the door of a hermeneutics classroom—before I knew the difference between *exegesis*, *eisegesis*, and *extra-Jesus*—I tended to *use*—or rather, *abuse*—the Bible in personal debates. Whether I was arguing for the correctness of my theological tradition, defending a personal behavior or ethical standard, or sometimes even trying to manipulate a particular social situation, I had a knack for opening Scripture and finding just the answer I was looking for. I would like to think that, with spiritual maturity and a much better grasp of biblical backgrounds, languages, and interpretation, I have improved upon this tendency, but I also know that even with the

---

9. Hans-Georg Gadamer, *Truth and Method*, rev. ed., trans. Joel Weinsheimer and Donald G. Marshall (New York: Continuum, 2004), 272–273.

10. Grant R. Osborne, *The Hermeneutical Spiral: A Comprehensive Introduction to Biblical Interpretation*, rev. ed. (Downers Grove, IL: InterVarsity Press, 2006), 29; cf. 467.

11. William W. Klein, Craig L. Blomberg, and Robert L. Hubbard Jr., *Introduction to Biblical Interpretation*, 3rd ed. (Grand Rapids, MI: Zondervan, 2017), 44.

training I now marshal, I am not above traditional bias that hinders correct interpretation.

Researchers in the area of human cognition have shown that people in a wide array of fields trying to make judgments or decisions based on evidence are prone to a type of bias of which they are not aware—a type of bias "partial to existing beliefs, expectations, or a hypothesis in hand."[12] This phenomenon, which researchers call *confirmation bias*, is "the tendency to bolster a hypothesis by seeking consistent evidence while minimizing inconsistent evidence."[13] People work with a confirmation bias when they test their hypothesis only in ways that will support it and overlook information that does not support their bias.[14]

Research on confirmation bias shows that once a person "has taken a position on an issue, one's primary purpose becomes that of defending or justifying that position."[15] Natural scientists, psychologists, social scientists, and criminologists have explored the various ways in which confirmation bias hinders research in their respective fields. This chapter is an examination of the way in which our respective faith traditions can color, shape, or distort our theological disagreements, highlighting the way confirmation bias toward a particular theological tradition can shape the outcomes of our interpretations of Scripture.

In this chapter, I argue (1) there is evidence of confirmation bias in routine theological procedures like exegesis and proof-texting. Our faith tradition—either the one into which we are born or the first one we "make our own" as we mature—can foster this bias. Biblical interpreters are often less interested in the truth and more interested in justifying their own theological tradition or beliefs. I also acknowledge, with many psychological researchers, that (2) there are helpful procedures that can reduce or minimize the effects of confirmation

---

12. Raymond S. Nickerson, "Confirmation Bias: A Ubiquitous Phenomenon in Many Guises," *Review of General Psychology* 2, no. 2 (1998): 175. Though the designation of *confirmation bias* dates back to the work of Peter C. Wason in the 1960s, the phenomenon has been recognized much longer. Nickerson finds this recognition in Francis Bacon's *Novum Organum* (1620). See Nickerson, "Confirmation Bias," 176.

13. Barbara M. O'Brien, "Prime Suspect: An Examination of Factors that Aggravate and Counteract Confirmation Bias in Criminal Investigations," *Psychology, Public Policy, and Law* 15, no. 4 (2009): 315.

14. Barbara M. O'Brien, "Confirmation Bias in Criminal Investigations: An Examination of the Factors That Aggravate and Counteract Bias," PhD diss. (University of Michigan, 2007), 4.

15. Nickerson, "Confirmation Bias," 177.

bias in research. I will apply some of these procedures to tradition and theological method—such as giving deliberate attention to counterexamples and counterhypotheses—and offer some other proposals of my own.

Motivated and Unmotivated Biases

Confirmation bias plays a big role in every area of human life, every branch of human learning. Research psychologist Raymond Nickerson boldly suggests that if someone "were to attempt to identify a single problematic aspect of human reasoning that deserves attention above all others, the *confirmation bias* would have to be among the candidates for consideration."[16] He further speculates that this type of bias "by itself, might account for a significant fraction of the disputes, altercations, and misunderstandings that occur among individuals, groups, and nations."[17] Consequently, awareness of confirmation bias may help us better understand and advise interpretive and doctrinal diversity among us.

Though this type of bias may hinder the pursuit of theological truth, it is not, strictly speaking, a willful, nefarious enterprise born out of a simple refusal to believe the truth. As psychologists observe, confirmation bias is not a deliberate, conscious attempt to build a case or defend a particular thesis by ignoring or working around other evidence. This bias is not what a defense attorney does when legally defending a client she knows to be guilty, nor is it what a debate team member does when preparing to defend a claim he personally rejects. Rather, confirmation bias is a "less explicit, less consciously one-sided case-building process."[18] Confirmation bias in biblical studies and theology has to do with the *way someone unwittingly uses and selects the evidence that confirms his or her previously held belief or working hypothesis.*

Instances of confirmation bias tend to fall into one of two broad categories identified by Nickerson: *motivated* and *unmotivated* confirmation bias. Unmotivated bias relates to the tendency of human beings to be persistent in their beliefs about the world. Not much is at stake for us in maintaining these kinds of beliefs; we just tend to stubbornly

---

16. Nickerson, "Confirmation Bias," 175.
17. Nickerson, "Confirmation Bias," 175.
18. Nickerson, "Confirmation Bias," 175.

cling to what we think we know—even in matters of trivial importance. Motivated confirmation bias occurs when the researcher has something personal at stake; likely a deeply held and valued belief is at risk. Unmotivated confirmation bias surfaces when people "proceed in a biased fashion . . . in the testing of hypotheses or claims in which they have no material stake or obvious personal interest."[19] Both categories have apparent value in assessing biblical interpretation and theological method, with motivated confirmation bias bearing more weight.

The first experimental support for confirmation bias came from a simple math challenge given to a sample group of undergraduate psychology students by cognitive psychologist Peter Wason, the first modern psychologist to study the phenomenon. Wason's experiments document what Nickerson labels unmotivated confirmation bias. Wason was able to show that people generally tend to overlook evidence and possible hypotheses that do not coincide with their working hypothesis. The most famous of Wason's experiments was the "2–4–6 problem" experiment, which provided the first evidence for what he would later call confirmation bias.[20]

Wason's subjects were given three numbers—2, 4, 6—and told that there was a "simple rule" that explained the relationship between the numbers. The subjects were encouraged to discover the rule that explained the relationship between those numbers by writing their own sets of three numbers and the reasons why they thought their numbers fit the rules.[21] After the subjects wrote down their sets of three numbers and showed them to the experimenter, Wason would tell them whether their numbers conformed to the rule he had in mind. Upon hearing whether the new numbers proposed conformed to the rule, the subjects were asked to guess the rule—to offer a hypothesis—that best explained the relationship between the three numbers.

If the subject were to propose "8–10–12," the answer would be "yes."[22] If the subject proposed "107–109–111," the experimenter

---

19. Nickerson, "Confirmation Bias," 176.
20. Peter C. Wason, "On the Failure to Eliminate Hypotheses in a Conceptual Task," *The Quarterly Journal of Experimental Psychology* 12, no. 3 (1960): 129–140.
21. Wason, "On the Failure to Eliminate Hypotheses in a Conceptual Task," 130–131.
22. Peter C. Wason, "'On the Failure to Eliminate Hypotheses in a Conceptual Task . . .'—A Second Look," in *Thinking and Reasoning*, ed. P. C. Wason and P. N. Johnson-Laird (Baltimore: Penguin, 1968), 165–166.

could still affirm her as giving numbers that conformed to the rule. Looking at these sets of numbers, one might suggest that the rule consisted of any series of three numbers that rose by two, but this was not the rule Wason had in mind. The random numbers "6–16–17" would also have conformed to the rule Wason had in mind. Only when a subject proposed a sequence of numbers out of order, such as "3–17–12" or "8–4–83" and received a "no" response would she likely discover the very simple rule Wason was assuming: that the numbers are simply any series of ascending numbers.

While the students had little or no difficulty making guesses about the rule describing the relationship between the numbers, few students offered a set of numbers that did not conform to their preconceived hypothesis—that the rule consisted of any series of three numbers that rises by two. Only six of the original twenty-nine undergraduate psychology students surveyed by Wason guessed the rule correctly (any series of ascending numbers) on their first attempt. Thirteen guessed the rule after one incorrect guess. Nine correctly identified the guess after two or more incorrect attempts. One subject never identified the rule correctly.[23]

These experiments demonstrate confirmation bias in matters of little personal consequence to the participants. The same type of unmotivated confirmation bias can occur in everyday reasoning as well. Data shows that medical students, physicians, and psychiatrists tend to search for symptoms that correspond to their preliminary diagnosis in such a way that they can ignore or reject other types of evidence that surface.[24] Studies have also shown that criminal investigators, jury members, and court witnesses can display the same kind of bias.[25] Unmotivated confirmation bias seems to be a factor in some interpretative judgments of little theological consequence.

If bias plays a role in these smaller, less important matters, it also has the potential to play an even larger role in foundational beliefs

---

23. Wason, "On the Failure to Eliminate Hypotheses in a Conceptual Task," 138–139.

24. R. Mendel, E. Traut-Mattausch, E. Jonas, S. Leucht, J. M. Kane, K. Maino, W. Kissling, and J. Hamann, "Confirmation Bias: Why Psychiatrists Stick to Wrong Preliminary Diagnoses," *Psychological Medicine* 41 (2011): 2651–2659.

25. T. Lindholm and S. A. Christianson, "Intergroup Biases and Eyewitness Testimony," *Journal of Social Psychology* 138 (1998): 710–723; O'Brien, "Confirmation Bias in Criminal Investigations"; O'Brien, "Prime Suspect," 315–334.

that shape our other beliefs and behavior. Motivated confirmation bias protects something larger, such as a cherished belief or idea. Wason recognized that the results of his experiments could have implications for religious thinking as well, especially when people think within a "closed system."[26] Because we operate within particular traditions of the Christian faith, our attempts to think systematically about the contents of the Bible are susceptible to the same basic failure to acknowledge other hypothetical explanations of a particular biblical text. As Ben Witherington explains, "Sometimes one's theological system is so carefully worked out that one assumes that anything that does not fit the system must be a misinterpretation of the text."[27]

While Wason is correct to say confirmation bias can distort religious thinking in its dogmatic forms, confirmation bias can also inhibit the reasoning processes of anti-religious thinkers. Many atheists and agnostics who affirm naturalism a priori rule out the possibility of the bodily resurrection of Jesus as an explanation for the empty tomb accounts in the Gospels because, as it is often stated, "Dead men just don't come back from the dead." The evidence for the empty tomb and the post-resurrection appearances are summarily dismissed because they do not fit their closed worldview.[28]

Types of Confirmation Bias

Research psychologists agree that the way we choose to process information can affect our final judgments and conclusions: "People typically seem oblivious to the fact that the way they process information may itself influence their judgments and the questions they ask may determine the answers they receive."[29] Theologians and interpreters of Scripture can fall prey to the same kind of confirmation bias, even if they are unaware of it.

---

26. Wason, "'On the Failure to Eliminate Hypotheses in a Conceptual Task . . .'–A Second Look," 174.

27. Ben Witherington III, *The Problem with Evangelical Theology: Testing the Exegetical Foundations of Calvinism, Dispensationalism, Wesleyanism, and Pentecostalism*, rev. ed. (Waco, TX: Baylor University Press, 2016), 4.

28. For a sampling of naturalist arguments against the resurrection of Jesus, see Robert M. Price, ed., *The Empty Tomb: Jesus beyond the Grave* (Amherst, NY: Prometheus, 2005).

29. Charles G. Lord, Mark R. Lepper, and Elizabeth Preston, "Considering the Opposite: A Corrective Strategy for Social Judgment," *Journal of Personality and Social Psychology* 47, no. 6 (1984): 1231.

Nickerson calls confirmation bias a "ubiquitous phenomenon in many guises," meaning that it operates in different ways in different contexts. In its popular forms, confirmation bias leads to obsessing over the headlines of "fake news," mistrust of all media news reports associated with the "other side" of the political spectrum, rationalizing failing public policy, and finding connections between the newspaper horoscope and everyday life. Even the most well-intentioned Christians are guilty of many of the same irrational tendencies, especially when they use the Bible to justify their incorrect preunderstandings. This section covers just a few of the types of confirmation bias identified by Nickerson that can affect biblical interpretation and theology.

When We Have Something to Prove

Working with a hypothesis of some sort is a crucial step in the reasoning process, but the careless use of a working hypothesis can lead to both motivated and unmotivated forms of confirmation bias. Nickerson highlights some ways in which a restriction of attention to one working hypothesis can skew the research results. First, restriction to one working hypothesis can affect the selection of relevant data. If one is "strongly committed to a particular position, one may fail to consider the relevance of information to the alternative positions and apply it (favorably) only to one's own hypothesis or belief."[30] One may look only for evidence that supports his claim and ignore data that would support a contradictory claim. In theology, one may seek out biblical proof for a doctrine of eternal security while overlooking evidence in the text that may support a doctrine of soteriological apostasy, or vice versa.

Second, the restriction of attention to one working hypothesis can lead to preferential treatment of evidence. Nickerson is careful to note that this preferential treatment of data does not mean that researchers always ignore other data, but it does mean they give less weight or consideration to this data, by either discrediting it or explaining it away.[31] In Christian theology, this type of bias is more likely to surface when weighing texts more conducive to our

---

30. Nickerson, "Confirmation Bias," 177.
31. Nickerson, "Confirmation Bias," 178.

doctrinal position than when considering other texts that seem to challenge our position. For example, a group of biblical texts may seem to coincide with a given position on whether a true believer can genuinely apostatize from the faith after true belief. Other texts that seem to indicate a contrary position may be given less weight or harmonized with the texts supporting the given position. In the process of considering biblical texts pertinent to our theological conversation, we may also ignore relevant data that does not fit our presupposed conclusion.

Third, hypothesis-driven research enables people to "see in data the patterns for which they are looking, regardless of whether the patterns are really there."[32] Numerous experiments have demonstrated that individuals have the propensity to see in themselves and others the personality traits and characteristics that they are seeking to find.[33] Research has shown that not even professional counselors are immune to this type of bias.[34]

The same danger presents itself to interpreters of Scripture who would find patterns in it that represent their own thinking and preconceived notions of theology or ethics. As critics of historical Jesus research since Albert Schweitzer have often observed, many of its representative approaches tend to reflect the ideological interests of their adherents.[35] Liberal Protestants see patterns of a liberal Protestant Jesus in the text, feminists a feminist Jesus, social justice warriors another social justice warrior, and fundamentalists a fellow fundamentalist. For this reason, scholars should strive to be aware of their respective philosophical commitments

---

32. Nickerson, "Confirmation Bias," 181.

33. See Mark Snyder and Bruce Campbell, "Testing Hypotheses about Other People: The Role of the Hypothesis," *Personality and Social Psychology Bulletin* 6 (1980): 421–426; Mark Snyder, "Seek and Ye Shall Find: Testing Hypotheses about Other People," in *Social Cognition: The Ontario Symposium on Personality and Social Psychology*, ed. Edward Tory Higgins, C. Peter Herman, and Mark P. Zanna (Hillsdale, NJ: Erlbaum, 1981), 277–303; William B. Swann, Tony Giuliano, and Daniel M. Wenger, "Where Leading Questions Can Lead: The Power of Conjecture in Social Interaction," *Journal of Personality and Social Psychology* 42, no. 6 (1982): 1025–1035; Gershon Ben-Shakhar, Maya Bar-Hillel, Yoram Bilu, and Gaby Shefler, "Seek and Ye Shall Find: Test Results Are What You Hypothesize They Are," *Journal of Behavioral Decision Making* 11 (1998): 235–249.

34. See Douglas C. Strohmer and Victoria A. Shivy, "Bias in Counselor Hypothesis Testing: Testing the Robustness of Counselor Confirmatory Bias," *Journal of Counseling and Development* 73, no. 2 (1994): 191–197.

35. See Albert Schweitzer, *The Quest of the Historical Jesus: A Critical Study of Its Progress from Reimarus to Wrede*, trans. William Montgomery (London: Adam & Charles Black, 1910).

and presuppositions.[36] But even conservative seminary students, pastors, biblical scholars, and theologians face the same potential impediment to correct interpretation: seeing what they want to see in the biblical text rather than what is there by authorial design. As *sola Scriptura* Christians, our primary goal is to understand the theological content of Scripture, not defend our respective theological traditions.

Our Beliefs Are Sticky

In my family we frequently lament that the sports media and conference officials are conspiring against our favorite football teams. We act as if we have a strong belief that the referees are out to get us (because usually they are!). It is highly unlikely that such a belief could be proven, but the belief sticks because of the narrative of victimization and paranoia we bring to every game as fans of an underdog team. We use every bad or disputable call made against our team as confirming evidence of this thesis (and tend to overlook the bad calls that go in our favor). It's the same thing that happens with JFK conspiracy theorists, anti-vaccine Facebook moms, and myopic politicos determined to expose the hidden agenda of the political party they oppose. When we form a belief, it is hard to shake. Our beliefs have tremendous sticking power.

One well-documented phenomenon is what psychologists call *belief persistence*. Belief persistence is the notion that "once a belief or opinion has been formed, it can be very resistive to change, even in the face of fairly compelling evidence that it is wrong."[37] Francis Bacon once observed that the "human understanding, when it has once adopted an opinion (either as being the received opinion or as being agreeable to itself), draws all things else to support and agree with it."[38] Psychologists call the tendency of human beings to stick to an earlier formed opinion the *primacy effect*.[39] Nickerson describes

---

36. Andreas J. Köstenberger, L. Scott Kellum, and Charles L. Quarles, *The Cradle, the Cross, and the Crown* (Nashville: B&H Academic, 2009), 125.

37. Nickerson, "Confirmation Bias," 187.

38. Francis Bacon, *The Works of Francis Bacon*, vol. 4, ed. James Spedding, Robert Leslie Ellis, and Douglas Denton Heath (London, 1875), 56.

39. See Steven J. Sherman, Kim S. Zehner, James Johnson, and Edward R. Hirt, "Social Explanation: The Role of Timing, Set, and Recall on Subjective Likelihood Estimates," *Journal of Personality and Social Psychology* 44, no. 6 (1983): 1127–1143.

the phenomenon in this way: "When a person must draw a conclusion on the basis of information acquired and integrated over time, the information acquired early in the process is likely to carry more weight than that acquired later."[40]

In the natural sciences, belief persistence frequently becomes what Nickerson calls "theory persistence." He looks to the examples of individual scientists throughout the history of science who had tremendous difficulty letting go of favored theories when overwhelming evidence to the contrary presented itself to them. Only scientists who followed after them, without the same vested interests in the theories, were able to dismiss them.[41] Philosopher of science Thomas Kuhn makes very similar observations about the resistance of people entrenched in a particular paradigm to new theories that come along:

> Though a generation is sometimes required to effect the change, scientific communities have again and again been converted to new paradigms. . . . These conversions occur not despite the fact that scientists are human but because they are. Though some scientists, particularly the older and more experienced ones, may resist indefinitely, most of them can be reached in one way or another. Conversions will occur a few at a time until, after the last holdouts have died, the whole profession will again be practicing under a single, but now different, paradigm.[42]

The longer one holds a belief in a scientific theory, the more resilient it becomes in the mind of the individual who holds it. Kuhn likens the shift from one scientific paradigm to another to a conversion. It is a dramatic change in belief that does not come easily because it affects a whole group of other beliefs (like the change from Newtonian to Einsteinian physics).

In my experience, even the brightest seminary students (and sometimes even seminary professors) tend to attach themselves to one side of a theological debate if they do not immediately encounter

---

40. Nickerson, "Confirmation Bias," 187.
41. Nickerson, "Confirmation Bias," 195. Nickerson looks to the historical evidence presented in I. Bernard Cohen, *Revolution in Science* (Cambridge, MA: Harvard University Press, 1985) for support.
42. Thomas S. Kuhn, *The Structure of Scientific Revolutions* (Chicago: University of Chicago Press, 1962), 152.

alternative perspectives. Students whose first encounter with an articulate explanation of the biblical concept of predestination comes from a Reformed or Calvinistic framework tend to maintain that explanation, whereas students whose first such exposure comes from an explicitly Arminian or non-Calvinistic framework tend to safeguard that view. The young pastor who quickly adopts a millennial view has difficulty seeing biblical texts from another perspective.

Confirmation bias may also explain why many of my PhD students are hung up on the work of the same theologian from semester to semester, not wanting to consider the works of other scholars. In these cases, the bias is neither deliberate nor strongly motivated in the sense that something personal or foundational is at stake in the interpreter's choices. *Interpretive and theological decision makers tend to stick with the first convincing case or voice they hear.* The initial newness of the information, coupled with our brain's tendency to persist in the beliefs that we hold, can shape any further consideration we give to the matter.

We Tend to Find Something to Be Glad About

Another bias closely related to confirmation bias is positivity bias—what researchers have named "the Pollyanna principle."[43] Pollyanna, the eponymous protagonist of Eleanor H. Porter's 1911 novel, was known for her relentless optimism. Seeking to find something to be glad about in every situation, she was often incapable of seeing the fault in fellow human beings. She paints the cruel town she lives in and harsh circumstances she faces in an idyllic light. The Pollyanna principle simply means that some people—optimistic as the principle's fictional namesake—tend to believe propositions they would like to be true and reject propositions they would like to be false.[44] The positivity bias simply means "that people find it easier to deal with positive information than with negative."[45] This positivity bias closely reflects Jonathan Haidt's observation that we frequently *rationalize* the beliefs

---

43. See Margaret Matlin, "Pollyanna Principle," in *Cognitive Illusions: Intriguing Phenomena in Thinking, Judgment, and Memory*, 2nd ed., ed. Rüdiger F. Pohl (New York: Routledge, 2017), 315–336.

44. Nickerson, "Confirmation Bias," 197; Margaret Matlin and David Stang, *The Pollyanna Principle: Selectivity in Language, Memory, and Thought* (Cambridge, MA: Shenkman, 1978).

45. Nickerson, "Confirmation Bias," 202.

we *feel to be true* or *want to be true* rather than seek truth for the sake of truth.

This positivity bias also parallels a trait of Apple Computer founder and former CEO Steve Jobs that longtime Apple engineers described as Jobs's "reality distortion field." Software designer Bud Tribble coined the phrase to describe the way in which Jobs tended to have unrealistic expectations about himself, his employees, and what could be done in the real world. The positive side of Jobs's reality distortion field, his staff reported, is that he could motivate them to create technology people thought impossible and in remarkably quick timetables. The negative side, however, is that Jobs was prone to nonrational self-deception that would have negative impacts on his business, his relationships, and ultimately, his physical well-being.[46] Though positivity can have its benefits in research, it can also have distorting effects.

In Christian theology and Christian ethics, this positivity bias means reading texts in a way that is favorable to a belief or practice cherished by the interpreter, or at least a rejection of an interpretation that would have negative implications for their beliefs or practices. Interpreters skewed by this bias might phrase their respective positions like this: "Whatever the Bible says about spiritual gifts, it can't mean x"; "Whatever the Bible says about the role of women in the church, it must mean y"; and so forth and so on. The fundamentalist interpreter may be too confident in the theological distinctives of his particular tradition, unable to see other interpretations as possible options for a biblical text. The liberal interpreter may be overly optimistic about biblical writers sharing his value system, such as the assertion that Jesus would have supported gay marriage or abortion. Historical and theological revisionists often reject traditional theological and ethical positions and read Scripture in such a way that it confirms their beliefs.

A Pollyanna bias in theology may explain why escapism is so prominent in some sectors of popular eschatology. Some people hold a theological disposition that God will not allow his people to undergo suffering, which shapes their reading of prophetic books and events. The Pollyanna bias also undergirds much of the prosperity gospel:

---

46. See Walter Isaacson, *Steve Jobs* (New York: Simon & Schuster, 2011), 117–124.

because I want to be healthy and wealthy, God must want that for me too! The Pollyanna bias keeps many readers of Scripture from seeing the purpose God has in the suffering of the saints (Rom. 5:3–5; 2 Cor. 4:8–10, 17; Phil. 1:29; Heb. 2:10; James 1:2–4).

Scripture contains warnings about teachers and prophets who teach only what people want to hear (Jer. 6:14; Obad. 3–4, 8; Matt. 24:24–26; 2 Tim. 4:3). Readers of the Bible must likewise learn to be suspicious of their own biases and motivations to ensure they are not simply reading or seeing in the text what they want to see. Those who recognize biblical authority must call into question their interpretive desires and place themselves under the meaning of the text, even if that takes them to a place with which they are uncomfortable. This interpretive disposition is the hermeneutics of submission.

What If We're Wrong?

Confirmation bias can pose real-world problems. In the world of criminal investigation and courtroom trials, it can lead to false accusations and false convictions. As legal scholar Barbara O'Brien observes in her study of the impact of confirmation bias in criminology, detectives, lawyers, judges, and jury members must come to conclusions regardless of this risk of confirmation bias. Indecision is not an option, especially when justice is in the balance. The same can be said of confirmation bias in Christian theology, which can have detrimental effects on the teaching and practice of the church. When dealing with matters of eternal consequence, the effects of interpretive and theological bias are no less serious. Indeed, they are more serious. Some of the suggestions offered by O'Brien for combating confirmation bias in a criminal investigation can be helpful first steps for addressing the same potential for confirmation bias of traditional or denominational positions in biblical interpretation and theological method.[47]

First, we should investigate alternative hypotheses contrary to the hypothesis with which we work. In their 1984 study, research psychologists Charles Lord, Mark Lepper, and Elizabeth Preston demonstrated that many instances of unmotivated confirmation bias are

---

47. O'Brien, "Confirmation Bias in Criminal Investigations," 39–61; O'Brien, "Prime Suspect," 329–330.

a result of "inadequate cognitive strategies" that can be corrected by "adopting a new strategy" that promotes impartiality. These researchers showed evidence that decision makers can alleviate confirmation bias if they are encouraged to consider alternative proposals to their working hypothesis.[48] For O'Brien, this means jury members must consider alternative theories about what happened before making their decisions.

For theologians, this principle means that they should read deeply and widely in the broader Christian tradition. They must consult other faith perspectives and give serious consideration to theological positions contrary to their own. We should also consult the resources of global Christianity outside of our national or cultural perspective.[49] Sometimes this comes as a challenge for Christians who presume that they adhere to the same theological system as Jesus and the apostles. However, as Christians both aware of our interpretive fallibility and committed to the truthfulness of God's word, we should at least contemplate why other Bible-believing Christians throughout history have come to opinions contrary to our own. We should ask questions about *why* and ask honest questions about our own positions. When we ask these questions, we can either strengthen our case for our presumed tradition or move to a more biblically sound position.

One way to do this involves the *direct* instruction to consider what the data might mean if the expected conclusion were reversed.[50] In a theological classroom, we might ask students what sort of evidence we would need to acquire from the biblical text if we were arguing for the opposite position. Theologians should try and establish arguments not only in favor of their position but against it as well! In so doing, they either correct their erroneous position or strengthen their confidence and support for the position they hold.

My Baptist theology students would be well served to study the best arguments for the Presbyterian practice of paedobaptism (the baptism of infants), as would Presbyterian students benefit from assessing the best arguments for credobaptism (the baptism of believers). What argument or evidence from Scripture could falsify our claim that only

---

48. Lord, Lepper, and Preston, "Considering the Opposite," 1239.
49. Millard J. Erickson, *Christian Theology*, 3rd ed. (Grand Rapids, MI: Baker, 2013), 58.
50. Lord, Lepper, and Preston, "Considering the Opposite," 1232.

believers should be baptized? Both sides should consider what sort of exegetical evidence they may expect to find if the position opposite of theirs is true, and whether the biblical evidence weighs in favor of their position or of the contrary position. In so doing, we are encouraging our students to look at data they may not have considered and to reorient their selection biases.

Lord, Lepper, and Preston also offer an *indirect* way of pushing students to consider alternate hypotheses. Rather than asking students to imagine what sort of data they would expect to find if the opposite hypothesis were true, professors may simply encourage their students to read papers or research that offers conclusions different from their own. In this approach, "the professor neither describes the tendency to ignore alternative data patterns nor instructs the student to adopt any particular cognitive strategy, but instead relies on the recommended paper to render opposite possibilities more accessible."[51] One valuable pedagogical tool available to contemporary theological disciplines is the type of multiview books made available by various publishers. These books usually offer brief introductions to the key positions in a theological debate from some of their most capable exponents, as well as responses from their critics. I would add that we should follow a *principle of charity* and use the strongest possible arguments available for the opposing sides rather than subjecting students to "straw men" or patently inferior versions of the argument.

Second, we must assess our own theological opinions critically in light of contrary theories. Whether we are looking at previously established interpretations of biblical texts (i.e., undercoded abductions) or new interpretations (i.e., creative abductions), we must use abductive reasoning to compare our belief with the belief in question (i.e., meta-abduction). The criteria we used for assessing abductions in chapter 3 are also helpful for assessing hypotheses and theories contrary to our own:

(1) *Coherence*—Is the contrary hypothesis internally coherent "with everything else we hold true in the field"?[52] For theological assessment, this internal coherence extends to several levels

---

51. Lord, Lepper, and Preston, "Considering the Opposite," 1232.
52. Louis J. Pojman, *Philosophy: The Quest for Truth*, 4th ed. (Belmont, CA: Wadsworth, 1999), 30.

of theological inquiry. Does the contrary hypothesis about a particular theological disagreement cohere with the more universally accepted tenets of orthodoxy? If the position does not cohere with orthodoxy—the broadly established hermeneutical framework of the Christian faith—then it will be dismissed. If it is within the bounds of orthodoxy, the question becomes which theological opinion best fits with the larger collection of biblical data.

(2) *Simplicity*—Is the contrary hypothesis simpler than the working hypothesis? Which hypothesis—the working hypothesis or the contradictory hypothesis—requires the least amount of ad hoc solutions? Regarding exegesis, what is the simplest explanation of the text that best fits with its historical context?

(3) *Fruitfulness*—Which hypothesis—the working or the contradictory hypothesis—offers more explanatory power in addressing peripheral issues?

(4) *Comprehensiveness*—Which theory better accounts for all of the biblical data, the theory of my theological tradition or the theory of another tradition or theologian?

It is quite possible that an honest assessment of contrary theories may result in a change in our own doctrinal positions. Consequently, these criteria require intellectual virtue and honesty, matters we will turn to in the next chapter.

Third, accountability to others may assuage some instances of confirmation bias. In the psychological literature, accountability refers to the "social pressures to justify one's views to another."[53] The fear of the negative consequences associated with a failure to make such a justification, as well as the potential reward for demonstrating persuasive justifications for actions and beliefs, can keep decision makers accountable.[54] Presenting research at a professional meeting or for publication may encourage researchers to bring their best work to the table, to weigh all the relevant evidence, and to consider all the alternatives. A seminary student who must present his findings before his professor and peers is

---

53. Philip E. Tetlock and Jae Il Kim, "Accountability and Judgment Processes in a Personality Prediction Test," *Journal of Personality and Social Psychology* 52, no. 4 (1987): 700.

54. Jennifer S. Lerner and Philip E. Tetlock, "Accounting for the Effects of Accountability," *Psychological Bulletin* 125, no. 2 (1999): 255.

more likely to be held accountable than a student who receives no such feedback. On a larger scale, the historic Christian tradition serves as an important counterbalance to theological novelty. When the time does come for creative abductions or new theories in theology, they must be scrutinized critically under biblical authority.

Research has shown that accountability does not always curtail bias. Accountability can restrain confirmation bias in the early stages of belief formation, especially when individuals are told that they will need to provide a well-informed audience with justification for their actions or position.[55] However, after some people reach initial decisions in belief formation, accountability is of limited value because individuals at this stage tend to be more interested in publicly justifying their established positions than correcting their conclusions.[56]

Finally, we should ask questions about our motivations in research. Researchers are aware that self-justification can set people up for confirmation bias. It is also easy to assume that the other person is guilty of bias while naively assuming one's own objectivity. "The other interpreter is shaped by his theology while I am reading the text free of those bothersome presumptions!" Diagnostic questions can aid in curtailing some of the detrimental effects of this bias.

"Am I seeking self-justification or the truth? Do I want to be right in an argument more than I want to know what is right?" The integral question for the Christian theologian is whether we are ultimately placing ourselves under the authority of a favored tradition, a point of view, a perception, or Scripture itself. "Does our research methodology ultimately reflect a desire to be faithful to Scripture and a desire to honor and glorify God, or a desire to be esteemed by peers?" A word from the book of Lamentations is helpful here: "Let us test and examine our ways, and return to the LORD!" (Lam. 3:40).

Conclusion

Scripture warns us about making judgments based on appearances or preconceived notions (1 Sam. 16:7), but not every bias or prejudgment

---

55. O'Brien, "Confirmation Bias in Criminal Investigations," 39.
56. Tetlock and Kim, "Accountability and Judgment Processes in a Personality Prediction Test," 707.

is undesirable or unhelpful. We all have biases and presuppositions that help us navigate through life. We cannot theologize outside of some tradition of belief and practice. The historic Christian tradition provides a helpful framework for interpretation. Deeply held convictions rooted in tradition are helpful deterrents to being blown about with every wind of doctrine. However, tradition uncritically embraced or untested by the data of Scripture can lead to distorting confirmation bias.

Demonstrating whether a particular theologian or interpreter has been prey to confirmation bias is a difficult, if not impossible, task because we are not always aware of the circumstances and motivations of theological research. Unlike researchers in more formal sciences, theologians are not usually very good at explaining the processes by which they come to their conclusions. (This lacuna, by the way, is something more deliberate attention to theological method can alleviate.) While confirmation bias in theological method is difficult to prove, we who are engaged in the enterprises of biblical interpretation and Christian theology can and should strive to be conscious of our own bias tendencies and exercise various means to hold them in check.

Some may worry that discussion of our traditional biases opens interpreters up to hermeneutical relativism and uncertainty, the endless circling of hermeneutical loops. After all, how can I know I have not exercised some confirmation bias in this discussion about confirmation bias? Awareness of the possibility of confirmation bias in theology reminds me that I have an imperfect mind prone to mistakes in reasoning. But without acknowledging my potential for this kind of error, I am in even greater danger of ignoring these types of mistakes and judgments and becoming susceptible to interpretive pride. This awareness provides an important check on my theological tradition's sway over me as an interpreter of the Bible.

PART TWO

WHAT WE SHOULD DO ABOUT DOCTRINAL DISAGREEMENT

6

When Should We Change
Our Minds?

Insights from the Epistemology of Disagreement

Toward the end of his life, Augustine published his *Retractationes* (i.e., "re-treatments," "revisions," or "retractions"), a retrospective analysis of his earlier writings and theological works. Of his own theological development, Augustine wrote, "I do not claim . . . perfection for myself even now when I am old, and even less when, in early manhood, I had begun to write or to speak to the people, and so much authority was attributed to me that, whenever it was necessary for someone to speak to the people and I was present, I was seldom allowed to be silent and to listen to others and to be 'swift to hear but slow to speak.'"[1] Augustine recognized that his works were not beyond revision or correction, and he displayed a willingness to change his mind on some matters of theological controversy. He recognized his fallibility and sought to change his opinions where he deemed it necessary.

Other theological memoirs expose more dramatic changes of opinion. Upon his conversion to Roman Catholicism in 1845, John Henry Newman wrote his *Essay on the Development of Christian Doctrine*,

---

1. Augustine, *The Retractions*, trans. Mary Inez Bogan (Washington: Catholic University of America Press, 1968), 4.

in which he not only spelled out a defense of the unique developments of Catholic theology but also gave his reasoning for leaving the Anglican Oxford Movement he once led.[2] Some memoirs detail how self-proclaimed atheists become theists, while others record the opposite experience.[3] Some theological memoirs talk about the experiences that drove their authors out of evangelicalism,[4] while the works of others describe their shift from theological liberalism to historic Christian orthodoxy.[5] In each of these instances, a change in theological beliefs was preceded by a theological disagreement. Augustine was once skeptical of his mother's faith. Newman began as an opponent of the Roman Catholic doctrine he later embraced. Thomas Oden eventually came to reject the liberal existentialism of his theological training when he rediscovered the patristic tradition. Every change in theological belief begins with a point of difference.

The Bible tells us conversion begins with a change of mind. The most common term for repentance in the New Testament is the Greek word *metanoeō*, which means "to change one's mind." Repentance involves a person's decision to change his mind about his sinful behavior and disposition, moving from an embrace of sin toward a rejection of it. Biblical conversion entails people changing their minds about the direction of their lives and submitting to the lordship of Christ. Changes of mind are part of the human experience, part of how we learn and grow in sanctification. Some changes of mind can be good, while others can be harmful to our souls.

When we have disagreements about Scripture, we do so because we are active readers who bring to the text our own interpretative

---

2. John Henry Newman, *An Essay on the Development of Christian Doctrine* (London, 1893). Former evangelicals who become Catholics and former Catholics who become evangelicals still write similar spiritual and theological autobiographies. See Francis J. Beckwith, *Return to Rome: Confessions of an Evangelical Catholic* (Grand Rapids, MI: Brazos, 2009); Christopher A. Castaldo, *Holy Ground: Walking with Jesus as a Former Catholic* (Grand Rapids, MI: Zondervan, 2009); cf. Robert L. Plummer, ed., *Journeys of Faith: Evangelicalism, Eastern Orthodoxy, Catholicism, and Anglicanism* (Grand Rapids, MI: Zondervan, 2012).

3. Anthony Flew, with Roy Abraham Varghese, *There Is a God: How the World's Most Notorious Atheist Changed His Mind* (New York: HarperCollins, 2007); Dan Barker, *Godless: How an Evangelical Preacher Became One of America's Leading Atheists* (Berkeley, CA: Ulysses, 2009).

4. David P. Gushee, *Still Christian: Following Jesus out of American Evangelicalism*, rev. ed. (Louisville: Westminster John Knox, 2017); Gushee, *Changing Our Mind*, 3rd ed. (Canton, MI: Read the Spirit, 2017).

5. Thomas C. Oden, *A Change of Heart: A Personal and Theological Memoir* (Downers Grove, IL: InterVarsity Press, 2014).

limitations, reasoning processes, feelings, and biases. But recognition of our differences poses a few practical questions about our beliefs. *When we encounter disagreement with another believer, should we change our mind, withhold judgment, or steadily maintain our present belief? Should we hold onto a belief that people as smart as us or smarter reject? At what point are we being stubborn or closed-minded by holding on to our belief?*

For intramural Christian debates, the question becomes, *Why should I maintain this belief when other self-identifying Christians deny it?* I have less difficulty answering these types of questions when I am engaged in disagreements with theologians and philosophers who have rejected biblical authority and the gospel. But the problem gets much hairier when considering the differences between otherwise like-minded Christians who share similar convictions about the gospel, Scripture, and Christian mission. I endure some angst—epistemic and existential—when I have a major disagreement with someone who evidences the fruit of the Spirit and a deep and abiding love for the Lord.

A possible aid to these challenges comes from a sister discipline of hermeneutics: *epistemology*, the branch of philosophy dedicated to understanding how we know what we know.[6] Traditionally, epistemologists typically deal with questions about what constitutes knowledge and questions about how much warrant or justification is needed before we can say that we *know* something that we *believe*. For the last decade, many epistemologists have engaged in fruitful discussion over the nature of disagreement.[7] Epistemologists specializing in

---

6. While hermeneutics and epistemology share similar concerns and methods, the disciplines have notably different orientations and end goals. For a critical evaluation of these differences, see Anthony C. Thiselton, *Hermeneutics* (Grand Rapids, MI: Eerdmans, 2009), 7–12. According to Thiselton, one significant way hermeneutics differs from epistemology is in its focus. Hermeneutics highlights *understanding* or listening (*Verstehen*) to a text rather than *explaining* (*Erklärung*) an object (8–9).

7. Seminal works in the problem of epistemic disagreement include Richard Feldman, "Epistemological Puzzles about Disagreement," in *Epistemology Futures*, ed. Stephen Hetherington (New York: Oxford University Press, 2006), 216–236; Thomas Kelly, "The Epistemic Significance of Disagreement," in *Oxford Studies in Epistemology* 1, ed. John Hawthorne and Tamar Gendler Szabo (New York: Oxford University Press, 2006), 167–196; and Bryan Frances, "When a Skeptical Hypothesis Is Live," *Noûs* 39 (2005): 559–595.

Monographs and collected works in the area include Richard Feldman and Ted A. Warfield, eds., *Disagreement* (New York: Oxford University Press, 2010); David Christensen and Jennifer Lackey, eds., *The Epistemology of Disagreement: New Essays* (New York: Oxford University Press, 2010); Diego E. Machuca, ed., *Disagreement and Skepticism* (New York: Routledge, 2012); Bryan Frances, *Disagreement* (Malden, MA: Polity, 2014); Jonathan Matheson, *The Epistemic Significance of Disagreement* (New York: Palgrave Macmillan, 2015).

disagreement address both *theoretical* and *practical* concerns. Like others in their field, these philosophers grapple with traditional theoretical questions about the nature of knowledge, belief, truth, and the like. Epistemologists of disagreement not only seek to understand the significance of disagreement for beliefs and knowledge formation but also wrestle with the concrete question of *what we should do* when we encounter someone who disagrees with our beliefs.[8]

When we recognize disagreement, should we maintain our belief, change it, or suspend our judgment until more facts are available? Sometimes this question is relatively easy to answer. When we have good reason to believe we are in a better place to know something than the person with whom we take issue, we will maintain our belief. It is also easier to change our beliefs when we disagree with someone whom we believe has more expertise on the matter. The more difficult question is what we should do when we realize we disagree with a *peer*—someone who appears to be our equal in intelligence, know-how, and training. Applied to Christian theology, what should I do when I have a doctrinal disagreement with someone whom I recognize as being equally intelligent, well educated, and very skilled as an exegete of Scripture?

I am not an epistemologist, nor the son of an epistemologist. I have no aspirations of solving or even adequately addressing some of the complex issues raised by philosophers in this area. What I do want to do is introduce some of the key issues in the epistemology of disagreement to nonspecialists and make some application to this larger question we have about interpretive and doctrinal disagreement. I am primarily concerned with a practical question: what interpretive moves do we make when we encounter disagreement over the interpretation of a biblical text or a theological claim? When should we change our beliefs about the meaning of a biblical passage or Christian doctrine and when should we retain those beliefs? At what point should we withhold judgment?

For this chapter, I will be overlooking theological and interpretive differences we have with those outside of Protestant evangelicalism who maintain a different theological disposition toward Christian

---

8. Frances, *Disagreement*, 5–6.

belief and the Bible. Though many of the principles contained in this chapter would apply to these sorts of theological and interpretive disagreements, I will focus on the distinct problem faced by those Protestants who share the belief that the Bible is inerrant, infallible, and the final authority in Christian theology. Evangelical Protestants who differ over doctrine share the same body of evidence in Scripture. These Christians desire to agree with the Bible even if they feud with one another over what it means.

The structure of this chapter loosely follows epistemologist Bryan Frances's "rough procedure" for addressing epistemic disagreement. Frances offers the clearest, most practical assessment of the epistemology of disagreement I have seen to this point.[9] The first section is an exploration of the differences between genuine and illusory disagreement in biblical interpretation. Before we change our minds, we must ask whether we have a real disagreement or not. Context and language are important tools for assessing this question. The second section features "disagreement factors" that cause reasonable people to come to drastically different conclusions regarding a particular interpretation of a text. The third section covers what Frances calls the "Better Position Question," an important question for all intellectual disagreements. I conclude this chapter with some broad applications for biblical hermeneutics from the epistemology of disagreement that may be useful for assessing our theological differences.

Do We Really Disagree?

According to Frances, the first step in assessing disagreements is determining whether we genuinely disagree with one another. Sometimes we talk past one another, convinced of disagreement between us when there is no real disagreement. Not all apparent theological disagreements are genuine disagreements; some are merely *illusory disagreements*.

Differences in Expression

Now and then what appears to be a genuine disagreement is really an illusory disagreement rooted in *semantics* or the use of language.[10]

---

9. Frances, *Disagreement*, 110.
10. Frances, *Disagreement*, 11–12.

The biblical canon offers a few examples of this sort of apparent disagreement,[11] but perhaps none is more prominent than the apparent tension between Romans 4:1–25 and James 2:14–25. Many have read Paul and James to be contradicting each other on the issues of justification, faith, and works. This apparent disagreement led some, including Luther, to question the canonicity and apostolicity of the epistle of James.[12]

But are these biblical authors teaching contrary positions? At first glance, there are certainly reasons for thinking so. Both Paul and James use Abraham as illustrations for their arguments, and both cite Genesis 15:6 as scriptural support for their positions (cf. *1 Macc.* 2:52). Paul adamantly defends a position that Abraham was justified by faith and not by works, while James maintains that "a person is justified by works and not by faith alone" (James 2:24). On the surface, Paul and James seem to be in direct contradiction with each other, with Paul saying *A* ("faith alone and not works") and James saying not-*A* ("works and not faith alone").[13] Furthermore, if there were a genuine theological disagreement between them, it would certainly pose a major problem for theological assumptions about the truthfulness and inspiration of one or both of the writings (hence Luther's attitude toward James).

Though New Testament scholars vary in their respective approaches to this problem, one possible solution based on a closer examination of Paul and James's respective uses of *dikaioō* ("justify") and *ergon* ("works") can show that there is no real contradiction between them.[14] Whereas Paul uses a form of *dikaioō* to talk about the

---

11. See Klyne Snodgrass, *Between Two Truths: Living with Biblical Tensions* (Grand Rapids, MI: Zondervan, 1990); cf. James D. G. Dunn, *Unity and Diversity in the New Testament: An Inquiry into the Character of Earliest Christianity*, 3rd ed. (London: SCM, 2006). Many of these apparent discrepancies in the New Testament relate to the specific context of the author(s), as Dunn explains: "*Within the NT itself we have not simply diverse kerygmata, but in fact kerygmata which appear to be incompatible—that is, gospels which are incompatible when compared directly with each other without reference to their different life settings*" (26, italics original).

12. LW 35:362.

13. For a sampling of New Testament scholars who see Paul and James to be in direct contradiction with one another, see Rudolf Bultmann, *Theology of the New Testament*, 2 vols. (Waco, TX: Baylor University Press, 2007), 2:162–163; Gunther Bornkamm, *Paul* (New York: Harper & Row, 1971), 153–154; and J. B. Souček, "Zu den Problemen des Jakobusbriefes," *Evangelische Theologie* 18 (1958): 460–468.

14. Douglas J. Moo, *The Epistle to the Romans*, New International Commentary on the New Testament (Grand Rapids, MI: Eerdmans, 1996), 261n28.

event by which God declares a person legally right in Christ, James appears to use the term to speak about a public demonstration of faith.[15] In the context of Romans 4, Paul appears to use *ergon* to mean *ergōn nomou* ("works of the law"; cf. Gal. 2:16; 3:2, 5, 10)— religious rituals associated with the law of Moses such as circumcision or food laws.[16] James, on the other hand, seems to have almsgiving and care for the poor in mind in his use of the term *ergon* (see James 1:27–2:13).[17] Given their respective contexts and messages, James and Paul apparently offer no genuine disagreement of ideas.

Conceptual Variation

Another example of illusory disagreement goes beyond mere semantics to conceptual variety. Sometimes the charge is brought against the doctors of Nicaea that they taught a fundamentally different doctrine of Christ than Paul taught. Critics charge that Paul was in disagreement with Nicene Christology because of the obvious Greco-Roman metaphysical influence on the language of the creed, especially in its description of Christ as *homoousios* ("same substance"). This difference would be what David Kelsey calls "conceptual discontinuity."[18]

True, it would be anachronistic to assume Paul thought in the same terms and concepts as fourth-century metaphysics. However, as David Yeago demonstrates, the difference in *conceptual presentation* between Paul and the Nicene Creed does not entail a difference in their *patterns of judgment* related to Christ. Nicaea described Jesus as "being of one substance with the Father." Paul described Jesus as being "in the form [*morphē*] of God" (Phil. 2:6), making him worthy of all allegiance (Phil. 2:10). Nicaea may have used different conceptual categories than Paul to describe the deity of Jesus, but Paul and Nicaea make the same judgment about Jesus's identity.[19] Paul and Nicaea are in agreement, even if they have distinctive philosophical frameworks.

---

15. Ralph P. Martin translates *dikaioutai* as "proved righteous." See Martin, *James*, WBC 48 (Nashville: Thomas Nelson, 1988), 95.

16. Thomas R. Schreiner, *Romans*, BECNT (Grand Rapids, MI: Baker, 1998), 215–217.

17. Martin, *James*, 82–83.

18. See David H. Kelsey, *Proving Doctrine: The Uses of Scripture in Modern Theology* (Harrisburg, PA: Trinity, 1999), 188.

19. David S. Yeago, "The New Testament and Nicene Dogma: A Contribution to the Recovery of Theological Exegesis," in *Theological Interpretation of Scripture: Classic and Contemporary Readings*, ed. Stephen E. Fowl (Cambridge, MA: Blackwell, 1997), 93.

So long as Christians are cross-cultural in their communication of the gospel, they will need to *contextualize* the biblical message. Contextualization faithful to Scripture may apply different terms, concepts, and illustrations to give new expressions to its claims and judgments in different contexts.[20] The differences of expression and even conceptual framing do not necessarily entail theological disagreements.

Differences in Comparison Classes

Another type of illusory disagreement Frances describes is apparent disagreement provoked by different *comparison classes*.[21] Suppose we point to a number of texts in the Old Testament that regulate slavery (e.g., Gen. 16:3; Ex. 12:44; 20:10; 21:2, 20–21; Lev. 22:11; 25:46; Deut. 5:14; 15:12–14; 23:15–17) and texts in the New Testament that speak about the ways in which slaves and masters should treat one another (e.g. Eph. 6:5–9; Col. 4:1; 1 Tim. 6:1–3), and then you were to say to me, "The Bible sanctions slavery," and I were to say to you, "The Bible does not sanction slavery." What is an apparent contradiction—it appears you are saying *A* and I am saying not-*A*—might not be a real contradiction at all, depending on the way we are using comparison classes.

By "the Bible sanctions slavery," you mean the Bible *does not prohibit slavery explicitly*. Therefore, if compared to a nineteenth-century American abolitionist document that explicitly calls for an end to all forms of slavery, one could argue that the Bible sanctions slavery—at least by restricting or regulating it rather than abolishing it. By my saying, "The Bible does not sanction slavery," I mean to say that biblical authors do not wholeheartedly endorse slavery as an *ideal practice* but rather address the practical realities of slavery in the ancient world. (It is also worth noting that slavery in the Greco-Roman world was very different from its Western counterpart.[22]) I may agree with you that, when we compare the biblical texts to abolitionist literature, they appear rather tolerant of slavery—at least in the sense of being permis-

---

20. Kevin J. Vanhoozer, *The Drama of Doctrine* (Louisville: Westminster/John Knox, 2005), 130.

21. Frances, *Disagreement*, 12–13.

22. For a brief summary of the differences between later Western slavery and slavery in the ancient world, see David A. deSilva, *Honor, Patronage, Kinship, and Purity: Unlocking the New Testament Culture* (Downers Grove, IL: InterVarsity Press, 2000), 190–193.

sive rather than prohibitive. You may likewise agree that the Bible, when compared to other ancient Near Eastern texts on slavery, takes a far more restrictive, less favorable approach to the subject matter. Once we define the comparison classes with which we argue, it may become apparent that the disagreement we believed we had is illusory.

What these types of illusory disagreements illustrate is the crucial importance of context in apparent interpretive disagreements. Context is likewise crucial for assessing genuine disagreements that initially appear to be agreements. If one were to overhear an early-fourth-century conversation between Arius and Athanasius, they might superficially appear to agree with one another when each of them labels Jesus the "Son," the "Begotten," and the "Word."[23] Despite their shared vocabulary, however, it is clear that they had very different understandings as to what these titles mean. By the descriptor "Begotten," Arius means the Son was "made" by God, begotten in time. Athanasius, on the other hand, uses the term to mean "not made," begotten in eternity. Arius conceives of Jesus as the created Son; Athanasius believes him to be the eternal Son.

In this historical instance, we see the verbal similarity in these respective Christological expressions, but this similarity is quite superficial and masks a deep disagreement between the fourth-century theologians. Theologians can use the same terms and be working from different dictionaries. The same sort of thing happens today with charlatans and contemporary cults who use biblical and theological vocabulary but mean something different than what Scripture or the broader Christian tradition teaches. A Mormon missionary may call Jesus "the Christ" and talk about salvation in language familiar to evangelicals, but the substantive difference between the Mormon Jesus and the Jesus of the historic Christian faith is irreconcilable.

Can Reasonable, Intelligent People Disagree with One Another?

We have seen that Christians are divided over doctrine because they read imperfectly, they exegete differently, reason individually, have

---

23. There is even textual evidence that Arius in his later writings consciously borrowed the language of the Nicene Creed that had anathematized him. See Rudolf Lorenz, *Arius judaizans? Untersuchungen zur dogmengeschichtlichen Einordnung des Arius* (Göttingen: Vandenhoeck & Ruprecht, 1979), 192–193.

varying emotional responses, and work from distinct biases. But when faced with theological disagreement, we may be tempted to jump to the automatic conclusion that those who disagree with us are the ones making the exegetical mistakes, being irrational in their thinking, or working from a distorting prejudice or emotion. But epistemologists of disagreement show us that *not all disagreements stem from such irrationality*. Even reasonable people of similar intelligence can disagree without necessarily being irrational.

Frances lists and discusses what he calls a few "easier" questions about disagreement that help us explain why *reasonable people may disagree about a given issue*. The answer to each of these questions is "yes," but each explanation also exposes what Frances calls *disagreement factors*. With these basic questions about disagreement, Frances identifies several disagreement factors that contribute to differences of opinion among reasonable persons, including, but not limited to, (1) data or evidence, (2) time, (3) ability, (4) background knowledge, and (5) circumstances of the investigation.[24]

(Q1) *Can two intelligent people come to <u>reasonable yet different answers</u> to a single question?* Yes, this type of disagreement happens all the time. Frances illustrates the answer with a story about Pro and Con, who, during a murder trial, each hear only one side of the case. Pro hears the prosecution only; Con hears the defense only. Even if both have *justified* beliefs about the guilt or innocence of the murder suspect, one of them has a justified *false* belief. Pro and Con may both be reasonable individuals in that they are neither unintelligent nor uneducated, but (1) they have radically different beliefs *because they are forming their belief based on radically different bodies of evidence*.[25] Reasonable people can come to conflicting religious beliefs when attempting to interpret different religious texts. The religious disputes between Muslims and Christians are more than disagreements over the meanings of texts; they reason from entirely different sources of authority (i.e., the Qur'an and the Bible). While the answer to this particular question may be obvious, it does little to help those of us who are in disagreement over the meaning(s) of the same text.

---

24. Frances, *Disagreement*, 26.
25. Frances, *Disagreement*, 18–19.

(Q2) *Can two intelligent people come to reasonable yet different answers to a single question when they share the <u>same data</u>?* This question has more pertinence for hermeneutics because it addresses a disagreement between reasonable people over the same data. The answer here is likewise affirmative, because (2) reasonable people can have different *background knowledge* or expertise that affects the outcome of the interpretation of the data.[26]

This disagreement factor describes the sort of interpretive difference a seminary-trained pastor and a medical doctor might have over the meaning of a biblical passage. Both individuals may be intelligent, reasonable persons, but the pastor's additional background knowledge in biblical history, languages, and interpretation gives him an *epistemic advantage* over someone trained in an unrelated field like medicine. Notably, the epistemic disadvantage of the medical doctor says nothing about her intelligence. She may very well be more intelligent than the seminary-trained pastor is, but she does lack training in this area and pertinent background knowledge. Were the shoe on the other foot, I certainly would give the medical doctor epistemic advantage in making a medical prognosis. Having a PhD in biblical studies does not make a pastor an expert in medicine, even if he knows how to Google his symptoms!

(Q3) *Can two intelligent people come to reasonable yet different answers to a single question when they share the same evidence and relevant <u>background knowledge</u>?* Yes, reasonable people with similar background knowledge or training looking at the same evidence can come to different conclusions. Frances notes that "reasonable" here is a loose term simply meaning *"not stupid,"* but it does not specify the *ability* or *skill level* of the persons in disagreement.[27] Disagreements over biblical passages may arise between two reasonable people who have similar training if one involved in the disagreement is more skilled than the other in translating the nuances of Hebrew or Greek syntax. Biblical interpreters with similar training and *shared factual knowledge* (3) can still display different degrees of *skill competency*. One scholar may be more competent in the translation of Biblical

---

26. Frances, *Disagreement*, 19–20.
27. Frances, *Disagreement*, 21–22.

Hebrew than another scholar in the same field. Frances also observes that even two persons with similar background knowledge and cognitive ability can disagree over the interpretation of the data due to one person having a *temporary* cognitive deficit (i.e., making errors in judgment or mistakes).

(Q4) *Can two intelligent people come to reasonable yet different answers to a single question when they share the same evidence, relevant background knowledge, and similar <u>cognitive ability</u>?* Yes. Frances chalks this possibility up to (4) *time spent researching the problem.*[28] Two biblical scholars with similar training and similar cognitive ability can likewise come to drastically different conclusions regarding a passage depending on how much time they spend investigating the text in question.

(Q5) *Can two intelligent people come to reasonable yet different answers to a single question when they share the same evidence, relevant background knowledge, similar cognitive ability, and have worked on the same question for a <u>comparable time period</u>?* Again, the answer is yes, because two equally reasonable persons can spend comparable time studying the same problem and (5) come to different results because of the *circumstances of the investigation.*[29] Constant distractions or interruptions, unhelpful input from other colleagues, and some other factors can affect the outcome of an investigation by a reasonable individual.

In biblical interpretation, as with any other disagreement of great significance, we also recognize that disagreements over the meaning of a text may relate to larger, more fundamental disagreements at the level of presuppositions or worldview. Even disagreements over more foundational issues such as worldview share many of the same disagreement factors listed above. We may have a clear disagreement about the existence of God with an atheist who is working from a different set of evidence or who has not spent the same amount of time considering the question of God's existence. Disagreement at this more fundamental level of worldview can cause disagreements about more specific interpretive issues, such as the veracity of the miracle accounts in the Gospels.

---

28. Frances, *Disagreement*, 24–25.
29. Frances, *Disagreement*, 26.

Do Both Disagreeing Parties Display Epistemic Virtue?

To these basic disagreement factors listed by Frances, we could add differences in our respective *epistemic virtues* that drive our disagreements. Virtue epistemology is another specialized area within the field of epistemology that speaks about *the intellectual character of the inquirer*. W. Jay Wood describes these epistemic or intellectual virtues as moral and intellectual habits or qualities that individual thinkers develop over time. Curiosity, intellectual honesty, teachability, patience, discernment, creativity, and wisdom are just a few of the virtues of intellectual inquiry.[30]

Like moral virtues, these epistemic virtues encourage human flourishing and reflect back positively on the thinker. The intellectually virtuous display a love for and openness to truth, wherever their inquiry may take them. By contrast, epistemic vices such as being simpleminded, haughty, closed-minded, gullible, or uncritical reflect back poorly on a person's intellectual life.[31] The deepening of intellectual virtues can also accompany growth in the Christian faith, as these characteristics correspond to the fruit of the Spirit grown in believers (Gal. 5:22–23).

How do differences in epistemic virtues give rise to disagreement? Reasonable people who have different study habits or levels of studiousness will have divergent opinions and levels of knowledge. Studiousness is a virtue celebrated in Scripture. Biblical authors frequently commend those who are diligent in their pursuit of the truth found in the Scriptures (Pss. 1:2; 119:18; 2 Tim. 2:15). Luke recounts Paul and Silas's encounter with the Jews at Berea who were open to the gospel message (Acts 17:10–15). Luke describes them as being people of "noble" character or being "noble-minded" (*eugenesteroi*) because of their open-mindedness toward the message and their commitment to examine Paul and Silas's message in light of the Scriptures (v. 11). The intellectual virtue of the Bereans is in stark contrast to the closed-mindedness and refusal to believe the Scriptures on the part of the Thessalonians (v. 13).

---

30. For an extended discussion on epistemic virtues, see W. Jay Wood, *Epistemology: Becoming Intellectually Virtuous* (Downers Grove, IL: InterVarsity Press, 1998), 33–76; Robert C. Roberts and W. Jay Wood, *Intellectual Virtues: An Essay in Regulative Epistemology* (New York: Oxford University Press, 2007).

31. Wood, *Epistemology*, 16, 47–48.

Disagreement can ensue when one person practices intellectual honesty while another practices the epistemic or interpretive vice of self-deception. Those who practice this vice see only what they want to see. The intellectually honest pursue internal consistency with their beliefs and are perturbed when they sense internal conflicts in their belief systems.[32]

The Bible is a complex literary work that requires great diligence and time in interpretation. It's not a one-and-done read like a magazine or a mystery paperback. Patience and persistence are crucial epistemic virtues in matters of great importance in its interpretation, and the more challenging the interpretive question, the more persistence is required. The interpretation of God's word calls for studiousness and discipline.

Epistemic humility is a general willingness to admit the possibility of one's being wrong. Such humility is not an automatic admission of being wrong or a claim that all truth is relative. It is simply cognizance of our imperfection as thinkers and interpreters, remaining open to change if compelling evidence to the contrary presents itself.[33] The Bible has a lot to say about the teachable spirit. Wise men grow in their wisdom, but fools hate reproof and correction (Prov. 12:1; cf. 1:25, 30; 5:12). The "one who accepts correction will be honored" (Prov. 13:18 CSB). Those who can accept correction are open to the work of God's Spirit (Prov. 1:23). The one open to correction is wise (Prov. 15:5, 31; 1 Pet. 5:5). Submission to Scripture's authority entails openness to its corrective influence (2 Tim. 3:16).

Kevin Vanhoozer has applied these intellectual virtues to hermeneutics and biblical interpretation. The hermeneutically virtuous have a "disposition of the mind and heart that arises from the motivation for understanding, for cognitive contact with the meaning of the text."[34] In other words, they approach texts in general and the biblical text in particular with a desire to know the meaning of the text as its authorship intended. They are *open* to the otherness of the text, not wanting to impose their agendas or meanings on it.

---

32. Wood, *Epistemology*, 48.

33. We could also use John Piper's phrase, "humble affirmation," to describe the same epistemic humility. See John Piper, *Let the Nations Be Glad! The Supremacy of God in Missions*, 2nd ed. (Grand Rapids, MI: Baker, 2003), 120n15.

34. Kevin J. Vanhoozer, *Is There a Meaning in This Text? The Bible, the Reader, and the Morality of Literary Knowledge* (Grand Rapids, MI: Zondervan, 1998), 376.

Who Is in a Better Interpretive Position?

The more difficult questions about disagreement are questions about *what to do* when people realize they are in disagreement. We clearly disagree. Now what? Should we (1) maintain our belief, (2) change our belief, or (3) suspend our belief temporarily? When faced with genuine disagreement, we will choose one of these three options in part based on a crucial question that Frances calls the *Better Position Question*.[35] For disagreements in biblical interpretation, this question is whether you are in a better position to interpret this passage than the person who disagrees with you about its meaning.

The disagreement factors mentioned above play a considerable role in answering this question. With this question, the person realizing disagreement asks herself whether the person or persons with whom she disagrees may know information relevant to the disagreement that she does not know.[36] Does the person with whom we differ have the same evidence we have at our disposal? Have they spent more time, less time, or the same amount of time dealing with the problem? Do they have a comparable ability and background knowledge? Does the person with whom we disagree exhibit external evidence of intellectual virtues like studiousness and humility? Do I exhibit these characteristics?

If after examination of these disagreement factors one deems the person with whom she disagrees *not* to be in a better epistemic position in the debate, then that person is her *epistemic inferior*. (Note: the term *inferior* here is not a pejorative term of derision but a simple assessment of who is in a better place to answer the disputed question at hand.) The most reasonable response to the realization of disagreement with an epistemic inferior is *maintaining one's own beliefs*.[37] In biblical interpretation, this option means that we can continue to believe that a given biblical passage means *x*, despite someone else arguing it means *y*, because the person arguing for *y* does not appear to be in a better position to know the meaning of the text. Again, we do not mean that the person with whom we disagree is not a reasonable person or that she is our epistemic inferior in every disagreement that

35. Frances, *Disagreement*, 30–32.
36. Frances, *Disagreement*, 28.
37. Frances, *Disagreement*, 27.

we may have. We simply mean that she is our epistemic inferior based on some of the disagreement factors listed above (e.g., evidence, time, ability, background knowledge, etc.).[38]

On the other hand, if one deems the person with whom she disagrees to be in a better epistemic position regarding this specific disagreement, then that person is her *epistemic superior*. Upon recognition of a disagreement with an epistemic or interpretive superior, usually the most reasonable thing to do is change one's belief. In a disagreement over biblical interpretation, we can reject our prior belief that the given biblical passage means x in favor of a new belief that the passage means y (or for that matter, r, s, or t). This change of mind occurs at various stages of the Christian life, as we move from overly simplistic readings of biblical passages toward more informed, nuanced readings by encountering interpretive disagreement with those who have spent more time studying a topic or who have more ability, background knowledge, or evidence.

Finally, one may deem the person with whom she disagrees an *epistemic peer*—someone who from all outward appearances is in a roughly equivalent epistemic position with regards to disagreement factors.[39] An epistemic peer is someone a person judges, at least from the outset of the disagreement, to have no readily evident epistemic advantage or disadvantage. In other words, the epistemic peer is someone who seems equally capable of coming to a correct conclusion.[40] Awareness of epistemic peers raises the central problem of the epistemology of disagreement: what are we to believe when we are facing disagreement with those who seem to have "no discernible epistemic advantage" in the disagreement?[41]

---

38. Kelly, "Epistemic Significance of Disagreement," 173–174.

39. Philosophers disagree somewhat about the parameters of epistemic peerhood, whether peerhood extends beyond disagreement about a particular issue (i.e., whether they are generally reliable in a field) or whether peerhood requires the same evidential grounds. See Earl Conee, "Rational Disagreement Defended," in Feldman and Warfield, *Disagreement*, 69–90. For our purposes here, we will describe an interpretive peer as someone who works from the same data and has roughly the same background knowledge, training, and ability.

40. Bryan Frances, "Disagreement," in *The Routledge Companion to Epistemology*, ed. Sven Bernecker and Duncan Pritchard (New York: Routledge, 2013), 68.

41. Kelly, "Epistemic Significance of Disagreement," 168. Kelly, who first appropriated this term in the epistemology of disagreement, borrows it from Gary Gutting, *Religious Belief and Religious Skepticism* (Notre Dame, IN: University of Notre Dame Press, 1982), 83.

How Should We Respond to Disagreement with a Peer?

Epistemologists tangle over two broad options in cases of disagreement with epistemic peers: the *steadfast* position and the *conformist* position. Both positions have potential application in hermeneutics. Those who argue that it is sometimes reasonable to maintain belief in the midst of a disagreement with an epistemic peer embrace the steadfast position (also called the "nonconformist" position). Someone who holds to a steadfast position does not change his beliefs when he has a theological disagreement with a peer who seems just as smart and just as capable of coming to the right conclusion. Someone who holds to a conformist position will either change his mind or refrain from making a judgment when confronted with peer disagreement.

Advocates for the steadfast position give different reasons for belief maintenance among epistemic peers. Some argue that since there are no normative epistemic criteria for resolving disagreements between peers, it is reasonable to maintain one's belief.[42] Other steadfast epistemologists such as Thomas Kelly contend that while peer disagreement can be psychologically unsettling, it may not provide sufficient reason for abandoning one's position.[43] One may discover that someone who they originally believed to be an epistemic peer is not a peer after all. Assuming that a person with whom we disagree is our equal with regard to disagreement factors may be a subtle way to "beg the question in favor of the skeptical view."[44]

We cannot make presumptions about the other person's general intelligence or know-how based on one issue on which we disagree. Even people who are normally our epistemic superiors make mistakes. As Kelly explains, "I need not assume I was better qualified to pass

---

42. See John Hawthorne and Amia Srinivasa, "Disagreement without Transparency: Some Bleak Thoughts," in Christensen and Lackey, *Epistemology of Disagreement: New Essays*, 9–30. Hawthorne and Srinivasan take a steadfast yet skeptical approach to peer disagreement, suggesting that there is no "general and intuitively satisfying answer" to be found "to the question that is at the centre of the disagreement debate" (28). They conclude that since there is no universally normative criteria for what we ought to do when faced with disagreement, the conformist position fails.

Richard Fumerton takes a similar skeptical steadfast position in Fumerton, "You Can't Trust a Philosopher," in Feldman and Warfield, *Disagreement*, 91–110. Fumerton disparages the philosophical enterprise as a typically unreliable or unsettled enterprise—something he admits creates additional problems for his own argument for philosophical skepticism.

43. Kelly, "Epistemic Significance of Disagreement," 192–193.

44. Kelly, "Epistemic Significance of Disagreement," 179; cf. David Christensen, "Epistemology of Disagreement: The Good News," *Philosophical Review* 116, no. 2 (2007): 195–196.

judgement on the question than they were, or that they are likely to make similar mistakes in the future, or even more likely to make such mistakes than I am. All I need to assume is that *on this particular occasion* I have done a better job with respect to weighing the evidence and competing considerations than they have."[45] The positive outcome of this steadfast position is that awareness of interpretive disagreement with a fellow Bible scholar need not result in either a general distrust of her interpretive knowledge and capability or skepticism about one's own interpretive stance.

Even when we disagree with a peer, we may choose to maintain our belief, especially if we believe our position to be coherent with other beliefs we believe to be true.[46] Suppose that John and Jacob are two theologians who come to a disagreement about the meaning of Romans 9:6–18—difficult as that may be to imagine! John interprets Romans 9:6–18 to mean E—that God unconditionally elects some individuals to salvation and others to damnation, based solely on his sovereign will. Jacob, on the other hand, argues not-E. Jacob believes he and John are epistemic peers with similar training, background knowledge, intelligence, skill, etc. He likewise knows that John has the same evidence before him, namely the text of Romans 9:6–18. But Jacob remains steadfast in his position that whatever this text means, it cannot mean E. Is Jacob acting rationally in maintaining his belief if he believes that he and John are interpretive peers? The supporter of the steadfast position says yes, if Jacob believes that not-E coheres better than E with his *other* justified belief L—that God desires to save every person. The champion of the steadfast position could likewise say that John may rationally maintain his belief E if it better coheres with his belief S—that God exercises meticulous providence in all human affairs.

The other epistemic option—the conformist position—says one cannot maintain a belief that contradicts one held by an epistemic peer—at least not without further investigating the cause of the disagreement. David Christensen, who calls the conformist position "epistemic modesty," says peer disagreement should make us consider

---

45. Kelly, "Epistemic Significance of Disagreement," 180, italics original.
46. Kelly, "Epistemic Significance of Disagreement," 193.

whether or not we made an error in coming to our conclusions. Even if we do not revise our beliefs, we should at least reconsider the level of confidence we have in the disputed belief.[47]

One conformist option, similar to what one does when she realizes she is the epistemic inferior in the disagreement, is to surrender one's belief and (a) *adopt the opposing position.* Adopting the opposing position is easier to do in disagreements of lesser consequence than it is on matters foundational to one's worldview. I am more likely to concede an argument with an epistemic peer in a relatively trivial matter, such as a debate over the length of Jesus's earthly ministry, than I am to concede an argument with a very intelligent New Testament scholar who disagrees with me about Jesus's divine identity. One disagreement weighs heavily in my worldview; another does not.

Another conformist option, named "The Equal Weight View," recommends "retreat into a state of agnosticism" when confronted with a disagreement with an epistemic peer.[48] If someone believes the person with whom they disagree to be their equal about disagreement factors and epistemic virtue, they may choose to (b) *suspend judgment until a later time.*[49] This suspension of judgment occurs when, in disagreement, we encounter compelling but not completely convincing reasons to cease believing *x*.

Applied to biblical interpretation, this option means we withhold final judgment about the meaning of a given biblical passage if we have good reason not to reject a previously held interpretation but have good reason to consider the alternative position as well. Withholding judgment in interpretation does not mean that one is skeptical about texts having an objective meaning, nor does it downplay their importance. It simply means that we are not, at this present time, capable of making a judgment with great confidence. We who are believers have the hope for fuller understanding of the texts in question—and the divine subject matter addressed in the texts—in the eschaton (1 Cor. 13:12).

---

47. David Christensen, "Epistemic Modesty Defended," in Christensen and Lackey, *Epistemology of Disagreement: New Essays,* 77–99; Christensen, "Epistemology of Disagreement: The Good News," 188–189.

48. Thomas Kelly, "Disagreement and the Burdens of Judgment," in Christensen and Lackey, *Epistemology of Disagreement: New Essays,* 34.

49. Frances, *Disagreement,* 43.

On this epistemic option, Frances makes the important observation that "*suspending judgment ≠ not acting.*"[50] A doctor may suspend judgment about her beliefs about the diagnosis of a patient's
ailments, but her agnosticism on the matter does not keep her from
attempting to treat the symptoms. The same may be true of interpretive judgments as well. Suppose Sue interprets the warning passage
in Hebrews 6:1–8 to mean that a believer may apostatize from the
faith, i.e., may genuinely lose his or her regenerate state before God.
Now suppose Sue encounters a convincing argument from Stan, who
argues that the warning passage in Hebrews 6:1–8 is *not* about a
genuine believer apostatizing but rather about persecuted Christians
losing their vocational and ministerial effectiveness if they cower
under persecution.[51]

Sue believes Stan to be epistemically virtuous and her peer with
regards to disagreement factors, as they both have similar training in
New Testament studies and have spent considerable time studying the
warning passages in Hebrews. Following her exchange with Stan, Sue
may suspend her judgment about the meaning of the passage but still
choose to *act* in a certain way in the interim. Christians who believe
in the possibility of genuine apostasy after conversion and those who
believe that genuine Christians necessarily persevere to the end *practice* the suggestions of the warning passages in similar ways, staying
faithful to Jesus in the midst of persecution whether the consequence
of not staying faithful is losing their salvation or simply losing their
effectiveness as ministers of reconciliation.

Most epistemologists of disagreement engaged in the debates over
steadfast and conformist positions suggest that "conciliatory responses
are appropriate in some cases and steadfast responses in others."[52]
They also raise additional questions in the debate that complicate matters further, questions like the role of "higher-order evidence" such as
expert opinions,[53] controversial beliefs,[54] disagreement between split

---

50. Frances, *Disagreement*, 36.
51. See Herschel H. Hobbs, *Hebrews: Challenges to Bold Discipleship* (Nashville: Broadman, 1971), 56–66.
52. David Christensen and Jennifer Lackey, "Introduction," in Christensen and Lackey, *Epistemology of Disagreement: New Essays*, 1; cf. Frances, *Disagreement*, 196–197.
53. Thomas Kelly, "Peer Disagreement and Higher-Order Evidence," in Feldman and Warfield, *Disagreement*, 111–174.
54. Frances, *Disagreement*, 85–86, 95–98, 201–203.

experts,[55] and questions about what to do when the Better Position Question cannot be answered.[56] While many of these questions remain unanswered, the rough procedure outlined here gives us a helpful starting point for assessing our disagreements.

Dealing with Theological Disagreement

Here we must summarize the insights of Frances and Wood which are relevant to theological and interpretive disagreement. *We begin by asking whether our disagreement is a genuine disagreement or an illusory one.* Remember: not all apparent theological disagreements truly are disagreements, nor are all apparent agreements true agreements. We must ask whether we are defining terms in the same way and using the same comparison classes.

Second, we must ask ourselves about our epistemic or interpretive position. Am I epistemically superior or inferior to my challenger? In other words, am I really in a better place to know the meaning of the text than the person or persons with whom I disagree?

(1) Are *we working with the same body of evidence?* Scripture is the primary data of Christian theology, but Christians can come to different theological conclusions when they are considering different biblical texts. The first step in the actual task of developing evangelical systematic theology is gathering all the relevant biblical materials on the doctrine in question.[57] The selection process itself requires basic knowledge of biblical contents and some exegetical acumen. If both parties still disagree about the doctrine after looking at the same bodies of evidence in Scripture, then we may proceed to the next important question.

(2) *If I disagree with a tenet from a particular tradition, am I interacting with its best and most sophisticated representations or with a straw man?* An intellectually honest interpreter of Scripture, driven by a desire for the truth rather than simply reassurance of her own position, will want to assess theological points of view contrary to her own (as noted in chapter 5), but she will also want to seek out the best representations of a particular idea and not simply easily defeasible straw men.

---

55. Frances, *Disagreement*, 152–156.
56. Frances, *Disagreement*, 148–151.
57. Millard J. Erickson, *Christian Theology*, 3rd ed. (Grand Rapids, MI: Baker, 2013), 53–56.

(3) *Who exhibits a more thorough understanding of the relevant background material?* If the person with whom I disagree displays a less critical understanding of the pertinent biblical texts and the doctrine in question, I will more than likely regard him as being in an epistemically inferior position and will therefore maintain my own belief. On the other hand, if my opponent does display adequate background knowledge, I will move on to evaluating his skill set.

(4) *Who exhibits greater theological acumen and exegetical skill?* Does the person with whom I disagree theologically demonstrate competence in theological reasoning and biblical exegesis? If so, does he do so with greater skill than I? Because of my training, I frequently dismiss the conclusions of those who disagree with me theologically more readily if they do not display equal or better interpretive know-how. But I also find myself disagreeing, at times, with biblical scholars and theologians who I believe to be more intelligent and skilled than I. In disagreements where I become convinced that they have the epistemic upper hand, I change my belief. In disagreements where I am convinced that they are typically more intelligent than I but am *unconvinced* by their current arguments and reasoning, I will likely maintain my own belief. In disagreements where I am convinced that each of our arguments is equally compelling, I will withhold final judgment on the matter. But in each of these cases, an epistemically virtuous person will give further consideration to the matter at hand, not simply disregard positions contrary to his own.

(5) *Do both parties evidence adequate time spent accessing the disputed issue?* I may be convinced that a person is generally as intelligent as I or more intelligent than I but be unconvinced that he or she has spent as much time dealing with the issue at hand. I know several atheists who have much higher IQs than I and who have spent much more time considering questions in the natural sciences than I have. To them, I may yield their epistemic superiority on matters in the sciences not pertinent to the existence of God or the Christian worldview. (For instance, I would easily buckle in a debate about string theory and loop quantum gravity theory because on those subjects I would likely be an epistemic inferior to everyone else in the room.) But most skeptics with whom I am acquainted have spent considerably less time

than I researching the philosophy of religion and arguments for God's existence. As such, I tend to be more dubious about their conclusions. For disagreements with theologians who have spent considerable time studying topics in which I have done only a little research, I may be more likely to yield beliefs when met with a compelling argument. But I will be more reluctant to change my mind when I disagree with generally more intelligent theologians who disagree with me in one of my research concentrations.

(6) *Do both disagreeing parties display the intellectual virtues such as curiosity, studiousness, persistence, and intellectual honesty?* Possession of intellectual virtues does not guarantee a correct conclusion any more than possession of intellectual vices necessitates an incorrect belief. But these qualities are good and helpful indicators as to whether a person is an epistemic inferior, superior, or peer.

(7) *Does the person with whom I disagree exhibit the fruit of the Spirit?* To these epistemic virtues, we may also add Christian virtues that brand a follower of Jesus. Jesus told us to test prophets by their fruits (Matt. 7:15–20), which I take to mean blessing and success stemming from a life of obedience (John 15:1–16). Paul asserts that a lack of virtue can be a good indicator of false teaching: "If anyone teaches false doctrine and does not agree . . . with the teaching that promotes godliness, he is conceited and understands nothing" (1 Tim. 6:3–4 CSB).

Once we have addressed these questions, we can state whether the person or party with whom we disagree is an *interpretive inferior, superior,* or *peer.*

Third, if we discern that we are obvious epistemic inferiors to the opposing party, it is reasonable to change our interpretive belief, or at least to call our own belief into question. If I have a long-held belief that people become angels when they die and I encounter someone who has actually read the Bible and rejects this belief, then it is reasonable to reject my belief. For more substantial disagreements with someone who appears to be an epistemic superior, it is at least worth suspending present belief and investigating the matter further.

Fourth, if we determine conclusively that we are in a better epistemic position than our interlocutors, the most reasonable thing to do is maintain our belief. This move is reasonable and virtuous when we have considered all the textual support of a position and have properly answered all the disagreement questions pertinent to the issue. However, a reasonable person should revisit the matter when he encounters an epistemic peer or epistemic superior who holds the position previously rejected on the grounds of epistemic inferiority.

Fifth, if, following an evaluation of the Better Position Question, we discover that we are epistemically equal to the person with whom we disagree, we must decide whether we will be conformist or steadfast in our responses and if we have justification for our choice in the matter. This question is the central debate in the arena of the epistemology of disagreement. Those who hold conformist positions suggest that we should either *change our belief* or *withhold judgment* when we disagree with someone we reckon to be our epistemic peer. Those who hold the steadfast approach contend that we should *not change our beliefs* when we disagree with someone we believe to be our epistemic peer. I am presently convinced that the steadfast position is the more reasonable, intellectually honest position, though I know others in the field think differently.

Sixth, any explicitly Christian consideration of whether we should change our mind should include extended time in prayer and seeking God's wisdom. The Lord is the final source of wisdom in decision making (Prov. 2:6). We should seek his wisdom and his presence in every decision, including epistemic decisions (Prov. 3:5–6; 1 Chron. 16:11). As the Lord promised Jeremiah, "Call to me and I will answer you, and will tell you great and hidden things that you have not known" (Jer. 33:3). James tells us, "If any of you lacks wisdom, let him ask God, who gives generously to all without reproach, and it will be given him" (James 1:5). Let me first acknowledge a degree of subjectivity in the way we sense the leadership of the Holy Spirit in our lives. I also want to stress the fact that he will not lead you to believe or do something contrary to his expressed intentions in Scripture.

Finally, we can proceed to one of three interpretive choices: (1) maintaining our interpretive belief, (2) rejecting our interpretive belief and adopting a new one, or (3) suspending belief about the meaning of a specific passage. With regards to theological or interpretive disagreement, the wisest thing to do may be to evaluate what steps one should take on a case-to-case basis. When I disagree with someone whom I believe to be my peer in theology or biblical interpretation, I am more inclined to change my mind or withhold judgment on matters I believe to be of lesser consequence (e.g., millennial views, the order of God's decrees, etc.) and more likely to maintain beliefs I believe to be more foundational to my worldview (e.g., the authority and trustworthiness of Scripture, the deity of Christ, etc.).

Withholding final judgment may be temporary, or it may be lifelong. There are some matters in Scripture about which I have no deeply held beliefs because I feel I have not spent adequate time assessing them. I may arrive at a more confident position on a disputed topic after carefully assessing the evidence and arguments for each position. There are other matters in Scripture about which I suspect I will never have a strong belief because the backgrounds and contexts of certain texts seem lost to history (e.g., baptism for the dead in 1 Cor. 15:29). On relatively nonconsequential matters of the latter sort, I expect to reserve my final judgment until the *final judgment*, when I believe all these matters will be known with clarity (1 Cor. 13:12).

Conclusion

Many of the important questions about epistemic disagreement remain unsettled and difficult to assess. Interpretive disagreement has many of the same qualities as any other epistemic disagreement, and some of the discussion from the burgeoning field of the epistemology of disagreement may be helpful for evaluating these disagreements. The patterns of judgment we make regarding epistemic beliefs bear clear commonalities with the sorts of decisions we have to make in interpreting texts.

Disagreement affords us "opportunities for epistemic self-improvement,"[58] or, in the case of biblical interpretation, opportunities for sanctification and a better understanding of the living God. An intellectually virtuous assessment of disagreement entails appreciation for it, especially when the disagreement is with a peer. In the words of the proverb, "As iron sharpens iron, so a person sharpens his friend" (Prov. 27:17 NET). Disagreement does this in a number of ways. First,

---

58. Christensen, "Epistemology of Disagreement: The Good News," 187.

exposure to interpretive disagreement should raise introspective questions about the debated text. *Does the person with whom I disagree have additional evidence or resources that I have not considered? Have I spent adequate time wrestling with this text? How confident am I of the meaning of the text in question and its implications for Christian belief and practice?*

Second, awareness of interpretive disagreement makes us aware of different hermeneutical possibilities for an individual text. Disagreement may mean that one or more of the persons involved are wrong about the authorial intent, but a text, unlike debate over a proposition, occasionally opens more than one correct possibility of meaning. As Vanhoozer grants, "The Spirit's vitality in interpretation is also seen in the diversity of readings. Particular interpretations may make valuable contributions without needing to make the further claim that they have said everything that needs to be said. Just as many members make up one body, so *many readings may make up the single correct interpretation.*"[59]

Finally, awareness of interpretive disagreement can foster in us an attitude of hermeneutical humility. While disagreement with hermeneutical peers can signal an error on their part, it should at least make us aware of the possibility that we are mistaken in our own judgment about the meaning of a text. Disagreement reminds us of our own imperfections as interpreters and our need for ongoing growth and development. We should prayerfully, patiently, and humbly wade through the theological disagreements we have with one another. On occasion, this means changing our minds, while on other occasions it means remaining steadfast in our belief or suspending our judgment on a matter.

Thus far, we have discussed reasons why we disagree about doctrine and whether we should change our minds about our disagreements. Assuming that we can "agree to disagree" on a specific point of difference, we must now ask some hard questions about what types of disagreements can sustain Christian fellowship and which differences might make it impossible.

---

59. Vanhoozer, *Is There a Meaning in This Text?*, 420.

7

When Should Doctrine Divide Us?

On Theological Boundary-Making

I once heard a well-meaning pastor declare, "Denominations are inventions of the Devil himself. When God's people are divided over doctrine, Satan wins." The remark came in a sermon drawn from the so-called "High Priestly Prayer" of Jesus in John 17:1–26, a passage in which Jesus prays not once but four times that his followers would "be one" with one another as he is one with the Father (vv. 11, 21–23). "Because if Jesus prayed for unity, we should too," the pastor reasoned, "Quarrels over doctrine are distractions from the Devil which keep us from what is really important."

The earnest appeal for Christian unity here truly is appreciated. On this point I agree: If Jesus desired his followers to be one, his disciples should desire the same. Jesus is, after all, the head of the whole body, the Lord of all throughout history who call him Savior and Lord (Eph. 1:22–23; 1 Cor. 12:13). In the beginning, the church was "of one heart and soul" (Acts 4:32). The apostle Paul challenged the churches under his care to be of the same mind (Eph. 4:1–16; Phil. 2:2; Rom. 15:5). Because we have been reconciled to God through our faith in Christ, we should also seek reconciliation with others who belong to Christ (Col. 1:13–23).

This being said, the pastor's comments were also rife with problems. First, he gave our common enemy too much credit. No, the devil cannot make us do anything. The devil and demonic powers can deceive and wield manipulative influence, but they cannot *determine* human behavior or beliefs any more than they can make our heads spin and vomit pea soup.

Second, not every theological disagreement is attributable to internal or external evils. The Bible talks about "doctrines of demons" (1 Tim. 4:1 NASB), but this is not a reference to the ordinary differences of opinion and tradition that divide fellow believers. Not all of our theological disputes are necessarily the products of unbelief, sinfulness, or malicious intent. We have seen many ways in which fallible and well-intentioned interpreters can come to different conclusions regarding the meaning of disputed biblical texts.

Lastly, these comments display an unhelpful, cavalier attitude toward doctrine. Many ecumenists seem to believe that doctrine itself is the source of our problems and that abandoning confessions would remedy our ecclesial woes. Yet it is important to note that in the same prayer in which Jesus asked for unity among his disciples, he also prayed for them to be *sanctified in the truth* of the Father's word (John 17:17, 19). The pursuit of theological truth is no small matter in the life of the church, and true Christian unity cannot be attained without it. In the words of David F. Wells, "Without theology there can be no Church, because theology holds the key to Christian identity, to Christian continuity, to genuine piety, to serious worship, and to the sort of Christian thought that seeks to bring the import of God's Word into our world."[1]

The desire for true, gospel-centered Christian unity honors God and builds up the body of Christ, but practical questions remain for any who hope to have this kind of fellowship.[2] How do we draw the line between ordinary theological and interpretive disagreements and false doctrine which "does not agree with the sound teaching of our

---

1. David F. Wells, *No Place for Truth: Or Whatever Happened to Evangelical Theology?* (Grand Rapids, MI: Eerdmans, 1993), 292.
2. Evangelical theologians Peter Leithart and Kevin Vanhoozer have recently taken up this important topic in two very different yet important monographs. See Peter J. Leithart, *The End of Protestantism: Pursuing Unity in a Fragmented Church* (Grand Rapids, MI: Brazos, 2016); Kevin J. Vanhoozer, *Biblical Authority after Babel: Retrieving the Solas in the Spirit of Mere Protestant Christianity* (Grand Rapids, MI: Brazos, 2016).

Lord Jesus Christ and with the teaching that promotes godliness" (1 Tim. 6:3 CSB)?

To what degree should we who are believers embrace the plurality of compatible traditions, and to what extent should we call for separation from others who self-identify as the people of God? When should doctrine divide us, and when should we cooperate together despite our differences? How do we determine which expressions of doctrine are essential for us to believe and which are not? These are crucial questions for every follower of Christ.

Two flawed approaches to these types of questions arise. The first is an overemphasis on harmony at the expense of truth. The forms of liberal theology prevalent in the nineteenth and twentieth centuries built their brand on accommodation to modernity, discarding beliefs they believed to be outmoded, historical tenets such as the divinity and resurrection of Jesus Christ. The teaching of Jesus was stripped of its theological content in favor of ethics.

What emerged was a kind of *theological minimalism* that effectually *denies the need for any "essential" Christian doctrine or truth.* Postmodern theologians have continued the trend of minimizing doctrine, not out of the same modernistic, anti-supernatural bias but out of concern for how exclusive truth claims might be oppressive to outsider communities. Theological minimalism in both modern and postmodern veins tends to prioritize experience over doctrine and to reduce theology to ethics.[3]

At the other extreme, *theological maximalists* raise every doctrinal topic to the same level of practical importance.[4] For them, every doctrine is a major one.[5] Because they believe all doctrines to be expressions of God's truth, theological maximalists suggest that "*all* truth must be defended with equal vigor."[6] For the theological maximalist, every doctrine is an essential element of a rigid theological system.

---

3. Michael E. Wittmer, *Don't Stop Believing: Why Living Like Jesus Is Not Enough* (Grand Rapids, MI: Zondervan, 2008), 15–20.

4. The term "theological maximalism" comes from M. James Sawyer, *The Survivor's Guide to Theology: Investigation of the Critical Issues, Survey of Key Traditions, Biography of Major Theologians, Glossary of Terms* (Grand Rapids, MI: Zondervan, 2006), 145–146.

5. See R. Albert Mohler Jr. "A Call for Theological Triage and Christian Maturity," Albert-Mohler.com, July 12, 2005, http://www.albertmohler.com/2005/07/12/a-call-for-theological-triage-and-christian-maturity/. Mohler writes, "The misjudgment of true fundamentalism is the belief that all disagreements concern first-order doctrines."

6. Sawyer, *Survivor's Guide to Theology*, 145.

The rejection or redefinition of any doctrine, no matter how minor, is perceived as a rejection of the whole system. Deny their view of end-times events or of church government, and you may be accused of denying the authority of Scripture itself. In short, they "major on the minors" because they believe no doctrine to be of minor consequence.

Driven by this idea that every doctrine is of equal importance, and their conviction that they are defenders of the doctrinal purity of the church, theological maximalists tend to be *sectarian* in their thinking. Believing themselves to have the only possible correct understanding of disputed biblical texts, theological maximalists encourage personal and ecclesial separation from those who disagree with them. Fundamentalists take texts that speak about separation from those in immoral practices (Eph. 5:11; 2 Cor. 6:14–18) and false teachers (Rom. 16:17) to extend to every theological or political rift. Some within fundamentalism go so far as to encourage a "second degree of separation" from those who may agree with them theologically but who do not (in their minds) practice proper separation with others who do not share their theological tenets.[7]

For centuries, theologians have formulated or implicitly held to *doctrinal taxonomies* (also called *dogmatic ranks*) that sort doctrines according to their significance and authoritative role in the broader Christian tradition. Protestants have been creating taxonomies of doctrine since the first generation of the Reformation, something made necessary by the Protestant insistence that the people of God ought to be able to read the Bible for themselves. Doctrinal taxonomies can be helpful tools for correcting the mirroring errors of a theological minimalism which turns a blind eye to colossal errors and a theological maximalism which casts every dissenting opinion as a heresy.

More foundational doctrines are given greater weight and authority in a theological system, while other doctrines take a place of secondary or tertiary importance. These taxonomies draw boundaries

---

7. Some of the more detailed discussions of the practice of doctrinal and ecclesial separation in the fundamentalist tradition are in Fred Moritz and Mark Sidwell, eds., *"Be Ye Holy": The Call to Christian Separation* (Greenville, SC: Bob Jones University Press, 2000); Ernest D. Pickering, *Biblical Separation: The Struggle for a Pure Church*, rev. ed. (Arlington Heights, IL: Regular Baptist Press, 2008); Pickering, *The Tragedy of Compromise: The Origin and Impact of the New Evangelicalism* (Greenville, SC: Bob Jones University Press, 2000); Mark Sidwell, *Set Apart: The Nature and Importance of Biblical Separation* (Greenville, SC: Bob Jones University Press, 2016).

between "sound doctrine" (1 Tim. 4:6 NASB) and the "doctrines of demons" (1 Tim. 4:1 NASB; cf. 1:3; 2 Tim. 4:3), as well as between essential and nonessential Christian beliefs. Essential Christian beliefs divide the followers of Jesus from those who are not (Matt. 10:34–36). Taxonomies provide guardrails in which faithful Christians can navigate their different readings of Scripture. The guardrail separates essential doctrines from nonessential tenets. A guardrail is an important metaphor because it gives the driver freedom to move across different lanes while also protecting her from driving off the cliff. No one concerned for their own well-being wants to ride right up against the guardrails.

Such taxonomies also function as requirements for fellowship and provide a common ground for Christians from diverse traditions to serve together in Christian mission. While some in both theological maximalist and theological minimalist camps cringe at the notion of doctrinal boundary-making, this practice has deep roots in Christian history. It was the practice of apostolic anathemas and creedal formulations of the early church. Biblical writers allowed for some variation in practice in the early church but stressed agreement on matters "of first importance" (1 Cor. 15:3).

This chapter is an examination of the concept of doctrinal taxonomies. I begin with a biblical-theological assessment of doctrinal diversity and heresy. I next examine the concept of doctrinal taxonomy. When should Christians who place themselves under the authority of Scripture tolerate other beliefs, and when should they regard differences in belief as a potential threat to orthodoxy? I conclude this chapter with a series of tests that can help us sort the differences between us by their importance. These tests, I hope, will help us think through the question of fellowship and ministry together with Christians who may interpret Scripture differently than us.

The Nature of Heresy and False Teaching

The term *heresy* is an important historical term used to describe theological deviations from "the faith that was once for all delivered to the saints" (Jude 3). Some bandy the term about too frivolously, labeling any idea with which they find grievance "unorthodox" or "heretical."

Theological maximalists, who make every tenet of their systems a nonnegotiable article of belief, are quick to drop the "H-bomb." ("If you don't agree with my position on spiritual gifts, you're unorthodox." "If you don't agree with my view on immigration policy, you're probably a communist heretic!") The heresy hunters of the digital age closely monitor the boundaries of their theological tribes, anxiously waiting to pounce on any who they believe cross the line. Given enough time, they will gleefully devour any deviants within their own ranks (Gal. 5:15).

By contrast, theological minimalists are often too hesitant to label a doctrine *unorthodox* when the vast majority of Christians throughout history would have applied that label without hesitation. They tend to be pragmatists more concerned with carrying out a particular agenda than with teaching Christian truth. Those who trivialize doctrine have difficulty recognizing or acknowledging heterodoxy when they see it, even if it is in their own ranks. The Bible explicitly condemns such a passive approach to doctrine: "Everyone who goes on ahead and does not abide in the teaching [doctrine] of Christ, does not have God. Whoever abides in the teaching has both the Father and the Son. If anyone comes to you and does not bring this teaching, do not receive him into your house or give him any greeting, for whoever greets him takes part in his wicked works" (2 John 9–11). The passive acceptance of heresy in a local church is often tantamount to participation in it.

The term *heresy* does not apply to every interpretive mistake or error but rather to those teachings or beliefs so egregious that "those who believe [them] . . . must be considered to have abandoned the faith."[8] I take some positions held by my dear brothers to be erroneous, but these differences don't make them heretics. Furthermore, not every belief or idea contrary to the Christian faith is a heresy, at least in the classical sense of the word. Secular humanism, for instance, is a contrary worldview rooted in unbelief. It is not an aberration from within Christianity that invokes Christian language or elements. It is a false teaching but is not, strictly speaking, a heresy.

---

8. Harold O. J. Brown, *Heresies: The Image of Christ in the Mirror of Heresy and Orthodoxy* (Grand Rapids, MI: Baker, 1994), 1.

Heresies come from within and use "insider language." For example, modern-day cults like Mormons and Jehovah's Witnesses are deviations from the historic Christian faith that employ Christian authorities and terminology (even if they do so in ways that contradict the broad consensus of Christians throughout history). Whereas worldviews outside the Christian faith require an *apologetic* posture that defends the faith from external challenges, heresies need *polemical* responses that critique their peculiar elements because they threaten the faith from within. Apologists counter challenges outside of the Christian faith like atheism or Islam, while polemicists tackle internal challenges like the prosperity gospel or Gnosticism, false teachings or ideas advocated by people who claim to be Christians.

Etymologically speaking, *heresy* has its roots in doctrinal diversity.[9] Before it became a pejorative term used to describe a false teaching contrary to *orthodoxy* ("right teaching," "true teaching"), it was simply a Greek word meaning "party," "sect," "grouping," or "school of thought" (*hairesis*). In the first century, *hairesis* described any variation within a larger group. It was used to describe the various groups or parties within Judaism, such as the Sadducees (Acts 5:17), the Pharisees (Acts 26:5), and even followers of Christ (Acts 24:5; 28:22).[10]

The term also has a negative connotation in the New Testament, tangentially but not always directly related to false teaching. In 1 Corinthians 11, Paul addresses the problem of *haireseis* or "factions" that divide the body of Christ (v. 19), but the problem there is not false teaching but mistreatment and humiliation of those who have nothing (vv. 21–22). Elsewhere Paul puts "factions" (*haireseis*) in a list of the works of the flesh that stand in opposition to the fruit of the Spirit (Gal. 5:20 CSB).

The closest biblical association of *haireseis* with false teachers is in 2 Peter 2:1: "But false prophets also arose among the people, just as there will be false teachers among you, who will secretly bring in destructive *heresies*, even denying the Master who bought them, bringing upon themselves swift destruction." Scholars are divided over whether *haireseis* in this context refers to the false teachings themselves—the

---

9. Alister E. McGrath, *Heresy* (New York: HarperOne, 2010), 37–39.
10. Josephus, *Bellum Judaicum* 2.118; *Antiquitates Judaicae* 13.171.

definition of heresy most frequently used from the second century onward—or the schisms that were forged as a consequence of the false teaching.[11]

Even if biblical authors do not use the term *heresy* in the sense in which it came to be understood in the following centuries, they do have much to say about "false teachers" (*pseudodidaskaloi*) and "false prophets" (*pseudoprophētai*) relevant to the discussion of heresy. Hebrew prophets condemned those prophets of Israel who prophesied according to their own imagination (e.g., Deut. 18:20–22; Jer. 23:9–32; Ezek. 13:1–23). The apostles repeatedly confronted teachings that they believed to be erroneous, counterfeit, and even sinister in origin. The Pauline Epistles tackled legalistic religion (Gal. 6:12ff.), denials of a future resurrection for believers (1 Cor. 15:12ff.; 2 Tim. 2:18), the worship of angels (Col. 2:18), genealogical myths common to so-called mystery religions (1 Tim. 1:3–4), and esoteric practices that denied the goodness of creation (1 Tim. 4:3–4). John condemned a teaching spreading around churches in Asia Minor that denied the coming of Christ in human flesh (1 John 4:2ff.; 2 John 7).

One of the primary apostolic concerns was protecting churches from the corruption and strife caused by these aberrant teachings. Some of the weightiest theological formulations within the New Testament were, in fact, ad hoc responses to the particular doctrinal controversies their congregations faced (e.g., 1 Corinthians 15; Col. 1:15–21). Just as the true prophets of Israel had to deal with the prophets of foreign gods and false prophets from among the people of the land, the apostles confronted false teaching from within the church and from without.

The New Testament Epistles offer several characteristics of false teachers and those susceptible to their teachings. *First, false teaching preys on the spiritually immature.* Paul repeatedly expresses concern for the minds of believers who may be "led astray" by belief in a different Jesus, a different spirit, and a different gospel (2 Cor. 11:3–4; cf. Gal. 1:6–7). Elsewhere, he asserts that believers will have true "unity of the faith" only when they will *"no longer be children,*

11. Thomas R. Schreiner, *1, 2 Peter, Jude*, New American Commentary 37 (Nashville: B&H Academic, 2003), 328; Richard J. Bauckham, *Jude, 2 Peter*, WBC 50 (Waco, TX: Word, 1983), 239–240.

tossed to and fro by the waves and carried about by every wind of doctrine, by human cunning, by craftiness in deceitful schemes" (Eph. 4:13–14).

Second, false teaching can be the product of distorted interpretations of Scripture by those not firmly established in the truth. Some pervert the meaning of Scriptures that are "hard to understand," doing so "to their own destruction" (2 Pet. 3:16). The emphasis made here is not on a particular method of interpretation or the difficulty of the texts themselves but on the type of people who distort the Scriptures—"ignorant and unstable" people (*hoi amatheis kai astēriktoi*). The term "unstable" (*astēriktoi*) shares a cognate (*stērizō*) with another word used in 2 Peter 1:12 to describe those "firmly established" (*estērigmenous*) in the truth (NIV). With the same group of terms, Peter contrasts those deeply rooted in the truth with those who are not (*astēriktous*), who are more susceptible to the deception of false prophets (2 Pet. 2:14).[12]

Third, false teaching grows out of ungodly ambition, ignorance, and conceit. Paul cautioned Timothy about false teachers who "wandered away into vain discussion, *desiring to be teachers* of the law, without understanding either what they are saying or the things about which they make confident assertions" (1 Tim. 1:6–7). These teachers had ambition but lacked proper understanding of the things they taught. Elsewhere in the same letter, Paul warned, "If anyone teaches a different doctrine and does not agree with the sound words of our Lord Jesus Christ and the teaching that accords with godliness, he is *puffed up with conceit* and *understands nothing*. He has an *unhealthy craving for controversy* and for quarrels about words" (1 Tim. 6:3–4). The ambition for power can be an impetus for false teaching as well. John challenged a false teacher who "put himself first" and denied the apostolic authority of John's teaching, speaking "wicked nonsense" against him (3 John 9–10).

Fourth, false teaching sometimes stems from a desire for material gain. This tendency is very apparent in the modern world, where faith-healing televangelists and prosperity preachers prey upon the underprivileged to finance their extravagant lifestyles, but the same kind of

---

12. See "στηρίζω," in *NIDNTTE* 4:375.

greed motivated false prophecy and teaching in the early church (2 Pet. 2:3). As Paul defended his apostleship from this charge, "We are not, like so many, peddlers of God's word, but as men of sincerity, as commissioned by God, in the sight of God we speak in Christ" (2 Cor. 2:17). The same type of charge appears in the Pastoral Epistles: "From these come . . . constant disagreement among people whose minds are depraved and deprived of the truth, who imagine that godliness is a way to material gain. . . . For the love of money is a root of all kinds of evil, and by craving it, some have wandered away from the faith and pierced themselves with many griefs" (1 Tim. 6:4b–5, 10 CSB).

Fifth, false teaching can result from and lead to inappropriate sensuality and sexual immorality. The idolatrous fixation on immoral behavior can yield false teaching. These false teachers "do not serve our Lord Christ, but their own appetites [or "belly"; *koilia*]" (Rom. 16:18). As Peter observes, "many will follow their sensuality [*aselgeiais*], and because of them the way of truth will be blasphemed" (2 Pet. 2:2). Teaching rooted in immoral desires yields immoral behavior. The risen Lord warns the churches in Pergamum and Thyatira about teachings that lead his "servants to practice sexual immorality [*porneusai*]" (Rev. 2:20; cf. 2:14). In a post–sexual revolution Western culture, people still "[follow] their own sinful desires [*epithymias*]" (Jude 16) and "accumulate for themselves teachers to suit their own passions" (2 Tim. 4:3). Sensual urges and lust still motivate many to deny biblical truth about God's design for sex and marriage and to justify atrocities like human abortion.

Sixth, false teaching is sometimes attributed to demonic deception. Some who depart the faith do so because they pay attention "to deceitful spirits and teachings of demons" (1 Tim. 4:1). Paul cautions against affirming false apostles who are like Satan, who masquerades as "an angel of light" (2 Cor. 11:13–14). Paul forewarns Galatian Christians not to believe any other gospel even if "an angel from heaven should preach to you a gospel contrary to the one we preached to you" (Gal. 1:8). Not every spiritual work is from God. The spirit of the messenger and the message must be tested because, as John insists, spirits who do "not confess Jesus" are "not from God" (1 John 4:3).

Seventh, false teachers seek to divide the body of Christ. Paul cautioned the church at Rome about "those who cause divisions and create obstacles contrary to the doctrine that you have been taught" (Rom. 16:17). In his admonition to Titus to avoid "foolish controversies" and "quarrels about the law" (Titus 3:9), Paul remarks, "As for a person who stirs up division, after warning him once and then twice, have nothing more to do with him, knowing that such a person is warped and sinful; he is self-condemned" (Titus 3:10–11). Those who cause division are worldly, "devoid of the Spirit," and are relentlessly pursuing their own ungodly passions (Jude 18–19).

Finally, false teaching can come from apostates and deviant teachers within the church. False teachers from "among the people [*en tō laō*] . . . secretly bring in destructive heresies" (2 Pet. 2:1). Jesus warned about false prophets from among the people who outwardly come in "sheep's clothing but inwardly are ravenous wolves" (Matt. 7:15). Paul blames the Galatian conflict on false teachers who had covertly entered their ranks: "This matter arose because some false brothers [*pseudadelphous*] had infiltrated our ranks to spy on the freedom we have in Christ Jesus in order to enslave us" (Gal. 2:4 CSB). Some of the false teachers addressed in the Pastoral Epistles appear to be former coworkers of Paul (1 Tim. 1:3; 2 Tim. 1:15; 2:15–18).[13] John states that his "antichrist" opponents, those who deny that Jesus is the Christ, came out of the fellowship with the churches because "they did not belong" there in the first place (1 John 2:19 CSB). In instances where theological matters of first importance are denied, rejected, or replaced, doctrine does divide the people of God from those who are not.

Biblically speaking, "false doctrine" is more than an incorrect propositional belief about some aspect of Christian doctrine. It is not a simple interpretive mistake; it is an act of volition that stems from spiritual immaturity, unbelief, arrogance, and illicit desire. While these characteristics identified are helpful in addressing false gospels and heresies that do "not agree with the sound teaching of our Lord Jesus Christ" (1 Tim. 6:3 CSB), they do not describe the sorts

---

13. E. Earle Ellis, "Paul and His Opponents," in *Christianity, Judaism, and Other Greco-Roman Cults, Part 1*, ed. Jacob Neusner (Leiden: Brill, 1975), 297.

of intramural conflicts that come between sincere, faithful believers who are devoted to Christ, Scripture, and the proclamation of the gospel. Even believers who exhibit the fruit of the Spirit sometimes come to distinct conclusions regarding the meaning of biblical texts and doctrines.

By the second century, Christian writers were already using the term *heresy* to describe false teaching that was contrary to *orthodoxy* ("right opinion" or "right belief"), the normative standard of Christian belief prescribed in Scripture and expressed through creeds and confessions.[14] Throughout history, Christians have recognized the guardrails or essential beliefs which make them Christian and heretical beliefs which would properly deny them that title. The tribe of Christ, like every other tribe, has boundary markers that define whether one is in it or outside of it. This is why councils have anathematized ideas like Arianism, Apollinarianism, Nestorianism, Eutychianism, and Pelagianism, condemning them as heresies or false teachings contrary to sound teaching or orthodoxy. Diversity on some matters has been allowed, while other issues mark a boundary for who is in the faith and who is not.

While not formally recognized as a heresy until Nicaea, the ideas of Arianism were already *heretical* in substance because they contradicted the implicit orthodoxy presupposed by Christian believers and the explicit statements of Scripture regarding the true divinity of Jesus. New and improved versions of heresy rear their ugly heads in every generation, and simple appeals to the formulated creeds of the past do not always address them. An appeal to the ecumenical creeds would not directly answer some of the heretical developments of the Word-Faith movement popular in the late twentieth and early twenty-first centuries. Because heresy develops in every age, there is an ongoing need for doctrinal development anchored in the normative direction of Scripture in every age as well.[15]

Protestants and evangelicals can and should have a deep appreciation for the creedal formulations that helped clarify the boundaries between heresy and orthodoxy. They are helpful guides in establish-

---

14. See McGrath, *Heresy*, 39ff.

15. I argue for faithful doctrinal development extensively in *In Defense of Doctrine: Evangelicalism, Theology, and Scripture* (Minneapolis: Fortress, 2015).

ing what unites believers across different faith traditions.[16] But *sola Scriptura*–affirming Protestants recognize that such creeds *affirm* orthodoxy; they *do not invent* it. The Apostles' Creed, the Nicene Creed (in both its 325 and 381 renditions), and the Chalcedonian Definition provide helpful guardrails for Christology and the doctrine of God. Recognition of the beauty of these creeds and their derivative authority does not mean Protestants and evangelicals offer unilateral consent to all the proceedings and findings of these and subsequent councils. (I have yet to meet a Protestant who takes the condemnation of iconoclasm coming out of the Second Council of Nicaea in 787 as binding on all Christians.) Scripture, not a creed or a council, has the ultimate say in what matters should distinguish believers from unbelievers.

Not every theological or interpretive error is a "heresy" in the historical sense or a "false doctrine" in the biblical sense of the phrase. Some doctrines or interpretations are simply factually or hermeneutically wrong, not nefarious in intent or deceptive by design. Doctrinal taxonomies are helpful tools for differentiating between outright heresy, interpretive errors of lesser significance, and unsettled questions. But at the end of the day, I am more concerned with the broader pastoral implications of doctrines than I am with tidy categorizations of heretical and orthodox teaching. Paul stressed the importance of this when he told Timothy, "Keep a close watch on yourself and on the teaching. Persist in this, for by so doing *you will save both yourself and your hearers*" (1 Tim. 4:16). Teaching cardinal truth is paramount for protecting flocks, but imperfect interpreters must also have the freedom to differ on nonessential matters.

"In Essentials Unity, in Nonessentials Liberty, in All Things Charity"

In necessariis unitas, in non necessariis libertas, in omnibus caritas. The exact origin of this oft-quoted adage is unknown, but seventeenth-century Christians used the phrase in an effort to defuse religious tensions during the Thirty Years' War.[17] Whatever its original historical

---

16. R. Albert Mohler Jr., *The Apostles' Creed: Discovering Authentic Christianity in an Age of Counterfeits* (Nashville: Thomas Nelson, 2019), xxii–xxiii.

17. Rupertus Meldenius, *Paraenesis votiva per Pace Ecclesiae* (Rottenberg, 1626), 62. Henk J. Nellen has shown that Marco Antonio de Dominis (1560–1624) used the phrase in a prior

context, it is one of the earliest known expressions of dogmatic ranking. The church historian Philip Schaff once labeled it "the motto of
Christian irenics" and the "watchword of Christian peacemakers."[18]
It is one of the earliest Protestant statements about the need for doctrinal taxonomy.

In essentials unity (In necessariis unitas). Those doctrines labeled
necessariis are those essential or necessary to be called a Christian in
any historically meaningful sense. The seventeenth-century Lutheran
theologian Rupertus Meldenius (1582–1651) maintained that essential dogmas are (1) beliefs necessary for salvation, (2) beliefs stated
explicitly in Scripture, (3) beliefs universally recognized by Christian
creeds, and (4) those agreed upon by the church as necessary.[19] In
these matters, Christians must be unified. These beliefs distinguish the
people of God from unbelievers and heretics.

In nonessentials liberty (in non necessariis libertas). The Christian
experiences freedom to disagree over matters nonessential for salvation. Another version of the motto uses the phrase "in doubtful things
liberty" (*in dubiis libertas*), which refers to issues where no consensus
has been reached. For Meldenius, nonnecessary doctrines included
(1) those not explicitly found in Scripture, (2) those not shared by
all Christian traditions, (3) those not unanimously taught, (4) those
which are doubtful because of their sources, and (5) those which are
not necessarily edifying for all.[20] Whereas deviation on essential issues demands church discipline, discrepancy over nonessential issues
requires some level of tolerance.[21]

In all things charity (in omnibus caritas). Coupled with this taxonomy is an exhortation to be charitable when we agree and when
we are at variance with one another. Love should characterize the
conflicts that Christians have among themselves over nonessentials
and their disputes with non-Christians who deny the essential tenets

publication. See H. J. Nellen, "De Zinspreuk 'In Necessariis Unitas, In Non Necessariis Libertas, In
Utrisque Caritas'," *Nederlands archief voor kerkgeschiedenis* [*Dutch Review of Church History*]
79, no. 1 (1999): 99–106. The Puritan theologian Richard Baxter (1615–1691) later popularized
it among English-speaking Christians.

18. Philip Schaff, *History of the Christian Church*, 8 vols. (Grand Rapids, MI: Eerdmans,
1958), 6:650.

19. Schaff, *History of the Christian Church*, 6:651.

20. Schaff, *History of the Christian Church*, 6:651.

21. Grant R. Osborne, *The Hermeneutical Spiral*, rev. ed. (Downers Grove, IL: InterVarsity
Press, 2006), 400.

of the faith. Even heretics and false teachers are made in the image of God and endowed with human dignity. Efforts to compel them into orthodox belief should stem from concern for them and not from a desire to win arguments.

Mohler's Theological Triage

Like this classic statement of doctrinal taxonomy, most contemporary rankings make a distinction between essential and nonessential doctrines, or major doctrines and minor doctrines.[22] Others add categories or tiers to understand the way in which traditions or denominations relate to one another. Just as these taxonomies come in many shapes and sizes, theologians have particular ways of filling them out. It has become a common practice among evangelical theologians to use a three-tiered doctrinal taxonomy that distinguishes between primary, secondary, and tertiary levels of doctrine.[23] Two-tiered taxonomies separate Christian beliefs from non-Christian beliefs, but taxonomies with three or more tiers can define the parameters of various theological traditions. They can describe which theological matters Christians in the same local church or denomination can differ over and still maintain close fellowship and cooperation.

One of the more creative uses of a three-tiered taxonomy is R. Albert Mohler's "doctrinal triage," which classifies doctrines according to their level of urgency in the same way an emergency room sorts patients according to the seriousness of their ailments. Mohler drew his inspiration for the analogy from his mother, who worked for many years as a triage nurse. The practice of medical triage (from the French term *trier*, which means "to separate") originated on the battlefield to separate the mortally wounded from the critically wounded and the critically wounded from the noncritically wounded. In a modern-day emergency room, patients with gunshot wounds and heart attacks are given greater priority than those with severe colds and sprained ankles. A theological triage can distinguish between the acute errors of heterodoxy and the less significant in-house disputes

---

22. Wayne Grudem, *Systematic Theology* (Grand Rapids, MI: Zondervan, 2000), 29–30.
23. See Stanley J. Grenz and Roger E. Olson, *Who Needs Theology? An Invitation to the Study of God* (Downers Grove, IL: InterVarsity Press, 1996), 70–77; Vanhoozer, *Biblical Authority after Babel*, 204–206.

that divide us.[24] Mohler states that the discipline of "theological triage would require Christians to determine a scale of theological urgency that would correspond to the medical world's framework for medical priority."[25]

With the metaphor of triage, Mohler offers a taxonomy with both *descriptive* and *prescriptive* characteristics. The theological triage separates Christian beliefs from non-Christian beliefs, beliefs distinctive to denominations and traditions, and conflicting opinions within a tradition. In Mohler's doctrinal triage, first-level theological doctrines are those that are "most central and essential to the Christian faith."[26] "These first-order doctrines represent the most fundamental truths of the Christian faith, and a denial of these doctrines represents nothing less than an eventual denial of Christianity itself." According to Mohler, "Those who deny these revealed truths are, by definition, not Christians."[27] These beliefs distinguish authentic Christian belief from apostasy or heresy. Mohler places doctrines like the authority of Scripture, the Trinity, and the divinity of Jesus in this first level or tier.[28]

Second-level doctrines in Mohler's triage are issues that generate "significant boundaries" between fellow Christians: "Christians across a vast denominational range can stand together on the first-order doctrines and recognize each other as authentic Christians, while understanding that the existence of second-order disagreements prevents the closeness of fellowship we would otherwise enjoy."[29] Second-tier disagreements shape traditions as distinct movements within orthodox Christianity.

Third-level doctrines in the triage are of even lesser significance. According to Mohler, third-level doctrines are doctrines "over which evangelicals may disagree and yet remain in close fellowship, even

---

24. R. Albert Mohler, interview by author, Louisville, KY, September 8, 2016.
25. R. Albert Mohler, "Confessional Evangelicalism," in *Four Views on the Spectrum of Evangelicalism*, ed. Andrew David Naselli and Collin Hansen (Grand Rapids, MI: Zondervan, 2011), 78.
26. Mohler, "Confessional Evangelicalism," 78.
27. Mohler, "Call for Theological Triage"; Grenz and Olson, *Who Needs Theology?* 73. Elsewhere Mohler's language on denials of first-tier matters is slightly more nuanced: "Denying these doctrines represents nothing less than *eventually* denying Christianity itself" ("Confessional Evangelicalism," 79, italics mine).
28. Mohler, "Call for Theological Triage"; cf. Grenz and Olson, *Who Needs Theology?* 74. Mohler adds that the "essential truths of the incarnation [also] include the death, burial, and bodily resurrection of the Lord Jesus Christ" (Mohler, "Confessional Evangelicalism," 79).
29. Mohler, "Call for Theological Triage."

within local congregations."[30] Division over third-level doctrines typically occurs in the interpretation of certain biblical texts deemed un-
usually difficult to understand, like the apocalyptic books. Mohler
explicitly states that Christians who "affirm the bodily, historical, and
victorious return of the Lord Jesus Christ may differ over the timetable
and sequence without rupturing the fellowship of the church."[31] In
other words, we can affirm that the second coming of Jesus is a first-
tier belief while allowing for differences of opinion regarding its timing
and place in biblical eschatology.[32]

There may be a need for more tiers in a taxonomy than two or
three, especially when understanding how theological movements relate to one another. Much of the discussion within evangelicalism
over evangelical identity has been over *theological boundaries* that
define the movement itself.[33] The boundaries of evangelicalism are
broader than those which shape denominations within evangelicalism
but more restrictive than the boundaries that divide the Christian from
the non-Christian. One item in that debate over evangelical identity
has been the doctrine of biblical inerrancy. If biblical inerrancy is determined to be a litmus test for evangelical identity but not a requirement for Christian belief, then we may need a tier that goes between
the level of gospel belief and that of denominational belief. Issues like
inerrancy also create coalitions broader than our ecclesiological differences. An evangelical Baptist committed to the doctrine of biblical
inerrancy may feel more at home with an evangelical Presbyterian or
Wesleyan congregation that affirms this view of Scripture than with a
mainline Baptist congregation which denies it, even if the Baptists have
more in common with one another on matters of polity and baptism.

---

30. Mohler, "Call for Theological Triage"; cf. Mohler, "Confessional Evangelicalism," 80.

31. Mohler, "Confessional Evangelicalism," 80.

32. Grenz and Olson, *Who Needs Theology?* 76.

33. Grenz and Olson have argued against the use of boundary marking to define evangelicalism as a movement, preferring instead to think of the gospel as the "center" of the movement.
Prior to his death, Grenz argued that while churches properly retain the designation "boundaried
people," the same description cannot be predicated of a renewal movement within the church
such as "evangelicalism" because the term does not describe an elect, covenant community with
the ability to practice church discipline. See Stanley J. Grenz, "*Die Begrenzte Gemeinschaft* ('The
Boundaried People') and the Character of Evangelical Theology," *JETS* 45, no. 2 (2002): 301–316.
Olson recently commented that "evangelicalism has no definable boundaries and cannot have
them" because "an organization has boundaries" and a "movement does not" (Roger E. Olson,
"Postconservative Evangelicalism," in Naselli and Hansen, *Four Views on the Spectrum of Evangelicalism*, 163).

It is important to remember that these taxonomies are human theological constructs, efforts on the part of fallible believers to make sense of what is most important in the word of God and the Christian tradition. Because Protestants and evangelicals have no magisterium for dictating doctrine, what counts as a primary, secondary, or tertiary issue may vary from person to person or tradition to tradition. These rankings are somewhat subjective, framed by the theological priorities of their authors. Nevertheless, movements like evangelicalism have demonstrated that they are capable of a general consensus on those theological matters most important to them.[34]

Stratifying Doctrine: Three Tests

Theologians still squabble over which doctrines should be classified as first-tier, second-tier, and third-tier matters. One of the first major controversies following the death of Luther was the Adiaphora Controversy, in which Lutheran figures such as Philip Melanchthon (1497–1560) and Matthias Flacius (1520–1575) collided over what doctrines or practices counted as adiaphora ("matters of indifference") or nonessentials.[35] Some evangelicals today insist that the Protestant doctrine of justification by faith alone is a first-tier issue, essential to properly being called a Christian.[36] Other evangelical theologians assume the doctrine necessary to be a Protestant but consider it a second-level doctrine overall.[37] The former position excludes from the fold of the

---

34. For a fine example of this effort, see J. I. Packer and Thomas C. Oden, *One Faith: The Evangelical Consensus* (Downers Grove, IL: InterVarsity Press, 2004).

35. For them, it was fundamentally a debate over which Roman Catholic practices were the least abhorrent to them. For summaries of this debate, see Clyde Leonard Manschreck, *Melanchthon: The Quiet Reformer* (New York: Abingdon, 1958), 277–292. Calvin believed Melanchthon to be soft on adiaphora but considered their friendship too dear to divide over this matter. See H. J. Selderhuis, ed., *The Calvin Handbook*, trans. Henry J. Baron, Judith J. Guder, Randi H. Lundell (Grand Rapids, MI: Eerdmans, 2009), 59–61.

36. Mohler, "Call for Theological Triage." This first-tier status may be implied in the proverb commonly attributed to Luther that the Protestant doctrine of justification is "the article by which the church stands or falls" (*justificatio est articulus stantis et cadentis ecclesiae*). The original statement by Luther (WA 40.3.352) was worded slightly differently: "Because if this article stands, the church stands. If it falls, the church falls" (*quia isto articulo stante stat Ecclesia, ruente ruit Ecclesia*). See Alister E. McGrath, *Iustitia Dei: A History of the Christian Doctrine*, 3rd ed. (Cambridge: Cambridge University Press, 2005), vii.

37. Sawyer, *Survivor's Guide to Theology*, 169. Notably, the doctrine of justification by faith is a statement about one being justified by faith and trust in the person and work of Christ, not a statement about how we are justified by an intellectual affirmation of the doctrine of justification by faith. Calling for some tolerance on the matter, John Frame notes, "It is difficult to find anyone before Luther who had a clear understanding of 'justification by faith.'" See John M.

faith those Roman Catholics who affirm the condemnations made of justification by faith at the Council of Trent. The latter view draws the boundary widely enough to include even Trent-affirming Catholics.

Doctrinal taxonomies outside of evangelicalism are even more diverse.[38] Take for instance the dogmatic ranking of process theologian David Ray Griffin. His revisionist list of primary doctrines includes fairly standard statements about the goodness of God, the goodness of creation, God's revelatory act in Christ, and the hope of life after bodily death but excludes numerous other doctrines represented in the ecumenical creeds such as the Trinity, the deity of Jesus, etc.[39] For Griffin, traditional Christian doctrines regarding human sinfulness, the miracles of Jesus, and the atoning death of Jesus are afforded secondary and tertiary status, but they are also reinterpreted in light of his process philosophy. Griffin suggests that some of these doctrines contain truth expressed through a mythological form while others, such as the belief that God was incarnate in Christ, "should be discarded as simply false."[40] As a result, this taxonomy represents a rejection of the gospel preached by the apostles and agreed upon by the church throughout history.

The diversity of dogmatic ranks leaves us with a pressing methodological question: is there a better way to identify what doctrines go where in a doctrinal taxonomy? Here I recommend three primary "tests" for doctrines that I believe are helpful for placing them in the proper tiers: the hermeneutical test, the gospel test, and the praxis test. Coupled with an implicit appreciation for the broader Christian tradition throughout history expressed in the creeds of the major ecumenical councils and later confessions, these tests can help us distinguish between matters of first importance, things that divide denominations or theological traditions, and matters over which we have the freedom to disagree.

Frame, *Evangelical Reunion: Denominations and the Body of Christ* (Grand Rapids, MI: Baker, 1991), 88.

38. The doctrinal taxonomy of postliberal theologian George Lindbeck distinguished between *permanent* and *temporary* or *conditional* doctrines. He suggested that changes in Christian belief on sexual ethics can be informed by developments in science, technology, and culture. See George A. Lindbeck, *The Nature of Doctrine* (Louisville: Westminster John Knox, 1984), 85.

39. David Ray Griffin, *Two Great Truths: A Synthesis of Scientific Naturalism and the Christian Faith* (Louisville: Westminster John Knox, 2004), 31.

40. Griffin, *Two Great Truths*, 36.

The Hermeneutical Test: Clearer Things Come First

For those who affirm the sufficiency and clarity of the Bible, the first and most important test for doctrinal taxonomies is biblical and hermeneutical. Some doctrines are *clearly*, explicitly stated in Scripture, while others are mere implications or interpretations of biblical ideas. Some biblical teachings are easier to understand than others. Some biblical concepts and ideas are more challenging. Once more, this observation is consistent with the Protestant doctrine of the clarity of Scripture. As the divines behind the Westminster Confession of Faith (1646) acknowledge,

> All things in Scripture *are not alike plain in themselves, nor alike clear unto all* (2 Pet. 3:16); *yet those things which are necessary to be known*, believed, and observed for salvation, are so clearly propounded, and opened in some place of Scripture or other, that not only the learned, but the unlearned, in a due use of the ordinary means, may attain unto a sufficient understanding of them (Ps. 119:105, 130).[41]

The divines here state that those things which are clearer in Scripture are those "which are necessary to be known, believed, and observed for salvation." Those things in Scripture that are not "alike clear unto all" become disputed matters.

How do we assess the difference between these levels of doctrine hermeneutically and methodologically? Millard Erickson offers a helpful way of ranking doctrine that distinguishes between those doctrines clearly stated in Scripture, those directly implied by Scripture, those doctrines possibly implied by Scripture, and inferences from Scripture that are probable but not foregone conclusions.[42] Erickson contends that the more closely a doctrine can be tied to a biblical passage, the more authority it bears. Doctrines more clearly expressed in Scripture are more primary, while contested doctrines and inferences take more of a secondary or tertiary status.

The first and most critical level of authority Erickson describes is comprised of "direct statements of Scripture." By this, I take Erickson to mean doctrines that use the explicit language of Scripture without

---

41. The Westminster Confession of Faith 1:7, italics mine.
42. Millard J. Erickson, *Christian Theology*, 3rd ed. (Grand Rapids, MI: Baker, 2013), 65–66.

the need for much further qualification.[43] The manifold biblical statements about one God (Deut. 6:4; Isa. 45:18; 1 Cor. 8:6, etc.), the deity of Jesus (John 1:1; Rom. 9:5; Col. 1:15, etc.), and his substitutionary death for sinners (Rom. 5:8; 1 Pet. 2:24; 1 John 2:2) are so direct, so clear, that Christians from every tradition affirm these beliefs as central to their faith. The Scripture openly, repeatedly states that Jesus was sinless (2 Cor. 5:21; Heb. 4:15; 1 Pet. 2:22). Gospel writers clearly affirm the virginal conception of Jesus, and the only way to deny this doctrine is to reject their explicit testimony (Matt. 1:18–25; Luke 1:26–38). The theological statement "Christians are saved by faith, not by works" belongs in this first tier because its language is almost directly derived from Ephesians 2:8–9. Because the condemnation of same-sex erotic behavior comes directly from biblical language (1 Cor. 6:9; cf. Lev. 18:22; 20:13; Rom. 1:24–27), its prohibition is a first-tier issue that evangelicals will not waver on. Yet it is important to acknowledge, as Erickson does, that even biblical texts quoted directly in doctrinal formulations need to be interpreted and placed in their proper historical context.

Erickson next distinguishes between the varying levels of authority between "direct implications of Scripture" and "probable implications of Scripture."[44] Direct implications are not direct statements of Scripture but logical implications drawn from direct statements in Scripture. Nowhere in the Bible do we find the explicit statement "the Holy Spirit is God," but the deity of the Spirit is a clear, direct implication of what Scripture does say about God and the Holy Spirit. Consider these syllogisms:

(1) Ananias lied to the Holy Spirit (Acts 5:3).
(2) Ananias did not lie to people but to God (Acts 5:4).
∴ (3) Ananias lied to the Holy Spirit, who is God.

(1) You are God's temple, and the Spirit of God lives in you (1 Cor. 3:16).
(2) You are a temple of the Holy Spirit who is in you (1 Cor. 6:19).
∴ (3) You are a temple of God the Holy Spirit, who lives in you.

---

43. Erickson, *Christian Theology*, 65. These are akin to the "overcoded abductions" described in chapter 3.
44. Erickson, *Christian Theology*, 65.

Compounded with evidence mounted elsewhere regarding the divine activity of the Holy Spirit, it becomes clear that Scripture teaches his deity. Because this implication is a logical necessity of what Scripture explicitly states, this doctrine is an essential, primary doctrine. The Council of Constantinople (381) took this direct implication as a primary doctrine and anathematized the Pneumatomachians ("spirit-fighters") who denied the deity of the Spirit. The Council's more developed doctrine of the Spirit's deity is explicitly stated in the Niceno-Constantinopolitan Creed. The doctrine of the Trinity, a logically necessary deduction from biblical statements about the Father, the Son, and the Spirit, also fits into this category of direct implications from Scripture.

Probable implications, on the other hand, are inferences drawn from arguments wherein one or more of the premises is contested.[45] The introduction of open theism, or openness theology, in the 1980s ignited one of the most heated debates in the history of contemporary evangelicalism.[46] Open theists maintain that for human beings to be truly free, the future must not be settled, and God cannot know with certainty an uncertain future. Classical theists assert God's perfect foreknowledge to be part of his omniscience. Biblical, theological, and philosophical cases have been made for both sides.[47] Were there a direct statement on the foreknowledge of God in Scripture, or even a direct implication to be made, the conflict would more than likely be over. But differing assumptions about time, human freedom, and knowledge keep the debate alive.[48]

This simple syllogism explaining the classic position on divine foreknowledge (i.e., that God knows all future events) illustrates a probable implication from Scripture:

---

45. Erickson, *Christian Theology*, 66.

46. See Richard Rice, *The Openness of God: The Relationship of Divine Foreknowledge and Human Free Will* (Nashville: Review & Herald, 1980); William Hasker, *God, Time, and Knowledge* (Ithaca, NY: Cornell University Press, 1989); Clark Pinnock, Richard Rice, John Sanders, William Hasker, and David Basinger, *The Openness of God: A Biblical Challenge to the Traditional Understanding of God* (Downers Grove, IL: InterVarsity Press, 1994); Clark Pinnock, *Most Moved Mover: A Theology of God's Openness* (Grand Rapids, MI: Baker, 2000).

47. Open theists frequently appeal to passages where God appears to change his mind (Gen. 6:6; Ex. 32:9–14; Jonah 3:10) as evidence that he does not know future events. Classical theists contend these descriptions of God are anthropomorphic expressions meant to help us relate to God, not to describe his inner being. See Michael F. Bird, *Evangelical Theology: A Biblical and Systematic Introduction* (Grand Rapids, MI: Zondervan, 2013), 129.

48. These paradigms for understanding God's knowledge and foreknowledge in Scripture are like "undercoded abductions" because the interpreter must choose from a number of available interpretive options when deciding which premises are true.

(1) The Bible directly says God knows all things (1 John 3:20; cf. 1 Cor. 2:10).

(2) Knowledge of all things necessarily entails all things past, present, and future.

∴ (3) God knows all things past, present, and future.

Classical theists and open theists may agree about (1) but will differ on (2) because the open theist commonly argues that "all things" cannot entail future events that are not yet realized. The open theist argues these events are not decided because the future has not yet happened. Because premise (2) is not directly stated in Scripture, this syllogism is better described as a probable implication of biblical teaching rather than a direct and necessary implication of biblical teaching.[49]

Another doctrinal category is what Erickson calls "inductive conclusions from Scripture."[50] Though he never gives an extended definition of what he means by "inductive conclusions," Erickson does seem to conflate *inductive* and *abductive* reasoning (see ch. 3). Whatever the case, he appears to suggest that doctrines that begin as inferences to the best explanation of a larger body of biblical texts are of a lesser level of authority because of the possibility of interpretive fallibility on the part of the one making the inference. Doctrines such as the doctrine of eternal security or unconditional election fit into this category because they are inferences made on the part of the interpreter that are tested by inductive means. While biblical texts may be used in support of these inferences, these positions are more tentative than direct statements of or deductions from Scripture.

The penultimate tier of Erickson's taxonomy includes conclusions inferred from general revelation. Theologians who affirm the notion of general revelation usually speak of its numerous means, including *nature, reason, conscience,* and *history.* Inferences made from nature may include the general observation of the physical environment or data from the natural sciences. Inferences from reason may

---

49. While I do not consider a doctrine of exhaustive divine foreknowledge something a person *must* believe to be a Christian, I do consider it something a reasonable Christian *ought* to affirm in order to be consistent with other biblical claims made about God's power and character. See Bruce A. Ware, *God's Lesser Glory: The Diminished God of Open Theism* (Wheaton, IL: Crossway, 2000). In his doctrinal taxonomy, Wittmer describes the perfections of God as something Christians *should* believe. See Wittmer, *Don't Stop Believing,* 43.

50. Erickson, *Christian Theology,* 66.

also include the work of philosophers of religion and philosophical theologians. Philosophical theology may provide reasonable and help-ful ways of clarifying and arranging theological concepts laid out in Scripture, but such concepts ultimately have little binding authority on all Christians everywhere, given their tentative qualities. Philo-sophical theologians differ among themselves about what it means for God to be eternal. Is God atemporal, i.e., outside of time, or does he experience time like we do but only in an everlasting manner? While this debate is interesting and possibly elucidating to other theological controversies, Christians are not required by Scripture to take any one side on the matter. The results of inferences from general revelation are third- or fourth-level issues, theological opinions that in no way draw the lines of orthodoxy or Christian fellowship.

The final type of theological inference is that of outright specula-tion. Speculation about whether all dogs go to heaven or why God chose to create this world instead of another has no direct connec-tion to Scripture, inferences about its message, or general revela-tion. Many Roman Catholic doctrinal developments, such as the doctrines of the immaculate conception and assumption of Mary, fit in this category because they do not stem from a direct statement of Scripture, a direct implication of Scripture, a probable implication, or an inductive conclusion. Their only "authority" comes from the teaching office or tradition that proffers such speculation. Theologi-cal speculation often embodies the Pollyanna principle described in chapter 5, and offers no real answers or binding stipulations on groups of Christians. Erickson notes that speculation becomes a "serious problem" when Christians draw lines of fellowship and authority along these lines.[51]

The leap from the Bible to doctrine sometimes involves taking clear, indisputable statements from Scripture, while other times taking direct implications from clear statements. These are first-tier matters over which reasonable interpreters can have a great deal of confidence.[52] Because of their clarity, these doctrines are more binding to a larger group of people. On other occasions, inferences need to be made when

---

51. Erickson, *Christian Theology*, 66.
52. Sawyer, *Survivor's Guide to Theology*, 166.

assessing difficult biblical passages or how groups of biblical passages relate to one another. Making these inferences is both a science and an art, involving creative reasoning and human fallibility. These creative inferences should be more tentatively held than direct statements and direct implications. Therefore they belong to the category of second-, third-, and fourth-tier levels of doctrine.

The Gospel Test: Things Central to the Gospel Take Priority

The second test, closely related to the first, is what I call the "gospel test." We determine matters of primary doctrinal importance in relationship to the gospel itself. *What is the gospel (euangelion) of Jesus Christ? What must a person believe to become a Christian?* Given the centrality of the gospel in the New Testament and its importance in the identification of what it means to be a disciple of Christ, we must get it right (Jude 3–4).

When we assess where a doctrine fits in a taxonomy, we must ask how that doctrine relates to the gospel. Is it (1) an essential component of the gospel message itself; (2) something that buttresses the gospel, or that hinders it when it is rejected; or (3) something that is a theological or practical by-product of the gospel? The goal in this discussion is not to endorse some form of lowest-common-denominator belief or to minimize the importance of second- and third-tier beliefs but to establish the base level of Christian cooperation in the gospel itself.

The Explicit New Testament Gospel

Not every doctrinal matter that has "gospel" slapped on it is the gospel. For the past few years, evangelical thought leaders have made a habit of labeling various theological and ethical matters "gospel issues": "Racial reconciliation is a gospel issue." "The eternal, functional subordination of the Son is a gospel issue." "Our position on women in ministry is a gospel issue." "The immigration crisis is a gospel issue." Evangelicals have stopped short of saying "Chick-fil-A consumption is a gospel issue," but I won't be surprised if I hear it. When a favorite soapbox becomes a "gospel issue," having the right opinion on the issue essentially gets elevated to the level of a primary doctrine. Polemicists seem to use this designation to give a pressing theological, social, or political issue more weight, prioritizing the issue above other theological and social matters less important to them.

As D. A. Carson rightly notes, the phrase "gospel issue" has not been clearly defined by many who use it. Sure, the gospel can affect every area of life, but not every area of life is the gospel. While there are many important theological issues that are organically related to the gospel in the nexus of God's revealed truth, "gospel issue" ceases to be a useful category if it describes every biblical truth or its implication.[53] It is vital for us to make the distinction between something that is essential to the gospel and something that is merely an implication of the gospel. As Blake Newsom remarks, "If everything is the gospel, then nothing is the gospel."[54]

What then is the gospel, according to the New Testament? The most succinct biblical explanation of the gospel comes in 1 Corinthians 15:1–8:

> Now I would remind you, brothers, of the gospel I preached to you, which you received, in which you stand, and by which you are being saved, if you hold fast to the word I preached to you—unless you believed in vain.
>
> For I delivered to you as of first importance what I also received:
>
> > that Christ died for our sins in accordance with the
> > > Scriptures,
> > that he was buried,
> > that he was raised on the third day in accordance with the
> > > Scriptures,
> > and that he appeared to Cephas, then to the twelve.
>
> Then he appeared to more than five hundred brothers at one time, most of whom are still alive, though some have fallen asleep. Then he appeared to James, then to all the apostles. Last of all, as to one untimely born, he appeared also to me.

---

53. D. A. Carson, "What Are Gospel Issues?" *Themelios* 39, no. 2 (2014): 215–219.
54. Blake Newsom, "What Is the Gospel?" *Journal for Baptist Theology and Ministry* 11, no. 2 (2014): 5.

Here Paul wants to "make clear" for his readers the gospel he received and the gospel he was passing along to them. We are told that these are the matters of "first importance" (*prōtois*; 15:3): Jesus is the Messiah who died for our sins. He rose again, just as the Scriptures foretold and the disciples bore witness.

When Jesus himself speaks of the gospel, he usually talks about the in-breaking kingdom of God that is manifest in his ministry (e.g., Matt. 4:23; 9:35; 24:14; Luke 4:43; 8:1; 16:16). After the resurrection of Jesus, his followers paint his life and deeds as an indispensable component of that kingdom in-breaking. The earliest apostolic proclamations of the gospel were "about the kingdom of God *and the name of Jesus Christ*" (Acts 8:12). In their presentations of the gospel, they declared Jesus to be the Messiah (5:42) and the grace of God as a gift given through Jesus (20:24).

Throughout his corpus, Paul lists eight elements in his description of the gospel: (1) the gospel of God was promised through the Prophets (Rom. 1:1–2); (2) Jesus is the Messiah (Rom. 1:3; 1 Cor. 15:3); (3) Jesus was born a son of David (Rom. 1:3); (4) Jesus died for our sins (1 Cor. 15:3); (5) Jesus was buried (1 Cor. 15:4a); (6) Jesus was raised from the dead "in accordance with the Scriptures" (1 Cor. 15:4b); (7) the risen Jesus appeared to his disciples (1 Cor. 15:5–8); and (8) Jesus is the future agent of God's judgment (Rom. 2:16).

This is the gospel in simple biblical expression: Jesus died in the place of sinners and was raised from the dead on the third day. God laid our sin on him (Isa. 53:6). Although he committed no sin (1 Pet. 2:22), he bore the wrath of God on behalf of sinners (1 Pet. 3:18). His "chastisement . . . brought us peace" and "with his wounds we are healed" (Isa. 53:5). His resurrection was confirmed by eyewitnesses who beheld his majesty. This announcement of Jesus's victory over sin and death also comes with a call for faith and repentance. A person is not saved by his or her works but by faith in Jesus (Eph. 2:8–9). Those who turn from their sins and believe this message of God's saving activity in Christ will themselves be saved (Mark 1:15; Acts 20:21; Rom. 10:9–13). Any denial of these claims or the preaching of any gospel contrary to these claims is under apostolic anathema (Gal. 1:9; cf. 1 Cor. 15:12–19).

To this point, my primary focus has been on the way that doctrine divides us, but doctrine can also unite us. A common theological framework can bind people together from every race, every socioeconomic background, every culture, and every political party. The doctrine that unites such a diverse global community is the gospel of Jesus Christ. Only the gospel provides a real eschatological hope of an end to our worldly tensions and conflicts.

With the gospel, all Christians share a *metanarrative* or overarching story that speaks of God's redemptive act in Christ. God created the world. It was broken by sin. God revealed himself through Israel and gave the Messiah through them. God has acted through the death, burial, and resurrection of Jesus to save us from our sin and make things right again. We share a common *hope*: Jesus is literally coming again to bring an end to suffering and evil forever. While the early ecumenical creeds like the Apostles' and Nicene Creeds spell out these tenets plainly, we recognize that the Bible is the primary source of this grand story and the authoritative measuring rod for its faithful retellings in differing contexts. Gospel unity across various Christian traditions is impossible without the recognition of these essential, first-tier components.

How the Gospel Relates to Other Doctrines

So how does the explicit New Testament gospel relate to other doctrines? In his defense of the necessity of Christian belief, Michael Wittmer offers a taxonomy of sorts that divides first-tier doctrines into three categories: what Christians *must believe*, what Christians *must not reject*, and what Christians *should believe*. This model is helpful for showing the relationship between direct statements about the gospel, other matters derived from Scripture that make the gospel possible, and issues related to the gospel but which do not directly alter its essential message.

First, Wittmer lists two central theological tenets that Christians *must believe* at conversion: that we are sinners and that Jesus can save us from our sin. A person may become a Christian simply by believing these two elements of the explicit New Testament gospel without yet understanding other biblical doctrines that support it. Wittmer draws biblical support from biblical conversion narratives, such as the moment when Peter tells Cornelius that "everyone who believes in [Jesus] receives forgiveness of sins through his name" (Acts 10:43). Wittmer also stresses that repentance—a biblical prerequisite for regeneration—means "at minimum, that we believe we are sinners and that Jesus saves us from our sin."[55] I would add belief in the bodily resurrection of Jesus to this category of *must believe*. The resurrection is in every apostolic proclamation of the gospel recorded in the New Testament,[56] and Paul also expressly says this belief in Jesus being raised from the dead is a prerequisite for salvation (Rom. 10:9).

The second category in Wittmer's taxonomy includes things Christians *must not reject*. He includes here the doctrines of the Trinity, the true deity and humanity of Christ, and the general historical reliability of the gospel accounts. Included in this latter category would be the miracles of Jesus and the virgin conception of Jesus by the Holy Spirit. The earliest Christian creeds considered these doctrines essential beliefs. The authors of the Nicene Creed (325) condemned Arian heretics who denied the true deity of Jesus, and in turn, the doctrine of the Trinity. In response to Eutychian and Nestorian heresies, the Chalcedonian Definition (451) describes Jesus Christ as "truly God and truly man." The *hypostatic union* describes the way in which the two natures of Christ are joined together in one Person or subsistence (*hypostasis*).

This is not to say that every new believer must understand the doctrine of the Trinity or the hypostatic union upon conversion. It took the church centuries to articulate these beliefs in the first place! Furthermore, it would be unrealistic, unhealthy, and unbiblical to expect everyone who becomes a believer to pass some sort of detailed theological examination as a requirement for conversion. What this prohibition means is that if a person *denies* these things he probably does not understand the gospel in the first place.[57] Many Christian beliefs such as the doctrine of the Trinity begin as implicit dispositions

---

55. Wittmer, *Don't Stop Believing*, 39.
56. Acts 1:22; 2:24–32; 3:15; 4:10; 5:30; 10:40; 13:30, 34, 37; Rom. 4:24, 25; 6:4, 9; 7:4; 8:34; 10:9; 1 Cor. 6:14; 15:1–58; 2 Cor. 4:14; 5:15; Gal. 1:1; Eph. 1:20; 2:6; Col. 2:12; 3:1; 1 Thess. 1:10; 2 Tim. 2:8; 1 Pet. 1:21; 3:21; Rev. 1:5.
57. Mohler, interview by author.

that are made explicit beliefs when "a new set of circumstances confronts us" that bring these beliefs "to self-awareness."[58] When this doctrine is denied, the person or people denying it are no longer recognized as Christian.

Orthodox Christians of every stripe reject the Christological viewpoints of groups like the Church of Jesus Christ of Latter-day Saints (Mormons) and the Watchtower Bible and Tract Society (Jehovah's Witnesses), who explicitly deny the true divinity and eternal sonship of Jesus. (In the theological systems of both groups, Jesus is a created being who is subordinate to God.) But what are we to make of members of Trinity-denying sects like Oneness or "Jesus Only" Pentecostals who affirm the deity of Jesus but who claim Jesus and the Father are the same Person? If we must not reject the doctrine of the Trinity, can someone who subscribes to Oneness Pentecostal doctrine still be a Christian?

The earliest Christian theologians condemned the Oneness heresy (also known as Modalism, Sabellianism, or patripassianism). Oneness Pentecostals may endorse the biblical teaching of the divinity of Jesus Christ (John 1:1; Phil. 2:6–8; Col. 1:15–18, etc.), but they also ignore the explicit biblical distinctions between the Father, the Son, and the Holy Spirit (Luke 10:21; John 5:26–27; 15:26–27; Rom. 15:30). Because they conflate the identities of the Father and the Son, they also deny the unique preexistence of the Son (John 1:2; 17:5). The Son does not eternally coexist with the Father; the Father becomes the Son in the incarnation. Oneness Pentecostals often reject the doctrine of the Trinity because they misunderstand its orthodox formulation, believing Trinitarians to worship three distinct gods. While I suppose it is possible that a genuine Christian who lacks discipleship and discernment can be taken captive by the apparent simplicity of Oneness doctrine, I do not think anyone who understands the doctrine of the Trinity and rejects it can be a Christian. Oneness Pentecostals make other serious theological errors. First, based on their interpretation of Acts 2:38, they assert that only those baptized with the formula "in Jesus's name" are truly Christian. Second, they believe a person must speak

---

58. Anthony C. Thiselton, *The Hermeneutics of Doctrine* (Grand Rapids, MI: Eerdmans, 2007), 28.

in tongues in order to be assured of his or her salvation. Much like the false teaching that infiltrated the Galatian church, these legalistic (and unbiblical) requirements belong to "a different gospel" (Gal. 1:6), one contrary to the gospel proclaimed by the apostles (Gal. 1:8–9).[59]

Finally, Wittmer includes the category of things Christians *should believe*. The force of this language is important. Disciples should embrace beliefs in all three categories he mentions, but the first two categories are *musts* derived from the direct statements related to the gospel and the direct implications of the gospel. The third category of *should believe* doctrines consists of doctrinal matters clearly stated by Scripture but not directly associated with the gospel in its explicit presentations throughout Scripture, though their implied relationship is palpable. Wittmer lists here the perfections of God, the authority of Scripture, the nature of humanity made in God's image, the nature of the church as Christ's body, and the fall of humanity and its redemption and ultimate consummation. These are all still theological matters of the utmost importance, but not necessarily issues someone would be expected to grasp upon their initial faith in Christ.

The biblical gospel is a declaration of Christ's redemptive activity that calls for a response on the part of its hearers. Many of the precious doctrines of Scripture cherished by Protestants and evangelicals *directly support* the gospel, while others *indirectly support it*. The evangelical doctrine of *penal-substitutionary atonement* directly supports the gospel message by clarifying what Jesus did on behalf of sinners. The biblical teaching of humanity's creation as male and female, while crucial for understanding the created order, indirectly supports the gospel message proclaimed by the disciples. Other doctrines are *important ramifications* for living in light of the gospel message. Not every issue tangentially related to the gospel *is* the gospel. We must believe some doctrines upon conversion (i.e., the death of Jesus for sinners and his resurrection), while beliefs about other doctrines must come with discipleship and growth in the faith. Other disputed matters may remain unsettled or unresolved.

---

59. For a thorough evangelical assessment of Oneness Pentecostal theology from a former adherent, see Gregory A. Boyd, *Oneness Pentecostals and the Trinity* (Grand Rapids, MI: Baker, 1994).

To Wittmer's three categories we could add another: *things some Christians believe*, which would include the second- and third-tier matters in other taxonomies like Mohler's triage. These doctrinal differences are not over the gospel itself ("the who and the what of the gospel") but over the mechanics of *how* the gospel works (i.e., election, theories of atonement, the order of salvation, etc.) and the implications of the gospel for Christian practice.[60] Calvinists and Arminians all agree that God predestines us—that is a direct statement of Scripture (Rom. 8:29–30)—but they tussle over how that works.

Other second-, third-, and fourth-tier matters are explanations of first-tier matters such as the authority of Scripture, the doctrine of creation, the sinfulness of human beings, and the return of Christ. We agree that the Bible is authoritative in the life of the Christian even if we disagree about "what adjectives we use to describe it."[61] All Christians agree that God created everything—this is a first-tier matter—but there is disagreement on the timing and mechanisms involved, as well as the key texts in the debate. We likewise agree that Jesus is returning again to set things right, though we differ about the timetable and the order of events. From this distinction we can build on the motto of irenics mentioned above: in the grand story of the gospel, unity; in the details and application of the gospel story, freedom for interpretive diversity; in our gospel unity and interpretive differences, love and genuine concern for one another.

The Praxis Test: How Important Is What We Do to Us?

We may have relational fellowship on the gospel and other theological matters without the possibility of having organized or formal fellowship as a local church or denomination.[62] We may have unity of belief in the gospel and even in a soteriological system like Calvinism or Arminianism but still be incapable of having organizational unity because of our differences about the organization and practice of the church. These are "significant boundaries between believers."[63] When are these lines drawn and why? The third and final test for doctrinal

---

60. Kevin J. Vanhoozer, *Biblical Authority after Babel*, 206.
61. Mohler, interview by author.
62. Iain H. Murray, *Evangelicalism Divided* (Carlisle, PA: Banner of Truth, 2000), 2.
63. Mohler, "Confessional Evangelicalism," 79.

taxonomies is the praxis test that helps address this issue. The pastoral question is, "What doctrines and practices are vital for fellowship and partnership in ministry?" Again, this is where taxonomies of more than two tiers are most helpful.

The primary difference between second-tier matters that organize a denomination or a local church and third-tier issues about which Christians in a denomination or local congregation agree to disagree about seems to be the question of *practice* or *action*. Christians committed to the authority of Scripture can understand obedience to Scripture in the local church in sundry ways. Some agreement between Christians is necessary for the assembly of believers. As Wesley notes in his quotation of Amos 3:3, "Two cannot walk together unless they be agreed."[64] Stronger disagreements on practice will likely result in a parting of ways.

My home denomination, the Southern Baptist Convention, has historically been divided over Calvinism, Arminianism, and a hybrid position sometimes called "Traditionalism." (All Baptists since the seventeenth century have had similar groupings.) Yet Southern Baptists can rightly relegate this parochial difficulty to third- or fourth-tier status because this difference in interpreting key passages in Scripture on election *has little or no impact on their shared practices or priorities as a tradition or denomination.* They still share the same gospel and essential tenets, as well as those second-tier articles that make them Baptist. In the same way, Baptists who clash over the timetable of the eschaton display no substantive difference in action on matters like church government, the ordinances, or a priority like personal evangelism. But Baptists and Presbyterians who agree on Calvinistic soteriology may still choose not to covenant together in a local church because of the great divide between them on the matter of baptism. These theological differences affect the practice of the local church. Where practices or actions differ, the lines of organizational fellowship or unity are drawn more tightly.

What Kind of Fellowship?

An important note about practical fellowship between doctrinally and practically divided churches: functional unity can mean different things

---

64. John Wesley, "The Catholic Spirit," in *The Works of John Wesley,* ed. Thomas Jackson, 14 vols. (London, 1872), 5:496; §1.10.

in different contexts. Theologians recognize multiple categories of unity and models of fellowship among churches that are mainly divided by praxis: *spiritual unity, mutual recognition and fellowship, conciliar unity,* and *organic unity.* Spiritual unity is defined as the notion that "all Christians are one by virtue of being committed to and serving the same Lord."[65] This is the *invisible church* made up of all true believers throughout history. This body is divided by space, time, and discordant beliefs but will be reunited in the eschaton. We are united spiritually by first-tier issues no matter what tradition we presently recognize as home.

Mutual recognition is another level of fellowship whereby Christians from one tradition recognize Christians from another tradition as belonging to true churches.[66] Of this kind of unity Wesley asked, "Although a difference in opinion about the modes of worship may prevent an entire external union; yet need it prevent our union in affection? Though we cannot think alike, may we not love alike?"[67] Christians from different traditions who mutually recognize one another as believers in good fellowship may preach in one another's churches and share in Communion with one another. They may choose to participate in ministry together for a season but still be incapable of having a permanent affiliation or organizational unity. The Billy Graham crusades of the twentieth-century fit the profile for this kind of fellowship.[68]

Conciliar unity takes this type of partnership one step further in forming permanent associations between churches of different denominations without eliminating their denominational differences.[69] The World Council of Churches birthed in the ecumenical movement fits in this category. These approaches to church unity recognize differences in practice between traditions and relegate these differences to second-tier status that may divide them congregationally or denominationally but not missionally.

The final category of fellowship is *organic unity,* an effort to merge or eliminate denominational traditions within Christianity.[70] Those

---

65. Erickson, *Christian Theology,* 1011.
66. Harding Meyer, *That All May Be One: Perceptions and Models of Ecumenicity* (Grand Rapids, MI: Eerdmans, 1999), 89–93.
67. Wesley, "Catholic Spirit," 5:493, proem 4.
68. Erickson, *Christian Theology,* 1011–1012.
69. Meyer, *That All May Be One,* 141–150; Erickson, *Christian Theology,* 1012.
70. Meyer, *That All May Be One,* 94–100; Erickson, *Christian Theology,* 1012.

striving for this kind of unity seem to believe doctrinal compromise is a necessary step for achieving organic, organizational unity. Doctrine is of minimal importance in light of church unity. Protestants and evangelicals have shied away from this kind of unity since the dawn of the Reformation.

Differences in Priorities

Cooperation among Christian traditions, denominations, and churches is often defined by the respective priorities of those involved. Timothy George has written about an "ecumenism in the trenches" forged by shared social and political interests. Protestants may ally together with Roman Catholics on political and social matters in the public square (e.g., pro-life causes, traditional marriage) without capitulating their distinctive doctrinal convictions, but this kind of relationship does not entail theological or ecclesial unity.[71] Such agreement is unattainable if core Protestant beliefs and Catholic tradition are maintained. Most evangelicals would be wary of organizational fellowship with other Protestant Christian groups that do not value or prioritize personal evangelism and disciple making. The same applies to mainline Protestant groups who contend that social justice is the central aim of the Christian church.

These differences in priority can be first-tier matters. Ecumenical and evangelical priorities are often different, making mutual or conciliar fellowship impossible. As Kevin Vanhoozer explains, "In sum, we need to distinguish between ecumenical unity—visible unity of an organizational kind—and evangelical unity, where the focus is on the gospel, which both unites (in Christ) and divides."[72] Evangelicals across denominational lines may have partnerships of mutual recognition when their shared priority is the gospel and its proclamation.

Government Matters

Evangelicals argue about which model of church government—episcopal, presbyterian, congregational, or nongovernmental—best reflects

---

71. Timothy George, "Catholics and Evangelicals in the Trenches," *Christianity Today* 38, no. 6 (May 1994): 16.
72. Vanhoozer, *Biblical Authority after Babel*, 187.

the apostolic church of the New Testament. Some stress a top-down model of government, while others endorse a model that emphasizes the leadership of the congregation. Why the difference?

The creeds of the early church do not explicitly address the details of ecclesial structures, largely because unchallenged models were already in place when the creeds were developed. Christians differ on this issue not necessarily because they do not believe in biblical authority but because biblical writers themselves do not address these issues directly.

The New Testament offers no church planting manual complete with detailed instructions about the structure of church government or how to run business meetings. Instead, it offers ad hoc instructions that address specific situations cropping up in already established churches. When instruction about leadership is given, it is related to the character of leadership, not its formal organization (1 Tim. 3:1–13; Titus 1:5–9). Interpreters may strive to reconstruct the model of church leadership they believe most closely resembles the apostolic church, but they do so by an imperfect abductive process (see ch. 3).

Christians with different convictions about church government may work together in coalitions of churches across denominational lines on matters most important to them, either in mutual recognition or conciliar unity, but deeply held beliefs about biblical church government and practice often restrict formal association beyond this kind of partnership. Organic or organizational unity between Christians who hold competing models of church government is difficult to achieve, though some have attempted such unity. One example coming out of the twentieth-century ecumenical movements is the United Church of Canada, founded in 1925. Initially a coalition of Methodists, Presbyterians, and Congregationalists, this mainline Protestant denomination that once represented a variety of governmental models now has a modified Presbyterian model. The only way to achieve organizational unity of this magnitude is the capitulation of beliefs and convictions on matters related to church government.[73]

---

73. Erickson, *Christian Theology*, 1012. Notably, amid many of the changes in Canadian culture, this mainline ecumenical tradition eventually abandoned its evangelical identity. For a history of this change, see Kevin N. Flatt, *After Evangelicalism: The Sixties and the United Church of Canada* (Kingston, ON: McGill-Queen's University Press, 2013). Also see Jeff Seaton,

Whether one's tradition favors a bottom-up approach or a top-down approach to rule and polity, groups seeking this kind of unity will have to concede and possibly surrender their biblical convictions on the matter. Matters related to church government are often mutually exclusive because one form of government or another must be practiced in a local church or denomination. Consequently, these are boundary-making categories of the second tier.

One Lord, One Faith, One Baptism?

The Bible does not address infant baptism directly, nor does its authorship explicitly say that believer's baptism is the normative standard for all followers of Jesus. Since the Reformation, Christians have been divided over the practice and interpretation of baptism. Church historians debate when infant baptism became the norm, and theologians and biblical interpreters are divided over how to make sense of narratives from the early church that describe only the baptism of believers. However, both views are vital parts of their respective traditions.

Credobaptists and paedobaptists build their doctrines of baptism in different houses, from different starting places. Paedobaptism, as practiced by those in the Reformed tradition, is an entryway into the covenant, something central to the ecclesiology of their churches. By contrast, many Baptists do not recognize the baptism of infants as biblical baptism and assert that the only proper candidates for baptism are regenerate believers who have expressed conscious understanding of faith and repentance. For the credobaptist, baptism is witness and proclamation to the work of God in the life of the believer. Because of their convictions on this matter, many Baptists do not recognize Presbyterians who are not baptized after conscious faith in Christ as having been baptized, a necessary prerequisite for membership in their fellowship.

Again, mutual recognition of one another as believers in Christ is very achievable despite differences of interpretation on the ordinance or sacrament of baptism. However, formal organizational union is

---

Who's Minding the Story? The United Church of Canada Meets a Secular Age (Eugene, OR: Pickwick, 2018).

hindered by differences in practice. For these Christians, this practical difference makes this a second-tier boundary. Some churches practice a compromise on the matter, allowing members from both types of baptism. Yet this is possible only when those who hold these differences either (a) concede their own beliefs or (b) relegate them to a matter of practical insignificance. No effort at unity on this matter should violate the biblically directed consciences of those encouraged to conform.

Can We Have Communion?

Communion, or the Lord's Supper, is another practice that divides Christians who have varying interpretations of it. In his treatment on unity among "mere Protestant Christians," Vanhoozer contends that the Communion table is one place where evangelical Protestants should be gathering for fellowship. I agree with his lament over the irony "that Protestants broke fellowship over the very doctrine and practice intended to symbolize it."[74] So, the question for my local church becomes whether we should continue to exclude from the table fellow Christians who may share essential commitments to first-tier gospel issues but who nevertheless wrangle over the meaning of the Supper and its proper candidates.

For some Protestants, the differences in the way we conceptualize and receive the Lord's Supper are not trivial. Luther believed that Zwingli's rejection of the sacramental dimension of the Supper was tantamount to a refusal of God's grace. Despite Zwingli's tear-soaked pleas at Marburg, Luther refused to acknowledge the Swiss Reformer as his brother. But was this sort of practical separation appropriate?

Some take up the opinion that the *practice*, not the *interpretation* of the Supper, is ultimately what matters. According to this view, a Protestant can practice Communion with any church where the performance of the Supper is uniform.[75] In his *Letters to Malcolm*, C. S. Lewis briefly addresses the theological controversy surrounding the Supper and observes that obedience must take priority over compre-

---

74. Vanhoozer, *Biblical Authority after Babel*, 183.
75. There is greater variety in the practice of the Supper outside of Protestantism. Roman Catholics often give only bread to the laity. Theological cults like Mormons substitute wine or grape juice with water.

hension of what is happening in the meal: "The command, after all, was Take, eat: not Take, understand."[76]

However, the interpretation of the practice is not unimportant. Luther believed Jesus to be literally and physically present in the Lord's Supper. Zwingli rejected this notion and contended that the Supper was a memorial for Christ's atoning work. Calvin offered a mediating position that suggested the Supper was a proclamation of the Word of God and a source of nourishment for believers who experience Christ's spiritual presence in the Supper.[77] While I have no real difficulties with either the Zwinglian or the Calvinistic interpretations of the Supper—two positions I believe can be compatible—I personally would find it difficult to participate in any Communion service where the meaning is explicitly defined as transubstantiation or consubstantiation. I hold this conviction partly because scholars have convinced me of the importance of paying attention to authorial intent, which in this case would be the intention behind the performance of the Supper. Because I would have a fundamentally different "reading" of the Supper's signs than a Lutheran or a Roman Catholic officiant, I cannot in good conscience mislead him to believe I affirm his explanation of the event.

Unity on matters such as the Supper and baptism may be only an eschatological hope. Christian traditions of all stripes will be slow to embrace these calls to unity, sometimes with very good reason. In the interim, while we are all sorting through hermeneutical questions, we can prayerfully and patiently "keep loving one another earnestly," knowing that "love covers a multitude of sins" and interpretive differences. We can always show "hospitality to one another without grumbling" (1 Pet. 4:8–9).

Conclusion

Doctrinal taxonomies are a vital tool for theological discourse and relationships between fellow Christians. They help us distinguish between heresy and orthodoxy and between what beliefs are essential for Christian fellowship and those that are not. Apart from tools like

---

76. C. S. Lewis, *Letters to Malcolm: Chiefly on Prayer* (New York: Harvest, 1992), 104.

77. See I. John Hesselink, "Reformed View: The Real Presence of Christ," in *Understanding Four Views on the Lord's Supper*, ed. John H. Armstrong (Grand Rapids, MI: Baker, 2007), 59–71.

these, theologians can give in to theological minimalism that diminishes Christian doctrine altogether or theological maximalism that creates unnecessary strife and contention between Christians. Fellowship is achievable between Christians of differing faith traditions, but this sort of fellowship need not require an ecclesial union or organizational unity. For evangelicals, this fellowship is primarily defined by the gospel and a mutual desire to proclaim it. Things that are clearly defined in Scripture are given first priority, while room is allowed for differences on disputable interpretive matters. Matters of practical difference must distinguish us now because we have arrived at different conclusions from Scripture.

All Christians agree on the *who* of the gospel: the God revealed in Christ Jesus. We agree on the *what*: that God has acted through Jesus's death and resurrection to redeem sinners. Yet we do not always agree on the *hows* and *whys* of the gospel. This is partly because we lack comprehensive knowledge of God's intentions and because we struggle as imperfect interpreters of Scripture trying to comprehend its thought world. Praise be to God, the faith that saves is not comprehension of God's saving purposes but *trust in the person of Christ* and his saving activity. Imprisoned and facing his imminent death, Paul's consolation was not "I *understand* what I have believed" but rather "I *know whom I have believed*, and I am convinced that he is able to guard until that day what has been entrusted to me" (2 Tim. 1:12).

Some doctrines do and should divide us, separating believers from the nonbelieving world, those who know Christ from those who do not. Other beliefs divide us out of necessity for the time being, such as those between fellow believers on less important matters related to Christian practice and worship. However, Christian love and concern should characterize all of our theological differences. It is this topic we must take up in our final chapter.

8

How Then Shall We Disagree?

Lessons from Whitefield and Wesley

What would a letter written by an apostle look like in the age of the internet? If Paul were writing a blog in the twenty-first century, what sort of ethical instruction would he give? Would he admonish against us Netflix binge-watching, or would he grant liberty to cord-cutters with stronger consciences? Would he ever tell his Twitter followers who they should vote for or tell them to refrain from political involvement altogether? Most importantly for the present topic, how would he have handled the very public theological battles in which Christians now embroil themselves on social media? Ancient writers were silent on these matters not because they are unimportant to the faith but because these things are unique to our time and place in history.

New Testament writers do not directly address intramural struggles over the interpretation of Scripture in the church. Yes, they called out factions and personality cults (1 Cor. 1:10–17). And yes, even first-century believers had their practical and doctrinal differences. They disagreed about food (Rom. 14:1–23; 1 Cor. 8:1–13), the expectations placed on Gentile believers (Acts 15:1–35; Gal. 2:11–5:15), and the use of spiritual gifts (1 Cor. 14:1–40). The apostles also repeatedly rebuked false teaching that diminished the gospel and threatened the doctrinal integrity of the church. But anathemas were not directed at the kind of interpretive conflicts that shape our divisions in evangelicalism. They were directed against false teachers who denied the authority of the apostolic proclamation and who introduced idolatrous alternatives to their gospel. These teachings were condemned not because they were mere intellectual misjudgments but because they had a spiritual character rooted in unbelief and rebellion.

The historical reasons for New Testament silence on addressing exegetical differences between fellow believers are clear. When the New Testament was being written, the apostles handpicked by Jesus and inspired by the Holy Spirit were still around to settle any theological questions and disputes that would arise. The idea of a more formal, systematic theology had not yet developed, so Christians were not yet arguing about how best to convert the situational theologies of biblical writings into more organized systems.

For these reasons, we need an *improvised Christian ethic* of doctrinal disagreement that is consistent with the explicit instruction of Scripture. This final chapter is a constructive, provisional attempt at formulating such an ethic. The method used here loosely resembles what John Webster called a "theology of retrieval," a creative effort to address a contemporary problem with both Scripture and the resources of church history and historical theology.[1] Theologies of retrieval concern themselves not only with the world behind the biblical text but also the world in front of the text. They are concerned with the ways Christians throughout history have read and applied the Bible to their situations. Theologies of retrieval view every period of history as an arena of the Spirit's work. They are witness to ontological and theological continuity with the church of the past and the church of the present. They do not neglect the wisdom and experience of the faithful dead who still provide valuable guidance for our situation.[2]

One of the most notorious theological feuds in church history, the controversy between George Whitefield (1714–1770) and John Wesley (1703–1791) over Calvinism and Arminianism, will be the

---

1. See John Webster, "Theologies of Retrieval," in *The Oxford Handbook of Systematic Theology*, ed. John Webster, Kathryn Tanner, and Iain Torrance (New York: Oxford University Press, 2007), 583–599.

2. See W. David Buschart and Kent D. Eilers, *Theology as Retrieval: Receiving the Past, Renewing the Church* (Downers Grove, IL: InterVarsity Press, 2015), 1–37.

basis of the constructive ethic of disagreement formulated here. The personal and theological journeys of these evangelical giants were so intertwined that it is, in the words of one of their biographers, "impossible to seek a true understanding of the one without seeking also a true understanding of the other."[3] These men, both instrumental in the formation of modern evangelicalism, were at one time colaborers in the same field of ministry but for a season were made bitter rivals because of their theological differences.[4]

Like the public dispute between Luther and Zwingli, their conflict divided a movement and forged new rivalries. Yet as Whitefield and Wesley grew in God's grace and in their love for each other, they moved from being dogmatic opponents to becoming models for fellowship despite theological disagreement. Their practice of biblical principles demonstrates that interpretive disagreement between brothers and sisters in Christ need not hinder love for one another, nor should their love for one another diminish their commitment to their individual convictions. This chapter examines their unique narrative and its relationship to biblical commands about Christian relationships, and draws practical implications for our public disputes in the present.

Wesley, Whitefield, and the "Free Grace" Controversy

Wesley and Whitefield first became acquainted in 1733, when Charles Wesley, John's younger brother, invited Whitefield to join a small religious group at Oxford University known derisively by many around the university as "The Holy Club." Infamous for its strict behavior and methodical rigor, the Holy Club acquired many other nicknames, including the "Bible Moths," "Bible Bigots," and the "Supererogation Men," but the moniker that they eventually embraced was the "Methodists." The leadership of the group naturally fell to the older and more experienced John Wesley, who had recently returned to the university to teach courses in Greek. Still steeped in high church

---

3. Arnold A. Dallimore, *George Whitefield: The Life and Times of the Great Evangelist of the Eighteenth-Century Revival*, 2 vols. (Edinburgh: Banner of Truth, 1970, 1980), 1:67.

4. One of the best secondary sources on the debate between Wesley and Whitefield is Allan Coppedge, *John Wesley in Theological Debate* (Wilmore, KY: Wesley Heritage, 1987), 41–22; Coppedge, *Shaping the Wesleyan Message* (Nappanee, IN: Evangel, 2003), 31–98. Though clearly favorable to Wesley, Coppedge avoids an over-idealized hagiography. He writes fairly about all parties involved and provides a wonderful arrangement of the primary sources, on which my presentation here is dependent.

Anglo-Catholic theology and practice, the early group was a pale reflection of the gospel-centered, revivalistic preaching and theology later associated with Whitefield and the Wesleys.[5]

Though Wesley and Whitefield initially went their separate ways after their Holy Club days at Oxford—the Wesleys went to America while Whitefield stayed in Oxford—their immediate lives followed very similar trajectories. When the Wesley brothers left England to do missionary and social service work in the colony of Georgia, Whitefield briefly assumed leadership over the Methodists. Across the ocean that divided them, John Wesley and Whitefield both continued to experience frustration and disillusionment with their burdensome forms of religion. Eventually both men went on to experience dramatic, liberating new birth conversions: Whitefield at Oxford in 1735, and Wesley at Aldersgate in 1738.

In a wave of spiritual renewal that spread like a flame throughout England, Whitefield gained great notoriety as an open-air preacher and evangelist—a ministry he later recruited Wesley to take up with him. Whitefield charged Wesley to take over the evangelistic and congregational work he began in Bristol. Their ministry partnership flourished for a season until seeds of doctrinal disagreement grew into controversy over Calvinism and Arminianism.

Wesley and Whitefield offer concrete, historical examples of the reasons for theological disagreement described in this book. Both were finite interpreters of Scripture, shaped by their own cognitive limitations and cultural milieu. Wesley and Whitefield approached the same biblical texts with different exegetical and hermeneutical considerations, resulting in conflicting conclusions. They reasoned through the major themes of the Bible in distinctive ways, often choosing different interpretive models for key passages in question. But they were also inventive. Wesley's controversial doctrine of perfection is a clear example of a creative abduction because of its uniqueness.[6]

The disparity in the theological traditions that nourished Wesley and Whitefield also contributed to their differences.[7] Immersing him-

---

5. Dallimore, *George Whitefield*, 1:71–72.

6. For a history of the development of this doctrine, see T. A. Noble, *Holy Trinity: Holy People: The Theology of Christian Perfecting* (Eugene, OR: Cascade, 2013), 44–96.

7. Iain Murray, "Prefatory Note to 'A Letter to the Rev. Mr. John Wesley in Answer to His Sermon Entitled *Free Grace*,'" in *George Whitefield's Journals* (Edinburgh: Banner of Truth, 1960), 564–565.

self in the theological tradition of the Reformers and the Puritans, Whitefield began to embrace a Calvinistic understanding of predestination, reprobation, and perseverance (though he initially didn't care much for the label "Calvinist").[8] Wesley, on the other hand, was influenced by the theology of Jacob Arminius.[9] In spite of their shared love of Scripture, Wesley and Whitefield also proved to be men of very different theological intuitions with unique emotional responses to the issues at hand. Whereas Whitefield drew great comfort from the Calvinistic doctrine of predestination, Wesley grew very uneasy with it, concerned that it painted God in an abhorrent light.[10]

The Public Dispute: "Holy God as Worse than the Devil"?

The seeds of controversy were sown in 1739 when Wesley wrote and began preaching a sermon entitled "Free Grace," a message directed against the Calvinistic doctrine of predestination—something he was initially reluctant to do given his ministry context. To call the message "strongly worded" would be an understatement; it was a battle cry. Wesley pulled no punches in his description of the teaching, calling it "a doctrine full of blasphemy" that makes the "whole Christian revelation . . . contradict itself." He sincerely believed that the determinism entailed in the system inevitably led to antinomian or lawless behavior. It made preaching vain and cut out the motivation for evangelism and missions. Wesley argued that if the biblical notion of predestination were as the Calvinists described it, then "Holy God [would be] worse than the devil . . . more false, more cruel, and more unjust" because his expressed desire to save all (1 Tim. 2:4; 2 Pet. 3:9) would blatantly contradict his secret will to decree some unto salvation and others unto damnation.[11]

Several of Wesley's friends, including Whitefield himself, urged him not to publish the "Free Grace" sermon. Though Wesley refrained

---

8. Scholars disagree about when precisely Whitefield became more Calvinistic in his thinking. Dallimore contends that seeds of Reformed thought show up in his journals as early as 1735 (see Dallimore, *George Whitefield*, 1:84–85), but others contend that Calvinistic ideas do not explicitly appear in his sermons until 1739. See Luke Tyerman, *The Life of the Reverend George Whitefield*, 2 vols. (New York: Anson D. F. Randolph, 1877), 1:305; Coppedge, *John Wesley in Theological Debate*, 52, 83.

9. Rusty E. Brian, "John Wesley the Faithful Arminian," in *Embracing the Past—Forging the Future: A New Generation of Wesleyan Theology*, ed. Wm. Andrew Schwartz and John M. Bechtold (Eugene, OR: Pickwick, 2015), 157–170.

10. Coppedge, *John Wesley in Theological Debate*, 42.

11. See Coppedge, *John Wesley in Theological Debate*, 47–49.

from publishing it for a while, he sent it to the printers almost immediately after Whitefield left again for America in August of 1739.[12] Joined to the publication of the sermon was a hymn by Charles Wesley entitled "Universal Redemption" that presented a more positive, poetic expression of the Arminian theology of the Wesleys. The next year, Wesley would publish yet another treatise on predestination and reprobation, largely building off an earlier work by Isaac Watts.[13]

In 1740, the discord between Wesley and Whitefield was purely theological. The named personal attacks and critiques had not yet begun. Throughout that year, while Whitefield was in America, Whitefield and Wesley maintained regular, cordial correspondence. Even with the fraternal spirit that typified the letters, however, the entrenchments in their viewpoints were deepening. Whitefield became more convinced of the role of Calvinistic doctrine in America's Great Awakening, while Wesley further developed the implications of his Arminian theology with his doctrine of the possibility of Christian perfection.[14]

After more than a year of public silence on the matter, Whitefield felt compelled to publish his "Answer" to Wesley's "Free Grace." The letter, published first in America and later in England, changed the whole tenor of the conversation. Whitefield directly responded to several of the claims made in "Free Grace" and left others unanswered. He argued that a doctrine of divine reprobation does not create contradictions in the interpretation of Scripture and does nothing to deter from the practice of personal holiness. He flatly denied Wesley's charge that the doctrine of reprobation is blasphemous, countering with the accusation that the doctrine of universal redemption is even more profane. Whitefield did so by equating universal redemption with universalism, a move common to critics of the doctrine.

In the letter, Whitefield also raised two other issues unrelated to "Free Grace," the first being Wesley's doctrine of sinless perfection. The second criticism was more personal. Whitefield publicly censured

---

12. Murray, "Prefatory Note," 565.

13. John Wesley, *Serious Considerations of the Doctrine of Election and Reprobation* (London, 1740).

14. Coppedge, *John Wesley in Theological Debate*, 81–82.

Wesley for his use of casting lots to determine whether he would publish the sermon, something that Wesley had mentioned in their private correspondence.[15] Wesley's critics would use this disclosure against him for decades to come.[16] Whitefield later expressed great remorse for this harsh revelation.[17]

Though Wesley himself never took up a pen to write a public response to Whitefield's "Answer," he did continue to publish on the subject of predestination, including five works in 1741 alone.[18] The Wesleys used hymnody to combat Calvinistic doctrines, publishing numerous hymns defending the universality of the gospel call and the atonement.[19] The publication of these hymns drew great ire from the Calvinists because of some of the unpleasant names bestowed upon them: "Advocates of the Devil, Carnal Saints, etc."[20] In response, Whitefield increasingly incorporated Calvinistic distinctives into his sermons, including one occasion in which he preached on the absolute decrees of God in the presence of Charles Wesley.[21]

The Fallout of the Debate: "They Are Both Cheats, Deluders, and Imposters"

The debate had several personal ramifications for those involved. *First, the personal relationship between Whitefield and the Wesleys was strained, eventually to the point of complete estrangement.* In their first private meeting following the publication of Whitefield's letter in England, Whitefield asserted that they preached two different gospels and denied the Wesleys the right hand of fellowship (much like the reaction Luther had to Zwingli at the end of the Marburg Colloquy). Whitefield defended his public criticism of the Wesleys and promised to continue making such critiques, despite earlier promises to the contrary. Meanwhile, Wesley and Whitefield's respective defenders continued to stoke the fires of the debate, which took heavy

---

15. Whitefield, *George Whitefield's Journals*, 572.
16. Coppedge, *John Wesley in Theological Debate*, 93.
17. Dallimore, *George Whitefield*, 2:77.
18. See Richard Green, *The Works of John and Charles Wesley: A Bibliography* (London: C. H. Kelly, 1896), 17–21.
19. Coppedge, *John Wesley in Theological Debate*, 103–106.
20. Coppedge, *John Wesley in Theological Debate*, 113.
21. Coppedge, *John Wesley in Theological Debate*, 95; John Wesley, "A Letter to the Rev. Mr. Thomas Maxfield" (London: J. Fry, 1778), 9.

emotional tolls on both men. To his credit, Wesley never publicly named Whitefield in a sermon or in print.

Second, the Methodist movement itself was divided along theological lines, with its membership taking sides in the debate. The local societies were split over the predestination issue. Calvinist Dissenters built a place of worship in close proximity to the Foundry Church where the Wesleys served. Whitefield and his associates began a Calvinistic newspaper that condemned the actions of the other side.[22] The Wesleyans accused the Calvinists of promoting antinomianism; the Calvinists blamed the Wesleyans of endorsing papalism. Though many of the leaders would later have personal reconciliation, the organizational division between the parties was permanent.[23]

Third, the debate brought some temporary harm to the gospel witness of Whitefield and Wesley. Critics of the evangelical movement saw blood in the water and used the debate as an opportunity to attack. As one contemporary journalist described the quarrel,

> The controversy is grown to so great a Height, that Mr. *Whitefield* tells his Auditors, that if they follow Mr. Wesley's Doctrines, they will be *damned, eternally damned.* On the other Hand, Mr. *Wesley* tells his Congregation, that if they follow Mr. *Whitefield*, and do not stick close to him, it will bring *Distraction and Confusion* at last. . . . Now here is Oracle against Oracle, Revelation against Revelation, and the *God* of truth in one is declared to be a liar, by what he mentions in the other. . . . From these Circumstances, it is very evident that they [Wesley and Whitefield] both are Cheats Deluders and Imposters.[24]

Much like the Catholic critics of the Reformation who highlighted the internal differences among the Reformers to discredit them, polemicists of the high church tradition in Anglicanism used the Methodist

---

22. Coppedge, *John Wesley in Theological Debate*, 97–98.

23. The Calvinistic wing of the Methodist movement, largely diminished by the beginning of the twentieth century, eventually became the Presbyterian Church of Wales. For a history of this movement following the Whitefield-Wesley debate, see David Ceri Jones, Boyd Stanley Schlenter, and Eryn Mant White, *The Elect Methodists: Calvinistic Methodism in England and Wales, 1735–1811* (Cardiff: University of Wales Press, 2012).

24. *The Gentleman's Magazine* 11 (June 1741): 321–323, italics original.

discord as an opportunity to defend the episcopacy against its dissenters, further damaging an already embattled movement.

Personal Reconciliation: "Let Us Hold Fast to the Essentials"

Providentially, the story of Wesley and Whitefield's friendship did not end with this public embattlement, though many of their respective supporters would have had it that way. Whitefield was the first to reach out to Wesley, sending more than one unanswered letter apologizing for the way in which he had publicly conducted himself, especially with regards to his public rebuke of Wesley's use of lots.[25] But the coup de grâce to the feud between Wesley and Whitefield began with the reconciliation between the Wesleys and Howell Harris, the Welsh pastor at the forefront of Calvinistic Methodist work in Wales. Harris, who himself was no stranger to controversy,[26] was initially very antagonistic toward the Wesleys and the Arminian wing of the Methodist movement. But following his reconciliation with John and Charles, he became committed to seeing the former fellowship of the Wesleys and Whitefield restored. In 1741 and 1742, Harris wrote to and visited with both Whitefield and the Wesleys, prompting conversations that otherwise might not have happened. The journals and correspondence of these men give evidence to their renewed affections for one another and their willingness to maintain personal fellowship regardless of their unshifting theological opinions.[27]

Though the doctrinal differences between Wesley and Whitefield were too great for there to be a shared organization between their respective societies,[28] they had a renewed commitment to do ministry together that never diminished. After the men reached personal reconciliation, under their leadership their respective societies were able

---

25. Dallimore, *George Whitefield*, 2:139–141; George Whitefield, *The Works of George Whitefield*, 6 vols. (London, 1771), 1:331.

26. Harris most famously found himself at odds with Daniel Rowland, another key leader in the Welsh Methodist Revival. See Geraint Tudur, *Howell Harris: From Conversion to Separation, 1735–1750* (Cardiff: University of Wales Press, 2002). See also Dallimore, *George Whitefield*, 2:295–303. The charges leveled against Harris include his advocating the teaching of patripassianism (i.e., the teaching that God the Father died on the cross) and imprudence or impropriety with a married woman. Dallimore links this strange behavior to physical exhaustion and a head injury.

27. Coppedge, *John Wesley in Theological Debate*, 112–114; Dallimore, *George Whitefield*, 2:142–146.

28. Dallimore, *George Whitefield*, 2:50.

to reach the level of fellowship dubbed *mutual recognition*. They recognized one another as true, Bible-believing Christians and were able to have occasional partnerships in gospel ministry.

Though Wesley and Whitefield still spoke candidly of their differences, such as their disagreement over Wesley's doctrine of perfect sanctification, they coupled those admissions with the affirmations of the greater priority they placed on their fellowship in the gospel. These men attended the conferences of their sister societies, despite new debates popping up from time to time among their followers. In their cease-fire, they shared their pulpits and resolved not to contradict each other publicly when doing so, staying clear of the minor disputes that divided them.[29]

The end of Whitefield and Wesley's earthly relationship was a testimony to the triumph of the gospel over their minor dissimilarities. They had agreed that whoever died first would preach the other's funeral. At the age of 55, Whitefield, who had been prone to generally poor health, died the morning after preaching his final sermon atop a barrel in Exeter, New Hampshire. Though he was buried in Massachusetts, Wesley would preach two memorial services to Whitefield's Calvinistic Methodist societies in London in November 1770.[30]

In the sermon, Wesley praised the breadth of Whitefield's transatlantic missionary field, claiming that no one since the apostles themselves had preached the gospel so widely across the globe. But the most striking comment Wesley made was about the things which united the men who were once so publicly divided:

> Let us keep close to the grand Scriptural doctrines which he everywhere delivered. There are many doctrines of a less essential nature, with regard to which even the sincere children of God (such is the present weakness of human understanding) are and have been divided for many ages. In these we may think and let think; we may "agree to disagree." But, meantime, let us hold fast the essentials of "the faith which was once delivered to the saints;" and

---

29. Coppedge, *John Wesley in Theological Debate*, 157–158.
30. Wesley, then 67, preached these sermons at two locations where Whitefield regularly preached: Tottenham-Court Road Chapel on November 18, 1770, and the Moorfields Tabernacle on November 23, 1770.

which this champion of God so strongly insisted on, at all times, and in all places![31]

Wesley and Whitefield had different convictions about the meaning of Scripture that were never resolved on this side of eternity. However, they grew to understand that doctrinal disagreement need not result in public hostility or personal resentment, especially among Christians committed to the gospel, biblical authority, and the kingdom of God. At the end of their lives, they came to embody the "catholic spirit" Wesley later wrote about.[32] Note that Wesley's use of the phrase "agree to disagree" here in this sermon is the first time the phrase ever appeared in print.[33]

Disagreements without Divisiveness

Wesley and Whitefield were both among the first evangelical heirs of the Protestant Reformation, committed to the unique authority of the Bible, the proclamation of the gospel, and the need for the new birth. Though they shared so much in common on first-tier and second-tier theological matters, they had competing paradigms for understanding third-tier doctrines like the nature of predestination, election, and human freedom. Despite their differences, no one can accuse either side of lacking sincerity, passion, or an earnest desire to follow Scripture wherever it leads.

The redemptive story of Wesley and Whitefield leaves us with important principles, supported by Scripture, for our disputes today. Some Christians seem to believe the only choice they have in these controversies is to give up their convictions or be contentious bullies. Neither is a biblically faithful option. We must be able to correct doctrinal error when we see it, challenge misconceptions where they lie, and do so in a way that seeks the ultimate restoration and reconciliation of our opponents. On other occasions, we set aside our intramural differences and recognize that our interpretive stalemates need not

---

31. John Wesley, "On the Death of George Whitefield," in *The Works of John Wesley*, ed. Thomas Jackson, 14 vols. (London, 1872), 6:177–178, §3.1.

32. See James L. Schwenk, *Catholic Spirit: Wesley, Whitefield, and the Quest for Evangelical Unity in Eighteenth-Century British Methodism* (Lanham, MD: Scarecrow, 2008).

33. Max Cryer, *Common Phrases . . . and the Amazing Stories behind Them* (New York: Skyhorse, 2010), 13. Wesley used a similar phrase ("agree to differ") in a letter to Charles dated January 27, 1767.

hinder us from concern for one another as fellow believers. Whitefield and Wesley eventually came to understand that they would not change one another's minds, but they also realized that on this side of heaven, they didn't have to do so.

We Must Love Our Opponents

The foundational maxim of all Christian ethics is that every single person is made in the image of God and is deserving of basic human dignity (Gen. 1:26–28; 9:6). In personal, ecclesial, and academic debates it becomes easy to forget that we are not merely addressing free-floating ideas but the hearts and minds that are attached to them. We must strive to remind ourselves that even those in theological error are men and women deeply valued by God. Our theological interlocutors are people we are instructed to *love*.

Love is central to the Christian ethic espoused by Jesus and the apostles: "For this is the message that you have heard from the beginning, that we should love one another" (1 John 3:11). Our love for one another is the proving ground of our relationship to Jesus: "By this all people will know that you are my disciples, if you have love for one another" (John 13:35). We are called to love one another in the same way God loved those who were his enemies: "In this is love, not that we have loved God but that he loved us and sent his Son to be the propitiation for our sins. Beloved, if God so loved us, we also ought to love one another" (1 John 4:10–11). Peter does not insist that verbal correction on every theological point is most important. Instead, he writes, "Above all, keep loving one another earnestly, since love covers a multitude of sins" (1 Pet. 4:8).

Such love does not always come easy to us. Wesley observed that there are two "grand, general hindrances" to these commands: (1) we do not all think alike and (2) we do not all act alike.[34] That Jesus calls us to love even the worst of our enemies (Matt. 5:44) is an easier pill for some to swallow than the necessary implication of such an extreme position: Jesus calls us to love even our brothers and sisters who don't see eye to eye with us. We tend to act more harshly toward those

---

34. Wesley, "Catholic Spirit," 5:493.

who are more like us than we do toward outsiders. This basic human tendency to be hypersensitive to deviations from our tribal identities is what Freud called "the narcissism of minor differences" (*der Narzissmus der kleinen Differenzen*). It was true of Jews in the first century just like it is true of Baptist groups and Presbyterian groups in the twenty-first.

So how do we love our theological interlocutor? *From the outset, we must value them as persons.* As Roger Nicole clarifies this principle, "We owe it to our opponents to deal with them in such a way that they may sense that we have a real interest in them as persons, that we are not simply trying to win an argument or show how smart we are, but that we are deeply interested in them—and are eager to learn from them as well as to help them."[35]

Whenever and wherever possible, we should make conscious efforts to forge or foster actual relationships with those with whom we disagree. Apart from having a personal relationship, Wesley and Whitefield may never have made peace with each other. What ultimately drove their reconciliation was their slow realization that their personal concern for each other mattered more than their agreement on nonessential theological matters. Their relationship fostered within them a much-needed sense of empathy and concern for the other's well-being, something that ultimately drove away any motive in their dispute simply to be proven correct.

The need for relationships in theological disagreement is made all the more necessary by a world of theological disputes disconnected from actual human interaction. The technology of instant global communication has been both a great connector and a great dehumanizer. It is particularly dehumanizing when disputes are reduced to exchanges of comments trying to "one-up" the opponent or gain notoriety by taking a stand against them rather than seeing them as persons for whom Christian love is demanded by God.

Though Luther and Zwingli did not come away from the Marburg Colloquy with the same opinion about the Lord's Supper or even the same opinion about each other, what it did was *humanize*

---

35. Roger Nicole, "Polemic Theology: How to Deal with Those Who Differ from Us," in *Standing Forth: Collected Writings of Roger Nicole* (Ross-shire, UK: Christian Focus, 2002), 14.

their dispute. Of this humanizing at Marburg, Hermann Sasse adds, "Men who had known one another from writings only—and polemical ones at that—had now become personally acquainted: all this helped remove old prejudices."[36] Without human interaction, Luther and Zwingli would have had even more deficient understandings of their respective positions.

We should practice the principle of charity in our disagreements. Practicing what philosophers call the "principle of charity" is one way an intellectually virtuous person lives out the Golden Rule in her disagreements.[37] We should do unto those with whom we have differing opinions what we would want them to do for us (cf. Matt. 7:12).[38] In the same way that I would want people to truly understand my beliefs and how I arrived at them before they criticize me, I should do the same for them. Only by understanding one another do we avoid bearing false witness against our neighbors (Ex. 20:16; Deut. 5:20). People on both sides of a theological argument can unfairly malign one another when they misrepresent each other's positions instead of seeking to understand their position and how they came to it.

In part, the principle of charity means not assuming the worst in your interlocutor. In philosophy, this means not beginning with the assumption that a contrary position is irrational. For intramural Christian disagreement, this means refraining from suspicion toward "the genuineness of the author's Christian faith" upon discovering their disagreement from your position.[39] Uche Anizor likewise warns about a fear of the unknown which functions like a kind of "theological xenophobia."[40] At the height of the controversy between Wesley and Whitefield, they displayed judgmental and suspicious attitudes toward each other.

Another element in the principle of charity involves intentionally looking for the best versions and best representations of a particular

---

36. Hermann Sasse, *This Is My Body: Luther's Contention for the Real Presence in the Sacrament of the Altar* (Philadelphia: Fortress, 1959), 273.
37. For excellent overviews of this principle in theology, see Uche Anizor, *How to Read Theology: Engaging Doctrine Critically and Charitably* (Grand Rapids, MI: Baker, 2018), 3–23; Alan Jacobs, *A Theology of Reading: The Hermeneutics of Love* (Boulder, CO: Westview, 2001).
38. Nicole, "Polemic Theology," 10.
39. Anizor, *How to Read Theology*, 13.
40. Anizor, *How to Read Theology*, 14.

position and working from there. There are reasons to think that Wesley's initial critique of predestinarian doctrine came from his reading of works by hyper-Calvinists, not those by more moderate Calvinists like Whitefield, and that Wesley may have generalized all Calvinists in this light.[41] In the same manner, Calvinists who take the time to read the works of Arminius may be surprised to discover he sounds much more Reformed than the straw man often drawn in his place.[42]

Wesley and Whitefield both took *possible implications* of their opponent's system as certain heresy in their belief structures. It does not necessarily follow that God is a hypocrite for decreeing reprobation any more than it necessarily follows that anyone who affirms universal atonement is a universalist. These are possible implications built on unspoken presuppositions often unshared by both parties, not necessary inferences of the respective theological systems. Those who affirm a doctrine of divine reprobation do not presuppose, as did Wesley, that biblical texts asserted in favor of universal atonement mean that God desires to save every individual person. Wesley's argument that God would be hypocritical for predestining some to damnation carries weight only if the biblical texts in question do in fact indicate that God desires to save every individual person—another exegetical point debated among these parties.

Advocates of universal atonement do not necessarily presuppose, as did Whitefield, that Christ's provision of atonement for an individual guaranteed that the sins of that individual would actually be atoned for without any action on that person's part. Whitefield's argument was contingent upon a very particular definition of atonement that is not agreed upon by both parties. Wesley, like most in the Arminian tradition, assumed that atonement becomes effective only when activated by personal faith. Therefore, universal atonement does not procure universal salvation in his schema.

---

41. See Coppedge, *John Wesley in Theological Debate*, 47–49. As Coppedge suggests, the sermon published in August 1739 may have contained stronger language than the sermon preached in April 1739 due to the fact that Wesley spent the intervening time reading and critiquing the works of John Gill, a figure sometimes accused of hyper-Calvinism.

42. I credit Free Will Baptist theologian J. Matthew Pinson for helping me discover the "Reformed Arminius." See his *Arminian and Baptist: Explorations in a Theological Tradition* (Nashville: Randall, 2015). See also F. Leroy Forlines, *Classical Arminianism* (Nashville: Randall, 2011).

We can critique the exegetical presuppositions of our theological rivals (e.g., their belief that God wills to save only some, or that atonement is a provision made available for all but not applied apart from faith), but we should abstain from charges as great as heresy when their beliefs are not explicit, direct contradictions of Scripture. Heresy is more than intellectual error or misjudging the implications of what we affirm; it stems from a sinful disposition that rejects the plain teaching of Scripture, the worship of God, and holy living.

At the very least, the *charity* principle means trying to understand our interlocutor's meaning and aims.[43] As George Hunsinger explains, the principle of charity sometimes involves a "sympathetic interpretation" that temporarily suspends judgment on the disputed matter and assumes the internal coherency of the other position. Rather than assuming the other person/position is wrong, we can work backwards from the assumption that it is right and try, to the best of our ability, to resolve any apparent contradictions we may find in the position. Hunsinger opines that we often too quickly jump the gun in rushing to expose contradictions in a system or position rather than attempting, from the other side, to resolve those contradictions from within. Were we to discover that those contradictions are more easily resolved than we formerly supposed, then it would be rational to change our mind about that position.[44]

We should pray for those with whom we have disagreements, and when possible, pray with them. The exhortation to prayer laid out by Paul in 2 Thessalonians 3 is an excellent model for this kind of prayer. Pray for them to be effective in ministry (2 Thess. 3:1a) and for the word of God to be honored among them (v. 1b). Pray for their protection (v. 3) and their obedience (v. 4). Pray for an ever-increasing love for God in their hearts (v. 5). These types of prayers will soften hearts and stir affections for even our estranged brothers and sisters in Christ.

Whitefield earnestly prayed that God would end his doctrinal dispute with Wesley quickly, so that they would "be closely united in principle and judgment as well as heart and affection."[45] Though Wesley and

---

43. Nicole, "Polemic Theology," 11–12.

44. George Hunsinger, *Reading Barth with Clarity: A Hermeneutical Proposal* (Grand Rapids, MI: Baker, 2015), xii–xiii.

45. Whitefield, *George Whitefield's Journals*, 570.

Whitefield were never again in their earthly lives "united . . . in judgment," they were nevertheless united in their affection for one another and their commitment to the gospel ministry until death separated them.

In a wonderful letter penned to a friend who was about to publish a public critique of a fellow minister for theological error, John Newton (1725–1807) wrote,

> As to your opponent, I wish that before you set pen to paper against him, and during the whole time you are preparing your answer, you may commend him by earnest prayer to the Lord's teaching and blessing. This practice will have a direct tendency to conciliate your heart to love and pity him; and such a disposition will have a good influence upon every page you write.[46]

In my own life and from what I have seen in the lives of Whitefield and Wesley, continual, heartfelt prayer for one another, even for those who have wronged us, can change our disposition toward them, making us more empathetic to them and more concerned about their well-being.

Timothy George recommends meeting for corporate prayer with disagreeing parties. George suggests "a round of prayer meetings in which representatives of both communities meet together to pray for one another, to seek the illumination of the Holy Spirit in our study of the Scriptures, in our joint projects on behalf of the least, the last and the lost all around us, and in our efforts to be both faithful to our conscientious convictions and also agents of reconciliation within the evangelical family."[47]

Loving our opponent occasionally means gently correcting or rebuking them, but this should happen only after these other steps have been carried out. When Luke introduces Apollos in Acts 18, he describes him as "an eloquent man, competent in the Scriptures" (v. 24). He is commended for his training in the Scriptures, his fervent spirit, and his teaching ability (v. 25). But Luke also comments that "when Priscilla and Aquila heard him, they took him aside and explained to him the way of God more accurately" (v. 26). Apollos was apparently

---

46. John Newton, "Letter 19, On Controversy," in *Forty-One Letters on Religious Subjects* (London: Religious Tract Society, 1799), 144.

47. Timothy George, "Egalitarians and Complementarians Together? A Modest Proposal," in *Women, Ministry, and the Gospel: Exploring New Paradigms*, ed. Mark Husbands and Timothy Larsen (Downers Grove, IL: InterVarsity Press, 2007), 287.

in need of gentle correction, which he received privately from two who loved him enough to do so.

The New Testament is filled with examples where public rebuke was necessary to rebut doctrinal error (Gal. 1:6–7; Col. 2:8–23; 1 John 4:2–3). Scripture is "profitable for . . . rebuking [and] for correcting" (2 Tim. 3:16 CSB). Yet this kind of correction must come with the proper attitude and motive. Correction is for the building up of the individual or party in the wrong (2 Tim. 3:17), not for acclamation or scoring points. It must also be epitomized by kindness, gentleness, and forgiveness (Eph. 4:32; Prov. 15:1). Whenever and wherever we disagree, our appeal must be made on the "basis of love" (Philem. 9 NET).

Whitefield regretted the public rebuke of Wesley's use of lots, believing he would have better served Wesley by private, gentle correction. However, there were times in the life of Wesley and Whitefield when public rebuke was made necessary. In opposition to a common notion of inherited faith prevalent in England in their day, Wesley and Whitefield were proponents of the need for genuine conversion and renewal in the Holy Spirit. In Wesley's words, "If men are not Christians till they are renewed after the image of Christ, and if the people of England, in general, are not so renewed, why do we term them so?"[48] Wesley and Whitefield could have settled for an uneasy peace with their opponents by going the way of theological minimalism, but they recognized a real need for correction.

Though correction and rebuke are sometimes necessary, many unfortunately skip straight to this step without love or gentleness, and certainly without trying to really understand a person's position in the best possible light. Hermann Sasse describes this principle as a matter of personal holiness: "Pride and self-glorification, lack of love and humility, failure to understand the other side's point of view, and acrimonious speech are some of the sins that threaten the souls of those who have to fight doctrinal controversies. There are sins and dangers in orthodoxy that the world sees with greater clarity than we theologians do, and in many cases the judgment of God on the orthodox

---

48. Quoted in Iain H. Murray, *Evangelicalism Divided* (Carlisle, PA: Banner of Truth, 2000), 158–159.

defender of the faith may be far more severe than his verdict on the erring soul of a heretic."[49]

We Must Watch the Way We Conduct Ourselves

Disagreement over the things of God offers us no immunity to commands about Christian behavior and speech. Several instructions are relevant here. *First and foremost, we should be slow to debate and quick to listen.* James's exhortation that "every person be quick to hear, slow to speak, slow to anger" (James 1:19) applies to theological disagreements as well. This proverb is also applicable: "A hot-tempered man stirs up strife, but he who is slow to anger quiets contention" (Prov. 15:18). The Lord hates discord sown among brothers (Prov. 6:16, 19).

Whitefield's initial public engagement with Wesley on the matter of Calvinism was colored by youthful zeal and impetuousness, behaviors he later regretted. He was, after all, twenty-six years old—the same age as many of my students who act and speak hastily on their newly concretized theological opinions. What would Wesley and Whitefield's initial debate have looked like had they been working more slowly to understand each other's positions, asking questions, and treating their ideas with charity?

We must exercise patience and grace toward those who disagree with us. This principle is closely related to the first. As John Frame notes, some measure of tolerance of other theological positions is necessary lest every doctrine no matter how small become a test of orthodoxy. Contra theological maximalism, Frame says that some degree of tolerance is a necessary corollary of the biblical observation *"that each believer is subject to growth in his understanding."*[50] Some may fidget because of the use of the word *tolerance* here, but I suggest that this is a simple outworking of the biblical command to be *patient* with one another. We bear with one another, even in our differences. In his extended discussion on church unity, Paul encourages the Ephesian Christians to "walk in

---

49. Sasse, *This Is My Body*, 135.
50. John M. Frame, *Evangelical Reunion: Denominations and the Body of Christ* (Grand Rapids, MI: Baker, 1991), 88, italics original.

a manner worthy of the calling . . . with patience, bearing with one another in love" (Eph. 4:1a, 2b).

Ultimately, we must remember the unbelieving world is watching. The contemporary critics of Wesley and Whitefield used their contentious dispute as evidence against evangelical doctrine and the authenticity of their faith, something both men eventually came to regret deeply. Behavior unbecoming of Christians can adversely impact the proclamation of the gospel to the unbelieving world. For this reason, Jesus repeatedly emphasized the need for his followers to love one another in their public witness to the world (John 13:35; 17:21, 23). With the same spirit, Paul discouraged law court disputes between Christians because of the impact it had on the unbelieving public (1 Cor. 6:1–6). A spirit of irenicism should permeate our debates and disagreements, especially in a post-Christian context in which believers are becoming a minority.

Even the early defenders of the faith made the same admonishment. The fourth-century Cappadocian father Gregory of Nazianzus was no stranger to theological controversy. He vigorously defended the doctrines of the Trinity and the deity of the Holy Spirit against the heresy of semi-Arianism. He defended the integrity of Christ's human nature in his opposition to Apollinarianism. But Gregory was also selective about which theological debates were fit for public consumption: "If we cannot resolve our disputes outright, let us at least make this mutual concession, to utter spiritual truths with the restraint due to them, to discuss holy things in a holy manner, and not to broadcast to profane hearing what is not to be divulged."[51] Gregory was concerned that the polemical nature of the intramural debates hindered the apologetic ministry among the pagan adulterers and practitioners of infanticide.[52] But although he believed that much of the argumentation over Scripture and doctrine should remain in-house, he encouraged a full-on public engagement with atheism, Platonism, and other philosophies that stand in opposition to Christ.[53]

---

51. Gregory of Nazianzus, Oration 27.5. This translation of Gregory's "An Introductory Sermon against the Eunomians" appears in *On God and Christ: The Five Theological Orations and Two Letters to Cledonius*, trans. Frederick Williams and Lionel Wickham (Crestwood, NY: St. Vladimir's Seminary Press, 2002), 25–35.

52. Gregory of Nazianzus, Oration 27.6.

53. Gregory of Nazianzus, Oration 27.10.

Russell Moore extends the same principle to the world of social media debates. He notices that for many young theologians, blogging and social media are ways of working out their burgeoning theological schemas. "They are trying to sort out their beliefs," Moore remarked, "but they don't realize they're not playing a video game; they are dealing with real people and real onlookers."[54] When dealing with matters peripheral to the gospel, extended silence is welcome and wise, especially when theological banter on the internet has both a public character and a permanence that one can later regret.

Had she lived to see our current climate, Thumper the rabbit's mother may have said, "If you can't say anything nice, stay off of Twitter." But better advice comes from the Proverbs, which tell us to "Leave the presence of a fool, for there you do not meet words of knowledge" (Prov. 14:7). Sometimes the fool must be answered in his folly (Prov. 24:5), but other times he must be ignored lest we share in his foolishness (v. 4). It takes wisdom to know when to respond to those provoking a fight and when to ignore them. The same wisdom probably applies to most "trolls" or self-appointed critics and mind-guards on the internet. Strangers on social media are valuable to God and worth praying for, but responding to them is not always fruitful. Guard your tongue so that you may not sin with your speech (Ps. 39:1–3). Prayer and discernment should always be used in deciding which critics are worth our time and energy.

We Must Be Aware of Our Own Limitations

Nicole notes that in polemic theology, one "should be prepared to learn . . . that I may be wrong and the other person may be right."[55] He is quick to note that for the Christian, the essentials of the faith are not held so tentatively but "apart from issues where God Himself has spoken so that doubt and hesitancy are really not permissible, there are numerous areas where we are temperamentally inclined to be very assertive and in which we can quite possibly be in error."[56] We must acknowledge our fallibility as interpreters and as theologians. Such recognition by no means discounts the clarity of Scripture but reminds us of our own condition before God, the Bible, and others.

---

54. Russell D. Moore, interview by author, New Orleans, LA, October 11, 2016.
55. Nicole, "Polemic Theology," 15.
56. Nicole, "Polemic Theology," 15.

We must be humble interpreters of the word of God. I have no need to belabor the constant theme of this book that interpretive and theological disagreements are born out of our limitations as historically contingent human beings, people with different creative-reasoning impulses, different feelings, and different traditions. In his later writings on the "catholic spirit," Wesley explained this principle and used it to encourage humility: "It is an unavoidable consequence of the present weakness and shortness of human understanding, that several men will be of several minds in religion as well as in common life."[57]

We should refrain from argumentative and unyielding dogmatism in theological opinions that are mere inferences from other biblical ideas or other theological concepts. We make theological inferences or abductions whenever we attempt to draw a logical relationship between biblical doctrines. Whitefield believed Paul affirmed the idea of divine reprobation—that God foreordained some to unbelief—even though Paul does not explicitly say so in the biblical text. Whitefield was initially very critical of Wesley and his followers for not making the same inferences. Eventually, Whitefield acknowledged regret for the dogmatic attitude he had toward the doctrine: "I had written an answer, which though revised and much approved by some good and judicious divines, I think had some too strong expressions about absolute reprobation, which the apostle leaves rather to be inferred than expressed."[58]

Because theological inferences like this one are not explicit in Scripture, they are tenable and open to correction or revision. If someone makes a logical error in trying to make these connections, it does not mean, as Whitefield originally thought, that they do not believe the biblical text. Readers can place supreme confidence in the biblical text as the source of revelation and still falter in their understanding of its logical connections. When we have theological disagreements with those who arrive at different theological inferences than we do, we must be gracious and humble, acknowledging our limitations as interpreters and theologians. We must not presume the worst in our opponent because they do not make the same logical connections we make.

---

57. Wesley, "Catholic Spirit," 5:494, §1.3.
58. Quoted in Daniel Newell, *The Life of George Whitefield* (New York: R. T. Young, 1853), 79.

We should be careful about how much we let our personal trials color our disagreements. Whitefield was not wholly unjustified in writing a response to Wesley, particularly when one of his deeply held convictions appeared to be under attack. Where he erred was in making his critique of Wesley's theology personal, something he later acknowledged was partly due to the stress of his own personal circumstances. Historian Allan Coppedge lists several: When Whitefield wrote his "Answer" to Wesley, he was over a thousand pounds in debt, facing potential legal consequences. Whitefield's friend and financial supporter William Seward had been stoned to death in Wales following Seward's open-air preaching. The crowds that heard Whitefield's preaching dropped from tens of thousands to hundreds. Friends abandoned him. His publisher refused to work with him. His marriage proposal to Elizabeth Delamotte was rejected, and she was soon married to another man. While still only in his mid-twenties, Whitefield's health was very poor.[59] The stress Whitefield carried likely colored the way he received Wesley's "Free Grace" sermon.

We Must Be Aware of Our Own Motives

Some invoke controversy because they like the attention they receive from it. They appear to take comfort from the failure (or perceived failure) of others. Paul cautioned Timothy about teachers who have an "unhealthy craving for controversy and for quarrels about words" (1 Tim. 6:4). Gregory of Nazianzus warns against turning theology into a spectator sport used for personal glory: "They have undermined every approach to true religion by their complete obsession with setting and solving conundrums. They are like the promoters of wrestling-bouts in the theaters, and not even the sort of bouts that are conducted in accordance with the rules of the sport and lead to the victory of one of the antagonists, but the sort which are stage-managed to give the uncritical spectators visual sensations and compel their applause."[60] The same critique would apply to bloggers and theological shock jocks who seek to raise their "click counts" and podcast rankings with sensational headlines and unfounded accusations of

59. Coppedge, *John Wesley in Theological Debate*, 86–87.
60. Gregory of Nazianzus Oration 27.2.

heresy. They may build their "platform" with likes on their posts, re-tweets, and "followers," but they already have their reward in full.

Unlike fame-seeking rabble rousers, "people pleasers" avoid confrontation at all costs, even when it is necessary. People pleasers would rather keep the peace than make it (Matt. 5:9). Though the desire to pick public fights and the desire to please people come from different people of different demeanors and personalities, they can be expressions of the same foundational sin: the desire for human approval. Whether we are speaking about a cantankerous polemicist or an irenicist with a backbone of jelly, we should be wary of practicing our righteousness before others in order to be seen by them and receive their praise (Matt. 6:1–4). Paul makes it clear that there is a time for rebuke, even if it does not win the approval of people (Gal. 1:10).

We should seek to glorify God, not ourselves, in our theological disagreements. This desire should be the shared aim of Christian believers with conflicting theological ideas and convictions. Paul repeatedly pleaded that believers would be of the "same mind" (*auto phronein*; Rom. 15:5; cf. 12:16; 1 Cor. 1:10; Phil. 2:2, 5; 4:2). This was not a plea for "rote uniformity of thought, but for a common attitude and purpose."[61] The church at Rome to which Paul wrote his epistle had practical and philosophical differences between its Jewish and Gentile members, differences Paul did not expect would go away instantaneously. He did, however, long to see them cling to a central identity— a same-mindedness or harmony forged "in accord with Christ Jesus" (Rom. 15:5). Paul wanted to see them love one another in spite of their differences. Only this kind of same-mindedness would enable them to glorify God together with "one mouth" or "one voice" (*heni stomati*; v. 6). The fact that Paul prays for this kind of unity is indicative that it is something only God can grant; we cannot achieve it on our own. Christian unity is a gift from God that brings glory and honor to him.[62]

The desire to glorify God does not mean we never clash or that we never challenge what we perceive to be theological mistakes of fellow Christians. There is "a time to keep silence, and a time to speak" (Eccles. 3:7b). Loving rebuke is necessary and helpful on the right

---

61. James D. G. Dunn, *Romans 9–16*, WBC 38b (Nashville: Thomas Nelson, 1988), 746.
62. Thomas R. Schreiner, *Romans*, BECNT (Grand Rapids, MI: Baker, 1998), 749–750.

occasion. Just as there is a time for irenic theology, there is also a time for polemic theology. Yet even our attempts to correct or rebuke fellow believers should be driven by a desire to glorify God and to build up one another. As Iain Murray writes his description of Wesley and Whitefield's dispute, "Error must be opposed even when held by fellow members of Christ, but if that opposition cannot co-exist with a true love for all saints and a longing for their spiritual prosperity then it does not glorify God nor promote the edification of the Church."[63]

We must keep the gospel central in order to keep the "main thing" the "main thing." In 1748, after premature obituary reports on both sides of the Atlantic declared that "George Whitefield . . . the Founder of the Methodists" had died, Whitefield became determined to unshackle himself from the leadership of the Whitefieldian Methodist societies. His reasoning: he knew that his long-term association with those societies would prompt an unending rivalry with the Wesleyan Methodists, and he was determined to prevent the schismatic behavior among the British societies that he had seen in the colonies.[64] Whitefield not only disengaged from the societies that bore his name, he lent public support to Wesley's ministry, drawing their ire. He responded, "Let my name be forgotten, let me be trodden under the feet of all men, if Jesus may thereby be glorified."[65]

What matters first for the believer is the explicit gospel of the New Testament, not every other doctrine that supports it or results from it. It is what Paul called the matter of "first importance" (1 Cor. 15:3). The story of the gospel, more than our theological distinctives that attempt to explain its inner workings, should ultimately be what defines us in our relationship to other believers. Whitefield wholeheartedly believed this. In defense of his shared ministry with Wesley, with Presbyterians, with Baptists, and with others, he wrote, "I truly love all that love the glorious Emmanuel, and though I cannot depart from the principles which I believe are clearly revealed in the book of God, yet I can chearfully [sic] associate with those that differ from me, if I have reason to think they are united to our common Head."[66] This

---

63. Murray, "Prefatory Note," 568.
64. Dallimore, *George Whitefield*, 2:248–249.
65. Dallimore, *George Whitefield*, 2:257.
66. Dallimore, *George Whitefield*, 2:257; Whitefield, *Works*, 2:242.

association did not mean that Whitefield surrendered his distinctive theological beliefs. Instead, he served the larger body of Christ while recognizing that which was of central importance.

Conclusion

Followers of Jesus cling desperately to the hope of a future conscious and embodied life after death on a new earth where everyone recognizes God's rule and where evil and suffering have been permanently vanquished (1 Cor. 15:28). We pin our hopes on a future wherein God's people are truly united with one another (Col. 1:19–20), where schisms are no more, and where the knowledge of God is unshackled from its present impediments (1 Cor. 13:12; 1 John 3:2). All doctrinal disputes will eventually be resolved "when the perfect comes" (1 Cor. 13:10). This belief in a world without religious or interpersonal conflict is not mere wishful thinking but confident anticipation tethered to the life, death, burial, and resurrection of Jesus of Nazareth.

In this interim period while we see through a glass darkly, the people of God will disagree about Christian doctrine and practice. The solution to our conflict is not indifference to doctrine or surrender of convictions. We should be keeping a close watch on ourselves and our teaching (1 Tim. 4:16). But we also recognize that even those with shared commitments to the gospel, the glory of God, and the authority of Scripture continue to reach different conclusions about the meaning of the Bible, the character of God, and the inner workings of God's redemptive plan. They are prone to errors in judgment and are often unaware of the way in which their traditions and places in history color their theological outlooks.

The frailty of human interpretation should give us pause from interpretive pride and theological arrogance. It should also remind us of our great need for God's much greater grace in helping us understand the message of Scripture. Because we are recipients of God's grace, we should extend the same courtesy to those with whom we disagree. Love and patience should characterize our interpretive disagreements as imperfect readers of the Bible.

Acknowledgments

While this book is about doctrinal disagreement within the larger evangelical tent, it began as a labor of love for my home denomination, the Southern Baptist Convention. For two decades I have witnessed a deepening divide among Southern Baptists, not over theological liberalism or moral decay, as other Protestant denominations have more recently experienced, but over doctrinal matters thought by many to be secondary or tertiary issues. We have argued over the nature of election, the extent of the atonement, the timetable for Christ's return, and most recently, how best to apply our complementarian convictions in the life of the local church. Baptists have wrestled with many of the same questions since the seventeenth century and will probably do so until the Lord returns and corrects us all. But while the Lord tarries, I pray we will approach our differences in a holy and loving manner, recognizing all we have in common in the gospel, Scripture, and the Great Commission.

I must take a moment and acknowledge the many people who have helped me realize the vision of this project. Justin Taylor, Jill Carter, and the whole team at Crossway have been fantastic. Bill Deckard is a brilliant and gracious editor who made this book so much better with his keen editorial eye and helpful suggestions.

God has blessed me with a wonderful body of believers at the First Baptist Church of Kenner, Louisiana, where I have served as pastor of preaching and vision for nearly three years. They have very graciously allowed me to continue on in my capacity as a seminary professor, a writer, and a traveling lecturer. Balancing academic and pastoral ministries is a significant challenge, and I could not achieve this balance without an awesome ministry team around me. Chase Bell, Mary Helen Driver, Cody Killian, Danny Moore, Lindsey Hinkle, Nate Michel, and Clint Newsom are selfless servants who love God and the people he has entrusted to us. I also praise God for the deacons and leadership teams I have the privilege of serving with at FBC Kenner.

I must recognize Charles S. Kelley Jr., president emeritus of New Orleans Baptist Theological Seminary, who supported this book in every stage of its development. His contribution is clear in the Great Commission focus of this book.

I am indebted to the trustees of NOBTS, who granted me a sabbatical leave in the 2018–2019 academic year to complete this project among a few others. The Ola Farmer Lenaz Grant given to me in 2016 enabled me to travel and get important research done for the book.

I am also grateful for our provost, Norris Grubbs, who regularly advocates for the faculty and scholarly community in our institution.

Just days ago, our trustees elected James K. Dew as the ninth president of NOBTS. Dew is a gifted academic and administrator with a pastor's heart. I am rejoicing in his election, and I am praying for great kingdom success in his new endeavor.

My mentors and colleagues in the theological and historical studies division at NOBTS have been helpful dialogue partners throughout the process. Thank you, Bob Stewart, Jeff Riley, Page Brooks, Rex Butler, Steve Lemke, Lloyd Harsch, and Adam Harwood. I am blessed to work with such a doctrinally diverse group of Baptist theologians!

Thanks also to former students like Patrick Cochran, Andrew Hollingsworth, Richard Clark, Michael Steinmetz, Derek Kitterlin, Tim Walker, and David Gamble, all of whom read and critiqued portions of the book as it was being developed. I am grateful to Dean Treloar for transcribing the audio of my research interviews. My former assistant Kimberly Steinmetz's editorial eye was also a lifesaver with the earlier drafts.

I am grateful for Jason K. Allen, Gregg Allison, R. Albert Mohler Jr., Russell Moore, R. Stanton Norman, and Keith Whitfield, all of whom found a place for me in their busy schedules to discuss specific themes for this book. I also want to thank Kevin Vanhoozer, Timothy George, Michael Bird, and Ben Witherington III for their encouraging conversations and suggestions. I am also very appreciative of Matt Emerson, Luke Stamps, Brandon D. Smith, and the Center for Baptist Renewal (http://www.centerforbaptistrenewal.com/). Their contribution to the discussion of method, tradition, and hermeneutics in Baptist life is so very important.

I want to express special gratitude to David Dockery, one of my theological heroes, whose encouragement and endorsement helped me cross the finish line. His ministry of "big-tent," irenic evangelical theology has been a model to replicate in my own ministry. I am so honored to have him write the foreword for this book.

Of course, I am indebted to my loving wife and helpmate, Micah. Without her untiring support and sacrifice, this book would never have seen the light of day. Our children, Ben and Annie, always brought me joy when I came home from a long day at the office. Every day I pray Luke 2:52 over them—that like Jesus, they would grow in wisdom, in stature, and in favor with God and men. My in-laws, Collin and Marcia Elder, have always jumped in to help us whenever we have needed them along the way.

Finally, I dedicated this book to my parents, Glen and Diane Putman, who have spent more than forty years in ministry together. As a pastor, my dad has always had a heart for rebuilding declining congregations. As a counselor, he has labored to help hurting families and marriages in disrepair. My mother has always wowed me with her heart for the downtrodden and the sojourner, boldly and faithfully sharing the gospel with people from all walks of life. My parents have long modeled Christian peacemaking for me, and this project is in many ways a continuation of that ministry.

Soli Deo gloria
Rhyne Putman
June 13, 2019

Bibliography

Abdelsayed, Linda M., Joy M. Bustrum, Theresa Clement Tisdale, Kevin S. Reimer and Claire Allan Camp. "The Impact of Personality on God Image, Religious Coping, and Religious Motivation among Coptic Orthodox Priests." *Mental Health, Religion, and Culture* 16 (2013): 155–172.

Alcorn, Randy. *Heaven*. Carol Stream, IL: Tyndale, 2004.

Aldag, Ramon and Sally Riggs Fuller. "Beyond Fiasco: A Reappraisal of the Groupthink Phenomenon and a New Model of Group Decision Processes." *Psychological Bulletin* 113, no. 3 (1993): 533–552.

Allen, Michael and Scott R. Swain. "In Defense of Proof-Texting." *Journal of the Evangelical Theological Society* 54, no. 3 (2011): 589–606.

Allen, Michael and Scott R. Swain. *Reformed Catholicity: The Promise of Retrieval for Theology and Biblical Interpretation*. Grand Rapids, MI: Baker, 2015.

Allison, Gregg. *Historical Theology*. Grand Rapids, MI: Zondervan, 2011.

Allison, Gregg. "The Protestant Doctrine of the Perspicuity of Scripture: A Reformulation on the Basis of Biblical Teaching." PhD diss., Trinity Evangelical Divinity School, 1995.

Anderson, Douglas. "Peirce's Common Sense Marriage of Religion and Science." In *The Cambridge Companion to Peirce*, edited by Cheryl Misak, 181–185. Cambridge: Cambridge University Press, 2004.

Anizor, Uche. *How to Read Theology: Engaging Doctrine Critically and Charitably*. Grand Rapids, MI: Baker, 2018.

Armstrong, David. *The Mind-Body Problem: An Opinionated Introduction*. Boulder, CO: Westview, 1999.

Arnold, Clinton E. *Ephesians*. Exegetical Commentary on the New Testament. Grand Rapids, MI: Zondervan, 2010.

Augustine. *The Retractions*. Translated by Mary Inez Bogan. Washington: Catholic University of America Press, 1968.

Austin, J. L. *How to Do Things with Words*. 2nd ed. Cambridge, MA: Harvard University Press, 1962.

Bacon, Francis. *The Works of Francis Bacon*, vol. 4. Edited by James Spedding, Robert Leslie Ellis, and Douglas Denton Heath. London, 1875.

Baldwin, Henry Scott. "An Important Word: Αὐθεντέω in 1 Timothy 2:12." In *Women in the Church: An Analysis and Application of 1 Timothy 2:9–15*. 2nd ed., edited by Andreas J. Köstenberger and Thomas R. Schreiner, 39–51. Grand Rapids, MI: Baker, 2005.

Banaji, Mahzarin R. and Anthony G. Greenwald. *Blind Spot: Hidden Biases of Good People*. New York: Delacorte, 2013.

Barclay, John M. G. "Deviance and Apostasy: Some Applications of Deviance Theory to First-Century Judaism and Christianity." In *Modelling Early Christianity: Social-Scientific Studies of the New Testament in Its Context*, edited by Philip F. Esler, 114–127. New York: Routledge, 1995.

Barclay, John M. G. *Paul and the Gift*. Grand Rapids, MI: Eerdmans, 2015.

Barker, Dan. *Godless: How an Evangelical Preacher Became One of America's Leading Atheists*. Berkeley, CA: Ulysses, 2009.

Barr, James. *Biblical Words for Time*. London: SCM, 1962.

Barr, James. *The Semantics of Biblical Language*. Oxford: Oxford University Press, 1961.

Barth, Karl. *Nein! Antwort an Emil Brunner*. Zürich: Theologischer Verlag, 1934.

Barth, Markus. "The Faith of the Messiah." *Heythrop Journal* 10 (1969): 363–370.

Bateman, Herbert W. IV, ed. *Four Views on the Warning Passages in Hebrews*. Grand Rapids, MI: Kregel, 2007.

Bauckham, Richard J. *Jude, 2 Peter*. Word Biblical Commentary 50. Waco, TX: Word, 1983.

Bauer, David R. and Robert A. Traina. *Inductive Bible Study: A Comprehensive Guide to the Practice of Hermeneutics*. Grand Rapids, MI: Baker, 2011.

Beckwith, Francis J. *Return to Rome: Confessions of an Evangelical Catholic*. Grand Rapids, MI: Brazos, 2009.

Beker, J. Christiaan. *Paul the Apostle: The Triumph of God in Life and Thought*. Philadelphia: Fortress, 1980.

Ben-Shakhar, Gershon, Maya Bar-Hillel, Yoram Bilu, and Gaby Shefler, "Seek and Ye Shall Find: Test Results Are What You Hypothesize They Are." *Journal of Behavioral Decision Making* 11 (1998): 235–249.

Best, Ernest. *A Critical and Exegetical Commentary on Ephesians*. Edinburgh: T&T Clark, 1998.

Bird, Michael F. *Evangelical Theology: A Biblical and Systematic Introduction*. Grand Rapids, MI: Zondervan, 2013.

Bird, Michael F. *What Christians Ought to Believe: An Introduction to Christian Doctrine through the Apostle's Creed*. Grand Rapids, MI: Zondervan, 2016.

Bird, Michael F. and Preston M. Sprinkle, eds. *The Faith of Jesus Christ: Exegetical, Biblical, and Theological Studies*. Grand Rapids, MI: Baker, 2010.

Blomberg, Craig L. *Interpreting the Parables*. 2nd ed. Downers Grove, IL: InterVarsity Press, 2012.

Bock, Darrell L., ed. *Three Views on the Millennium and Beyond*. Grand Rapids, MI: Zondervan, 1999.

Bonfantini, Massimo A. and Giampaolo Proni. "To Guess or Not to Guess?" In *The Sign of Three: Dupin, Holmes, Peirce*, edited by Umberto Eco and Thomas A. Sebeok, 119–134. Bloomington: Indiana University Press, 1983.

Bornkamm, Gunther. *Paul*. New York: Harper & Row, 1971.

Boyd, Gregory A. *Oneness Pentecostals and the Trinity*. Grand Rapids, MI: Baker, 1994.

Brian, Rusty E. "John Wesley the Faithful Arminian." In *Embracing the Past—Forging the Future: A New Generation of Wesleyan Theology*, edited by Wm. Andrew Schwartz and John M. Bechtold, 157–170. Eugene, OR: Pickwick, 2015.

Briggs, Richard S. *Words in Action: Speech Act Theory and Biblical Interpretation, Toward a Hermeneutic of Self-Involvement*. Edinburgh: T&T Clark, 2001.

Bromiley, G. W. *Zwingli and Bullinger*. Philadelphia: Westminster, 1953.

Brown, Harold O. J. *Heresies: The Image of Christ in the Mirror of Heresy and Orthodoxy*. Grand Rapids, MI: Baker, 1994.

Bruce, F. F. *The Epistles to the Colossians, to Philemon, and to the Ephesians*. Grand Rapids, MI: Eerdmans, 1984.

Brunner, Emil and Karl Barth. *Natural Theology: Comprising 'Nature and Grace' by Professor Dr. Emil Brunner and the reply 'No!' by Dr. Karl Barth*. Translated by Peter Fraenkel. Eugene, OR: Wipf & Stock, 2002.

Bultmann, Rudolf. *Jesus Christ and Mythology*. Upper Saddle River, NJ: Prentice Hall, 1958.

Bultmann, Rudolf. *Theology of the New Testament*. 2 vols. Waco, TX: Baylor University Press, 2007.

Burk, Denny. "New and Old Departures in the Translation of Αὐθεντεῖν in 1 Timothy 2:12." In *Women in the Church*. 3rd ed., edited by Andreas J. Köstenberger and Thomas R. Schreiner, 279–296. Wheaton, IL: Crossway, 2016.

Buschart, W. David and Kent D. Eilers. *Theology as Retrieval: Receiving the Past, Renewing the Church*. Downers Grove, IL: InterVarsity Press, 2015.

Caird, George B. "The Descent of Christ in Ephesians 4, 7–11." In *Studia Evangelica*, edited by F. L. Cross. 7 vols. 2:535–545. Berlin: Akademie, 1964.

Caird, George B. *The Language and Imagery of the Bible*. Philadelphia: Westminster, 1980.

Calvin, John. *Commentaries on the Epistle of Paul the Apostle to the Romans*. Translated by John Owen. Grand Rapids, MI: Baker, 2009.

Calvin, John. *Commentaries on the Epistles of Paul to the Galatians and Ephesians*. Translated by William Pringle. Grand Rapids, MI: Baker, 2009.

Calvin, John. *Institutes of the Christian Religion*. 2 vols. Edited by John T. McNeill. Translated by Ford Lewis Battles. Louisville: Westminster John Knox, 1960.

Carson, D. A. *Exegetical Fallacies*. 2nd ed. Grand Rapids, MI: Baker, 1996.

Carson, D. A. *The King James Debate: A Plea for Realism*. Grand Rapids, MI: Baker, 1979.

Carson, D. A. "What Are Gospel Issues?" *Themelios* 39, no. 2 (2014): 215–219.

Carson, D. A., Peter T. O'Brien, and Mark A. Seifrid, eds. *Justification and Variegated Nomism*. 2 vols. Tübingen: Mohr Siebeck, 2001, 2004.

Casanowicz, I. M. "Hapax Legomena—Biblical Data." In *The Jewish Encyclopedia*. 12 vols. 6:226–228. New York, 1906.

Castaldo, Christopher A. *Holy Ground: Walking with Jesus as a Former Catholic*. Grand Rapids, MI: Zondervan, 2009.

Catechism of the Catholic Church. 2nd ed. New York: Doubleday, 2012.

Christensen, David. "Epistemic Modesty Defended." In *The Epistemology of Disagreement: New Essays*, edited by David Christensen and Jennifer Lackey, 77–99. New York: Oxford University Press, 2010.

Christensen, David. "Epistemology of Disagreement: The Good News." *Philosophical Review* 116, no. 2 (2007): 187–217.

Christensen, David and Jennifer Lackey, eds. *The Epistemology of Disagreement: New Essays*. New York: Oxford University Press, 2010.

Clark, David K. *To Know and Love God: Method for Theology*. Wheaton, IL: Crossway, 2003.

Clayton, Philip. *Explanation from Physics to Theology: An Essay in Rationality and Religion*. New Haven, CT: Yale University Press, 1989.

Clouse, Robert G., ed. *The Meaning of the Millennium: Four Views*. Downers Grove, IL: InterVarsity Press, 1977.

Cohen, I. Bernard. *Revolution in Science*. Cambridge, MA: Harvard University Press, 1985.

Cole, Graham A. *He Who Gives Life: The Doctrine of the Holy Spirit*. Wheaton, IL: Crossway, 2007.

Comfort, Philip Wesley. *A Commentary on the Manuscripts and Text of the New Testament*. Grand Rapids, MI: Kregel, 2015.

Conee, Earl. "Rational Disagreement Defended." In *Disagreement*, edited by Richard Feldman and Ted A. Warfield, 69–90. Oxford: Oxford University Press, 2010.

Cooper, John W. *Body, Soul, and Life Everlasting: Biblical Anthropology and the Monism-Dualism Debate*. Grand Rapids, MI: Eerdmans, 1998.

Coppedge, Allan. *John Wesley in Theological Debate*. Wilmore, KY: Wesley Heritage, 1987.

Coppedge, Allan. *Shaping the Wesleyan Message*. Nappanee, IN: Evangel, 2003.

Corcoran, Kevin. "The Constitution View of Persons." In *In Search of the Soul: Four Views of the Mind-Body Problem*, edited by Joel B. Green and Stuart L. Palmer, 153–185. Downers Grove, IL: InterVarsity Press, 2005.

Corrington, Gail Paterson. "Redaction Criticism." In *To Each Its Own Meaning: An Introduction to Biblical Criticisms and Their Application*, edited by Steven L. McKenzie and Stephen R. Haynes, 87–99. Louisville: Westminster John Knox, 1993.

Cranfield, Charles E. B. *The Epistle to the Romans*, vol. 1. International Critical Commentary. Edinburgh: T&T Clark, 1975.

Crockett, William, ed. *Four Views on Hell*. Grand Rapids, MI: Zondervan, 1996.

Croy, N. Clayton. *Prima Scriptura: An Introduction to New Testament Interpretation*. Grand Rapids, MI: Baker, 2011.

Cryer, Max. *Common Phrases . . . and the Amazing Stories behind Them*. New York: Skyhorse, 2010.

Cullmann, Oscar. *Christ and Time: The Primitive Christian Conception of Time and History*. Translated by Floyd V. Filson. London: SCM, 1951.

Dallimore, Arnold A. *George Whitefield: The Life and Times of the Great Evangelist of the Eighteenth-Century Revival*. 2 vols. Edinburgh: Banner of Truth, 1970, 1980.

Darwin, Charles. *The Descent of Man and Selection in Relationship to Sex*. Vol. 1. Rev. ed. London: John Murray, 1888.

Dawkins, Richard. *The Selfish Gene*. New York: Oxford University Press, 1976.

Dennett, Daniel C. *Breaking the Spell: Religion as a Natural Phenomenon*. New York: Viking, 2006.

Descartes, René. *Discourse on Method and Meditations on First Philosophy*. Translated by Donald A. Cress. Indianapolis: Hackett, 1980.

Descartes, René. *Oeuvres de Descartes*. Vols. 1–12. Rev. ed. Edited by Charles Adam and Paul Tannery. Paris: J. Vrin/C.N.R.S., 1964–1976.

DeSilva, David A. *Honor, Patronage, Kinship, and Purity: Unlocking New Testament Culture*. Downers Grove, IL: InterVarsity Press, 2000.

DeYoung, Kevin. *Taking God at His Word*. Wheaton, IL: Crossway, 2014.

Dixon, Thomas. *From Passions to Emotions: The Creation of a Secular Psychological Category*. New York: Cambridge University Press, 2003.

Dorrien, Gary. *The Making of American Liberal Theology: Idealism, Realism, and Modernity, 1900–1950*. Louisville: Westminster John Knox, 2003.

Doyle, Arthur Conan. *The Adventures of Sherlock Holmes*. London, 1901.

Dunn, James D. G. *Christology in the Making: A New Testament Inquiry into the Origins of the Doctrine of the Incarnation*. 2nd ed. Grand Rapids, MI: Eerdmans, 1996.

Dunn, James D. G. *The Epistle to the Galatians*. Black's New Testament Commentary. Peabody, MA: Hendrickson, 1993.

Dunn, James D. G. *Jesus, Paul, and the Law: Studies in Mark and Galatians*. Louisville: Westminster John Knox, 1990.

Dunn, James D. G. *Romans 9–16*. Word Biblical Commentary 38b. Nashville: Thomas Nelson, 1988.

Dunn, James D. G. *Unity and Diversity in the New Testament: An Inquiry into the Character of Earliest Christianity*. 3rd ed. London: SCM, 2006.

Easter, Matthew C. "The *Pistis Christou* Debate: Main Arguments and Responses in Summary." *Currents in Biblical Research* 9, no. 1 (2010): 34–42.

Eco, Umberto. *The Limits of Interpretation*. Bloomington: Indiana University Press, 1990.

Eco, Umberto. *Semiotics and the Philosophy of Language*. Bloomington: Indiana University Press, 1984.

Eco, Umberto and Thomas A. Sebeok, eds. *The Sign of Three: Dupin, Holmes, Peirce*. Bloomington: Indiana University Press, 1983.

Edwards, Keith J. "The Nature of Human Mental Life." In *Christian Perspectives on Being Human: A Multidisciplinary Approach to Integration*, edited by J. P. Moreland and David M. Ciocchi, 175–205. Grand Rapids, MI: Baker, 1993.

Ehrman, Bart D. *The Orthodox Corruption of Scripture: The Effect of Early Christological Controversies on the Text of the New Testament*. New York: Oxford University Press, 1993.

Eichrodt, Walter. *Theology of the Old Testament*. Translated by J. A. Baker. 2 vols. Louisville: Westminster, 1967.

Ellis, E. Earle. "Paul and His Opponents." In *Christianity, Judaism, and Other Greco-Roman Cults, Part 1*, edited by Jacob Neusner, 264–298. Leiden: Brill, 1975.

Emerson, Matt. *He Descended to the Dead: An Evangelical Approach to Holy Saturday*. Downers Grove, IL: InterVarsity Press, 2019.

Erasmus, Desiderius and Martin Luther, *Luther and Erasmus: Free Will and Salvation.* Translated and edited by E. Gordon Rupp and Philip S. Watson. Philadelphia: Westminster, 1969.

Erickson, Millard J. *Christian Theology.* 3rd ed. Grand Rapids, MI: Baker, 2013.

Erikson, Erik H. *Young Man Luther: A Study in Psychoanalysis and History.* New York: Norton, 1958.

Estep, William R. *Baptists and Christian Unity.* Nashville: Broadman, 1966.

"Evangelicals and Catholics Together: The Christian Mission in the Third Millennium." *First Things* (May 1994).

Evans, Craig A. *Mark 8:27–16:20.* Word Biblical Commentary 34b. Nashville: Thomas Nelson, 2000.

Feldman, Richard. "Epistemological Puzzles about Disagreement." In *Epistemology Futures,* edited by Stephen Hetherington, 216–236. New York: Oxford University Press, 2006.

Feldman, Richard and Ted A. Warfield, eds. *Disagreement.* New York: Oxford University Press, 2010.

Flatt, Kevin N. *After Evangelicalism: The Sixties and the United Church of Canada.* Kingston, ON: McGill-Queen's University Press, 2013.

Flew, Anthony and Roy Abraham Varghese. *There Is a God: How the World's Most Notorious Atheist Changed His Mind.* New York: Harper-Collins, 2007.

Forlines, F. Leroy. *Classical Arminianism.* Nashville: Randall, 2011.

Frame, John M. *Evangelical Reunion: Denominations and the Body of Christ.* Grand Rapids, MI: Baker, 1991.

Frances, Bryan. *Disagreement.* Malden, MA: Polity, 2014.

Frances, Bryan. "Disagreement." In *The Routledge Companion to Epistemology,* edited by Sven Bernecker and Duncan Pritchard, 68–74. New York: Routledge, 2013.

Frances, Bryan. "When a Skeptical Hypothesis Is Live." *Noûs* 39 (2005): 559–595.

Freeman, Curtis. *Contesting Catholicity: Theology for Other Baptists.* Waco, TX: Baylor University Press, 2014.

Fumerton, Richard. "You Can't Trust a Philosopher," in *Disagreement,* edited by Richard Feldman and Ted A. Warfield, 91–110. Oxford: Oxford University Press, 2010.

Gadamer, Hans-Georg. *Truth and Method*. Rev. ed. Translated by Joel Weinsheimer and Donald G. Marshall. New York: Continuum, 2004.

Garrett, James Leo. *Systematic Theology*, vol. 1. 3rd ed. North Richland Hills, TX: BIBAL, 2007.

Gentleman's Magazine, The 11 (June 1741): 321–323.

George, Timothy. "Baptists and Ecumenism: An Interview with Timothy George." Interview by Everett Berry and Winston Hottman. Center for Baptist Renewal. April 6, 2017. http://www.centerforbaptist renewal.com/blog/2017/4/6/baptists-and-ecumenism-a-discussion -with-timothy-george.

George, Timothy. "Catholics and Evangelicals in the Trenches." *Christianity Today* 38, no. 6 (May 1994): 16.

George, Timothy. "Egalitarians and Complementarians Together? A Modest Proposal." In *Women, Ministry, and the Gospel: Exploring New Paradigms*, edited by Mark Husbands and Timothy Larsen, 266–288. Downers Grove, IL: InterVarsity Press, 2007.

George, Timothy and Thomas G. Guarino, eds. *Evangelicals and Catholics Together at Twenty: Vital Statements on Contested Topics*. Grand Rapids, MI: Brazos, 2014.

Gombis, Timothy G. *The Drama of Ephesians: Participating in the Triumph of God*. Downers Grove, IL: InterVarsity Press, 2010.

Graham, Jesse, Jonathan Haidt, and Brian A. Nosek. "Liberals and Conservatives Rely on Different Sets of Moral Foundations." *Journal of Personality and Social Psychology* 96 (2009): 1030–1040.

Green, Joel B. and Stuart L. Palmer, eds. *In Search of the Soul: Four Views of the Mind-Body Problem*. Downers Grove, IL: InterVarsity Press, 2005.

Green, Richard. *The Works of John and Charles Wesley: A Bibliography*. London: C. H. Kelly, 1896.

Greenspahn, Frederick E. *Hapax Legomena in Biblical Hebrew: A Study of the Phenomenon and Its Treatment since Antiquity with Special Reference to Verbal Forms*. SBL Dissertation Series 74. Chico, CA: Scholars, 1984.

Greenwald, Anthony G., Debbie E. McGhee, and Jordan L. K. Schwartz. "Measuring Individual Differences in Implicit Cognition: The Implicit Association Test." *Journal of Personality and Social Psychology* 74 (1998): 1464–1480.

Gregory of Nazianzus. *On God and Christ: The Five Theological Orations and Two Letters to Cledonius*. Translated by Frederick Williams and Lionel Wickham. Crestwood, NY: St. Vladmir's Seminary Press, 2002.

Grenz, Stanley J. "*Die Begrenzte Gemeinschaft* ('The Boundaried People') and the Character of Evangelical Theology." *Journal of the Evangelical Theological Society* 45, no. 2 (2002): 301–316.

Grenz, Stanley J. and Roger E. Olson. *Who Needs Theology? An Invitation to the Study of God*. Downers Grove, IL: InterVarsity Press, 1996.

Griffin, David Ray. *Two Great Truths: A Synthesis of Scientific Naturalism and the Christian Faith*. Louisville: Westminster John Knox, 2004.

Grudem, Wayne. "He Did Not Descend into Hell: A Plea for Following Scripture instead of the Apostles' Creed." *Journal of the Evangelical Theological Society* 34, no. 1 (1991): 103–113.

Grudem, Wayne. *Systematic Theology*. Grand Rapids, MI: Zondervan, 2000.

Gunton, Colin E. *A Brief Theology of Revelation*. London: T&T Clark, 1995.

Gushee, David P. *Changing Our Mind*. 3rd ed. Canton, MI: Read the Spirit, 2017.

Gushee, David P. *Still Christian: Following Jesus out of American Evangelicalism*. Rev. ed. Louisville: Westminster John Knox, 2017.

Gutting, Gary. *Religious Belief and Religious Skepticism*. Notre Dame, IN: University of Notre Dame Press, 1982.

Haidt, Jonathan. "The Emotional Dog and Its Rational Tail: A Social Intuitionist Approach to Moral Judgment." *Psychological Review* 108 (2001): 814–834.

Haidt, Jonathan. *The Happiness Hypothesis: Finding Modern Truth in Ancient Wisdom*. New York: Basic, 2006.

Haidt, Jonathan. "Moral Psychology and the Misunderstanding of Religion." In *The Believing Primate: Scientific, Philosophical, and Theological Reflections on the Origin of Religion*, edited by Jeffrey Schloss and Michael J. Murray, 278–291. New York: Oxford University Press, 2009.

Haidt, Jonathan. "Morality." *Perspectives on Psychological Science* 3 (2008): 65–72.

Haidt, Jonathan. *The Righteous Mind: Why Good People Are Divided by Politics and Religion*. New York: Vintage, 2012.

Hansen, Collin. "Young, Restless, Reformed." *Christianity Today* (September 2006): 32.

Hansen, Collin. *Young, Restless, Reformed: A Journalist's Journey with the New Calvinists*. Wheaton, IL: Crossway, 2008.

Harman, Gilbert H. "Enumerative Induction as Inference to the Best Explanation." *Journal of Philosophy* 64 (1967): 529–533.

Harman, Gilbert H. "Inference to the Best Explanation." *Philosophical Review* 74 (1965): 88–95.

Harmon, Steven R. *Ecumenism Means You, Too: Ordinary Christians and the Quest for Christian Unity*. Eugene, OR: Cascade, 2010.

Harmon, Steven R. *Toward Baptist Catholicity*. Eugene, OR: Wipf & Stock, 2006.

Harris, Sam. *Free Will*. New York: Free Press, 2012.

Harris, W. Hall III. "The Ascent and Descent of Christ in Ephesians 4:9–10." *Bibliotheca Sacra* 151 (1994): 198–214.

Hasker, William. *God, Time, and Knowledge*. Ithaca, NY: Cornell University Press, 1989.

Hawthorne, John and Amia Srinivasa. "Disagreement without Transparency: Some Bleak Thoughts." In *The Epistemology of Disagreement: New Essays*, edited by David Christensen and Jennifer Lackey, 9–30. New York: Oxford University Press, 2010.

Hays, Richard B. *The Faith of Jesus Christ: An Investigation of the Narrative Substructure of Galatians 3:1–4:11*. Chico, CA: Scholars, 1983.

Hays, Richard B. "ΠΙΣΤΙΣ and Pauline Christology: What Is at Stake?" In *Pauline Theology*, vol. 4, edited by E. Elizabeth Johnson and David M. Hay, 35–60. Atlanta: Scholars, 1997.

Heidegger, Martin. *Being and Time*. Translated by John Macquarrie and Edward Robinson. New York: Harper & Row, 1962.

Heil, John. *Philosophy of Mind*. 2nd ed. New York: Routledge, 2004.

Heine, Ronald E. *The Commentaries of Origen and Jerome on St. Paul's Epistle to the Ephesians*. New York: Oxford University Press, 2002.

Helm, Paul. *Faith, Form, and Fashion: Classical Reformed Theology and Its Postmodern Critics*. Eugene, OR: Cascade, 2014.

Henry, Carl F. H. *God, Revelation, and Authority*. 6 vols. Wheaton, IL: Crossway, 1999.

Hesselink, I. John. "Reformed View: The Real Presence of Christ." In *Understanding Four Views on the Lord's Supper*, edited by John H. Armstrong, 59–71. Grand Rapids, MI: Baker, 2007.

Hirsch, E. D. Jr. "Meaning and Significance Reinterpreted." *Critical Inquiry* 11 (1984): 202–225.

Hirsch, E. D. Jr. *Validity in Interpretation*. New Haven, CT: Yale University Press, 1967.

Hobbs, Herschel H. *Hebrews: Challenges to Bold Discipleship*. Nashville: Broadman, 1971.

Hodge, Charles. *Systematic Theology*. 3 vols. New York: Scribner, Armstrong, 1873.

Horton, Michael. *The Christian Faith: A Systematic Theology for Pilgrims on the* Way. Grand Rapids, MI: Zondervan, 2011.

Hume, David. *A Treatise on Human Nature*. 2 vols. London: Longmans, Green, 1874.

Hunsinger, George. *Reading Barth with Clarity: A Hermeneutical Proposal*. Grand Rapids, MI: Baker, 2015.

Isaacson, Walter. *Steve Jobs*. New York: Simon & Schuster, 2011.

Jacobs, Alan. *A Theology of Reading: The Hermeneutic of Love*. Boulder, CO: Westview, 2001.

Janis, Irving L. *Groupthink: Psychological Studies of Policy Decisions and Fiascoes*. 2nd ed. New York: Houghton Mifflin, 1982.

Janis, Irving L. *Victims of Groupthink: A Psychological Study of Foreign Policy Decisions and Fiascoes*. New York: Houghton Mifflin, 1972.

Janis, Irving L. and Leon Mann. *Decision Making: A Psychological Analysis of Conflict, Choice, and Commitment*. New York: Free Press, 1977.

Johnson, Roger A., ed. *Psychohistory and Religion: The Case of Young Man Luther*. Philadelphia: Fortress, 1977.

Jones, David Ceri, Boyd Stanley Schlenter, and Eryn Mant White. *The Elect Methodists: Calvinistic Methodism in England and Wales, 1735–1811*. Cardiff: University of Wales Press, 2012.

Kelly, Thomas. "Disagreement and the Burdens of Judgment." In *The Epistemology of Disagreement: New Essays*, edited by David Christensen and Jennifer Lackey, 31–53. New York: Oxford University Press, 2010.

Kelly, Thomas. "The Epistemic Significance of Disagreement." In *Oxford Studies in Epistemology*, vol. 1, edited by John Hawthorne and Tamar Gendler Szabo, 167–196. New York: Oxford University Press, 2006.

Kelly, Thomas. "Peer Disagreement and Higher-Order Evidence." In *Disagreement*, edited by Richard Feldman and Ted A. Warfield, 111–174. New York: Oxford University Press, 2010.

Kelsey, David H. *Proving Doctrine: The Uses of Scripture in Modern Theology.* Harrisburg, PA: Trinity, 1999.

Kennedy, George A. *New Testament Interpretation through Rhetorical Criticism.* Chapel Hill, NC: University of North Carolina Press, 1984.

Kittel, Gerhard and Gerhard Friedrich, eds. *Theological Dictionary of the New Testament.* Translated by G. W. Bromiley. 10 vols. Grand Rapids, MI: Eerdmans, 1977.

Klein, William W. *The New Chosen People: A Corporate View of Election.* Rev. ed. Eugene, OR: Wipf & Stock, 2015.

Klein, William W., Craig L. Blomberg, and Robert L. Hubbard Jr. *Introduction to Biblical Interpretation.* 3rd ed. Grand Rapids, MI: Zondervan, 2017.

Klink, Edward W. III and Darian R. Lockett. *Understanding Biblical Theology: A Comparison of Theory and Practice.* Grand Rapids, MI: Zondervan, 2012.

Knight, G. W. III. "ΑΥΘΕΝΤΕΩ in Reference to Women in 1 Timothy 2.12." *New Testament Studies* 30 (1984): 143–157.

Knust, Jennifer. *Unprotected Texts: The Bible's Surprising Contradictions about Sex and Desire.* New York: HarperOne, 2011.

Köhler, Walther. *Zwingli und Luther. Ihr Streit über das Abendmahl nach seinen politischen und religiösen Beziehungen.* 2 vols. Leipzig, 1924; Gütersloh, 1953.

Komoszewski, J. Ed, M. James Sawyer, and Daniel B. Wallace. *Reinventing Jesus: How Contemporary Skeptics Miss the Real Jesus and Mislead Popular Culture.* Grand Rapids, MI: Kregel, 2006.

Köstenberger, Andreas J., L. Scott Kellum, and Charles L. Quarles. *The Cradle, the Cross, and the Crown.* Nashville: B&H Academic, 2009.

Kroeger, Catherine Clark. "Ancient Heresies and a Strange Greek Verb." *Reformed Journal* 29 (1979): 12–15.

Kroeger, Richard Clark and Catherine Clark Kroeger. *I Suffer Not a Woman: Rethinking 1 Timothy 2:11–15 in Light of Ancient Evidence.* Grand Rapids, MI: Baker, 1992.

Kuhn, Thomas S. *The Structure of Scientific Revolutions.* Chicago: University of Chicago Press, 1962.

Kümmel, Werner Georg. *Römer 7 und Das Bild des Menschen im Neuen Testament*. Munich: C. Kaiser, 1974.

Ladd, George Eldon. *The Gospel of the Kingdom: Scriptural Studies in the Kingdom of God*. Grand Rapids, MI: Eerdmans, 1959.

Latourette, Kenneth Scott. "Ecumenical Bearings of the Missionary Movement and the International Missionary Council." In *A History of the Ecumenical Movement, 1517–1948*. 2nd ed., edited by Ruth Rouse and Stephen C. Neil, 355–362. Philadelphia: Westminster, 1967.

Lawrence, Richard T. "Measuring the Image of God: The God Image Inventory and the God Image Scales." *Journal of Psychology and Theology* 25, no. 2 (1997): 214–226.

Layman, C. Stephen. *The Power of Logic*. 3rd ed. New York: McGraw-Hill, 2005.

Lehmann, Karl, Michael Root, and William G. Rusch, eds. *Justification by Faith: Do the Sixteenth-Century Condemnations Still Apply?* London: Bloomsbury, 1997.

Leithart, Peter J. *The End of Protestantism: Pursuing Unity in a Fragmented Church*. Grand Rapids, MI: Brazos, 2016.

Lerner, Jennifer S. and Philip E. Tetlock. "Accounting for the Effects of Accountability." *Psychological Bulletin* 125, no. 2 (1999): 255–275.

Letis, Theodore, ed. *Majority Text: Essays and Reviews in the Continuing Debate*. Grand Rapids, MI: Institute for Biblical Textual Studies, 1987.

Lewis, C. S. *Letters to Malcolm: Chiefly on Prayer*. New York: Harvest, 1992.

Lewis, C. S. *Mere Christianity*. New York: HarperOne, 2001.

Lincoln, Andrew T. *Ephesians*. Word Biblical Commentary 42. Nashville: Thomas Nelson, 1990.

Lindbeck, George A. *The Nature of Doctrine*. Louisville: Westminster John Knox, 1984.

Lindholm, T. and S. A. Christianson. "Intergroup Biases and Eyewitness Testimony." *Journal of Social Psychology* 138 (1998): 710–723.

Lints, Richard. *The Fabric of Theology: A Prolegomenon to Evangelical Theology*. Grand Rapids, MI: Eerdmans, 1993.

Lipton, Peter. *Inference to the Best Explanation*. 2nd ed. New York: Routledge, 2004.

Locke, John. *An Essay Concerning Human Understanding*. Edited by Peter H. Nidditch (New York: Oxford University Press, 1975.

Lord, Charles G., Mark R. Lepper, and Elizabeth Preston. "Considering the Opposite: A Corrective Strategy for Social Judgment." *Journal of Personality and Social Psychology* 47, no. 6 (1984): 1231–1243.

Lorenz, Rudolf. *Arius judaizans? Untersuchungen zur dogmengeschichtlichen Einordnung des Arius*. Göttingen: Vandenhoeck & Ruprecht, 1979.

Louw, J. P. *Semantics of New Testament Greek*. Atlanta: Scholars, 1982.

Luther, Martin. *D. Martin Luthers Werke*. Kritische Gesamtausgabe. 73 vols. Weimar: Herman Böhlaus Nachfolger, 1883–2009.

Luther, Martin. *Luther's Works*. Edited by Jaroslav Pelikan, Helmut T. Lehmann, and Christopher Boyd Brown. 75 vols. Philadelphia: Fortress; St. Louis: Concordia, 1955–.

Luther, Martin, and Desiderius Erasmus. *Luther and Erasmus: Free Will and Salvation*. Translated and edited by E. Gordon Rupp and Philip S. Watson. Philadelphia: Westminster, 1969.

Lutzer, Erwin W. *The Doctrines That Divide: A Fresh Look at the Historical Doctrines That Separate Christians*. Grand Rapids, MI: Kregel, 2015.

MacArthur, John and Richard Mayhue, eds. *Biblical Doctrine: A Systematic Summary of Bible Truth*. Wheaton, IL: Crossway, 2017.

Machuca, Diego E., ed. *Disagreement and Skepticism*. New York: Routledge, 2012.

Manschreck, Clyde Leonard. *Melanchthon: The Quiet Reformer*. New York: Abingdon, 1958.

Marsh, John. *The Fullness of Time*. London: Nisbet, 1952.

Marshall, I. Howard and Philip H. Towner. *A Critical and Exegetical Commentary on the Pastoral Epistles*. International Critical Commentary. Edinburgh: T&T Clark, 1999.

Martin, Dale B. *Biblical Truths: The Meaning of Scripture in the Twenty-First Century*. New Haven, CT: Yale University Press, 2017.

Martin, Dale B. *Pedagogy of the Bible: An Analysis and Proposal*. Louisville: Westminster John Knox, 2008.

Martin, Dale B. *Sex and the Single Savior: Gender and Sexuality in Biblical Interpretation*. Louisville: Westminster John Knox, 2006.

Martin, Ralph P. "Approaches to New Testament Exegesis." In *New Testament Interpretation: Essays on Principles and Methods*, edited by I. Howard Marshall, 220–251. Exeter, UK: Paternoster, 1977.

Martin, Ralph P. *James*. Word Biblical Commentary 48. Nashville: Thomas Nelson, 1988.

Matheson, Jonathan. *The Epistemic Significance of Disagreement*. New York: Palgrave Macmillan, 2015.

Matlin, Margaret. "Pollyanna Principle." In *Cognitive Illusions: Intriguing Phenomena in Thinking, Judgment, and Memory*. 2nd ed., edited by Rüdiger F. Pohl, 315–336. New York: Routledge, 2017.

Matlin, Margaret and David Stang. *The Pollyanna Principle: Selectivity in Language, Memory, and Thought*. Cambridge, MA: Shenkman, 1978.

McCall, Thomas H. *An Invitation to Analytic Christian Theology*. Downers Grove, IL: InterVarsity Press, 2015.

McGrath, Alister E. *Christianity's Dangerous Idea*. New York: HarperOne, 2007.

McGrath, Alister E. *Heresy*. New York: HarperOne, 2010.

McGrath, Alister E. *Iustitia Dei: A History of the Christian Doctrine*. 3rd ed. Cambridge: Cambridge University Press, 2005.

McGrath, Alister E. *The Science of God*. Grand Rapids, MI: Eerdmans, 2004.

McGrath, Alister E. *A Scientific Theology*. 3 vols. Grand Rapids, MI: Eerdmans, 2001–2003.

McClendon, James Wm. Jr. and James M. Smith. *Convictions: Defusing Religious Relativism*. Valley Forge, PA: Trinity, 2002.

Meldenius, Rupertus. *Paraenesis votiva per Pace Ecclesiae*. Rottenberg, 1626.

Mendel, R., E. Traut-Mattausch, E. Jonas, S. Leucht, J. M. Kane, K. Maino, W. Kissling, and J. Hamann. "Confirmation Bias: Why Psychiatrists Stick to Wrong Preliminary Diagnoses." *Psychological Medicine* 41 (2011): 2651–2659.

Merrill, Eugene H. *Everlasting Dominion: A Theology of the Old Testament*. Nashville: B&H Academic, 2006.

Metzger, Bruce M. and Bart D. Ehrman. *The Text of the New Testament: Its Transmission, Corruption, and Restoration*. 4th ed. New York: Oxford University Press, 2005.

Meyer, Ben F. *Reality and Illusion in New Testament Scholarship: A Primer in Critical Realist Hermeneutics.* Collegeville, MN: Liturgical Press, 1994.

Meyer, Harding. *All May Be One: Perceptions and Models of Ecumenicity.* Grand Rapids, MI: Eerdmans, 1999.

Mohler, R. Albert Jr. *The Apostles' Creed: Discovering Authentic Christianity in an Age of Counterfeits.* Nashville: Thomas Nelson, 2019.

Mohler, R. Albert Jr. "A Call for Theological Triage and Christian Maturity." AlbertMohler.com, July 12, 2005. http://www.albertmohler .com/2005/07/12/a-call-for-theological-triage-and-christian-maturity/.

Mohler, R. Albert Jr. "Confessional Evangelicalism." In *Four Views on the Spectrum of Evangelicalism,* edited by Andrew David Naselli and Collin Hansen, 68–96. Grand Rapids, MI: Zondervan, 2011.

Moo, Douglas J. *The Epistle to the Romans.* New International Commentary on the New Testament. Grand Rapids, MI: Eerdmans, 1996.

Moreland, J. P. "Restoring the Substance to the Soul of Psychology." *Journal of Psychology and Theology* 26 (1998): 29–43.

Morgan, Amy C. "The Impact of Adverse Childhood Experiences on God Images." PhD diss., New Orleans Baptist Theological Seminary, 2017.

Morgan, Christopher W. "Toward a Theology of the Unity of the Church." In *Why We Belong: Evangelical Unity and Denominational Diversity,* edited by Anthony L. Chute, Christopher W. Morgan, and Robert A. Peterson, 19–36. Wheaton, IL: Crossway, 2013.

Moritz, Fred and Mark Sidwell, eds. *"Be Ye Holy": The Call to Christian Separation.* Greenville, SC: Bob Jones University Press, 2000.

Moroney, Stephen K. *The Noetic Effects of Sin: A Historical and Contemporary Exploration of How Sin Affects Our Thinking.* Lanham, MD: Lexington, 2000.

Morris, James P., Nancy K. Squires, Charles S. Taber, and Milton Lodge. "Activation of Political Attitudes: A Psychophysiological Examination of the Hot Cognition Hypothesis." *Political Psychology* 24, no. 4 (2003): 727–745.

Mounce, William D. *Pastoral Epistles.* Word Biblical Commentary 46. Nashville: Thomas Nelson, 2000.

Murphy, Nancey. *Bodies and Souls, or Spirited Bodies?* (Cambridge: Cambridge University Press, 2006.

Murray, Iain H. *Evangelicalism Divided*. Carlisle, PA: Banner of Truth, 2000.

Murray, Iain H. "Prefatory Note to 'A Letter to the Rev. Mr. John Wesley in Answer to His Sermon Entitled *Free Grace*.'" In *George Whitefield's Journals*, edited by Iain H. Murray, 564–565. Edinburgh: Banner of Truth, 1960.

Neil, Stephen and N. T. Wright. *The Interpretation of the New Testament, 1861–1986*. 2nd ed. Oxford: Oxford University Press, 1988.

Nellen, Henk J. "De Zinspreuk 'In Necessariis Unitas, In Non Necessariis Libertas, In Utrisque Caritas.'" *Nederlands archief voor kerkgeschiedenis* 79, no. 1 (1999): 99–106.

Neufeld, Dietmar. *Reconceiving Texts as Speech Acts: An Analysis of John*. Leiden: Brill, 1994.

Newbigin, Lesslie. *The Gospel in a Pluralist Society*. Grand Rapids, MI: Eerdmans, 1989.

Newell, Daniel. *The Life of George Whitefield*. New York: R. T. Young, 1853.

Newman, John Henry. *An Essay on the Development of Christian Doctrine*. Rev. ed. London, 1893.

Newsom, Blake. "What Is the Gospel?" *Journal for Baptist Theology and Ministry* 11, no. 2 (2014): 2–15.

Newton, John. *Forty-One Letters on Religious Subjects*. London: Religious Tract Society, 1799.

Nicene and Post-Nicene Fathers, Series 1. Edited by Alexander Roberts, James Donaldson, Philip Schaff, and Henry Wace. 14 vols. Peabody, MA: Hendrickson, 1994.

Nicene- and Post-Nicene Fathers, Series 2. Edited by Alexander Roberts, James Donaldson, Philip Schaff, and Henry Wace. 14 vols. Peabody, MA: Hendrickson, 1994.

Nickerson, Raymond S. "Confirmation Bias: A Ubiquitous Phenomenon in Many Guises." *Review of General Psychology* 2, no. 2 (1998): 175–220.

Nickerson, Raymond S. *Reflections on Reasoning*. Hillsdale, NJ: Lawrence Erlbaum, 1986.

Nicole, Roger. *Standing Forth: Collected Writings of Roger Nicole*. Ross-shire, UK: Christian Focus, 2002.

Noble, T. A. *Holy Trinity: Holy People: The Theology of Christian Perfecting*. Eugene, OR: Cascade, 2013.

Oberman, Heiko. *Forerunners of the Reformation: The Shape of Late Medieval Thought.* Translated by Paul L. Nyhus. New York: Holt, Rinehart, & Winston, 1966.

O'Brien, Barbara M. "Confirmation Bias in Criminal Investigations: An Examination of the Factors That Aggravate and Counteract Bias." PhD diss., University of Michigan, 2007.

O'Brien, Barbara M. "Prime Suspect: An Examination of Factors That Aggravate and Counteract Confirmation Bias in Criminal Investigations." *Psychology, Public Policy, and Law* 15, no. 4 (2009): 315–334.

O'Collins, Gerald and Daniel Kendall. "The Faith of Jesus." *Theological Studies* 53 (1992): 403–423.

Oden, Thomas C. *Change of Heart: A Personal and Theological Memoir.* Downers Grove, IL: InterVarsity Press, 2014.

Oden, Thomas C. *John Wesley's Teachings.* 4 vols. Grand Rapids, MI: Zondervan, 2012.

Olson, Roger E. *Against Calvinism.* Grand Rapids, MI: Zondervan, 2011.

Olson, Roger E. "Postconservative Evangelicalism." In *Four Views on the Spectrum of Evangelicalism*, edited by Andrew David Naselli and Collin Hansen, 161–187. Grand Rapids, MI: Zondervan, 2011.

Osborn, Carroll D. "ΑΥΘΕΝΤΈΩ (1 Timothy 2:12)." *Restoration Quarterly* 25 (1982): 1–12.

Osborne, Grant R. "The Flesh without the Spirit: Romans 7 and Christian Experience." In *Perspectives on Our Struggle with Sin*, edited by Terry L. Wilder, 7–48. Nashville: B&H Academic, 2011.

Osborne, Grant R. *The Hermeneutical Spiral: A Comprehensive Introduction to Biblical Interpretation.* Rev. ed. Downers Grove, IL: InterVarsity Press, 2006.

Packer, J. I. and Thomas C. Oden. *One Faith: The Evangelical Consensus.* Downers Grove, IL: InterVarsity Press, 2004.

Pannenberg, Wolfhart. *Basic Questions in Theology*, vol. 1. Translated by G. H. Kelm. Philadelphia: Fortress, 1970.

Panning, Armin J. "AUTHENTEIN —A Word Study." *Wisconsin Lutheran Quarterly* 78 (1981): 185–191.

Pate, C. Marvin, ed. *Four Views on the Book of Revelation.* Grand Rapids, MI: Zondervan, 1998.

Peirce, Charles Sanders. *The Collected Papers of Charles Sanders Peirce.* 8 vols. Edited by Charles Hartshorne and Paul Weiss (vols. 1–6) and

Arthur W. Burks (vols. 7–8). Cambridge, MA: Harvard University Press, 1931–1958.

Pickering, Ernest D. *Biblical Separation: The Struggle for a Pure Church.* Rev. ed. Arlington Heights, IL: Regular Baptist Press, 2008.

Pickering, Ernest D. *The Tragedy of Compromise: The Origin and Impact of the New Evangelicalism.* Greenville, SC: Bob Jones University Press, 2000.

Pierce, Ronald W. and Rebecca Merrill Groothuis, eds. *Discovering Biblical Equality: Complementarity without Hierarchy.* Downers Grove, IL: InterVarsity Press, 2005.

Pinnock, Clark. *Most Moved Mover: A Theology of God's Openness.* Grand Rapids, MI: Baker, 2000.

Pinnock, Clark, Richard Rice, John Sanders, William Hasker, and David Basinger. *The Openness of God: A Biblical Challenge to the Traditional Understanding of God.* Downers Grove, IL: InterVarsity Press, 1994.

Pinson, J. Matthew. *Arminian and Baptist: Explorations in a Theological Tradition.* Nashville: Randall, 2015.

Piper, John. *The Future of Justification: A Response to N. T. Wright.* Wheaton, IL: Crossway, 2007.

Piper, John. *Let the Nations Be Glad! The Supremacy of God in Missions.* 2nd ed. Grand Rapids, MI: Baker, 2003.

Piper, John and Wayne Grudem, eds. *Recovering Biblical Manhood and Womanhood.* Wheaton, IL: Crossway, 1991.

Plummer, Robert L., ed. *Journeys of Faith: Evangelicalism, Eastern Orthodoxy, Catholicism, and Anglicanism.* Grand Rapids, MI: Zondervan, 2012.

Pojman, Louis J. *Philosophy: The Quest for Truth.* 4th ed. Belmont, CA: Wadsworth, 1999.

Price, Robert M., ed. *The Empty Tomb: Jesus Beyond the Grave.* Amherst, NY: Prometheus, 2005.

Putman, Rhyne R. *In Defense of Doctrine: Evangelicalism, Theology, and Scripture.* Minneapolis: Fortress, 2015.

Putman, Rhyne R. "Why I Did Not Affirm the 'Traditional' Statement: A Non-Calvinistic Perspective." *Journal for Baptist Theology and Ministry* 10, no. 1 (2013): 71–80.

Reasoner, Mark. *Romans in Full Circle: A History of Interpretation.* Louisville: Westminster John Knox, 2005.

Reed, Stephen K. *Cognition*. 4th ed. Pacific Grove, CA: Brooks/Cole, 1996.

Rice, Richard. *The Openness of God: The Relationship of Divine Fore-knowledge and Human Free Will*. Nashville: Review & Herald, 1980.

Richards, E. Randolph and Brandon J. O'Brien. *Misreading Scripture with Western Eyes: Removing Cultural Blinders to Better Understand the Bible*. Downers Grove, IL: InterVarsity Press, 2012.

Rizzuto, Ana-Maria. *The Birth of the Living God: A Psychoanalytic Study*. Chicago: University of Chicago Press, 1979.

Roberts, Robert C. and W. Jay Wood. *Intellectual Virtues: An Essay in Regulative Epistemology*. New York: Oxford University Press, 2007.

Rohrbaugh, Richard L., ed. *The Social Sciences and New Testament Interpretation*. Grand Rapids, MI: Baker, 2003.

Ryle, Gilbert. *The Concept of Mind*. Chicago: University of Chicago Press, 1949.

Sanders, E. P. *Judaism: Practice and Belief, 63 BCE–66 CE*. Minneapolis: Fortress, 2016.

Sanders, E. P. *Paul and Palestinian Judaism*. Minneapolis: Fortress, 1977.

Sasse, Hermann. *This Is My Body: Luther's Contention for the Real Presence in the Sacrament of the Altar*. Philadelphia: Augsburg Fortress, 1959.

Sasse, Hermann. *We Confess*. Translated by Norman Nagel. 3 vols. St. Louis: Concordia, 1984–1986.

Sawyer, M. James. *The Survivor's Guide to Theology: Investigation of the Critical Issues, Survey of Key Traditions, Biography of Major Theologians, Glossary of Terms*. Grand Rapids, MI: Zondervan, 2006.

Schaap-Jonker, Hanneke, Elisabeth Eurelings–Bontekoe, Piet J. Verhagen, and Hetty Zock, "Image of God and Personality Pathology: An Exploratory Study among Psychiatric Patients." *Mental Health, Religion, and Culture 5* (2002): 55–71.

Schaff, Philip. *History of the Christian Church*. 8 vols. Grand Rapids, MI: Eerdmans, 1958.

Schelkle, Karl Hermann. *Paulus, Lehrer der Väter: die alkirchliche Auslegung von Römer 1–11*. Düsseldorf: Patmos–Verlag, 1959.

Schleiermacher, Friedrich D. E. *Hermeneutics: The Handwritten Manuscripts*. Translated by James Duke and Jack Forstman. Atlanta: Scholars, 1977.

Schreiner, Thomas R. *1, 2 Peter, Jude*. New American Commentary 37. Nashville: Broadman, 2003.

Schreiner, Thomas R. *Romans*. Baker Exegetical Commentary on the New Testament. Grand Rapids, MI: Baker, 1998.

Schweitzer, Albert. *The Quest of the Historical Jesus: A Critical Study of Its Progress from Reimarus to Wrede*. Translated by William Montgomery. London: Adam & Charles Black, 1910.

Schwenk, James L. *Catholic Spirit: Wesley, Whitefield, and the Quest for Evangelical Unity in Eighteenth-Century British Methodism*. Lanham, MD: Scarecrow, 2008.

Searle, John. *Speech Acts*. Cambridge: Cambridge University Press, 1969.

Seaton, Jeff. *Who's Minding the Story? The United Church of Canada Meets a Secular Age*. Eugene, OR: Pickwick, 2018.

Selderhuis, H. J., ed. *The Calvin Handbook*. Translated by Henry J. Baron, Judith J. Guder, and Randi H. Lundell. Grand Rapids, MI: Eerdmans, 2009.

Sherman, Steven J., Kim S. Zehner, James Johnson, and Edward R. Hirt. "Social Explanation: The Role of Timing, Set, and Recall on Subjective Likelihood Estimates." *Journal of Personality and Social Psychology* 44, no. 6 (1983): 1127–1143.

Shweder, Richard A. "In Defense of Moral Realism: Reply to Gabennesch." *Child Development* 61 (1990): 2060–2067.

Shweder, Richard A., Nancy C. Much, Monamohan Mahapatra, and Lawrence Park. "The 'Big Three' of Morality (Autonomy, Community, and Divinity), and the 'Big Three' Explanations of Suffering." In *Morality and Health*, edited by Allan M. Brandt and Paul Rozin, 119–172. New York: Routledge, 1997.

Sidwell, Mark. *Set Apart: The Nature and Importance of Biblical Separation*. Greenville, SC: Bob Jones University Press, 2016.

Silva, Moisés. *Biblical Words and Their Meaning: An Introduction to Biblical Semantics*. Rev. ed. Grand Rapids, MI: Zondervan, 1994.

Silva, Moisés, ed. *New International Dictionary of New Testament Theology and Exegesis*. Rev. ed. 5 vols. Grand Rapids, MI: Zondervan, 2014.

Singal, Jesse. "Psychology's Favorite Tool for Measuring Racism Isn't Up to the Job." *New York Magazine*, January 2017, https://www

.thecut.com/2017/01/psychologys-racism-measuring-tool-isnt-up-to
-the-job.html.

Smith, Christian. *The Bible Made Impossible: Why Biblicism Is Not a Truly Evangelical Reading of Scripture.* Grand Rapids, MI: Brazos, 2012.

Smith, James K. A. *Desiring the Kingdom: Worship, Worldview, and Cultural Formation.* Grand Rapids, MI: Baker, 2009.

Smith, James K. A. *The Fall of Interpretation: Philosophical Foundations for a Creational Hermeneutic.* Rev. ed. Grand Rapids, MI: Baker, 2012.

Snodgrass, Klyne. *Between Two Truths: Living with Biblical Tensions.* Grand Rapids, MI: Zondervan, 1990.

Snyder, Mark. "Seek and Ye Shall Find: Testing Hypotheses about Other People." In *Social Cognition: The Ontario Symposium on Personality and Social Psychology,* edited by Edward Tory Higgins, C. Peter Herman, and Mark P. Zanna, 277–303. Hillsdale, NJ: Erlbaum, 1981.

Snyder, Mark and Bruce Campbell. "Testing Hypotheses about Other People: The Role of the Hypothesis." *Personality and Social Psychology Bulletin* 6 (1980): 421–426.

Souček, J. B. "Zu den Problemen des Jakobusbriefes." *Evangelische Theologie* 18 (1958): 460–468.

Sprinkle, Preston, ed. *Four Views on Hell.* 2nd ed. Grand Rapids, MI: Zondervan, 2016.

Sproul, R. C. *Getting the Gospel Right: The Tie That Binds Evangelicals Together.* Grand Rapids, MI: Baker, 2003.

Spykman, Gordon J. *Reformational Theology: A New Paradigm for Doing Dogmatics.* Grand Rapids, MI: Eerdmans, 1992.

Stegemann, Ekkehard W. and Wolfgang Stegemann. *The Jesus Movement: A Social History of the First Century.* Minneapolis: Fortress, 1999.

Stephens, W. P. *Zwingli: An Introduction to His Thought.* Oxford: Clarendon, 1994.

Stewart, Robert B. "The Case of the Unexpected Sermon: Discovering the Values (and Dangers) of Abductive Preaching." *Preaching: The Professional Journal for Preachers* 19, no. 1 (July–August 2003): 14–17, 48.

Stewart, Robert B., ed. *The Reliability of the New Testament: Bart D. Ehrman and Daniel B. Wallace in Dialogue.* Minneapolis: Fortress, 2011.

Stott, John. *Romans: God's Good News for the World.* Downers Grove, IL: InterVarsity Press, 1994.

Strohmer, Douglas C. and Victoria A. Shivy. "Bias in Counselor Hypothesis Testing: Testing the Robustness of Counselor Confirmatory Bias." *Journal of Counseling and Development* 73, no. 2 (1994): 191–197.

Sturtz, Harry A. *The Byzantine Text-Type and New Testament Textual Criticism.* Nashville: Thomas Nelson, 1984.

Swann, William B., Tony Giuliano, and Daniel M. Wenger. "Where Leading Questions Can Lead: The Power of Conjecture in Social Interaction." *Journal of Personality and Social Psychology* 42, no. 6 (1982): 1025–1035.

Tafilowski, Ryan. "Marburg Colloquy." In *Encyclopedia of Martin Luther and the Reformation*, vol. 2, edited by Mark A. Lamport, 498–500. Lanham, MD: Rowman & Littlefield, 2017.

Tate, W. Randolph. *Biblical Interpretation: An Integrated Approach.* Peabody, MA: Hendrickson, 1991.

Tetlock, Philip E. and Jae Il Kim. "Accountability and Judgment Processes in a Personality Prediction Test." *Journal of Personality and Social Psychology* 52, no. 4 (1987): 700–709.

Thielman, Frank. *Ephesians.* Baker Exegetical Commentary on the New Testament. Grand Rapids, MI: Baker, 2010.

Thiselton, Anthony C. "'Behind' and 'in Front of' the Text: Language, Reference, and Indeterminacy." In *After Pentecost: Language and Biblical Interpretation*, edited by Craig Bartholomew, Colin Green, and Karl Möller, 97–117. Grand Rapids, MI: Zondervan, 2001.

Thiselton, Anthony C. *Hermeneutics.* Grand Rapids, MI: Eerdmans, 2009.

Thiselton, Anthony C. *The Hermeneutics of Doctrine.* Grand Rapids, MI: Eerdmans, 2007.

Thiselton, Anthony C. *New Horizons in Hermeneutics: The Theory and Practice of Transforming Biblical Reading.* Grand Rapids, MI: Zondervan, 1992.

Thiselton, Anthony C. "Semantics and New Testament Interpretation." In *New Testament Interpretation: Essays on Principles and Methods*, edited by I. Howard Marshall, 75–104. Exeter, UK: Paternoster, 1977.

Thiselton, Anthony C. *Systematic Theology.* Grand Rapids, MI: Eerdmans, 2015.

Thiselton, Anthony C. *The Two Horizons: New Testament Herme-neutics and Philosophical Description with Special Reference to Heidegger, Bultmann, Gadamer, and Wittgenstein.* Carlisle: Pater-noster, 1980.

Thomas, Robert L. *Evangelical Hermeneutics: The New Versus the Old.* Grand Rapids, MI: Kregel, 2002.

Thompson, Mark D. *A Clear and Present Word: The Clarity of Scripture.* Downers Grove, IL: InterVarsity Press, 2006.

Thompson, Mark D. *A Sure Ground on Which to Stand: The Relation of Authority and Interpretive Method in Luther's Approach to Scripture.* Eugene, OR: Wipf & Stock, 2006.

Thornbury, Gregory Alan. *Recovering Classical Evangelicalism: Applying the Wisdom and Vision of Carl F. H. Henry.* Wheaton, IL: Crossway, 2013.

Thornhill, Chad. *The Chosen People: Election, Paul, and Second Temple Judaism.* Downers Grove, IL: InterVarsity Press, 2015.

Torbet, Robert G. *Ecumenism: The Free Church Dilemma.* Valley Forge, PA: Judson, 1968.

Treier, Daniel J. "Proof Text." In *Dictionary for Theological Interpreta-tion of the Bible,* edited by Kevin J. Vanhoozer, Craig G. Bartholomew, Daniel J. Treier, and N. T. Wright, 622–624. Grand Rapids, MI: Baker, 2005.

Treier, Daniel J. *Virtue and the Voice of God: Toward Theology as Wis-dom.* Grand Rapids, MI: Eerdmans, 2006.

Trench, Richard Chenevix. *On the Study of Words.* New York, 1856.

Trenchard, Warren C. *Complete Vocabulary Guide to the Greek New Testament.* Rev. ed. Grand Rapids, MI: Zondervan, 1998.

Troeltsch, Ernst. *Gesammelte Schriften.* 4 vols. Tübingen: J. C. B. Mohr, 1913–1925.

Trueman, Carl R. "Illumination." In *Dictionary for Theological Inter-pretation of the Bible,* edited by Kevin J. Vanhoozer, Craig G. Bar-tholomew, Daniel J. Treier, and N. T. Wright, 316–318. Grand Rapids, MI: Baker, 2005.

Tudur, Geraint. *Howell Harris: From Conversion to Separation, 1735–1750.* Cardiff: University of Wales Press, 2002.

Turner, Nigel. *Syntax,* vol. 3 of *A Grammar of New Testament Greek.* 3rd ed. Edited by James Hope Moulton. Edinburgh: T&T Clark, 2000.

Tyerman, Luke. *The Life of the Reverend George Whitefield.* 2 vols. New York: Anson D. F. Randolph, 1877.

Vanhoozer, Kevin J. *Biblical Authority after Babel: Reviving the Solas in the Spirit of Mere Protestant Christianity.* Grand Rapids, MI: Brazos, 2016.

Vanhoozer, Kevin J. *The Drama of Doctrine.* Louisville: Westminster/ John Knox, 2005.

Vanhoozer, Kevin J. *First Theology: God, Scripture, and Hermeneutics.* Downers Grove, IL: InterVarsity Press, 2002.

Vanhoozer, Kevin J. *Is There a Meaning in This Text? The Bible, the Reader, and the Morality of Literary Knowledge.* Grand Rapids, MI: Zondervan, 1998.

Vanhoozer, Kevin J. *Remythologizing Theology: Divine Action, Passion, and Authorship.* New York: Cambridge University Press, 2012.

Van Huyssteen, J. Wentzel. *The Shaping of Rationality: Toward Interdisciplinarity in Theology and Science.* Grand Rapids, MI: Eerdmans, 1999.

Vitz, Paul C. *Faith of the Fatherless: The Psychology of Atheism.* 2nd ed. San Francisco: Ignatius, 2013.

Wallace, Daniel B. *Greek Grammar beyond the Basics: An Exegetical Syntax of the New Testament.* Grand Rapids, MI: Zondervan, 1996.

Ware, Bruce A. *God's Lesser Glory: The Diminished God of Open Theism.* Wheaton, IL: Crossway, 2000.

Wason, Peter C. "On the Failure to Eliminate Hypotheses in a Conceptual Task." *The Quarterly Journal of Experimental Psychology* 12, no. 3 (1960): 129–140.

Wason, Peter C. and P. N. Johnson-Laird. *Thinking and Reasoning.* Baltimore: Penguin, 1968.

Webster, John. *Holy Scripture: A Dogmatic Sketch.* New York: Cambridge University Press, 2003.

Webster, John. "Theologies of Retrieval." In *The Oxford Handbook of Systematic Theology*, edited by John Webster, Kathryn Tanner, and Iain Torrance, 583–599. New York: Oxford University Press, 2007.

Wells, David F. *No Place for Truth: Or Whatever Happened to Evangelical Theology?* Grand Rapids: Eerdmans, 1993.

Wesley, John. *The Works of John Wesley.* Edited by Thomas Jackson. 14 vols. London, 1872.

Westcott, B. F. *Epistle to the Ephesians*. Grand Rapids, MI: Eerdmans, 1952.

Westfall, Cynthia Long. "The Meaning of αὐθεντέω in 1 Timothy 2.12." *Journal of Greco-Roman Christianity and Judaism* 10 (2014): 138–173.

White, James R. *The King James Only Controversy: Can You Trust Modern Translations?* 2nd ed. Grand Rapids, MI: Bethany House, 2009.

Whitefield, George. *George Whitefield's Journals*. Edinburgh: Banner of Truth, 1960.

Whitefield, George. *The Works of George Whitefield*. 6 vols. London, 1771.

Whitlock, Luder G. Jr. *Divided We Fall: Overcoming a History of Christian Disunity*. Philipsburg, NJ: P&R, 2017.

Wilder, Terry L., ed. *Perspectives on Our Struggle with Sin: Three Views of Romans 7*. Nashville: B&H Academic, 2011.

Witherington, Ben III. *New Testament Rhetoric: An Introductory Guide to the Art of Persuasion in and of the New Testament*. Eugene, OR: Wipf & Stock, 2009.

Witherington, Ben III. *The Problem with Evangelical Theology: Testing the Exegetical Foundations of Calvinism, Dispensationalism, Wesleyanism, and Pentecostalism*. Rev. ed. Waco, TX: Baylor University Press, 2016.

Witherington, Ben III. *Women in the Earliest Churches*. Cambridge: Cambridge University Press, 1988.

Witherington, Ben III and Darlene Hyatt. *Paul's Letter to the Romans: A Socio-Rhetorical Commentary*. Grand Rapids, MI: Eerdmans, 2004.

Wittmer, Michael E. *Don't Stop Believing: Why Living Like Jesus Is Not Enough*. Grand Rapids, MI: Zondervan, 2008.

Wolters, Al. "The Meaning of Αὐθεντέω." In *Women in the Church*. 3rd ed., edited by Andreas J. Köstenberger and Thomas R. Schreiner, 65–115. Wheaton, IL: Crossway, 2016.

Wolters, Al. "A Semantic Study of Αὐθέντης and Its Derivatives." *Journal of Greco-Roman Christianity and Judaism* 1 (2000): 145–175.

Wood, W. Jay. *Epistemology: Becoming Intellectually Virtuous*. Downers Grove, IL: InterVarsity Press, 1998.

Wright, N. T. *Justification: God's Plan and Paul's Vision*. Rev. ed. Downers Grove, IL: InterVarsity Press, 2016.

Wright, N. T. *The New Testament and the People of God*. Minneapolis: Fortress, 1992.

Wright, N. T. *Paul and the Faithfulness of God*. Minneapolis: Fortress, 2013.

Wright, N. T. *Pauline Perspectives: Essays on Paul, 1978–2013*. Minneapolis: Fortress, 2013.

Wright, N. T. *The Resurrection of the Son of God*. Minneapolis: Fortress, 2003.

Yeago, David S. "The New Testament and Nicene Dogma: A Contribution to the Recovery of Theological Exegesis." In *Theological Interpretation of Scripture: Classic and Contemporary Readings*, edited by Stephen E. Fowl, 87–100. Cambridge, MA: Blackwell, 1997.

Yinger, Kent L. *The New Perspective: An Introduction*. Eugene, OR: Wipf & Stock, 2011.

Yount, William R. *Created to Learn: A Christian Teacher's Introduction to Educational* Psychology. Nashville: B&H Academic, 1996.

Zwingli, Ulrich. *Huldreich Zwingli's Werke*. Edited by M. Schuler and J. Schulthess. Zurich, 1828–1842.

Zwingli, Ulrich. *Huldreich Zwinglis sämtliche Werke*. 10 vols. Berlin, Leipzig, Zurich: Heinsius, 1905–1991.

General Index

Scripture Index